Congressional Travels

Places, Connections, and Authenticity

RICHARD F. FENNO, JR.
UNIVERSITY OF ROCHESTER

PEARSON
Longman

New York   Boston   San Francisco
London   Toronto   Sydney   Tokyo   Singapore   Madrid
Mexico City   Munich   Paris   Cape Town   Hong Kong   Montreal

Editor-in-Chief:	Eric Stano
Senior Marketing Manager:	Elizabeth Fogarty
Production Manager:	Denise Phillip
Project Coordination, Text Design, and Electronic Page Makeup:	Stratford Publishing Services
Cover Design Manager:	Wendy Ann Fredericks
Cover Designer:	Base Art Co., Ltd.
Cover Illustration/Photo:	Richard E. Fenno, Jr. photographer by Richard Baker
Manufacturing Buyer:	Roy Pickering
Printer and Binder:	Courier Corporation
Cover Printer:	Phoenix Color Corporation

Library of Congress Cataloging-in-Publication Data

Fenno, Richard F., 1926-

    Congressional travels: places, connections, and authenticity/Richard F. Fenno,
      p. cm.
    Includes index.
    ISBN 0-321-47071-0
    1. legislators—United States—Biography.   2. United States Congress—
Biography.   3. JK1030.F46 2007

328.73092'2—dc22   2006034954

Please visit us at www.ablongman.com

ISBN 0-321-47071-0

1 2 3 4 5 6 7 8 9 10—CRW—09 08 07 06

To all the University of Rochester students who have researched and written about the United States Congress.

Contents

PART II
Tracking Politicians

Preface

Congressional Travels is the culmination of one political scientist's lengthy adventure studying America's national-level politicians—its representatives and its senators. The underlying thrust of my research has been this: For anyone with an interest in our representatives and senators—what they are like and what they do—it is helpful to go to *the places* where they work and to talk with them about how they go about their business there. My early efforts took me to Washington as the place to watch them and talk to them about decision making in their committees. My later efforts took me outside Washington to the places from which they have been elected. Along the way, my basic question broadened from a legislative question, "How do they organize and make decisions in committee?" to a representational question, "How do they connect with their constituents?"

This study tackles the representational connections question by asking of some U.S. House members: "What are they really like?" The answer, I suggest, can be found by examining their constituency connections in the places where those connections are formed, tested, and maintained.

The first part of the book presents the upside possibilities of a constituency-centered research focus on our elective politicians. It develops the central idea that two research venues—Washington and the constituency—are better than one venue in answering the "What are they really like?" question. It further suggests—with some evidence, analysis, and argument—that Washington-based journalists could, and should, devote more attention to the constituency-level relationships of our elected Capitol Hill politicians. Our surveys tell us that most constituents, most of the time, do think well of their own member of Congress. But individual performance is not much studied, nor is the question of representation.

To indicate what political scientists and journalists might look for, and find, in the constituencies, I explore the idea of "authenticity"—a widely held standard in making judgments about politicians and in thinking about their constituency relationships. It is an idea that points us more toward the subject of representation than toward the more popular subject of legislation.

Because it was personal experience that drove my research from a Washington-centered venue to a constituency-centered venue, the book includes several autobiographical segments and a little research history. In those segments, I have tried to convey the pleasures and the rewards of the experience—as well as the appropriateness of it.

Three personal experiences were especially important in shaping the book. The first (see Chapter 2) was an event that impressed upon me the importance of a representative's perception of his or her constituency— and hence the need to go there—as a key to understanding constituency influence on his or her behavior. The second (see Chapter 2) came from a one-year residence in Washington and my disappointment with the performance of the Washington-based reporters as they related to the U.S. senators I was studying. The third influence (see Chapter 1) came from the local coverage, in 2001, of a congressman's funeral. It vividly reinforced the authenticating relevance of a constituency. And in so doing, the funeral launched this book.

The largest section of the book draws on my firsthand experiences to make three paired comparisons of U.S. House members in their districts. The first compares the constituency relationships of two Midwestern Republicans in the 1970s. It does so anonymously. The second is a comparison between the constituency connections of an identified New York City Democrat in the 1970s with the connections of his Democratic successor in a New York City–plus constituency in 1990. The third and most complex comparison examines Washington behavior, constituency connections, and Washington media analysis of two prominent members of the large takeover Republican class of 1994. Taken together, the three sets of stories argue in favor of constituency-centered analysis. Or so I would hope.

A favorite story of mine provides an appropriate summary. The Capitol Hill newspaper, *Roll Call*, once carried a feature ("Five Questions") in which they asked retired legislators: "What were you most proud of from your tenure in Congress?" Typically, the answers focused on some legislative effort—sometimes successful, sometimes not. When one of the most powerful and respected legislators of his day, former Senate Majority Leader George Mitchell, was asked that question, he gave a three-sentence answer. "I think most for me is that I was able to earn and retain the trust of the people of Maine. As you know, this is a time in which there is not a good deal of trust, and the public is often cynical about politics and elected officials. I worked hard at it and I think I was able to retain it." (July 13, 2000)

More than what he had accomplished as a legislative leader, George Mitchell took pride in what he had accomplished as a representative of his constituency. His answer is all about home connections. You could not, therefore, know what "this guy was really like" without watching him at work in Maine. Senator Mitchell's dominant sense of accomplishment in winning constituent trust is a measure of how very difficult the job of representation can be. And if that complex constituency connection could be won—for this unusually accomplished U.S. senator—only by "working hard at it," surely many other politicians' constituency connections are worthy of serious examination, too. His story is all about place, connections, and authenticity.

My political science friends will, of course, recognize the constituency-centric line of argument, together with the promise of constituency-based evidence in support of it. Given their strong preference for legislative-centric analysis, I am interested in their reaction. But I will let the presentation itself answer the reservations they may have. As for any reaction of Washington's resident journalists to my argument that "two venues are better than one" in studying our national politicians, I take a less benign view. Capitol Hill journalists could and should pay more attention than they now do to our representatives and senators in the world from which they have come—and upon which they depend for judgment and survival. For all of us, I argue, two venues are better than one venue in answering the question: "What are they really like?"

Richard F. Fenno, Jr.

Acknowledgments

I have accumulated a great many debts during these travels. The greatest of these are owed to the half-dozen members of the House of Representatives who allowed me to travel around with them in their constituencies. Unfailingly, each one welcomed me, educated me, and found a personal way to make my visit enjoyable and profitable.

For their good natured assistance, I wish to thank Gary Ackerman, David McIntosh, Lindsey Graham, and the two House members who remain anonymous. And, of course, the late Ben Rosenthal and his staff, especially Mike Goldenthal and Rachel Gordon.

From the McIntosh office and campaign staff, Scott Bowers, David Buskill, Jennifer Hallowell, and Jim Houston provided ready and helpful assistance. Jerry Scharfman's care and friendship were indispensable during my Ackerman visits. Alan Gershuny was unusually helpful, also, in that place. In South Carolina, David Woodard was responsible for getting me there, and he tutored me throughout. Denise Bauld provided her staffer's insights and helped with the manuscript. Greg Pierce provided company on the road. Edward Mercer, Jane Goolsby, and Pam Carpenter were helpful in the Anderson office.

On the academic side, I have been blessed with friends who read the manuscript at various stages and gave me a much-needed blend of encouragement and advice. In that cooperative enterprise, Larry Evans gave me early guidance; Doug Arnold provided the first overall perspective; Gerald Gamm helped me put it all together; and Mo Fiorina carried me across the finish line. I also received very illuminating and helpful feedback from several reviewers commissioned to read the manuscript by Longman: Tobin Grant, Southern Illinois University; Eric Uslaner, University of Maryland; Robert Sahr, Oregon State University; Bruce Oppenheimer, Vanderbilt University; and John Hibbing, University of Nebraska, Lincoln. I needed each contribution at each point of attack, and I am deeply in their debt.

In Rochester, Zak Talarek was a talented, dependable research assistant. The one person who improved the manuscript at every stage was Rosemary Bergin. She updated the various segments more often than I care to count, with her usual expertise and her encouraging good humor. I thank her, once again, for all of it.

At Longman I wish to thank, Editor-in-Chief Eric Stano for his confidence, Kathy Glidden for her professional project management skills, and Joy Matkowski for saving me embarrassment with her copyediting. They have been an easy team to work with.

Nancy knows, of course, how much all of this depends ultimately on her loving support. In that spirit, I thank her most of all.

CHAPTER I

A Story About Place:
Joe Moakley's Funeral

In the late spring of 2001, a member of the U.S. House of Representatives passed away in Massachusetts. From my summertime perch on Cape Cod, I watched a fascinating local drama unfold. A drama of remembrance, it posed, for several days, a simple question: "What was he like?"

At ground zero, the most striking aspect of Joe Moakley's funeral drama was the sheer amount and scope of interest in it. The new Republican president came. The previous Democratic president and his vice president came. The Republican speaker and the Democratic minority leader of the House came. From seven o'clock in the morning till late afternoon, the city's three major television stations provided live coverage of the day's activities—"an epic electronic requiem for a heavyweight," in the words of a media analyst.[1] For four days, commentary and remembrances filled the pages of Boston's two major newspapers. An unusual degree of national press coverage, too, was attracted to the occasion. It was as if a national hero had been lost. And the drama suggested that the "What was he like?" question would require a national-level answer.

As a lifelong observer of the Congress, however, I knew with near certainty that Representative John Joseph (Joe) Moakley was not a national hero. He was not a nationally known member of the House. He had registered no visible national accomplishments in Washington. He had never been pursued by the national media. He had never claimed national prominence, nor had anyone else ever made that claim on his behalf. Joe Moakley was not a national figure. He was, by any national measure, an obscure member of the House. To the extent that he had a Washington profile, it was one of likability. Why, then, this remarkable level of attention at the end of his life?

His record of congressional service did include a lengthy, but not exceptionally long, 28 years in the House. It was highlighted by a four-year stint as chairman of the very important House Committee on Rules. That particular committee, however, is probably the most private of all House committees, a characteristic that only underscores the absence of any publicly recorded national-level accomplishments. The Rules Committee is also, perhaps, the most partisan of House committees, a characteristic that would hardly account for the extraordinary bipartisan makeup of the mourners at his funeral. The congressman's service record in the House, I concluded, was of little help in explaining the extraordinary outpouring of attention to his funeral.

A more promising explanation lies in the ample evidence that those House colleagues who knew Joe Moakley and worked with him inside the institution liked him as a person. A senior Rules Committee Democrat described him as "a person of immense good humor and good will . . . even his political enemies could not dislike Joe Moakley."[2] And a senior Republican on the committee echoed, "I love Joe Moakley . . . it's a pleasure to talk with him and work with him."[3] House Speaker Dennis Hastert recalled "a good man and a good legislator, whose jokes always kept us laughing."[4] His Democratic Party leader, Dick Gephardt, called him "one of the most beloved, humane people I have ever met."[5]

The congressman's public, three-month battle with terminal cancer was well known to his colleagues. During his March 3, 2001, State of the Union Address to Congress, President George W. Bush had saluted Moakley as "a fine Representative and a good man." The warmth of the applause that followed was testimony to the affection and the sympathy of his colleagues. And, perhaps, the president had come to Boston to make another symbolic gesture.[6]

It is tempting to conclude that the attention paid to his passing was, indeed, the result of Joe Moakley's personality—that people came to his funeral because they had liked him. And yet, it is no denigration of Moakley to suggest that the 435-member House of Representatives has always been heavily populated with little-known "nice guys"—senior members who are noticeably well-liked and noticeably easy to work with—few of whom ever receive such a bipartisan national farewell. While his personal affability is certainly a positive factor, it was never the covering explanation for such national-scale attention fame in late May and early June 2001.

The explanatory story I wish to tell begins with a reminder: that a House member's designation, as prescribed in the U.S. Constitution, is not Congressman, it is *Representative*. And whereas "congressman" or "congresswoman" tends to call our attention to a House member's Capitol Hill activities and to his or her relationship with colleagues, "representative" points us toward a House member's activities in his or her home district and to relationships with constituents.

The two sets of activities and relationships are, of course, two parts of a single job—legislator and representative. As such, they are related to one another. For an outside observer, however, they generate two quite different perspectives. One is a distinctly Washington perspective; the other is a distinctly local perspective.

I believe that while the examination of Joe Moakley's activities and relationships in Washington provides, at best, a weak explanation of the ceremony after his death, an examination of his activities and relationships in his home constituency provides a strong explanation. We could know all there was to know about Moakley's life in Washington and not explain the attendance at his funeral. I will argue that he was not a memorable congressman but he *was* a memorable representative. The story of his funeral should not be read as a national story at all. It was primarily a local story.

Joe Moakley can be known best as someone with recognizable connections to a place and to a constituency, for it is these connections—and the strength of these connections—that made him a remarkable politician. Therefore, answers to the question "What is he like?" cannot be found in Washington. They can only be found at home. Answers to the question "Why did so many people come to memorialize him?" can only be found at home. Joe Moakley was, indeed, "a heavyweight"—not in Washington, but at home.

For those who knew him and/or wrote about him, his personality certainly mattered a lot. But what mattered more was the kind of representative he was—the durable pattern of relationships he developed with his constituents. Personal characteristics became important only as a trace element in the search for those *constituency connections* that determined the kind of representative he was. His connections formed a pattern—one that can be recognized, analyzed, and appreciated. It was his connective pattern that made Representative Joe Moakley a real person—and for that reason, a remarkable and memorable one.

The rock on which all his other representational connections rested was a *place*. And the place was South Boston. "Joe was South Boston to the core," said the friend who delivered the eulogy.[7] "He lived his entire life on this peninsula," and "it was here in this place where his character was shaped."[8] In nearly every article, it was said of him that "he never forgot where he came from."[9] Or "he never forgot his Southie roots."[10] And when asked what he wished to have inscribed on the new federal courthouse to be named after him, he had answered, "He never forgot where he came from."[11] South Boston was an Irish Catholic working-class neighborhood. And what Joe Moakley "never forgot" were the values and the loyalties he imbibed in that neighborhood.

"I learned very early as a child," he said, "that it is very important to never forget where I came from. In so doing, I learned the value of loyalty and that loyalty is, indeed, the holiest good in the human heart. And from there, I learned very quickly, in the old neighborhood, to live for the people upstairs, downstairs, over the back fence."[12] Of the tribal loyalties of that place, he said, "As soon as we're born, we're baptized into the Catholic Church, we're sworn into the Democratic Party and we're given union cards."[13]

Joe Moakley was a knowable representative largely because he was rooted in a knowable place, but also because his connections to the people in that place were equally knowable. They were dominantly *personal* connections. His former staffer, now Congressman Jim McGovern, recalled, "Joe's mentor, of course, was Speaker Tip O'Neill, who used to say all politics is local. I think Joe took that one step further. For him, all politics is personal."[14] He once described himself as "a bread and butter Democrat from South Boston who cares first and foremost about local issues affecting the people I represent. The problems of the people I represent are what I know about and that's why I went to Congress."[15] And similarly, "The politicians, when I was a kid, put you to work, put oil in your cellar, put food on your table, helped you get a job, get to school. That is the way I was brought up."[16]

That view expressed itself in countless acts of direct personal kindness and personally directed interventions with a variety of governmental bureaucracies. Such is the dominant impression given off in the outpouring of reminiscences in newspaper articles. Nearly all of them contain examples of one-on-one personal constituent service, and some of them are completely devoted to that theme.[17]

"Mr. Moakley concentrated on constituency services," wrote one political reporter, "at the expense of oratorical flourishes or media appearances. He was in the House 12 years before he hired his first press spokesman." And he quoted the congressman, "Most people view life through their kitchen windows."[18]

It was his personal touch—the "beloved," "compassionate," "down to earth," "just Joe" quality—that set him apart. In the variety of remembrances, he was described interchangeably as: "everyman congressman," "everyone's old friend," "friend of all friends," "champion of the people," "champion of the working people," "champion of the downtrodden," "a man of the people," "the people's congressman," and "a neighbor to all people."[19] Here is where Moakley's personality became crucial. But it was crucial in the context of a describable *place*, and of the describable values and practices that tied him to that place.

It is a further warrant of this full-blown, locally developed representational portrait that it was accepted in toto by the national press as well. The *New York Times*, the *Washington Post*, and the *Los Angeles Times* were captivated by the funeral—partly by the distinguished guests, but partly because it allowed them to present the picture of a classic representational pattern. The *Post* began its lengthy report that the man "known simply as 'Joe' to his constituents was hailed . . . as a powerful man who never forgot his working class South Boston roots." And the *Post* had no difficulty in recognizing the pattern as classic. He was, the *Post* agreed, "one of the last Boston Irish Democrats in the tradition of House Speaker John W. McCormack and Thomas P. 'Tip' O'Neill who believed 'all politics is local.'"[20]

In a pair of articles, the *Los Angeles Times*, too, recognized that "Moakley came from the same tradition of working class Irish American politics that produced (two) House Speakers." They quoted a description of him as "a lunch pail, neighborhood, stand-up, go-to kind of guy . . . somebody who never forgot where he came from."[21] They also described him as "'a bread and butter politician . . .' (who) was rarely identified with major national issues and thrived instead on helping constituents win a Social Security check or admission to a Veterans Affairs hospital." The *New York Times* also noted that Moakley "followed the adage of his mentor, Speaker Thomas P. O'Neill, Jr.—'all politics is local.'"[22] And they noted that "he had few equals when it came to bringing the political pork home to his state and district."[23]

This constituency-centered picture of Representative Joe Moakley was clearly painted, easily recognized, and widely accepted. The widespread adoption of the well-known "all politics is local" description of Moakley's connections made it easier to see him as exemplifying one recognizable pattern of representational behavior. The combination of person, place, and connections was classic. Anyone interested could easily answer the question "What is Joe Moakley like?" by knowing "where he came from" and examining his connection patterns at home. For anyone who recognized and wanted to honor the kind of representative he was, the appropriate place to do it was with his constituents in his home territory. And they did so.

The Joe Moakley story only hints at the many sorts of connections that might exist between a representative and a constituency. But it does make clear how fundamental to the understanding of a politician those constituency connections can be. At a minimum, it raises the question "Can we afford to ignore constituency connections in any effort to understand our representatives?" And relatedly, "Are there differences between Washington-centered and constituency-centered answers?" Those were the questions I asked myself at the time of the funeral. I had spent hundreds of hours in dozens of home constituencies. But I had never tackled either question. The clarity of the Moakley event gave me extra encouragement to do so.

Notes

1. Monica Collins, "Joe Moakley 1927–2001," *Boston Herald* (hereafter BH), June 2, 2001.
2. Ethan Wallison, "Colleagues Mourn Passing of Moakley," *Roll Call,* May 31, 2001.
3. Martin Nolan, "He Was a Rare Breed: A Gentle Soul Who Stood Firm," *Boston Globe* (hereafter BG), May 29, 2001.
4. Karen Forstel and Joe Schatz, "Massachusetts Rep. Moakley Dies; Remembered for Humane Spirit, Support for Less Fortunate," *Congressional Quarterly* (hereafter CQ), June 2, 2001.
5. Wallison, "Colleagues Mourn."
6. In the front row at the funeral, only one person away from the president, was Senator Edward Kennedy, with whom the president was then working most closely on his high-priority education legislation. If that calculation entered into the president's decision, it only raises the question as to why it might have meant so much to the senator that the president came. That puts the focus on Kennedy, to ask why Moakley might have meant so very much to him, which returns us to the original question, What is so special about Moakley?
7. Andrew Miga, "Joe Moakley 1927–2001," BH, May 29, 2001.
8. "The Nation," *Los Angeles Times,* June 2, 2001.
9. Brian Mooney and Szymon Twarog, "John Joseph Moakley, 1927–2001, Southie's Son; At Home He Always Had Time to Assist," BG, May 29, 2001; Thomas Farragher, "Courthouse Dedicated to Moakley," BG, April 19, 2001.

10. Miga, "Joe Moakley."
11. Collins, "Joe Moakley."
12. Farragher, "Courthouse Dedicated."
13. Miga, "Joe Moakley."
14. Rep. Jim McGovern, "For Joe Moakley, All Politics Was Personal," *Roll Call*, June 7, 2001.
15. Farragher, "Courthouse Dedicated."
16. Aaron Zitner, "Rep. Joseph Moakley; Longtime Lawmaker," *Los Angeles Times*, May 29, 2001.
17. For example, Brian Mooney and Douglas Belkin, "Moakley Remembered as a Friend to Those in Need," BG, May 30, 2001; David Guarino and Andrew Miga, "Southie Bids a First Goodbye to Its Favorite Son," BH, May 31, 2001; Peter Gelzinis, "Barber Knows Moakley Was a Cut Above the Rest," BH, May 31, 2001; Brian Mooney, "Moakley's Loss Deeply Felt Among the Many He Helped," BG, May 31, 2001; Marcella Bombardien, "Outside, They Told Stories of Joe," BG, June 2, 2001.
18. Mark Feeney, "People's Legislator Moakley Dies," BG, May 29, 2001.
19. In addition to those articles already cited, see Brian McGrory, "A Neighbor to All People," BG, June 1, 2001; Adrian Walker, "He Bridged Gaps, Even in Death," BG, June 2, 2001; Brian C. Mooney, "Powerful, Humble Alike Pay Tribute to John Joseph Moakley," BG, June 2, 2001; Peter Gelzinis, "Joe Moakley 1927–2001: Joe Was Guided by Own Decency," May 29, 2001.
20. Pamela Ferdinand, "'Regular Joe' Moakley Is Laid to Rest," *Washington Post*, June 2, 2001; David Stout, "Joe Moakley, Congressman from Boston, Dies at 74," *New York Times* May 28, 2001. See also Mary McGrory, "Bless Them Both," *Washington Post*, June 10, 2001.
21. *Los Angeles Times*, "Moakley Dies in His 15th Term" in *Milwaukee Journal*, May 29, 2001.
22. Zitner, "Rep. Joseph Moakley."
23. Stout, "Joe Moakley, Congressman from South Boston, Dies at 74."

CHAPTER 2

One Question, Two Perspectives

A QUESTION: WHAT
ARE THEY LIKE?

At the time of the Moakley funeral, I had spent 31 years writing to strangers, telephoning friends, negotiating with airlines, and renting automobiles, all for the purpose of insinuating myself into the daily lives of some American politicians. Thirty of them were members of the U.S. House of Representatives, and 16 of them were members of the U.S. Senate. As best as I can count, between 1970 and 2002, I made 70 separate trips to spend time with House members and 57 trips to visit with senators. These 127 trips took me to 27 states, from New York to California, Florida to Washington, New Mexico to Maine, and Minnesota to Texas. Any person who spends that much time away from home in that many places ought to have something to say for himself! Now that I have stopped doing all that, it seems natural to ask myself: What, if anything, did it all add up to?

As far as I have been able to determine, it all adds up to this: traveling around with them, talking with them, and watching them in their home constituencies provides a perspective on our elected politicians that cannot be learned as well or appreciated as much in any other way. From this perspective, they are *representatives*; they work to develop and protect representational-style relationships with their constituents, and they do this in a variety of constituency contexts across America. If the many questions I have asked about these elected representatives can be boiled down to a single one, it is probably this one: What are they like?

I favor this formulation, as in the Moakley case, because it is probably the most basic and unadorned question we can ask about our elected politicians. It is certainly among the most common. In an introductory author's note to his encyclopedic examination of six 1988 presidential candidates, Richard Ben Cramer writes that his purpose was to answer "the only questions that I (and I think, most voters) ever wanted to ask: Who are these guys? What are they like?"[1] Newsweek editor Benjamin Bradlee, in his chummy book Conversations with Kennedy, quotes the president: "'That's what makes journalism so fascinating,' the President commented, 'and biography so interesting . . . the struggle to answer that single question, What's he like?'"[2] In her posthumous memoir, veteran Washington Post journalist Meg Greenfield writes that "the hardest part of a Washington journalist's job is to discover and comprehend what these men and women are doing and why."[3] And the Post's media watchdog, Howard Kurtz, in a lengthy analysis of several presidential candidate profiles, poses "the question that all profile writers seek to answer: 'Who is this guy?'"[4]

An early effort of my own was a 1982 essay entitled "What Is He Like? What Is She Like? What Are They Like?"[5] So, I share the question and some elements of the analysis with each of the other authors. But I do not share all the elements with any of them. My politicians are members of Congress, my context is local, and the activity I study is representation. My contribution—if any—to the work of others in approaching our common "What are they like?" question is to think of elected politicians as representatives and to argue for the relevance and value of a constituency-level search for answers. I chose to answer our common question by going where the representatives go, seeing what they see, listening to what they hear, and talking with them about all of it.

This was not my first instinct as a political scientist. In the beginning, my interest in American politics focused on the executive branch. And that interest took me, eventually, to Washington—to interview people about the president's cabinet.[6] When my interest turned to relationships between executive officials and Congress, I began talking, in Washington, with members of the legislative branch.[7] With the latter group, I soon came to focus on what they were doing inside their committees and why. I thought of them primarily as legislators, and I studied their legislative work.[8] The legislative decisions of interest to me were being made in Washington, so the legislative process became my investigative focus.

Truth to tell, Capitol Hill politics was amply fascinating, energizing, and consuming. And I might never have left the Washington scene but for a chance experience close to home, one that suggested a different angle of vision and put me on a different path.

On the morning of the historic televised Kennedy-Nixon campaign debate in 1960, the top staff assistant to my own congressman called to tell me that he—the assistant—was in town. He almost never came. I invited him to share dinner and the debate with my wife and me, and I agreed to pick him up in downtown Rochester. We had become friends because I had often used the office of my congressman as "headquarters" on Capitol Hill—a hospitable home away from home—during my earliest Washington interview visits.

The makeup of the district was urban, suburban, and rural, in equal thirds, and the drive to my home wound through the city on the way out to the western suburbs. Because my guest was a stranger to the district, I said to him as we began, "I thought you'd like to see a little bit of your district." As we started driving through the large—and largely black—Third Ward city neighborhood, he looked at the people of color walking and shopping on the street and said, "This isn't our district." Then, "This can't be our district." Then, "Are you sure this is our district?" Each time, I assured him that it was. Nothing more was said. Silently, I reflected on a surprising anomaly: My congressman's top assistant does not know the makeup of his boss's district!

Sometime later, I began putting this experience together with reflections gathered from my occasional conversations in Washington with the congressman himself. At the end of the day, we would sometimes sit in his Longworth Building office and drink a little scotch while the congressman waxed lyrical about "my constituents." He would marvel at his comfort level with the people back home. "I love my constituents," he would say. "They are wonderful people. They trust me because they know me. They've known me all my life. As a boy, I used to deliver groceries to their back doors. Many times, we'd sit in the kitchen and talk. We think the same way." He had been born and lived all his life in the rural third of his district.

Putting one and one together, I thought I understood why his top aide (who came from Virginia) didn't know about the black constituents in this New York district. Nobody told him! Either the congressman didn't know about them, or if he did, he did not have them in mind when he talked about "my constituents." When he thought about "my constituents," he perceived mainly—perhaps only—the one-third of his constituents who lived in the rural part of the district. And his selective perception suggested the possibility that in his home connections and in his Washington decisions, he would be most heavily involved with, and responsive to, that particular segment of his district. My reflections on this pair of experiences turned my interest from the study of legislation toward the study of representation.

The insight I drew from my experiences was this: that the constituency an elected representative represents is, to an important degree, the constituency in the mind's eye of the representative. In the study of representation, therefore, perception matters a lot. From this view, a "constituency" becomes more complex than a set of census statistics—more even than the data in the pioneering *Almanac of American Politics*.[9] A constituency is, to an important degree, what the elected representative thinks it is. From that beginning, I gradually concluded that the best way for anyone to plumb House member perceptions of their home constituencies was to accompany some of them while they were at home—to look over their shoulders, watch them, and talk with them while they were connecting with their constituents. But for years, absorbed as I was in legislative politics, I did nothing about it.

In 1970, ten years after the Kennedy-Nixon debate, I finally decided to do something about it. I would pursue my early insight about perception by going home with some members of the House of Representatives to try to figure out what they saw there, what they did there, why, and with what consequences. And I have been at it ever since. Thus, my tour guide experience years ago with a Washington friend became—like the more recent Moakley funeral—a tributary flowing into this book.

The large subject of the book is *representation*, the dominant context is the *home constituency*, the motivating idea is the *perceptions* of the House member or senator, and the *activity of interest*, to me, is the *connections* between the constituency and the House member or senator. From those materials, I shall try to fashion some answers to the question "What are they like?"

TWO PERSPECTIVES: WASHINGTON AND CONSTITUENCY

Most of what we know about what our national politicians "are like" has been generated in Washington by reporters who live and work in Washington. They write about national politics for people interested in national politics. They keep the national political score for the rest of us on matters of governmental and individual performance. We are without doubt their beneficiaries. But we are also their prisoners. They write from the perspective of the nation's capital. And so, when we ask them "What are they like?" the answers we get are, perforce, *Washington* answers.

It is reasonable to ask, of course, "Why not simply accept Washington answers?" Can't we know all we want or need to know about our elected politicians by watching them in Washington? For sure, we can learn a lot, but what we get is a distinctive Washington perspective. And that perspective can result in a self-centered, incomplete, and potentially distorted picture of our elected politicians. Indeed, considerable testimony to that effect comes from the resident journalists themselves.

Washington's premier political reporter, David Broder, for example, has written that "the Washington-oriented journalists, politicians and bureaucrats with whom I spend my time . . . look with suspicion, if not contempt, on lesser breeds outside the beltway."[10] The esteemed columnist Russell Baker writes that "to be part of Washington is to live in a fever of narcissism. One cannot conceive of 'the country' being simply indifferent to Washington. . . . I suspect it simply doesn't give a damn. A repugnant idea to Washingtonians."[11] "I left Washington," he says, "and almost immediately I felt in touch with life again."[12] The idea that people live different lives inside and outside the nation's capital is a common one—broadly exemplified by the research of political scientist James Young and by the stories of novelist Ward Just.[13]

As a contemporary template, consider the views of longtime *Washington Post* editorial page editor and *Newsweek* columnist Meg Greenfield, in her valedictory effort to describe "what those real men and women are doing and why."[14] "The professional value system of political Washington," she writes in her book *Washington,* "entices those who came to it from elsewhere; [and] most adopt Washington-centered behavior patterns."[15] "The inhabitants of Washington become wrapped up in the peculiar life of this place," she writes, "and can no longer imagine caring so much about any other."[16] "It is as if everyone who came to the place were put into a witness protection program, furnished with a complete new public identity . . . a fake persona."[17] "Their daily lives and personal dealings [in Washington] seem more real and important to them than the distant abstraction they have taken to calling 'the American people,' which is spread throughout the great shapeless wilderness that has been designated as 'out there.'"[18] "Every year or so," she writes, "the traveling Washington-based press corps goes lyrical about . . . good old out there—as they fly together over the country."[19] The idea is, of course, that flying over it every year is okay, but you wouldn't want to go there to have a look around.

Media reporter Howard Kurtz, in one of his own "who is this guy?" articles, echoes the same theme. "In political Washington," he writes,

> Where past lives are shed like so much excess skin, anything is possible. . . . Washington is a city built upon the politics of expediency. Yesterday's campaign promise is today's lily-livered compromise. Positions shift with the ebb and flow of pundits and polls . . . intellectual consistency means nothing. . . . The capital is, in short, a landscape perfectly suited for public figures . . . who are constantly reinventing themselves. . . . Yes, anything is possible in this city of chameleons.[20]

Similarly, *New York Times* writer Michael Kelly paints Washington politicians as creating and dealing in images—which conceal more than reveal the person underneath.

> In the culture of Washington, what sort of person a politician actually is and what he actually does are not important. What is important is the perceived *image* of what he is and what he does. Politics is not about objective reality, but virtual reality. What happens in the political world is divorced from the real world. . . . Washington has become a strange and debased place, the true heart of a national culture in which the distinction between reality and fantasy has been lost.[21]

"Washington, after all, is a city that turns on reputation, . . ." echo two resident reporters, where "to be seen as bright or powerful is, to a degree, to be bright and powerful."[22]

To read these views of informed Washington observers is discouraging. If the politicians who operate there are "chameleons" with "fake personas" who "reinvent themselves" by manipulating their "images" and their "reputations," any pursuit of the "what are they like?" question may be a fool's errand. These opinions neither contemplate nor permit any extra Washington view of what a U.S. representative is like. These opinions come from within what one observer calls "the wind tunnel of Washington conventional wisdom."[23] And they invite only bewilderment in understanding Joe Moakley.

At the very least, we ought to worry about placing our "what are they like?" question entirely in the hands of Washington's journalists. As matters stand, however, this is pretty much what we have done. Of course, Washington observers have taught us a lot about what our politicians are like, and we will continue to learn from them. Even so, we might still ask, "Is their Washington perspective all there is?" and "Is it enough?"

Washington is, after all, only one world, and our elected politicians operate in at least two worlds. There is that other world "beyond the beltway"—the world Greenfield dismisses as "elsewhere" or "out there," the place where, she says, members of Congress will be found "gassing off in podunk."[24] Dictionaries define *podunk* as "a place of placid dullness and lack of contact with the progress of the world." It is popular Washington shorthand for the world beyond the beltway. It is, of course, the world from which all House and Senate members come, in which all of them spend a good part of their working lives, and to which all of them return for judgment.

Of course, Washington observers know that. But even as they acknowledge that relationship, they may give it short shrift. *Newsweek* columnist Jonathan Alter, for example, writes of "today's congressmen" that "their world—Congress world—is a fortress of unreality, its drawbridges only barely connected to life beyond the moat."[25] The assumption that there is another world—indeed, an important world—"beyond the moat" is accurate. But the companion assumption—that our politicians are "barely connected" to that world and, hence, hardly worth investigating in that place—is, like the Podunk putdown, a capital city conceit.

During my initial travels in House member constituencies, I had no interest whatever in the Washington media, their perspective, or their performance. My interest in these questions crystallized during a later experience watching them in Washington. Every day for a year (1981–1982), I rode the Metro from Dupont Circle to Capitol Hill to follow the Washington activities of ten U.S. senators in whose constituencies I had previously traveled.[26] In and around the Senate, I watched a few media people at close range. Subsequently, at a Harvard University roundtable discussion with media people and legislators, I discussed what I had learned.[27]

As chroniclers of congressional activity, the Washington press corps seemed to me to be performing two "scorekeeping" tasks. One was *institutional scorekeeping*, "where the press describes and evaluates progress toward some legislative outcome." The other was *individual scorekeeping*, "where the press describes and evaluates the activities of individual legislators." The Washington press, as I saw it, was doing "a better job at institutional scorekeeping than they were at individual scorekeeping."[28]

I had found reporters doing an excellent job of describing and evaluating progress toward legislative policy outcomes inside Congress. But I had found them doing an inadequate job of keeping a descriptive and/or an evaluative score on the activities of individual legislators. Media scorekeeping was essential in helping me keep track of the details and the legislative progress of the president's budget (the main story of the time). But I was getting very little help from the media in trying to understand the "who, what, and why" of the individuals who were making those budgetary decisions. Put differently, I had watched Capitol Hill journalists display a remarkable grasp of a legislative process but a much poorer grasp of what the relevant legislators "were really like."

In the mid-1970s and early 1980s, there had emerged a new group of elected politicians—more self-starting, more self-propelling, less dependent on party than before and, therefore, not easily portrayed in familiar, standardized ideological or partisan categories. They needed (and deserved) more definition—of the sort I had been learning by traveling with them in their districts. "You've got a lot of highly entrepreneurial, highly individualistic members of Congress, trying to push their own activity through the press . . . several hundred legislators singing, 'Hey, look me over' to the press. That's a new thing and it creates a booming, buzzing confusion."[29] Individual scorekeeping by the journalists, I argued, had become both more necessary and more difficult. So, "readers have to be given some guidance as to whether their members are doing a good job and not just from what the legislators tell them."[30]

My proposed remedy for the scorekeeping imbalance was simply for the Washington press corps to go more often to the place "beyond the moat" where individual members were grounded—the home constituency. The more that our politicians were becoming self-starting entrepreneurs, I argued, the more likely it was that they would have to be understood in their home contexts as well as in Washington. "The press pays more attention to what goes on in Washington," I concluded, "than what's going on at home; and I think that's a misallocation of their resources."[31] Although I would not make quite so categorical a statement today, my emphasis would be the same.

I look back on that 1981–1982 U.S. Senate experience and its lessons—along with the 1960 Rochester visit of my Washington friend and my observation of the Moakley funeral in 2001—as a third foundation stone of this book.

Washington media people do, of course, venture "out there," "beyond the moat" to write about members of the House and Senate. But when they do, they carry their Washington-centric perspective with them. Mostly, they leave Washington at election time to write about a few nationally interesting campaigns. They produce one-shot, in-and-out, on-the-run articles that focus on expectations about who will win. And as two students of the media put it, "The dogged methods of (Washington reporter) I. F. Stone are not frequently found on the congressional campaign trail."[32]

Media interest at campaign time centers on the activity of *winning,* because winners will soon become legislators, and because a winning legislator may become relevant on the Washington side—that is, the media's side—of "the moat." Washington media people are rarely interested in the activity of *representing* a constituency on the far side of "the moat."

Something very similar happens when Washington-based journalists venture into the countryside at presidential campaign time. Writing about the visiting journalists who pack off to the Iowa caucuses once every four years, a veteran political reporter of the statewide *Des Moines Register* summarizes, "They do know quite a lot about the positions of [a] specific candidate, about the tensions and jealousies of his staff, about the logistics of getting the candidates' entourage from one place to another. But they know nothing—and care less—about *the place* the candidate is campaigning in or *the people* he is trying to win"[33] (italics added). Needless to say, "place" and "people" are exactly what a "constituency" is all about.

Washington media people are not unaware of their Washington-centeredness, nor of a loss of influence that may result. They worry, for example, that their bias may have put them out of touch with something important—with "how people experience life."[34] They worry that talk radio may now be better than Washington journalists at connecting with popular concerns.[35] They worry that the gravitational pull of their Washington bias may be contributing to a widely acknowledged contemporary "disconnect"—felt by 60 percent of Americans in 1999—between citizens at home and their government in Washington.[36]

A prominent media analyst worries:

> The [national] press is now disconnected from the communities it serves . . . we don't know nearly as much about the neighborhoods . . . as the people that we are writing for do. There are a lot of people in the Washington bureau of the *LA Times* who have never really

spent any time in Los Angeles, including the two people who run the Washington Bureau of the *LA Times*.[37]

Retiring after 20 years covering national politics, veteran *New York Times* political reporter Adam Clymer spoke directly to these concerns. He had, he said, "some simple advice for Washington reporters: 'get out into the country as much as you can.'"[38] Journalists themselves recognize that Washington is not the only vantage point from which to view the nation's politics.

LOOKING AHEAD

My study of the members of Congress begins with the question: "What are they like?" My answer begins by recognizing that they do their work in two places—in a home constituency, where they pursue election, and in Washington, where they conduct the nation's business. The large argument of this book is that students of Congress can usefully pursue the "what are they like?" question in *both* places.

As political scientists, we have—for good reasons—expended most of our research energy on decision-making activity in the Washington workplace. And while I would not argue that we have overplayed activity there, I do argue that we have underplayed our legislators' representational activities in their home place. My bottom-line argument here is simply that for researching the question "what are they like?" two venues are better than one. And as a corollary, one venue—the constituency— has received less attention than it deserves.

There is also a stronger argument to be made. From time to time, and from case to case, I will make it: that the constituency is *a better place* than Washington in which to answer the "what are they really like?" question for our senators and representatives. I will base that argument largely on the shortcomings of our Washington-located and Washington-centered journalists in answering the "what are they really like?" question for us. If the Washington media were providing better answers, with more regularity, the case for more constituency-centered research would be a weaker one.

But the case would not be demolished, because political scientists always want to ask and answer questions—about representation, for example—that simply do not interest the Washington journalistic community. Moreover, many Washington journalists freely acknowledge their difficulties and their shortcomings in answering the "what are they like?" question. Intentionally or unintentionally, therefore, their worries and confessions invite political scientists to pursue the question in other places and in other ways.

Perhaps the view from the constituency will turn out to be identical to the view from Washington. But we cannot know that unless and until we go and take a look. Should increased attention to constituency-level politics prove enlightening, however, the larger idea of representational activity might prove worth looking at, too. In which case my own quarter-century of experience in the world "beyond the moat" might have some broader relevance. In that fond hope, I shall discuss some explorations in that world. But first, I have an idea that might be of some help as we go to "have a look" at the world beyond Washington.

Notes

1. Richard Ben Cramer, *What It Takes: The Way to the White House,* Random House (New York, 1992), p. vii.
2. Benjamin Bradlee, *Conversations with Kennedy,* W. W. Norton and Co. (New York, 1975), p. 144.
3. Meg Greenfield, *Washington,* Public Affairs Press (New York, 2001), p. 14.
4. Howard Kurtz, "Inside the Spin Machine," *Washington Post Weekly,* August 21–27, 1995.
5. Richard F. Fenno Jr., "What's He Like? What's She Like? What Are They Like?" reprinted in *Watching Politicians: Essays in Participant Observation,* IGS Press (Berkeley, CA, 1990).
6. Richard F. Fenno Jr., *The President's Cabinet: From Wilson to Eisenhower,* Harvard University Press (Boston, 1959); Fenno, "Now Is the Time for Cabinet Makers," *New York Times Magazine,* November 20, 1960; Fenno, "The Cabinet: Index to the Kennedy Way," *New York Times Magazine,* April 2, 1962.
7. Richard F. Fenno Jr., *The Power of the Purse: Appropriations Politics in Congress,* Little Brown (Boston, 1965).
8. Richard F. Fenno Jr., "The Internal Distribution of Influence: The House," in David Truman (ed.), *Congress and America's Future,* Prentice Hall (New York, 1965); Richard Fenno, *Congressmen in Committees,* Little Brown (Boston, 1972).
9. My first research trips were in 1970. The first *Almanac* was published in 1972. My initial efforts predated any knowledge of the *Almanac.* But the sense of constituency relevance was the same.
10. David Broder, "The States Drop the Ball," *Washington Post,* February 17, 1982.
11. Russell Baker, "Wise to Washington," *Boston Sunday Globe,* June 15, 1975. A recent play on Washington's self-centeredness is: David Brooks, "The Age of the Resume Gods," *New York Times,* February 12, 2005.
12. Russell Baker, "Letter from Washington," *New York Times Magazine,* February 15, 1976.

13. James Young, *The Washington Community, 1800–1828,* Columbia University Press (New York, 1966); Ward Just, *Echo House,* Houghton Mifflin (New York, 1997); Ward Just, "The Congressman Who Loved Flaubert," *Atlantic Monthly,* October 1972.

14. Greenfield, *Washington,* p. 14.

15. Ibid., p. 8.

16. Ibid., p. 20.

17. Ibid. See also Meg Greenfield, "Friendship in Washington," *Washington Post,* July 20, 1983.

18. Ibid., pp. 29–30.

19. Ibid., p. 68; Meg Greenfield, "The Two Washingtons," *Newsweek,* September 20, 1982.

20. Howard Kurtz, "The Irony of Al D'Amato," *Washington Post Weekly,* June 6–12, 1994, pp. 7–10.

21. Michael Kelly, "The Game," *New York Times Magzine,* October 31, 1993, pp. 64, 80.

22. Thomas Ricks and Michael Frisby, "How Inman Could Go from Star to 'Bizarre' in Such a Short Time," *Wall Street Journal,* January 21, 1994.

23. The phrase is that of journalist Hendrick Hertzberg. See Craig Lambert, "Hertzberg of the New Yorker," *Harvard Magazine,* January–February 2003.

24. Greenfield, p. 68.

25. Jonathan Alter, "The World of Congress: It's a Fortress of Unreality, with Its Laws, Logic and Codes of Behavior," Newsweek, April 24, 1989.

26. Especially relevant for my remarks at this stage was my experience writing, *The Emergence of a Senate Leader: Pete Domenici and the Reagan Budget,* CQ Press (Washington, DC, 1991).

27. Stephen Bates (ed.), *The Media and Congress,* Horizons (Columbus, OH, 1987), pp. 36–38.

28. Ibid.

29. Ibid.

30. Ibid.

31. Ibid.

32. Peter Clarke and Susan Evans, *Covering Campaigns,* Stanford University Press (Stanford, CA, 1983), as quoted in Richard E. Cohen "Covering Congress," *National Journal,* October 1983.

33. James Flansburg, "Don't Shoot Him, He's Only the Political Writer," *Des Moines Register,* December 17, 1979. Also, Richard Harwood, "Winking at Congress," *Washington Post Weekly,* June 6–12, 1998.

34. Jonathan Alter, "Sizzle over Substance," *Newsweek,* January 29, 1996; Paul Taylor, "The New Political Theatre," *Mother Jones,* November–December 2000; Albert Hunt, "Defining Politics Down," *Wall Street Journal,* October 7, 1999; David Shribman, "Hollywood, D.C.," *Boston Globe Magazine,* August 9, 1998; Gerald Seib, "Live from Hollywood, It's American Politics with Warren Beatty," *Wall Street Journal,* September 14, 1999.

35. Howard Kurtz, "The Year the Candidates Took to the Airwaves," *Washington Post Weekly,* November 2–8, 1992; James M. Perry, "Party May Be Over for Democrats, Republicans, As Candidates Use 'Teledemocracy' New Media," *Wall Street Journal,* November 4, 1992; Jonathan Alter, "Why the Old Media's Losing Control," *Newsweek,* June 8, 1992; Diane Rehm, "Power to the People," *Washington Post Weekly,* November 2–8, 1992.

36. The Hart-Teeter poll of May–June 1999 for the Council for Excellence in Government is from *Boston Globe*, September 1, 1999. See also Walter Cronkite, "How Television Lost the Game of Politics," *Boston Globe Magazine*, November 18, 1990; Gerald Seib, "Confidence Gap: Press Trapped in Own Cynicism," *Wall Street Journal*, August 31, 1994; Seib, "A Great Divide Between the Media and the Public," *Washington Post Weekly*, May 29–June 4, 1995; Seib, "Many Americans View Washington As a Mess and Just Tune It Out," *Wall Street Journal*, June 4, 1997; Howard Kurtz, "Turning Out the News," *Washington Post Weekly*, May 29–June 4, 1995.

37. Tom Rosensteil, "The 1994 Theodore H. White Seminar on Press and Politics," John F. Kennedy School of Government, Harvard University, 1994, pp. 46–47.

38. Ed Henry, "Heard on the Hill," *Roll Call*, April 28, 2003.

CHAPTER 3

An Idea: Authenticity

INTRODUCTION

The attraction of constituency-centered research begins with two propositions: that Washington is not the only important political place and that the Washington perspective on American politics is not enough. "Two venues, two looks" is preferable to "one venue, one look." My funeral story was an advertisement for that point of view—that we cannot know what Representative Joe Moakley "was like" without focusing on his connections in his home territory. Once we discover his connections to a particular place, and to the particular set of values and practices of that place, it becomes abundantly clear what Joe Moakley "was like." Furthermore, that discovery cuts across the grain of our pervasive Washington-insider journalism. There is no fake persona here, no chameleon shedding skin, no manipulation of appearances, reputations, or images. Joe Moakley is knowable and believable. He is who he says he is. He is a real person. He is grounded. What you see is what you get. We not only know what he is like, we know—to raise the standard—what he is "*really* like."

The idea that best invokes and captures that higher standard is, I suggest, *authenticity*. In a commonsensical way, it gets close to what we are trying to get at when we ask, "what is he or she *really* like?" In that sense, Joe Moakley comes across to us as an authentic political figure.

Authenticity is not easy to define.[1] It is a judgment that distinguishes what is real from what is fake, what is genuine from what is artificial, what is natural from what is contrived. It is certainly a familiar basis for

21

judgment. A search for *authenticity* on the *New York Times* Web site turns up dozens of entries, from reality TV to neighborhood preservation to fashion design. The fields of endeavor are too numerous to count. And the identity of the judges and their standards of judgment will differ from subject to subject and, perhaps, from time to time. But in every field, the label *authentic* is a judgment call. And to be judged as authentic is to be judged, nearly always, favorably.

In judging people, the idea is employed well beyond politics. When my boyhood hero and baseball star, Ted Williams, passed away in June 2002, he was praised for his authenticity almost as much as for his performance. He was described as "a man of diamond-like authenticity . . . [who] never stopped being himself," as "his own man to the end," and as "a completely authentic man [who] never bent to fashion."[2] In *Newsweek*'s retrospective picture essay on the September 11th attack, Henry Allen writes that "Marines, Rangers, SEALS, fighter pilots [are] the kind of guys who . . . do not talk a lot about 'authenticity' because they're what it means."[3] Speaking of favorable media judgments, one analyst writes that "combat veterans are magnets for goodwill, and authentic war veterans are off the charts."[4] Drawing on his business experience, corporate guru Jack Welch writes that the first question to be asked of a political leader should be: "Is he real . . .? [Because] Authenticity really matters. Does he know who he is . . .? He can't have an iota of fakeness [to achieve] the authority born of authenticity."[5] The idea is everywhere—and nowhere more so than in politics.

AUTHENTICITY IN POLITICS

When politicians talk to others and act before audiences, they are presenting themselves for judgment, and one judgment people in the audience make involves authenticity. Does the politician come across as "the genuine article" or a "phony," as "the real thing" or a "fraud"? Does he seem "comfortable in his own skin"? Can it be said of her that "What you see is what you get," or is there uncertainty—in persona and/or in message—about this or that person? Are you learning about the politician's core beliefs, or are you being served nostrums? Do the various parts of his or her persona fit together? In an open, gregarious society, voters have considerable faith in their ability to "size up" or "take the measure" of their politicians. Standards are hard to set, but confidence that "we'll know it when we see it" is strong.

It is not a judgment to be made quickly. It takes repetition, testing, and exposure. It is a judgment that gets made over time. And it is based upon the *connections* a politician makes with constituents.

In political journalist Joe Klein's popular novel about a presidential primary campaign, the narrator and close confidant of the winner passes judgment only on the very last page of the book: "his power came from the *authenticity* of his appeal. . . . There was very little artifice in him"[6] (italics in original). Readers were expected to recognize the relevant connections, to understand the standard, and to acknowledge the appropriateness of it as a final, summary basis for judgment.

The idea of authenticity is a staple of political reflection and commentary. One of America's most experienced national politicians has worried out loud, from his perspective, that "it's real easy in the profession of politics to *lose yourself* [italics added] in presenting yourself to others, and I think a lot of people do . . . get lost in the profession itself and in the forms of politics, the methods of politics."[7] Constituents will have the same worry. They will want to know whether a representative seems to have "lost" himself or herself and is, therefore, not authentic.

Campaigning for the presidency, another experienced national politician asks his listeners to "Look inside us . . . what makes us tick? *Are we real?* [italics added] Is it all politics? Do we really care about anybody?"[8] In 1984, when a front-running Democratic presidential candidate lost his early lead, his press secretary lamented, "It had almost nothing to do with the issues. We made a fatal mistake in the period after New Hampshire. We didn't answer the question, *Who is this guy?* [italics added] What's he all about?"[9] After presidential candidate Bill Clinton's first meeting with the two men who were soon to become his top campaign advisers, Paul Begala asks James Carville, "Is this guy for real?" And, adds Clinton biographer John Harris, Begala "would have numerous occasions in the year ahead to return to his original question."[10] These are all basic constituent questions about candidate authenticity.

The idea of authenticity appears, too, in blanket appraisals of our politicians. For example, "People have come to believe their elected officials and their candidates are not the real McCoy. They're not authentic. They're scripted, talking according to the polls, voting according to next November."[11] Politicians "won't act like a normal person. They won't say what they honestly think. They won't be real. They can't; they never will. TV won't let them. Today the average pol's public persona is more artificial than it ever was."[12] "Everybody is manipulating everybody else and seeming to have an awfully good time doing it. . . . Some of them have even gotten pretty good at faking authenticity. . . . But someone speaking in authentic tones is going to break through one of these days."[13]

Comments about specific individuals have the same ring to them. "Obviously, I wouldn't be married to my husband [a presidential candidate] if he weren't a man of total honesty and integrity. He's an authentic person. He's not a phony."[14] "When I lost, when I got beat, I lost my job. I didn't lose myself. I think it's important not to confuse who you are and what you do. . . . When I lost [the election] . . . I still had me intact."[15] A reporter imagined his upcoming interview with a prominent politician: "He's still *real* [italics added]. . . . He'd answer [me] . . . and I'd know I could take it to the bank."[16]

In the run-up to the 2002 midterm elections, evidence of a general authenticity standard was widespread. In the aftermath of Senator Paul Wellstone's death, a *Wall Street Journal* memoir headlined, "Paul Wellstone: Not A Faker, Just Plain Honest."[17] A *Washington Post* story about Elizabeth Dole's return to North Carolina to run for Senate headlined, "Is She For Real?"[18] When Al Gore began to move about, a *Roll Call* analyst commented, "Voters like candidates . . . who seem like genuine people, not packaged phonies. . . . The problem for Gore quite obviously is that he has already remade himself so often that any efforts to remake himself again would be met with more derision and cynicism . . . ."[19] One incumbent senator pitched his authenticity with the comment: "I'm not wearing a camouflage uniform. What you see is what you get."[20] Of a gubernatorial winner, it was explained, "He is just so comfortable in his own skin . . . people respond to that. He knows who he is no matter who he is with."[21] For independent-minded citizens, authenticity—as in the case of "authentic hero" John McCain—may be the primary consideration.[22]

Washington handicappers sometimes try, from their vantage point, to force-feed the requisite politician-constituency connections before they occur, especially in presidential campaigns. In January 2003, for example, well before the field of Democratic presidential candidates took shape, PBS pundits were already predicting that "authenticity will be the question" and suggesting prematurely who might be "the candidate of authenticity."[23]

When Iowa Senator Tom Harkin announced his support in his state's first and crucial presidential caucus, he began, "There is a powerful authenticity to Howard Dean."[24] John Kerry, who defeated Dean in Iowa, was quoted as saying, "I believe you have to be real, and people know it if you're not."[25] He then advertised himself as "the real deal," and he traveled New Hampshire in "The Real Deal Express." "This fall," an analyst wrote, "many will be looking especially hard at John Kerry, searching for . . . some kind of authenticity. They will want to know if he seems genuine enough to be President."[26] A seasoned supporter observed, "Spontaneity is not encouraged in politics today, but spontaneity often means genuineness and authenticity to people, and being genuine is so essential in this race."[27] A national columnist covering the Kerry campaign reported, "The questions *most asked* [italics added] of a political reporter go something like this: 'Ok, what's the real story? What is he really like?'"[28]

Afterward, the idea remained. A conservative columnist opined that President George "Bush enjoys the appeal of authenticity. He is a conviction politician, utterly comfortable with who he is and what he believes."[29] A *Newsweek* author wrote of Kerry's "weaknesses" that "chief among them was his inability (or refusal) to convey who he was."[30] A victorious Democratic Senate candidate explained, "I think what people are most hungry for right now is authenticity."[31] And a Democratic consultant argued generally that the party suffered in 2004 because "Democrats stopped being authentic." He suggested actions "to revive authenticity in the Democratic party."[32] Two years later, a Democratic gubernatorial candidate, who met Kerry, commented, "When he goes out to meet people, he doesn't come off real."[33] It is both a prescriptive and a descriptive idea.

In any search for authenticity in politics, in any search for what he or she "is really like," even the keenest observer never gets a full picture. My case in point is presidential speechwriter Peggy Noonan, who worried about authenticity in her book about the Reagan years. We have "Stepford candidates with prefab epiphanies," she began, "inauthentic men for an inauthentic age."[34] Ronald Reagan was her exception. But try as she might, she never quite figured out, as she put it, "who is this man?" "I would see him and I would wonder . . . who is he? My search for Reagan continued through the years. Who is this masked man?" After their final meeting, she concluded, however, that "I would never know him."[35] She knew parts, but not the whole of "what he was really like." Columnist Jonathan Alter, a less sympathetic Washington observer, concluded similarly, with respect to Reagan, that "great authenticity is also the paradoxical product of great mystery."[36] But *60 Minutes'* Mike Wallace had no reservations. "Ronald Reagan knew who the hell he was. He had his convictions. He was comfortable in his skin. I thought he was a superb President."[37]

It is best, I conclude, to think of authenticity as a broad and elusive judgment—one that matters a lot but defies precise formulation. A prominent subtext of Washington journalism, however, seems to be that authenticity is hard to find in the nation's capital. I have no doubt it does exist and can be found there. Senator John McCain, for example, assessed fellow Senator John Kerry this way: "You get to know people and you make decisions about them. I found him to be the genuine article."[38] Typically, however, interpersonal judgments about legislative colleagues are closely guarded and unavailable to the rest of us. If, therefore, we have a determined interest in the authenticity of our senators and House members, it would seem worthwhile to look in their home constituencies.

In a representative form of government, all ultimate judgments about an elected politician are made by constituents. And it is in the context of politician-constituent connections that authenticity can best be found and plumbed.

Appraisals of a representative's authenticity become increasingly relevant to political judgment whenever the influence of partisan allegiance on citizen judgment shrinks and whenever the influence of individual reputations on citizen judgment grows. The authenticity question will be asked of every elected politician, because in one form or another, authenticity is linked to constituent trust. And *trust* is the holy grail in producing positive, stable relationships between politician and constituents.

My beginning assumption is that authenticity is strongly related to place—as surely it was in the Moakley case. But how typical was he? His constituency connection pattern may be "classic," but is it a prototypical pattern? Is "place" as crucial for other politicians as it was for him? The answer is surely no—that the primacy of place can be diluted by population change, by redistricting manipulation, or simply by competing extra-constituency experiences. A home state observer of John Kerry's career mentioned "the fundamental local mistrust that he has never been able to shake. It's the idea that he is not really from here at all. He just drops in every few years and collects votes." "Maybe," he adds, "this is an unfair comparison with [Ted] Kennedy who *is* [italics in original] so manifestly from here."[39] Place is only one underpinning of authenticity. But place will always be a relevant reference point because every congressional politician's constituency is legally defined by its geographical boundaries. And whatever the full range of influences on an elected politician may be, many of them can profitably be discovered, plumbed, and evaluated within those boundaries.

My central contention is simply twofold: The study of home connections helps us to assess the authenticity of our elected politicians in Washington, and home connections deserve more attention. But a stronger contention cannot be summarily ruled out: that examining home connections gives us a *better chance* to look for, and to test for, the authenticity of our politicians than does observing them in Washington. Indeed, that is the furthest reach of my argument: that a politician's presentations and activities in his or her home constituency provide an especially advantageous context—better than contemporary Washington—in which to pursue questions of authenticity and trust.

DISCOVERING AUTHENTICITY

I was first attracted to the notion of authenticity when, after several trips to hang out with them in their statewide constituencies in the 1980s and 1990s, I began to think about the sheer durability of two long-serving, solidly entrenched U.S. senators, Claiborne Pell (D/RI) and David Pryor (D/AR). As I puzzled over their political longevity—30 years for Pell, 34 years for Pryor—the common key seemed to be their strong and unbroken sense of who they were. And the idea of authenticity seemed the most appropriate explanatory idea.

After several visits over several years with each senator, I concluded:

Within policy limits presented by liberal expectations in Rhode Island and by moderate-populist expectations in Arkansas, Pell and Pryor each fashioned a favorable and distinctive political persona. In one basic quality, however, their personae were remarkably similar. And that quality was their *authenticity* [italics in original]. However different the content of each senator's policy vehicle might be, each set of constituents finds its own senator's persona eminently believable. And that is the crucial commonality.[40]

David Pryor's authenticity derived from his identification with Arkansas as a distinctive and sustaining *place*. But Claiborne Pell's authenticity derived, instead, from his identification with *family traditions* that found nourishment in the political culture of a distinctive place—Rhode Island.

Two other ideas seemed to be close correlates of authenticity. I added, "Both senators' authenticity is buttressed by their *consistency*" and "There is a third ingredient in the Pryor-Pell recipe: *good character*" (italics in original).[41] All three ingredients were surely exemplified by Joe Moakley.

The idea of character is especially close to the idea of authenticity. Richard Ben Cramer, in his study, calls character "the coin of the realm."[42] And it has long been a central element in evaluating candidates. For a television special examining America's presidents, for example, PBS chose the title "Character Above All."[43] Presidential possibilities get assessed in articles headlined "Americans Yearn for a President with Character and Leadership," "Trying Presidential Character on for Size," "The Real Character Issues," and "Character Not Ideology."[44] In their texts, we read, "What is clear is that voters are looking for a new President who displays . . . character, consistency and candor."[45] "Assessing character is like eating soup with a fork," says one reporter, "but you know it when you see it."[46] There is, in other words, a kinship between character and authenticity.

Political philosopher Sisela Bok has expressed the linkages this way.

If candidates invoke principles that they plainly do not take seriously, it is their *character* [italics added], in the sense of integrity, that is in doubt; and this in turn gives reason to distrust not only their campaigning, but their conduct in office should they be elected. It is this connection between character and *trust* [italics added] that [Ralph Waldo] Emerson stressed in saying that we know very well "which of us has been just to himself." "In that man, though he knew no ill of him, he put no trust. In that other, though they had seldom met, *authentic signs* [italics added] had passed to signify that he might be *trusted* as one who had an interest in his own character."[47]

When character is suspect, authentic signs cannot be communicated, and trust cannot be established.

AUTHENTICITY AND TRUST: A STORY

Favorable constituent judgments about character produce favorable judgments about authenticity. And those judgments, in turn, feed into that degree of trust in the politician that is the most durable representational glue. The optimal condition for a relationship of trust is the belief, on the part of the constituent, that the representative has the interests of the constituent at heart and that the representative is *not* "in it for himself or herself." By word and by deed—particularly and most reliably by deed—elected politicians try to convey the idea that "I am working, and I will continue to work, on your behalf" or, in reverse form, "I am not in it for myself." Corollaries are that "I will level with you. I will not mislead you. I will encourage dialogue. I will bend over backwards to be open, frank, and forthcoming." If, the argument goes, I am not in it for myself, I have no reason to hide, cover up, mislead, or prevaricate. Over time, a constituent sense—that the representative is real, is not self-aggrandizing, and can be trusted—may grow, take root, and protect the incumbent. The authenticity of the representative will have been established.

A notorious case of winning and losing constituent trust is that of Gary Condit, a six-term Democratic representative from the Central Valley of California. In 2001, during six months of prime-time national exposure, he fell from a constituency relationship that seemed the very model of authenticity to a depth of constituency distrust that cost him the bedrock support of his party.

Representative Condit's authenticity rested on twin pillars: *a place* and *a personal style related to that place*. There was his "fierce loyalty to the Valley" and to what he called "Valley values," plus his independence in voting and in promoting the conservative policy preferences of "Condit Country" inside Congress.[48] There were also his down-to-earth, person-to-person relationships—his visits home every weekend to see and be seen; his responsiveness "whether you're a top official or just plain folk"; his comfortable, easygoing, unpretentious personal approach to a small-town, middle-class constituency.[49]

Of his policy connections, he commented, "We take a little heat from the extremists on either side, but I think the average man or woman in Merced or Ceres or Turlock understands what I'm trying to do. I think they get me and what I'm all about. In the final analysis, I think that's what's important."[50] A local reporter summed up a model representational relationship: "He listens. He remembers. And he votes the way Valley folks want. Condit prides himself on putting his constituent center-of-the-road interests far above party politics or self-promotion."[51]

Constituent judgments followed in kind: His "informal 'I'm your neighbor image' [has] paid off. People feel comfortable with him."[52] "Once he meets you, he remembers your name . . . you know, 'how are you' . . . 'how's your family.' He knows us and that's what's real important."[53] "I've always looked at him as a kind of Gary Cooper type . . . because he's got that folksy way about him and he's got a good sense of people."[54] He was a neighborly person, "one of us" with nothing to hide. A district reporter summed up: "He is almost a mini-god here. He has that reputation of being the home town boy that made good. . . . People have glowing praise of him. Seems like anybody's son, maybe your neighbor's son, somebody you could trust."[55]

Gary Condit seemed real, genuine, authentic; his representational relationships seemed unassailable. Yet he lost it all because, under pressure, he failed the acid test of an authentic relationship—a high degree of character-centered, constituent trust. A female Washington intern, with whom Condit had a "relationship" of some kind, disappeared without a trace. As her friend, Condit was questioned by the police, and, though he never was formally implicated, he was pursued, day and night, by the frenzied national media to tell "the whole story" of his friend, their relationship, and her disappearance. There was no leveling with his constituents, no dialogue—only excessive evasion and presumed cover-up. The fatal conclusion: "he must be hiding something." As one observer saw it, "The scandal has undermined the only capital he really had, his word and his bond. I don't see how we can trust him now. We don't know that he did anything, but we don't know that he didn't."[56]

Throughout the long, televised soap opera—which culminated in a ballyhooed prime-time interview seen by 23.7 million viewers, the largest TV audience of the summer—the representative remained detached and unhelpful.[57] Suspicion emerged, undermining established connections. He behaved as if he was indeed "in it for himself" and did indeed have something to hide. His behavior undermined the "I have your interests at heart" and the "I am not in it for myself" roots of his constituency relationship. In the end—except for those most personally loyal to him—few constituents were satisfied that he had "opened up" or told "everything he knew" or "told the truth." He did not express empathy or concern for the plight of her parents. His presentation, self-detached and evasive, was radically at variance from what they knew. The difference became a problem of his character, of his authenticity, and of their trust.

TV cameras captured angry constituents shouting "liar, liar, pants on fire."[58] "The thing I took from the [prime-time] interview," said one constituent, "was that his constituents deserved more after 30 years of support. . . . And then he sits up there with the interviewer and basically thinks he can fool all of his constituents . . . he thought he could fool all of his constituents all the time."[59] "He was highly regarded and loved," said another constituent. "Now we see he had a different side to him. We trusted him . . . and when you trust somebody, you expect the truth."[60] A constituency-based account of his unsuccessful primary campaign made it clear how badly he had lost touch with many long-time constituents.[61] He had lost his "mini-god" status, his "Gary Cooper image," and his "I'm your neighbor" linkage. He was no longer "one of us" and no longer trustworthy. His authenticity had been lost.

For most politicians, authenticity probably takes root in his or her early connecting activities. Once established, citizen judgments about character and trust are not easily changed. The Condit story, however, tells us how it might happen. The Condit story also suggests how indispensable constituency-centered stories might be in thinking about authenticity and the representational connections that are its underpinning.

IN SEARCH OF AUTHENTICITY: CAMPAIGNS AND CONNECTIONS

The idea of authenticity helps us to understand the limitations of Washington reporters. On the one hand, an ongoing election campaign provides the most promising occasion to test for candidate authenticity. On the other hand, normal election coverage focuses primarily on winning and on expectations about winning, concerns that invariably trump any straightforward reporting of constituent-candidate interaction. Authenticity, however, is precisely about constituent-candidate interaction. It is not about why or how a candidate wins. Winning does not answer the "what are they like?" question.

Winning may be relevant, but it does not tell us what we want to know about authenticity. Authenticity takes time to develop—and to erode—and cannot be captured in a one-time campaign snapshot. I have relied heavily on repeated campaign-time visits, because they produce the most concentrated display of representative-constituent interaction—not because of any interest in who wins.

Change in American campaign practices over the last quarter-century seems to have made it more difficult for a national reporter—even one so disposed—to discover and write about candidate connections and candidate authenticity. Television, in particular, has muddied—if not obstructed—any campaign-time search for authenticity. It has become the dominant medium

television / campaigning

through which candidates make positive presentations of themselves to constituents—touting their qualifications, their identifications, and their records. But what the electronic revolution giveth, it also taketh away. Television has proved to be particularly useful in attacking political opponents, and negative advertising has become a staple of televised political campaigns. The "political terrorism of those 30-second spots" has emerged as its worst manifestation.[62] The problem? This kind of campaign does nothing to reveal candidate authenticity and everything to hide it.

Consider this sequence of media commentary and the picture it paints of the increasingly negative impact on the search for, and the presentation of, candidate authenticity during all contemporary campaigns.

(1992) "In an era when . . . campaigns are fought primarily on television, radio commercials may seem to be a curiously antique form of weaponry. . . . Yet radio, political analysts say, remains the medium that candidates use for their meanest assaults."[63]

(1994) "Negative campaigning isn't new, but this year's barbs are more bitter than ever. So nasty have this year's campaigns been that voters are having a tough time telling the liars from the cheats."[64]

(1998) "Each [presidential] campaign has used more negative advertising, the so-called attack ads, than any campaign ever did before."[65]

(1989) "[In] the three leading [off-year] political contests of 1989, the negative ads have reached new levels of hostility, raising fears that this kind of mudslinging, empty of significant issues, is ushering in a new era of campaigns without content. Now, says a pioneer in political television, 'the idea is to attack first, last and always.'"[66]

(1990) "[T]he main question in a [House] member's mind every time he votes is, 'What kind of a 30-second spot are they going to make out of this vote?'"[67]

(1991) "I dare say the first thing that comes to my mind in a vote is: Can it [the issue] pass the 30-second test? How successful will my opponent be in applying it to a 30-second ad? It's a screen that comes up whenever there's a vote."[68]

Political television—positive and negative, presentation and counter-presentation, attack and counterattack—has been the main story of congressional campaigning in recent times.

For most constituents, campaign time is their best opportunity to answer the "what are they like?" question. But the kind of campaign they see is less and less helpful in providing the answer. The modern campaign has driven the citizenry further and further away from the candidate whose genuineness they are trying to assess.

Candidates are affected similarly. From their perspective, the campaign period can become their worst nightmare. They may have to spend an ever larger amount of their spare time raising the money to fund the television campaign. And most of that takes place away from their constituents, in staged fund-raisers or on the telephone with random samples. The change is summarized by one columnist.

> Not too long ago, gubernatorial and Senate candidates spent most of the fall feverishly appealing to *real voters* [italics added] at factory gates, Rotary Club luncheons, senior citizen centers and schools. Now, it is more common for major candidates to go for entire days without appearing in public or pressing any flesh. Instead, they are in the constant cycle of raising money to make more TV commercials.[69]

Worse still, the politician's search for television money has enticed the Washington media to dwell—sometimes exclusively—on the money chase as the key to winning elections. In which case, questions of candidate authenticity get left far behind. In the media-centered campaign, too, the need for "volunteers" has declined, causing another traditional point of direct citizen-candidate contact to disappear.[70] These changing campaign priorities and practices of "the permanent campaign" have conspired to obstruct the presentation of, and the search for, candidate authenticity.

In an effort to connect with voters, candidates have taken advantage of the "new media" of cable television and the Internet to communicate directly and positively with fragmented, specialized, and smaller segments of their constituency. On Web sites, they pose questions and deliver self-serving answers. Or they employ interview formats in which reporters ask questions, the candidates answer, and viewers and listeners make a judgment. Such interviews have increasingly come to focus on the personal and private relationships of the candidate.

In theory, these vehicles can help the constituents think seriously about authenticity. Often, however, these one-on-one interactions are mediated by celebrity involvement, and candidate association with celebrities is rarely authenticating. They also may be dominated by an increasingly aggressive cadre of "character cops" who have merely substituted negative interviewing for negative advertising.[71] "The politics of character," says one observer, "tend to drive out the politics of substance."[72] There can be a lot of "talk," therefore, about character without any gains in determining authenticity.

In theory, whenever direct interaction between politician and constituent takes place via the media—paid or free, in or out of the campaign—there are possibilities for testing the authenticity of the politician. All in all, however, a cursory look at various campaign trends in the electronic age does not yield a lot of optimism that campaign time activity alone will produce satisfying answers to the question "what are they really like?"

Is there, then, an alternative approach that might be helpful in discovering "what are they really like?" My answer is, of course, "yes." My suggestion is that journalists and academic observers of politics go to the constituency and observe the representational connections that elective politicians have established, or are establishing, in those places.

Observers ought to examine how those connections are developed and how they are maintained, without concern for "who wins." "Going there" will not change the politician or the campaign. But for those who do go, it will provide some underutilized leverage on the twin subjects of authenticity and representation. And while the search for authenticity may not yield easy answers, the search itself will make us more comfortable in thinking about the subject of representation in a large democracy.

Notes

1. Lionel Trilling, who worried about the ideas of sincerity and authenticity in the art world, concludes that "sincerity and authenticity are [words] which are best not talked about if they are to retain any force of meaning." Lionel Trilling, *Sincerity and Authenticity*, Harcourt Brace Jovanovich (New York, 1980), p. 112.
2. Editorial, "Bidding the Kid Adieu," *Boston Globe*, July 7, 2002; David Halberstam, "The Perfectionist at the Plate," *New York Times*, July 9, 2002.
3. Henry Allen, "Past, Present, Future," *Washington Post National Weekly*, September 9–15, 2002. See also Mark Shields, "American Politics, Before and After 9/11," *Miller Center Report* (University of Virginia), 18, no. 2 (Spring 2002), p. 9.
4. William Powers, "Goodwill Lacking," *National Journal*, December 20, 2002.
5. Jack Welch, "Five Questions to Ask . . . ," *Wall Street Journal*, October 28, 2004.
6. Anonymous (Joe Klein), *Primary Colors*, Random House (New York, 1996), p. 366.
7. Katherine Boo, "Al Gore's Search for Himself," *Washington Post National Weekly*, December 6–12, 1993.
8. John Harwood and Hilary Stout, "Dole Tries to Hold Lead in Iowa Caucuses," *Wall Street Journal*, February 12, 1996.
9. Edward Walsh, "Once More with Hart," *Washington Post Weekly*, February 9, 1987.
10. John F. Harris, *The Survivor: Bill Clinton in the White House*, Random House (New York, 2005), p. xiii.

11. Francis X. Clines, "Goodbye and Good Riddance: A 9-Term Congressman Departs, with No Longing Glance Back," *New York Times,* November 15, 1996.
12. Daniel Henninger, "Rudy the Real Defeats TV's Political Artifice," *Wall Street Journal,* October 5, 2001.
13. Meg Greenfield, "Virtual Reality," *Newsweek,* December 4, 1995. Also Greenfield, "Imitation Everything," *Newsweek,* March 13, 1995.
14. Bella English, "Bradley's Wife Learns to Cheer," *Boston Globe,* July 13, 1999.
15. Wayne Slater, "Former Texas Governor Still a Crowd Pleaser," *Dallas Evening News* printed in *Rochester Democrat and Chronicle,* November 26, 1995. See also John Broder, "Hubby's Scandal Sinking Utah Lawmaker," *Los Angeles Times,* printed in *Rochester Democrat and Chronicle,* December 10, 1995.
16. Nicholas Lemann, "The Quiet Man," *New Yorker,* May 7, 2001.
17. Fred Barnes, "Paul Wellstone: Not a Faker, Just Plain Honest," *Wall Street Journal,* October 28, 2002.
18. Mark Leibovich, "Is She For Real?" *Washington Post Weekly,* October 14–20, 2002.
19. Stuart Rothenberg, "Could Richard Nixon Be the Role Model for a New Al Gore?" *Roll Call,* September 11, 2002.
20. William Saletan, "Bible Beltway," www.Slate.com, October 23, 2002.
21. April Witt, "Straddling the Economic Divide," *Washington Post,* October 29, 2002.
22. Mark Shields, "Wanted: Democrat Like McCain," *Rochester Democrat and Chronicle,* January 14, 2003.
23. PBS, *The Newshour,* January 3, 2003.
24. CNN, *The Capitol Gang,* January 10, 2004.
25. Dale Russakoff, "Learning from Defeat," *Washington Post Weekly,* August 2–8, 2004.
26. David Denison, "Role of a Lifetime," *Boston Globe,* September 10, 2004.
27. Chuck Raasch, "Kerry Shops His Public Persona," *Rochester Democrat and Chronicle,* August 24, 2004.
28. Patrick Healy, "A Year on Trail, Kerry Projects Confidence," *Boston Globe,* June 6, 2004.
29. Kate O'Beirne, "After the Election of 2004, What's Next?" *Washington Post Weekly,* November 15–21, 2004.
30. Richard Wolfe, "That V Word," *Newsweek,* November 10, 2004. Web-exclusive commentary.
31. Amanda Ripley, "Obama's Ascent," *Time,* November 15, 2004.
32. Al Quinlan, "Authenticity Matters Most," www.greenbergresearch.com, March 21, 2006.
33. Blaine Harden, "Reality Politics," *Washington Post Weekly Edition,* September 12–18, 2005.
34. Peggy Noonan, *What I Saw at the Revolution: A Political Life in the Reagan Era,* Random House (New York, 1990), p. 108.
35. Ibid., pp. xiii, 262, 334.
36. Jonathan Alter, "Playing the Gipper Card," *Newsweek,* February 1, 1999.
37. "Newsmakers," *Rochester Democrat and Chronicle,* March 23, 2006.
38. John McCain speaking about John Kerry, John Aloysius Farrell, "At the Center of Power, Seeking the Summit," *Boston Globe,* June 21, 2003.
39. John Sedgwick, "All the President's Men," *Boston Globe,* September 5, 2004.
40. Richard F. Fenno Jr., *Senators on the Campaign Trail: The Politics of Representation,* Oklahoma University Press (Norman, 1996), pp. 323–327. These judgments were supported by interviews, statewide visits, and 86 pages of description and analysis.
41. Ibid.
42. Richard Ben Cramer, *What It Takes: The Way to the White House,* Viking Books, New York, 1992, p. 95.

43. *Character Above All*, Public Broadcasting System, May 29, 1996.
44. David Broder, "The Satisfied But Skeptical Voter: Americans Yearn for a President with Character and Leadership," *Washington Post Weekly Edition*, November 15, 1999; Charles Kenney, "Trying Presidential Character On for Size," *Boston Globe*, July 5, 1987; Jonathan Alter, "The Real Character Issues," *Newsweek*, March 10, 1992; Joe Klein, "Character Not Ideology," *Newsweek*, November 13, 1995; Daniel Golden, "Is Anyone Clean Enough to Be President," *Boston Globe*, September 27, 1987.
45. Broder, "The Satisfied But Skeptical Voter."
46. Alter, "The Real Character Issues."
47. Sisela Bok, "School for Scandal," Press Politics and Public Policy Center, John F. Kennedy School of Government, Cambridge, MA, April 1990, p. 3.
48. "Encore Presentation: Who Is Gary Condit?" CNN, *People in the News*, August 25, 2001; Carolyn Lochead, "A Power Broker Comes of Age," *San Francisco Chronicle*, December 18, 1996.
49. J. A. Sbranti, "To Valley Folks, He's Just Gary," *Modesto Bee*, July 18, 1998.
50. Vern Williams, "A Day in the Life of Congressman Condit," *Merced Sun-Star*, September 3, 1998.
51. Sbranti, "To Valley Folks."
52. Sbranti, "To Valley Folks." See also Paula Zahn, *People in the News*, CNN Programs.
53. "Is Gary Condit Staying or Going," *The Point with Greta VanSusteren*, CNN, September 7, 2001.
54. CNN, "Encore Presentation."
55. Ibid.
56. Stirling Newberry, "Stone Wheels: Covering the Ground in Condit Country," www.democrats.com, Democrats.com Unity, the best description of the economy of Condit's "place."
57. David Bauder, "Walters Beats '60 Minutes,'" *Boston Globe*, June 11, 2003. See also Kennedy School of Government, "One Expert's Opinion: Alex Jones Discusses Media Coverage of Gary Condit," *Press Politics*, August 23, 2001.
58. CNN, "Encore Presentation."
59. CNN, "Is Gary Condit Staying."
60. Carla Marinucci and Stacy Finz, "Once Loyal Supporters Have Crisis of Faith in Condit Country," *San Francisco Chronicle*, August 19, 2001.
61. Frank Bruni, "Gary Condit Is Still Running," *New York Times Magazine*, February 17, 2002. In the months of high-profile fixation on the Condit story, this article stands virtually alone as one drawn from traveling around with the congressman at home. It was a Central Valley political story. But it was not treated as one.
62. Tom Kenworthy, "Understanding Chicken-hearted Incumbents," *Washington Post Weekly*, November 19–25, 1990.
63. Elizabeth Kolbert, "Fueled by Words Alone, Radio Ads Are Nastier," *New York Times*, October 5, 1992.
64. Richard Wolf, "Charges Fly and Voters Are Listening," *USA Today*, November 1, 2001.
65. Michael Oreskes, "TV's Role in '88: The Medium Is the Election," *New York Times*, October 30, 1988.
66. James Perry, "The Negative Campaign Ad Comes of Age in Eastern Races, Stealing the Limelight," *Wall Street Journal*, November 2, 1989.
67. Michael Oreskes, "America's Politics Loses Way As Its Vision Changes World," *New York Times*, March 18, 1990.
68. Helen Dewar, "It's Better to Look Good Than to Do Good," *Washington Post National Weekly*, December 2–8, 1991.

69. Albert Hunt, "Campaign '94: Nasty and Expensive," *Wall Street Journal*, November 3, 1994.
70. Robin Gerber, "Where Are the Volunteers," *Washington Post Weekly*, October 23, 1994.
71. Tom Shales, "What Kind of Campaign Were the Networks Covering: Aggressive Personal Questions Took Over the News," *Washington Post National Weekly*, June 18, 1984; D. C. Denison, "Richard Ben Cramer," *Boston Sunday Globe Magazine*, August 9, 2000.
72. Oreskes, "America's Politics Loses Way."

CHAPTER 4

Washington Perspectives:
Practice and Possibility

JOURNALISTS AND
CONSTITUENCIES

I have been arguing, off and on, that Capitol Hill journalism is too Washington-heavy and too constituency-light—which raises a set of performance questions. Do we have any indicators of this disparity? What are the disincentives and the incentives that help to explain the disparity? What differences might it make if journalists did more reporting from the constituencies? And with what political effect?

To stimulate this kind of discussion, evidence from one small slice of reportorial performance is presented. It is followed by a discussion of the disincentives and the incentives that might affect reportorial activity in the constituency. The chapter closes with case studies of two: Senators Trent Lott of Mississippi and John Culver of Iowa.

A FRAGMENT OF EVIDENCE

In the 1970s, as my interest in national politicians grew, I began setting aside newspaper and magazine articles about them. It was a casual, intermittent, and unsystematic practice. When I happened upon some written work that centered on a single member of Congress—one that seemed interesting and was *not* simply a campaign story—I would clip it and throw it into the bottom drawer of a file cabinet. Two piles—one for

House members, one for senators—grew quite randomly, according to my attentiveness and my reading habits. I had no preconceived idea of how or why, or if ever, they might be useful to me—except, perhaps, that they might be useful somehow in my teaching or be a source of ideas for some later studies of individual politicians.

In thinking about the Washington-centeredness of the media's treatment of our elected national legislators, my haphazard collection of articles about these individuals became a resource. From it, I thought, I might get a provisional reading on the extent to which Washington journalists make non-campaign-time visits to the home constituencies of the legislators they write about. It is a fragment of evidence. You cannot "take it to the bank." But you can use it to start a discussion.

The House member pile of articles numbered 94; the senator pile numbered 157. The articles spanned 40 years, from 1961 to 2002. About a third were concentrated in the 1970s and 1980s. The reason: Those were the years before Congress abolished the member's *Congressional Record* allocation—years in which I received it and perused it daily. In no sense do I consider these articles to be an accurate sample of writing on individual politicians. They are simply a casual sampling of articles available to me, a sampling that provides a crude first cut into a pattern that deserves a broader and better discussion. If, in the collection of these materials, there was any unconscious bias, however, it would have tilted *in favor of* home-based reporting, because my ongoing research was focused on home activities. If anything, therefore, the collection overrepresents home-based analyses by Washington's journalists.

Two caveats are important. First, I eliminated articles that were written by local reporters carrying local datelines. Factors accounting for the activity of local reporters are beyond the scope of this inquiry. Happily, Douglas Arnold has studied the work of those reporters for us.[1] Second, most of the articles written about the senators I had studied individually were discarded and could not be included. Should the general subject prove interesting, a systematic survey would, of course, be necessary.

I read each article and asked the question: *Does this article contain any evidence that the writer ever journeyed, personally, to the home district or home state of the politician he or she was writing about?* The evidence in Table 4.1 tells us that the writer traveled to the home district of a House member in 23 percent of the cases—about once for every five articles. Those proportions certainly provide evidence of district-level reporting. They give a fairer shake to the Washington media,

TABLE 4.1
Articles About Individual House Members and Senators: A Collection

	TOTAL ARTICLES	HOME VISITS BY AUTHOR	PERCENT HOME VISITS BY AUTHOR
House Members	94	21	22%
Senators	157	24	15%
Total	251	45	18%

perhaps, than I have implied. On the whole, however, the lopsidedness of Washington-centric reporting supports the thrust of my argument.

In nearly 80 percent of these representative-centered articles, the writer was disinclined, or unable, to seek firsthand information by visiting the politician's constituency. A large majority of articles about individual House members appear to have been researched and written in Washington and distributed from there to the country. While it is often asserted that "all politics is local," it cannot be asserted that "all national coverage of politics is local." The apparent mismatch is surely suggestive.

Table 4.1 also describes a similar compilation of the Senate-related articles in my file drawer. Not surprisingly, given the greater public prominence of U.S. senators, the overall size of the collection (157) is 40 percent larger than the House collection. But the proportion of home-based to Washington-based research is smaller.

If we combine my two collections, we find that about one story in five written about individual members of the U.S. Congress reflects the author's visit to a home constituency. It tells us, also, that on average one article per year reflects a journalist's firsthand perspective on home connections. The very provisional conclusion I draw from my collection is that a remarkably large percentage of articles written about our elected representatives in Congress gets produced entirely *in Washington*.

There is, to be sure, a nonnegligible amount of reporting of home relationships by Washington-based reporters.[2] The 45 stories in the table provide evidence of that. But the denominator here is 251 stories. And the overall product, in my view, is in no way proportionate to the importance of the "what are they like?" question being asked about our representatives and their representational practices. Put differently, this output is not likely to convince political junkies of the importance of non-Washington

washington journalists rarely travel to districts

perspectives. My fragment of evidence supports the notion that the home connections of our elected politicians are understudied and underreported elements of our representational system of government.

In addition, among the 45 articles that do reveal a constituency presence, fewer still display any journalistic interest in the larger subject of representation. Reading the 21 "home-grown" stories about House members, we search in vain for much appreciation of, or an evaluation of, the process of representation. By the most generous of reckonings, not more than 3 of the 12 locally researched profiles even allude to the idea of representation. In the Senate cluster, it takes a similar stretch to place 4 of the 24 home-researched articles in a category that came close to the idea of representation. At best, therefore, only 2 percent of the articles in the collection demonstrate interest in the basic political process involved—representation.

This marked imbalance may reflect an assumption among journalists that legislative activity subsumes representational activity. Perhaps their idea is that representational activity is irrelevant to legislative activity. If so, both assumptions are wrong.

why so little focus on Representation?

LEAVING WASHINGTON: DISINCENTIVES

It will help us understand the dominant pattern of Table 4.1 if we consider some disincentives that might be operating when Washington reporters and/or their editors make their decisions about information gathering. The long-run disincentive is, of course, the dominant and mesmerizing decision-making activity at the nation's Capitol—all politics, all the time. But more manageable short-run calculations involving time, interest, and payoff also help account for the pattern of neglect.

The length of time involved is an obvious disincentive. Richard Ben Cramer's successful study of six presidential candidates—Bob Dole in small-town Kansas, Mike Dukakis in suburban Massachusetts, for example—is a superb home-based analysis. But it took him several years and multiple visits to do it—more time than most political reporters have available to them. "Campaign reporters," says Ben Cramer, "think they're in the character business; but they have no purchase on real character. It's long and difficult work to put the events of a life into context."[3] On-the-run, in-and-out constituency visits are very likely to produce sweeping and unsupported judgments. After a praiseworthy one-day visit with a U.S. senator in his home state, a *New York Times* reporter generalized: "He is, at age 51, a man who has based his career on avoiding unpopular stands."[4] Where, we might ask, did that sweeping conclusion come from? Surely not from a one-day visit!

A structural wrinkle in the matter of time constraints is the trend toward newspaper consolidation and the resulting decline in the number of available Washington reporters. Newspaper chains may have economized by hiring fewer Washington reporters to cover an expanding territory.[5] The reporters who remain will have a strong disincentive to increase their workload even more by traveling outside Washington—except, perhaps, in the heat of a temporarily interesting election campaign.

Consolidation decisions may result from a decided lack of interest in political reporting among publishers and editors. A 1992 study of the press and Congress concludes that "the views of those who cover Congress day in and day out differ from the views of those who manage the media organizations and make the decisions about what stories will be covered and what tone the coverage will take."[6] The media managers, that is, tend to think less well of Congress, to emphasize "day-to-day coverage," and to downplay congressional activity that "looks after voters and responds to their problems."[7] In sum, editors and publishers seem unlikely to give priority to beyond-the-beltway research when they assign their Washington reporters and analysts.

In addition, some reporters will lack the incentive to go out into the field to study politicians, even if they were given the time. "Why do you have to go out and talk to people including senators and presidential candidates," asks political journalist Richard Reeves, "when it's all on C-SPAN and the Internet?"[8] He is surely not alone in his inability to imagine what might be of reader interest or bring an extra payoff if he were to follow a politician at home.

And with some reason. Consider the discouraging experience of one who did—NPR journalist Linda Killian. She researched her book on the 1994 Republican freshmen in the House by traveling around with her central character in his Tennessee constituency. It was, like Ben Cramer's, an exemplary effort to explore home connections.[9] But it won her this putdown from the *New York Times* book reviewer. "All that we learn" from her home visit, he wrote, "is what Fred Barnes made clear in a memorable article some years ago: that the ins and outs of the average congressman's day are actually quite boring. Killian makes us feel it."[10]

Ho hum, nothing important here. One article by Fred Barnes settled that! For people accustomed to life on the Washington celebrity circuit, every-day life in the country—"out there" in Meg Greenfield's "podunk"—is easily written off as "boring."

By relying only on what they can learn in Washington, journalists not only miss what happens back home, but they risk overemphasizing easily available material at the expense of that which is hard to get. Consider, for example, money. Washington journalists have available to them, stored in the nearest computer, all they need to know about a candidate's political money—where it came from, how it is spent, and what special constituency interest is seeking access and votes from whom in return. As a result, money data get mined, probed, classified, charted, graphed, mas-saged, and compared endlessly and voluminously by interested groups and by the media, from one election cycle to the next. And the results cer-tainly do tell us a lot about our elected officials. But money data can eas-ily become a convenient and inadequate surrogate for a more complete and broad-gauged study of representational politics. If, of course, we let it happen. Much like the Washington reporters' focus on winning, a focus on money (and its impact on winning) can crowd out close-up questions about connectedness and authenticity.

In sum, a collection of disincentives—no time, no interest, no encour-agement, no support, no pizzazz, no payoff, no curiosity—probably serves to keep most reporters, most of the time, in Washington.

Capping all these individual calculations and disincentives, there is an enduring *comfort calculus* among Washington media people that keeps journalists satisfied with their Washington perspective and professionally disinclined to change. It is not my idea. It is theirs.

"Washington," writes media critic Howard Kurtz, "is an incredibly inbred and incestuous community in which everybody talks to the same seventeen people and arrives at the same conventional wisdom."[11] Journal-ists are part of the community, they profit from it, and they have little incentive to leave it. "We were once society's outsiders," Kurtz says, "but today [we] would rather be going to a Georgetown party with senator so and so and business leader so and so. . . . We now, many of us, are part of the game. Rather than identifying more with the plumbers out there, we identify with the policy-makers and the politicians."[12] The reward for playing the Washington game, he says, is "celebrityhood." Those who have tasted it want to keep it; those who aspire to it want to stay and play that game.

Reporters in Washington

"What's interesting to me," says former reporter Paul Taylor, "is the phenomenon of pack journalism . . . that in the end, we are fish in a school and we are oriented to one another. . . . [And] the nature of today's pack journalism is that you have ninety-nine percent of the energy going into covering one percent of the stories. . ."[13] "In Washington, DC," he writes, "it's the journalist who sits on the electronic throne and everybody else sort of comes and goes."[14] "In Washington," agrees Mark Hertsgaard, "you have a Palace Court Press. And they reflect the views within the palace that is known as official Washington . . . the problem with so much of the coverage in Washington is that the habits of mind that inform it, the sympathies that inform it are all with the people at the top. And not with the people outside the palace."[15] Doubtless, too, career promotions reflect and strengthen the calculus. All in all, there would seem to be little incentive to change focus or venue.

To be sure, there are a few—very few—reporters who regularly leave the capital, in David Broder's words, to do "very old fashioned shoe-leather reporting, walking the precincts, knocking on people's doors."[16] But Broder stands out as a practitioner. "David really gets out and talks to people," says the *Washington Post*'s one-time ombudsman Geneva Overholser. "But it's interesting that he should be so lauded for actually getting out there and talking to people. That's what reporters ought to be doing. And it shows how few do it anymore."[17] They don't. And her media colleagues have helped to explain why they don't.

The disincentives and the decisions that keep our journalists tied to Washington are partly individual and partly collective. Taken together, they help us understand the Washington-centeredness of our political journalism.

LEAVING WASHINGTON:
INCENTIVES

If it is true, as I believe it is, that Washington journalism is too tightly tied to the capital city, why would any of them leave their base of operations to travel with a politician at home? Given the manifold disincentives, what positive incentives might there be? The best reply I can think of is to get a better answer to the "what are they really like?" question or to get a better fix on an individual's authenticity. In each case, "better" means "better than you can get in Washington." And "different" means "different from what you get in Washington." Which leads me to ask, "Why might this be so?" My experience suggests several incentives.

At home, politicians are more likely to be *spontaneous*. They are relating to people who know them, who are familiar to them, and who know what they were like before they went to Washington. With these people, a politician is likely to be "more at ease," "unshirted," less guarded, more "natural." If he or she adopts a "fake persona," long-time acquaintances will recognize it. And they will not accept it as Washingtonians so often do—or, for lack of choice, must do.

I once heard campaign consultant Cathy Allen give advice to neophyte candidates who worried about how to present themselves to the electorate: "Make your case to your family and friends," she advised. "After that, it's all tactical." And she followed it up by advising consultants, "If you try to make a candidate something she or he is not, you will lose." People back home, who are closest to the politician, can best certify whether the candidate is the real thing. For their part, politicians work hardest to convey reassuring continuities when they are connecting with constituents at home. For observers, it is a prime vantage point from which to search for authenticity.

Traveling around with a politician permits observation in a great variety of contexts, as she presents herself to different individuals with their different interests, different sensitivities, and different historical connections with the politician. You can observe consistency of presentation and consistency in comfort level. (The "at homeness index," I have called it).[18] And you can listen afterward to the individual's reactions, appraisals, worries, and enjoyments. The sheer range of subject matter and experiences is conducive to a more reliable fix on what is repetition, what is common denominator, and what is variation.

When they are home, too, politicians usually have *more time* to talk and to reflect. They tend to be less harried by scheduling and find more moments of relaxation. Riding in the car from meeting to meeting often leaves a good bit of time to schmooze; reminisce; tell stories; compare events, individuals, groups, and places; and ruminate out loud—especially at the end of the day—about careers and connections. Observation at home is less constrained by time and subject matter than observation in Washington. Personal relationships between the observer and observed may develop to a degree that is impossible around the Capitol. In short, home provides more angles and more opportunities for the observer to cross-check experiences and reactions to events against one another, to assess consistency, character, and, hopefully, authenticity.

Experience tells me, finally, that the search for authenticity—this elusive idea—requires *stories:* personal stories, career stories, event stories, relationship stories. The best stories come from one-on-one conversations and firsthand observation of candidate-constituent connections and contexts. When I am asked what I want to do and see when I am in the district, I always say that I prefer to see the politician in as many different contexts as possible. And I avoid like the plague—if I have a choice—long-running events that eat up long periods of time and thus keep me away from the person I came to be with.

Frequent changes in activities and locations create valuable in-between time to talk or to tell stories while riding in the car, walking to and from a meeting, sitting in the home office, sharing a meal, and visiting friends—sometimes one-on-one, sometimes in the company of others. I call it "travel talk." It is the core of an exploratory research effort. It is also the core of the implicit bargain that has been struck when the politician agrees to let me come and "hang around–tag along" in the home constituency. Watching, listening, and talking inevitably yields events, the elaboration of events, and stories, all of which become critical in figuring out what another person is "really like."

When I completed my first 1970s study of 18 House members—and long before I entertained the idea of authenticity—I made a stab at answering the "what are they like?" question by noting some attitudes and behaviors I had observed during my constituency travels. They were attitudes and behaviors I had not known or appreciated from my earlier experiences with politicians on Capitol Hill. I wrote (in part),

> Intellectually, I knew that politicians required physical stamina. Having flogged myself around eighteen districts with them, I now think physical attributes are more important to political success than I previously believed. The second attribute . . . that has been highlighted by these visits is their sheer competitiveness . . . they *hate* to lose. We know they want to win; but they seem to be more driven by a determination not to lose. A third attribute that looms somewhat larger to me now is the politician's ability to keep from taking himself too seriously. It is something an outsider has less opportunity to observe on Capitol Hill where each House member seems to be a

king or queen in his or her own empire—isolated from everyday life, fawned over by staff, pampered by Capitol Hill employees, sought after by all manner of supplicants. In the district, they are more likely to be reminded of their ordinariness. When people ask me what they are like, I now stress stamina, competitiveness and a stabilizing perspective on themselves. I would not have stressed the same things after my Capitol Hill experiences.[19]

I recall these judgments not to give them any special weight but only to introduce the notion that we can learn some things by hanging around with politicians in their home districts—things like their connection patterns—that are hard to learn in Washington.

Compare, for example, a pair of media treatments of former Senate Majority Leader Tom Daschle. In 2001, C-SPAN went to South Dakota to televise "the most powerful Democratic legislator" on one leg of his "annual driving tour of his state." The managing editor of the Capitol Hill newspaper, *Roll Call*, reviewed the tape for his Washington readership. Under the title "On the Road with Daschle," the author began, "He motors himself around without staff and drops in on constituents in various *podunks* [italics added]. The video aired last week provided some hysterical scenes of Daschle doing everything from riding a monstrous fire truck to picking out beef jerky at a convenience store."[20] And so on for 12 snickering paragraphs. From his Capitol Hill perch, the writer watched the minority leader as he connected with his constituents—and found only terminal triviality. There are no reflections on "what is he like?" nor did the writer seem to expect any from the politician's constituency activities.

A second Washington reporter, observing that "Daschle's driving tours are the stuff of legend in South Dakota," decided to travel with the Senate minority leader in his constituency. From that vantage point, he produced a totally different picture of the same activity.[21] "Daschle," he reported, "is a politician of formidable interpersonal skills, many of which were on display when he traveled [home] last month to South Dakota." "Daschle's low key, low profile appearances at cattle auctions, health clinics and coffee shops," the author discovered, "are typical of his self-effacing approach to politics." They are consistent with his "soft spoken demeanor" as his party's leader in Washington. And this observer concludes, therefore, that "a trip to South Dakota offers clues to his remarkable rise" in Washington.[22]

He elaborates. One afternoon following "a morning of interviews, a question and answer session with constituents at a local restaurant," and "a meeting with elementary school teachers," the author observes that "Daschle seems to relish such encounters." And Daschle agreed. "It energizes me," he explained. "I really learn from them. I think it's awfully hard to get into a debate on the floor of the Senate without having experiences like that."[23] That comment, generated out of a Senator's ongoing home connections, links the study of representation to the study of legislation. The home-generated article puts a positive value on constituency connections instead of the routine podunk putdown in Capitol Hill's *Roll Call*.[24]

Going to the constituency and being there, I believe, made all the difference. A pair of case studies will, I hope, buttress that conclusion.

WASHINGTON MYOPIA: THE CASE OF TRENT LOTT

On December 20, 2002, incoming Senate Majority Leader Trent Lott of Mississippi resigned—under pressure—from the most powerful position in the U.S. Senate. It was a quintessential Washington story. It engaged, excited, and transfixed the Washington press corps for two weeks. It all began with a comment by Lott at a birthday celebration for 100-year-old South Carolina Senator Strom Thurmond. Referring to Thurmond's presidential candidacy in 1948, Lott commented, "I want to say this about my state. When Strom Thurmond ran for President, we voted for him. We're proud of him. And if the rest of the country had followed our lead, we wouldn't have had all these problems over all these years, either." C-SPAN's cameras rolled while numerous reporters listened. Since Thurmond had run a pro-states-rights, anti-integration campaign, Lott's comments could be, and quickly were, interpreted by civil rights advocates as racist—certainly in content, and arguably in intent.

Controversy soon erupted and grew. At first, however, the Washington press corps remained strangely silent, while other observers picked up Lott's comment and placed its racial implications on the public agenda. Press silence was interpreted by media watchdogs as a failure—prompting much wonderment and self-examination. Strangely, too, from my perspective, when Washington's journalists belatedly did pick up on the story—and massaged it to death—they failed to answer the questions: "Who is this guy?" "What is Trent Lott really like?" Indeed, they never asked.

What is especially remarkable about both journalistic failures is this: that Trent Lott was no ordinary Washington politician. For nearly eight years, he had been the second most important elected Republican leader (whip) in the U.S. House of Representatives. For two years, he had been the second-ranking Republican leader (whip) in the U.S. Senate. And for six years, he had been, arguably, the most powerful Republican in the U.S. Senate—first as minority leader, then as majority leader, and again as minority leader. On that lengthy and formidable record of personal and political accomplishment alone, Trent Lott *should have been among the most studied and the best known* U.S. senators of his day. Yet, when he spoke, the remarkable silence of the Washington press indicated otherwise.

The shortcomings of the Washington press corps, I would argue, resulted from their lack of interest in, and knowledge about, Trent Lott. In particular, they did not know, and were not curious about, Trent Lott in the context that had generated his controversial comments—Mississippi. The Trent Lott story was not just a Washington story. It was a Mississippi story, too. The sentiments he expressed were rooted in Mississippi. Had their personal assessments of Trent Lott been derived from experience in his Mississippi constituency, Washington journalists would have been primed with firsthand knowledge of race-related attitudes and activities in that place. They would have personally observed Lott's connections and listened to his philosophy. They would have been filled with firsthand knowledge of what Trent Lott was like. Under those conditions, they would, I believe, have responded quickly, knowledgeably, and contextually to his birthday party remarks. But they did not.

The day after Majority Leader Lott uttered his remarks, they appeared—not in the newspapers or on television—but on the Internet. On his Talking Points Web site, Joshua Micah Marshall noted that "Strom Thurmond's candidacy was based exclusively and explicitly upon the preservation of legalized segregation and opposition to voting rights and civil rights for blacks. Look at what incoming Majority Leader Trent Lott said about that candidacy yesterday."[25] A day later, he repeated that "Trent Lott seemed to implicitly endorse the pro-segregation, anti-civil rights platform Strom Thurmond ran for President on in 1948 . . . perhaps at a minimum, he'd like to apologize or take it back."[26] At that point, two days after Lott's comment, the controversy had captured the attention of numerous bloggers. Glenn Reynolds on Instapundit noted that Lott's remark had not yet appeared on the Democratic Party's Web site. "It seems the blogosphere's way ahead on this one," he wrote. "*Where's everyone else?*"[27] It is my question, too.

On that very same day, for example, CNN correspondent Jonathan Karl—who would become CNN's lead reporter on the story—interviewed Trent Lott. He conducted a chatty, friendly, and brief interview, focusing on the recent election—which would soon return Lott to the majority leader's job. "I've been smiling an awful lot lately," said Lott. "So I'm pretty happy." "Have you been gloating at all?" Karl asked. "No . . . I have tried very hard not to gloat."[28] That exchange carried the interview's tone and substance. There was nothing about Lott's remarks two days earlier. Blogger Marshall tracked Karl's interview. He wrote, "On [CNN's] *Inside Politics,* the John Kerry hair story made the cut, not the Trent Lott segregation story."[29]

The nation's bloggers were way ahead of Washington's press corps in recognizing an issue and shaping a Washington story. "By Monday," wrote media critic Howard Kurtz, "with the mainstream press still largely snoozing, Web writers were leading the charge."[30] So much so, indeed, that years later, another media analyst would call "the Lott resignation" story a watershed media event. It marked, he wrote, "the coming of age of the blogging world."[31] Indeed, the bloggers themselves would celebrate it, and they would use it to generate a lively internal discussion about their relationship to the mainstream media.[32] Students of the media, too, would use the Lott study to analyze this interrelationship.[33]

Five days after the Lott story surfaced on the web, the *Washington Post* printed its first major story, single authored, on page 13, where it shared a page with two other stories.[34] The next day's story—on page 6—had two authors. The third day, it reached page 1, where it remained, most every day, to the end. Lott's resignation story finally commanded a banner headline across page 1 plus seven separate Lott-related stories. In all, 16 *Washington Post* staff reporters captured bylines for the story—not to mention the work of the *Post*'s columnists. It was a big story. But they had not recognized it until they were hit over the head with it.

The *New York Times* reacted similarly—late on the uptake but, once engaged, going full throttle. Its Washington coverage also began five days late—with a 13-paragraph, single-authored story on page 28. The Lott saga reached the front page two days later, and it remained there for the duration. Lott's resignation-day story commanded a three-column headline plus six stories. In the end, 14 *Times* reporters had contributed to its coverage.

As Washington's journalists caught on and caught up, Trent Lott's troubles grew apace. A string of Lott apologies and repudiations never caught up with the growth of criticism. The developing story was described as "a brush fire turned into a bonfire," as "snowballing into an avalanche," and later as "a freight train going downhill without a brake."[35] After a week, the Washington press was engaged in what one observer called "a full blown, F-4 feeding frenzy from the media."[36] They chronicled "the daily tug of war, the hourly tug of war here in Washington."[37] After ten days, editorials had blossomed across the country, in newspapers large and small—some expressing outrage, others prudence—calling for Lott's resignation.[38]

As the story developed, however, press people continued to remark on its slow early development: "It grew slowly as a news story over this past weekend."[39] "Although the remarks were broadcast on C-SPAN, the story had little traction. . . ."[40] And they continued to puzzle: "Why were reporters caught napping when Trent Lott embraced the segregationist candidacy of Strom Thurmond?"[41]

Pushing that question aside for the moment, what did the Washington press corps contribute once they became seized of the story? Two things: *First,* they turned to their archives for information, and *second,* they kept the running score as the two-week controversy took its course. In doing so, they followed their professional instincts. To have done otherwise, like heading straight for Mississippi—my prescription—would have been contrary to instinct.

In their archives, the *Post* and the *Times* found that Lott had made the very same favorable comments about Thurmond back in 1980. They dug up his fairly lengthy voting record on race-related measures—such as his opposition to the Martin Luther King holiday and voting rights protections. They also revealed that, in college, he had favored keeping blacks out of his national fraternity. Some of their reports had originated in Mississippi newspapers. It was a record that only the major media could unearth, assemble, and authenticate—which they did, and did admirably.[42]

Second, the Washington press corps produced a daily—even hourly—updated assessment of relevant events and commentary, together with predictions about the outcome. Is this or that apology enough to save the senator? Is he going to survive? What does the president say? Which senators are for him and who against? Who is on whose side, why, and for how long? Does he have the votes? Every newspaper edition and every television show, day and night, were full of it—all Trent Lott, all the time.

Citizens could tune in at any time to learn the very latest findings, actions, comments, and betting odds. Once awakened, the Washington media gave us a textbook performance in nonstop political scorekeeping.

And yet, media watchers remained markedly self-critical. They continued to puzzle over their own performance, particularly their tardiness in recognizing and picking up the story. It was, said watchdog Kurtz, "a colossal misjudgment." "Why," he asked, "were Washington reporters . . . asleep at the switch? . . . Why did it take so long for most major newspapers to jump on the controversy even after it was mentioned?" "Lott's remarks were covered on C-SPAN, but the media seemed to kiss off the story."[43]

Washington journalists responded to these various queries predictably—that is, with media-centered rationales. They were slow, they explained, because the story was "buried under news about Iraq etc.," because "there were several other very big stories that day."[44] Or because too few favorite media "sources" were available: "The Senate isn't in session [so] you have 100 senators scattered all over the world."[45] Or if you miss a story during the first 24-hour news cycle, the story will perish or will get buried under newer breaking news.[46] These early explanations centered on the news-making system, not on the journalists themselves, their instincts, their routines, their preparation.

Self-criticism appeared, too. One focused on the younger reporters who, "because of their age," "were not familiar with Strom Thurmond's history" and "just didn't get it."[47] Or, "There's sort of a club with secret handshakes where reporters get friendly with senators like Trent Lott over the years and cut them plenty of slack."[48] One talk show host remembered "being confused by the pure weirdness of the remark . . . such an odd remark."[49]

After Lott's resignation, one media columnist focused attention on the journalists themselves—not to explain their early silence, but to explain their continuing lack of sympathy. *National Journal's* William Powers wrote, "Why the Lott story took off so slowly is a good question. But just as good is . . . why, once it did, it had staying power."[50] His answer to the entire puzzle was that the senator lacked any "cushion" of "goodwill" on the part of Washington journalists and other observers. Put simply, people didn't like Trent Lott.

"Based on the events of the last week," wrote Powers,

we can safely place Lott among the goodwill-deficient. It's true his story took several days to get traction, but once it did, it soon became clear that very few people in politics or the media had warm feelings of any kind about the Senate Majority Leader. If goodwill were a bank account, Lott had a shockingly low balance; especially for someone who has been in public life for so long and has risen so high. He rose without acquiring any appreciable goodwill among his colleagues, the media or the public at-large.

It was the only early effort I found to ask the "what is he like?" question regarding Trent Lott. The assertion is made that he was not likable and that Washington journalists knew him well enough to render personal judgments. But there is no supporting evidence for either assertion, nor does the author suggest or entertain any constituency-centered perspective on Trent Lott.

After Lott's fate was settled, Howard Kurtz directed another performance question at his colleagues. "Why," he asked, "did the press suddenly start savaging Lott's civil rights record after ignoring it for years?"[51] Newscaster Aaron Brown echoed that theme. "There is one nagging question that remains," he asked. "Why did it take so long? Trent Lott's affection for his good old days was hardly a secret. He'd been saying similar things for years."[52] And columnist Mark Shields agreed that "this is a man who has said . . . [these] things for a long, long time that haven't been covered. I mean like a tree falling in the forest. Now, all of a sudden, they're being covered."[53]

According to this view, the media—despite Trent Lott's high-ranking political position—had simply not been paying much attention to him. If Washington journalists hadn't been following him closely, it certainly helps to explain the sluggishness with which they came to recognize the possible impact of his remarks. And it raises, once again, the question of their inattentiveness to such an important player in the Senate.

New York Times media critic Frank Rich agreed with Kurtz about media tardiness. But he took the explanation in a different direction— one more in tune with my own view. When it was all over, Rich wrote:

> Mr. Lott's new offense almost fell through the journalistic cracks. Though his embrace of Mr. Thurmond's past took place in a room full of Washington reporters and politicos and was broadcast on C-SPAN, it was not at first reported in any paper (or on any evening TV news broadcast), even by those that did cover the Thurmond party. Why? It may be because the spectacle of a leading Republican back slapping with unreconstructed Dixiecrats did not initially strike anyone as big news.[54]

This was the least flattering explanation of all—that Washington media people had, indeed, become so much a part of the overall Washington culture that they had lost their professional perspective on what was happening there.

They had become Exhibit A of what Kurtz himself earlier had called "the inbred and incestuous community" in which journalists increasingly sought not "the story," but "celebrityhood." In the case of Trent Lott, the Washington press people attending his talk had become part of the performing cast and were no longer part of the critical audience. The upstart bloggers, of course, were neither so disoriented nor so compromised. They needed only a knowledge of some political history to get them engaged. Their unobstructed view and their personal independence remained intact. Indeed, they had been born to promote fresh perspectives—and controversy.

If any prescription for Washington's mainstream journalists were to follow from Frank Rich's view, it would be: "get out of Washington for a while and recover your perspective." And that is where I come in. From a management point of view, rotating assignments in and out of Washington would be one remedy. But if newspaper editors do not want to lose the valuable experience, knowledge, savvy, and contacts of their reporters, they might deliberately send them out into the country occasionally to scrape their encrusted antennae.

As I watched and read about Washington media performance in the Trent Lott case, I was struck by how little firsthand knowledge about him—or experience with him—was available to the journalists involved. I was struck, particularly, by how little usable constituency-centered experience and knowledge could be brought to bear on this high-ranking politician. Journalists were simply not primed to take his statements seriously. The idea of "priming" suggests that when certain attitudinal or informational stimuli are presented to people prior to their making observations or judgments, these prior stimuli will affect those people's subsequent observations and their judgments. Firsthand exposure to an elected politician's constituency relationships will prime a person to think about constituency relationships whenever the politician becomes an object of interest.

Had Washington journalists spent time in Trent Lott's constituency, traveled around with him, watched, talked, and listened to him in that *place*, I believe they would have been prepared to recognize his race-related, civil rights–related, segregationist-related comment. And they would have done so in a New York minute. But they were not primed to react to a Mississippi-centered comment. They did not know or think of Trent Lott in the context from which he came—his home constituency. Lacking the priming effects of exposure to his constituency context, they were ill prepared to raise or to answer the "what is he really like?" question. They flat-out missed the representational story.

The exception—which may prove the rule—was the immediate reaction to the Lott comment by Thomas Edsall of the *Washington Post*. He reacted because he was primed to do so. Almost alone, he had Mississippi stories to tell about Trent Lott—stories that were waiting to be "dug up" by the *New York Times*. Edsall did not attend the party, but he learned of it the next day from the *Post* reporter who had covered it as a social event. "I began to press that we should do a story on that [Lott] quote," he recalled.[55] After several rebuffs from the *Post*'s editors, who saw it as a nonstory, he was given a small space in the following day's paper—on page 6. Though buried and unnoticed, it was the first major newspaper story. Edsall reported (from his colleague's recollections) "an audible gasp and general silence" after the pro-segregationist comment. He solicited a "stunned" reaction from prominent civil rights leader, Representative John Lewis. And drawing on his own previous research, he described Senator Lott's earlier association with a "racialist" group in Mississippi.[56]

Reporter Edsall's out-front role had been generated out of his own extensive prior research in the South—some of which was about Trent Lott. There had been, first, his 1991 book, *Chain Reaction: The Impact of Race, Rights and Taxes on American Politics*.[57] In researching the book about "race-laden and race-driven conflict," Edsall wrote, "I followed the advice of my colleague, David Broder, and spent a substantial amount of time walking through the neighborhoods (many of them in the deep South, though not in Mississippi) going door-to-door."[58] In 1998 and 1999, he wrote several articles about Trent Lott's "sustained relations"— via speeches, meetings, pictures, visits—to the Mississippi Council of Conservative Citizens group "considered racist by conservatives and liberals."[59] Lott vigorously denounced the group and its views.[60]

When Trent Lott spoke, therefore, *one* journalist was primed to react. So far as I can discover, it was he and he alone who had positioned himself out in front of the story. Even so, Edsall had to wait two more days before his paper's management decided to let him do the Lott story (still placed near the back of the paper) that would launch the *Post*'s full-scale coverage.[61] Does one story demonstrate that journalists *had to* have firsthand knowledge about Lott's constituency to get a sense for what he was like? Probably not. But this journalist's prior research on Southern segregation politics generally, and Lott's connections in particular, is persuasive evidence in accounting for his unique response.

Once the Lott story hit the headlines, what other Washington reporting perception was available to help answer the "what is he like?" question? Not much. In my unsystematic research, I came across four pieces. The first, contained in my earlier Table 4.1 tally, was a 1996 *Congressional Quarterly* story about his "classic power struggle" for the job of Republican majority leader against his Mississippi colleague, Thad Cochran. They interviewed a number of informed Mississippians, but there was no evidence that the authors had ever been there.[62] People from the state were quoted concerning the common ambition, the "contrasting political styles," and their factional rivalries back home. It did touch slightly on Trent Lott's representational ties. But it was totally neglected during the 2000 uproar.

In my later reading, I came across only one reporter who was ready with a firsthand story to contribute to the 2002 Lott saga. Karen Tumulty of *Time* recalled that Lott had told her "in the mid-80's that he led a fight to prevent [his college] fraternity nationally from integrating." And she added, "At the time, it wasn't newsworthy. It was something that a Senator from Mississippi, who most people had never heard of, told me. But as this story got into the news . . . it became clear to me as a reporter that I had sort of a piece of the puzzle here."[63] As—almost alone—she did.

Support for the "priming" notion came from the experience, also, of reporter Gwen Ifil, who had gone to Mississippi "a few years ago" to inquire about a speech Trent Lott had reportedly made to an allegedly white supremacist group in the state. "I remember going to Mississippi at the time," she said, "and trying to do a story for NBC about his comments and about what people in Mississippi thought he meant. And it didn't ever gel."[64] That was all she said.

As an African American, however, Ifil was already primed to react immediately to Lott's birthday comments. And she was the first to display them on her *Washington Week in Review* television program just *two* days after he said it. "What was he thinking?" she asked. And she invited her audience to email their answers.[65] Understandably, leaders of the black community nationally were among the earliest to react to the story, and they became, to the end, the leading edge of Lott's critics.

I came across one article that mentioned a Mississippi contact with the senator. It was a brief, five-paragraph, 1999 story by *Newsweek* reporter

Julia Reed in which she recalled a 1996 interview with the new majority leader in his Pascagoula living room.[66] She described him as "a guarded and intensely private man" who told her that he was not accustomed to allowing "any look at my private life beyond my political life." By watching him continuously tidying up himself and his surroundings, she speculated that he had "an almost pathological need for order." He also told her, "I'm a lot more pragmatic than anybody realizes." Standing alone, these thoughts do not tell us much about what he is "really like." And while his first comment does not seem overly encouraging about traveling with him at home, the very fact of the interview suggests possibilities.

As far as I can tell, therefore, Washington's journalists had not asked and had not answered the question, "what is Trent Lott really like?" My suggestion to the media critics who asked each other, "Why did we take so long to pick up on the story?" is this: "You never had much interest in Trent Lott—certainly not proportionate to his power. You never went home with him to learn about him by observing his representational connections in his home constituency." The senator had begun his fateful comment with, "Let me tell you about my home state." For Lott himself—and for understanding Lott—"my home state" was crucial. His autobiography, published much later, makes that connection—"son of Mississippi," "Mississippi and I grew up together"—compellingly clear.[67] Because Washington's journalists had not gotten to know him in that place, they were not primed to react quickly and appropriately when he uttered his constituency-centered comments. And they didn't.

The most helpful journalistic summary I read was one in *Time*—of which Karen Tumulty was coauthor. It was helpful because it emphasized the importance of his constituency in thinking about Trent Lott. They quoted his Pascagoula press conference, where he had emphasized place. "I grew up in an environment that condoned policies and views that we now know were wrong and immoral."[68] He explained to *Time*'s reporters how he had come to change, by emphasizing the learning that came from traveling from place to place inside his home state.

"We lived in this cocoon in Pascagoula," he told them. "Everybody had a job. The schools were good. But it's different in the Delta. There, I've seen that a lot of people don't have the opportunity we had." He and his home place had changed together. "I have changed," he said. "People in Mississippi have changed."[69] They quoted a friend of his: "The most important thing to understand about Trent Lott is that he never left Mississippi. He did not grow in the sense of trying to understand the country. He's never outgrown who he is and where he comes from."[70] If someone had wanted to look for the authentic Trent Lott, some good advice would have been to go there, hang out with him, and see his home place through his eyes. Not to affect the outcome, of course, but to enlighten others who might be wondering, "who is this guy?"

When it was all over, the *Washington Post*'s Helen Dewar, the premier Capitol Hill observer of the U.S. Senate, wrote a "what is he like?" article. Under the title "For Lott, Power Rests on Friends More Than Followers," she described his Senate leadership behavior in these words: "relentless ambition, hard work, luck, cunning, southern collegiality, sharp elbows, a penchant for order and self-confidence."[71] She painted a picture of a complex person and leader. And she should know. But her appraisal came too late to inform the controversy. In any case, it rested entirely on his performance in Washington. It was a Capitol Hill look. There was nothing in it to stimulate a look at—or a visit to—Mississippi.

A more telling postmortem effort was the work by *New York Times* reporters David Halbfinger and Jeffrey Gentleson. They wrote *from* Mississippi, and their work suggests what might have been done earlier to prepare journalists for an immediate response to Lott's comment. The two men went to Mississippi—along with a lot of other Washington journalists—to cover the senator's press conference in his hometown. But unlike the others, they remained to look at Trent Lott's life in his constituency. They wrote two articles: "In Lott's Life, Long Shadows of Segregation" and "Black and White Doubt Their Senator's Seniority."[72] They did some on-the-spot library research—uncovering Lott's first Capitol Hill job with his own segregationist congressman, for example. And they talked, in context, to people who knew him.

Their conversations suggest the potential value of a constituency perspective. When asked (at the press conference) to describe and place in time his own conversion from supporting segregation to repudiating it, Mr. Lott had declined. "But asked again, as he was walking to his car," the authors wrote, "Lott told them he switched his thinking 'way back there.' 'What exactly had changed his mind?' 'Maturity,' he said. 'And experience, learning.'"[73] I could imagine a very enlightening follow-up conversation back and forth, riding in the car with him in the Mississippi setting. Such a conversation might even have generated a more many-sided and, hence, a more favorable view of the senator than the prevailing one.

In a conversation with a local Baptist minister, the *Times* reporters heard evidence illuminating the difference in black voter support for Senator Thad Cochran (32 percent) and Senator Lott (11 percent).[74] Said the minister,

"Senator Cochran has worshiped with us. But when Trent Lott is here, he worships at First Baptist on Live Oak. First Baptist is white."[75] As someone who has accompanied white Southern politicians in black churches there, I think the potential for elaborating that brief remark in an offhand, one-on-one conversation is large and crucial. Had Washington journalists done this sort of reporting before the birthday party, their work could have prepared others to pay prompt attention when the majority leader spoke at the party. But this exemplary work came too late to help anyone who might have wanted to know when it really "mattered."

Trent Lott had resigned his leadership position before any such home-centered attention appeared. In their time and in their way, Washington's press people gave us a valuable and necessary archival record, and they diligently kept score for us. But their archival and tally-keeping capabilities were superior to their reportorial and representational antennae. Because they had not observed him and talked to him in his native habitat, they and their professional colleagues knew remarkably little about Trent Lott. They were not primed to recognize the relevance of his comments at the point of controversy. Once the bloggers had signaled Lott's importance, Washington journalists responded. But from the time of Lott's triggering comments to the time of his resignation, the mainstream media remained surprisingly ill prepared and ill equipped to tell the rest of us what Senator Trent Lott "was really like." The Trent Lott story was not just a Washington story. It was a constituency story. Why hadn't Washington's media people been going off and on to Mississippi for years?

WASHINGTON INTERESTS: THE CASE OF JOHN CULVER

The business of Washington is legislation, and the activity of legislating is the main interest of the journalists who work there. On the other hand, the business of the constituency is representation, and Washington journalists are not interested in the activity of representing that takes place there. Or so I have been arguing: that certain kinds of political activity attract and support certain journalistic interests. For me, this notion got an appropriate test when a leading Washington journalist and I happened, by chance, to spend time studying the same member of Congress.

In the 1970s and 1980s, when I was busiest traveling the country, Elizabeth Drew reigned as one of Washington's most widely read and

widely respected resident political journalists. As Washington editor for
the *Atlantic,* as Washington correspondent for the *New Yorker,* as a talk
show regular, and as a topmost interviewer of Washington's political
people, she was the very prototype of a national scorekeeper. Among her
many books was one about U.S. Senator John Culver of Iowa.[76]

"In the summer of 1978," she explained,

> I spent some time with Culver, in the Senate and in Iowa, talking with
> him and watching him formulate strategies, push his legislation,
> decide how to cast his votes, deal with his constituents, respond to
> things that come at him and cope with the extraordinary pressures
> that a senator faces. Watching Culver as he worked through the
> cross-currents, hazards, and complications of Senate life, one could
> get a picture of that life, of what a senator actually does, and also of
> the workings of the Senate.[77]

Though he was only midway in his first term, she wrote, "Culver had
already established a reputation as one of the most effective members of
the Senate."[78] She described him as a senator who "gets in there and does
the hard work . . . of making the whole thing go."[79] She wrote an excellent book, informed, detailed, and insightful. It is appropriately titled
Senator. It presents Culver as very nearly a model of what a U.S. senator
should be. Her book is also a model of what Washington's journalists are
most interested in, which is legislative activity in Washington.

I, too, have written about John Culver. And my work, by contrast, is
more nearly a model of what constituency-centered researchers are interested in, that is, connecting activity in home constituencies. Our research
methods—observation and interviews—were the same. Our pictures of
John Culver's personal strengths were nearly identical, but our angle of
vision was quite different. She portrayed the politician-legislator. I portrayed the politician-representative. For that reason, our focus, our questions, and our end product were different. And that difference has nothing
to do with right or wrong, better or worse. It is entirely a matter of two
different interests—and, therefore, two different perspectives.

To her great credit, Drew did travel around with Culver—for a
weekend—in Iowa. Indeed, she devoted 20 percent of her book to it. And
it makes her book a more complete picture of the senator than anything I
could produce. The outline of her Iowa trip—a series of meetings with
constituents—was perfectly familiar to me.[80] But what I found most

striking in comparison was her near-total lack of interest, while she was in Iowa, in the patterns and problems of representation. She got him right, but she got him only half-right. And her dominating Washington perspective accounts for the difference.

In the book, she describes several constituency meetings—who says what to whom about what, concerning the issues at hand. When she generalizes about what is happening, she emphasizes the senator's intellectual strengths. And she simply assumes a two-way connection. "He reasons with them, shows them that he understands their problem and is trying to help them." "He wants to demonstrate to each group he meets with that he is knowledgeable about what it is doing and is interested in their problems." "He is teaching these people as well as responding to them."[81] Constituent satisfaction is assumed.

When she does record a couple of her conversations with constituents, they, too, emphasize Culver's intellect and his issue orientation. "One tells me that . . . what he appreciates most about Culver are his passion about issues and his intellect." Another says, "He is pleased that Culver is concentrating on the issues in Washington."[82] These comments fortify the book's theme: the senator's prowess as a legislator in Washington.

In a couple of instances, she picks up a hint that a two-way process of representation might be involved. In both instances, however, having mentioned it, she drops it without comment. One of the individuals just quoted, for example, tells her that meeting with constituents "does not come easily" for Culver, but that he, the constituent, disagrees with criticism of Culver for not connecting more.[83] She does not ask about this "criticism." Being interested in what a first-rate legislator he was, she had no interest in what his constituents might want or get by way of first-rate representation. Perhaps she simply assumed a positive connection between legislating and representing. If so, it is a common Washington mistake.

I traveled in Iowa with John Culver in 1974 and 1980, once before and once after Drew's visit. And I, too, wrote about him.[84] My conversations with the senator, however, centered on my interest in his connections with two home constituencies: a supportive "primary constituency" and a problematic "reelection constituency." With the first group—his strongest supporters—there was no problem. In several meetings with teachers, environmentalists, and labor unions—core elements of his strongly supportive primary constituency—he burnished his connections through energetic issue presentations, passionate partisan commitments, and recollections of past associations.

But in response to my questions, he worried about the weakness of his connection to the broader Iowa electorate, from which he would have to fashion a statewide supportive reelection constituency. "One thing I have not done since I have been in the Senate is to become well known in Iowa," he said. "Perhaps it has been a misuse of my incumbency. I have a very diffuse image." Or "In five years, I haven't become enough of an established personality in the state. There isn't much warmth of identification with me." With respect to broad constituent support, therefore, "I have a long way to go in this state. I have no illusions about that."[85] If, indeed, he was a model U.S. Senator, he would have to communicate its advantages—among other plus factors—to the Iowa voters.

"There was little doubt," I wrote, "that he had created a classic 'out of touch' problem for himself at home, that he had not kept his constituency career in an optimal balance with his Washington career." And I added, "This large vulnerability, incidentally, had gone unrecognized in Elizabeth Drew's admiring, but lopsidedly Washington-oriented study."[86] For Drew's legislatively competent Culver, widespread constituency satisfaction was taken for granted.

One small comparison might help illuminate the difference in our perspectives—legislating in Washington, and representing at home. During Drew's visit to Iowa, Culver held a meeting with some cattlemen. In three pages of commentary, she emphasizes the senator's preparation for the meeting, and she reports parts of their conversation back and forth, on the effect of beef imports on prices. She concludes by quoting one of the cattleman: "I think it's good for you to come out. There's problems out here, except when we have an election."[87] This hint of a possible connection problem, however, draws zero interest from the author. In her *very next sentence*, she is on the plane with Culver, listening to him discourse—for several pages in the book—about single-issue politics, John Gardner's recent book, and leadership in Washington. Not a syllable about his constituents.

When I traveled with Culver a year later, we also had contact with Iowa's cattlemen. He participated in the 1979 National Cattle Congress parade, and we toured the agricultural exhibits at the fairgrounds afterwards. Because I was then a visitor at the University of Iowa, I picked him up early and drove him all day in *my* car. I wrote,

> It struck me as odd that he would let himself be taken to the National Cattle Congress parade in my car with its New York license plates. As we left the Waterloo fairgrounds, having parked prominently near the entrance gate and having said goodbye to the

parade organizers, he parodied their likely reaction. "He's not from Iowa, they say." Where'd they ever get that idea? "He's arrogant, insensitive, out of touch." What makes them think that? Huh? "He votes more with the East than the Midwest." Where'd that idea come from? Huh? "All I'm doing is riding around with New York plates on my car!"[88]

"He was sensitive to his weakness," I noted, "but was not treating it seriously." He was not connecting, he knew it, and he mockingly chose to make light of it.

Later that same day, I reinforced my conclusion about his fragile representational connections—from listening to the senator swap stories with three college athletic coaches. About that connection, I wrote,

> It struck me that former star athlete [football] Culver was much more on the fringes of the conversation than he would have been had he "been around more" and kept in touch. The coaches' stories revolved around the current prospects of various Iowa athletes; and Culver's information seemed to end at the point where he went away [to Harvard] for college. "I think I played against him in high school," he said. Or, "Is he as good now as he was in college?" Culver's own stories were about freshman basketball at Harvard and his tattered hand-me-down sneakers given to him by his former Harvard roommate, Ted Kennedy. They were enjoyable stories, but they stamped him as Harvard, not Iowa.[89]

Thinking about authenticity, each of us had answers to the question "what is John Culver really like?" Drew's were legislative answers; mine were representational answers. We each had half an answer to the authenticity question. In her story, it would be Culver's fellow legislators who would determine what he was like, how they would work with him, and how much they would trust him. In my story, it would be his Iowa constituents who would size him up as a person and make their judgments of support and trust. We each examined half of the total judgment process. Drew did more than I did. Indeed, she put herself in a position to connect the two halves. But she had no interest in doing so. She was describing a legislator, not a representative. In her book, Culver appears unblemished and unbeatable. From my representational perspective, the blemishes were obvious and the electoral outcome became understandable. John Culver, the model legislator—but not the model representative—lost the election, 54 percent to 46 percent.

When we talked about it afterward in Washington, the senator first emphasized factors beyond his control. "From the time you left," he said, "the campaign continued upward so that I thought we were going to win. . . . The last minute suction turned it all around. That's about it." But one of his top campaign aides offered a different perspective.

Most people believe we lost it in the last week of the campaign. But Peter Hart (Culver's pollster) disagrees. He says we lost it in the first three and a half years—that Culver failed to make any impression. The Iowa polls on job performance consistently said 40 percent good job, 12 percent poor job, 48 percent no opinion. They never changed.

The Hart explanation squares with everything Culver (and I) had worried about during my trips—that he had yet to connect with a broad reelection constituency.

That conclusion also fit with poll results showing his relative weakness among rural, small-town, and farm voters—a factor Culver also emphasized. In concluding our postmortem, he said, "As near as I can tell, it was the sons of bitchin' rural vote that turned out in force. And that is poison to me. You just look at all these little towns—1000 votes, 2000 votes, 3000 votes. They killed me." I thought back to his visit with the cattlemen—not the public policy discussion in Drew's book, of course, but the representational discussion in my book. And I thought back to a story about farmers he told to friends over dinner. "Do you know how you can tell whether your baby is going to be a farmer? He's the one who cries before you hit him. That's just about it. But if you quote me on that, I'm dead." It expressed an attitude that was not helpful in building connections with his rural (think "cattlemen") constituents.

The senator's connection problems were well known, of course, to Iowa political observers. And to his victorious opponent—about whom one observer said that "his political strength is that Iowans view him as one of them, which he is."[90] Another observer added that Culver's opponent "hammered to death the idea that John was not an Iowan and did not care about folks here. He hit a nerve because some people thought there was a grain of truth to it."[91]

A top campaign aide stepped back to assess Culver's overall strengths and weaknesses.

Psychologically, John Culver is a mature, supremely self-confident man. He had been a senator for six years and he acted as if he belonged there. . . . Substantively, John Culver is a powerful intellect, an amazing intellect, an astounding intellect. He was absolutely certain what the campaign was all about, where the battle lines were drawn and where he stood on every single issue. . . . Stylistically, John Culver is a purebred. You brief him and put him before a crowd, and he takes it from there. With a crowd, he is superb. . . . [But] Culver was not good one on one. He would talk about the Trilateral Commission and things like that. He didn't like small talk. He tired of it. . . . It bored him. . . . Culver comes on like a bull; but he is threatening to people . . . he was not comfortable in rural areas. His campaign strategy began in the cities. He consolidated his strength there and then moved into the rural areas. It was too late. By that time, people saw him as a politician. By the time he got around to the small towns, people weren't interested.

It was a postmortem that included both the Drew and the Fenno perspectives.

Only a representational connections story, however, could explain his defeat. I had not gone to Iowa expressly to explain Culver's electoral fate. But my interest in his home connections helped me—even led me—to do that. Given Drew's legislative and policy-centered interests and perspectives, you could not explain the electoral outcome. Given my representation-centered interests and perspectives, you could.

After his defeat, John Culver left Iowa and took up permanent residence in Washington, where he could capitalize on his legislative strengths unaffected by his representational weaknesses. That choice—home or Washington—made "with his feet," suggests the further usefulness of a constituency-centered analysis.

CONCLUSION

This chapter has been part argument and part demonstration. It argues that representation is a crucial activity of Washington's elected politicians, and it demonstrates that representation has been neglected by Washington's journalists. It further argues that it would be useful to Washington journalists if they would go, on occasion, to the place—the constituency—where representation originates and gets practiced. The chapter suggests, in general terms, the benefit and the promise of that approach.

It describes cases where the lack of attentiveness to the constituency by Washington journalists resulted in an incomplete understanding of a Washington politician. Again, the concluding suggestion is that Washington journalists can usefully remedy the oversight by going— more than they do—to look at the representational connections of Washington politicians at home.

Notes

1. R. Douglas Arnold, *Congress, The Press and Political Accountability*, Princeton University Press (New York, 2004).
2. Most of these are reports about campaigns, done at campaign time, and I have tried to eliminate them. The very best is Richard Harris, "How's It Going," *New Yorker*, April 6, 1967.
3. D. C. Denison, "Richard Ben Cramer," *Boston Globe Magazine*, August 9, 2000.
4. David Rosenbaum, "Back Home, Senator Gets Support for Tax Bill," *New York Times*, June 2, 1986.
5. Brian Schaffner and Patrick Sellers, "The Structural Determinants of Local Congressional News Coverage. *Political Communication*, 20:1.
6. Kimberly Coursen Parkes, "How the Press Views Congress," in Thomas E. Mann and Norman J. Ornstein (eds.), *Congress, The Press and the Public*, American Enterprise Institute and the Brookings Institution (Washington, 1994), pp. 157–170. A 1976 study of network news coverage found one story out of 263 devoted to "constituency relations"; see Michael Robinson and Kevin Appel, "Network News Coverage of Congress," *Political Science Quarterly*, Fall 1979, pp. 407–417.
7. Parkes, "How the Press Views Congress," p. 159.
8. Shanto Iyengar, *Do The Media Govern?*, Sage Publications (Thousand Oaks, CA, 1977), p. xiii.
9. Linda Killian, *The Freshmen: What Happened to the Republican Revolution?* Westview (Boulder, CO, 1998).
10. David Greenberg, "A House In Shambles," *Washington Post National Weekly*, June 8, 1998.
11. Howard Kurtz, interview with Steve Talbot, "Why the Public Hates the Press, *Frontline*, PBS, www.pbs.org, June 1996.
12. Ibid.
13. Paul Taylor, interview with Steve Talbot, "Why the Public Hates the Press," *Frontline*, PBS, www.pbs.org, May 1996.
14. Ibid.
15. Mark Hertsgaard, interview with Steve Talbot, "Why the Public Hates the Press," *Frontline*, PBS, www.pbs.org, July 11, 1996.
16. David Broder, interview with Steve Talbot, "Why the Public Hates the Press," *Frontline*, PBS, www.pbs.org, July 11, 1996.
17. Geneva Overholser, interview with Steve Talbot, "Why the Public Hates the Press," *Frontline*, PBS, www.pbs.org, September 1996.
18. Fenno, *Home Style*, Scott Foresman & Co., (New York, 1978), p. 297.
19. Ibid., pp. 292–293. My third observation was better, more succinctly described by president-watcher, John Harris, as "detachment"—"the ability to step outside their public roles and comment, preferably by humor and irony, on their own performance." John F. Harris, "The President and the Press Corps," *Washington Post Weekly Edition*, January 8–14, 2001, p. 22.
20. Ed Henry, "Heard on the Hill," *Roll Call*, September 9, 2002.

21. John Lancaster, "The Uniter," *Washington Post Weekly*, April 16–22, 2001.
22. Ibid.
23. Ibid.
24. Two years later, another Washington reporter made the same trip. He noted, too, that "this face-to-face campaigning is key to his political survival," and he quotes Daschle: "I find this almost spiritual. I get closer to my state, my roots, and my thoughts." Mark Leibovich, "Grass-Roots Route," *Washington Post National Edition*, September 3, 2003.
25. Joshua Micah Marshall, "Talking Points Memo," www.talkingpointsmemo.com/, December 6, 2002.
26. Ibid., December 7, 2002.
27. Glenn Reynolds, "Instapundit," www.instapundit.com/ 11 A.M., December 7, 2002.
28. Interview, Jonathan Karl, *Inside Politics*, December 6, 2002.
29. Marshall, "Talking Points Memo," December 7, 2002.
30. Howard Kurtz, "A Hundred Candle Story and How to Blow It," *Washington Post*, December 16, 2002.
31. Andrew Kanter, "Cyber Speak: Sinclair Is the Latest to Feel the Power of the Blogs," *USA Today*, November 1, 2004.
32. Jay Rosen, "The Legend of Trent Lott and the Weblogs," www.presslink.com March 15, 2004. The story is now part of the history of blogging. See K. Daniel Glover, "The Rise of the Blogs," *National Journal*, January 21, 2006.
33. Esther Scott, "Big Media Meets the 'Bloggers': Coverage of Trent Lott's Remarks at Strom Thurmond's Birthday Party," Joan Shorenstein Center on the Press, Politics and Public Policy, Kennedy School of Government, Harvard University, 2004.
34. Thomas Edsall, "Poor Choice of Words, Lott Says: Senator Apologizes for Recent Remarks About Thurmond," *New York Times*, December 10, 2002.
35. John Martin, ABC News *Nightline*, December 10, 2002; CNN *Crossfire*, December 10, 2002; Gary Tuchman, CNN, December 20, 2002.
36. Paul Begala on CNN *Crossfire*, December 12, 2002.
37. CNBC, *The News with Brian Williams*, December 11, 2002.
38. The flow and the sweep of this controversy can best be followed through television programs and newspaper editorials collected and published every few days online by the Bulletin Board Faxing Network in its *The Bulletin's Frontrunner* accessible online via Lexis-Nexis.
39. CNBC, *The News with Brian Williams*, December 11, 2002.
40. ABC News, *Nightline*, December 10, 2002.
41. Howard Kurtz, "Reliable Sources," *Washington Post*, December 14, 2002.
42. See especially Carl Hulse, "Lott's Praise for Thurmond Echoed His Words of 1980," *New York Times*, December 11, 2002; Peter Applebome, "Lott's Walk Near the Incendiary Edge of Southern History," *New York Times*, December 13, 2002.
43. Howard Kurtz, *Reliable Sources*, CNN, December 21, 2002.
44. Stephen Hayes, "Why Did Press Pass on Trent Lott Story?" on *Reliable Sources*, December 13, 2002.
45. Ibid. Comments by Linda Douglas.
46. Rosen, "The Legend of Trent Lott."
47. Howard Kurtz on *Reliable Sources*, CNN, December 13, 2002.
48. Ibid. Comments by Howard Kurtz.
49. Tucker Carlson on *Reliable Sources*, December 21, 2002.
50. William Powers, "Goodwill Lacking," *National Journal*, December 20, 2002.
51. Howard Kurtz on *Reliable Sources*, CNN, December 21, 2002.
52. Aaron Brown, *Newsnight*, CNN, December 20, 2002.
53. Mark Shields on *The News Hour with Jim Lehrer*, December 13, 2002.
54. Frank Rich, "Bonfire of the Vanities," *New York Times*, December 21, 2002.
55. Rosen, "The Legend of Trent Lott."

56. Thomas Edsall, "Lott Decried for Part in Salute to Thurmond," *Washington Post,* December 7, 2002.
57. Thomas Edsall, *Chain Reaction: The Impact of Race, Rights and Taxes on American Policy,* W. W. Norton (New York, 1991).
58. Ibid., x.
59. Thomas Edsall, "Lott Renounces White 'Racialist' Group He Praised in 1992," *Washington Post,* December 16, 1998; Thomas Edsall, "Controversial Group Has Ties to Both Parties in South," *Washington Post,* January 15, 1999; Thomas Edsall, "Conservative Group Accused of Ties to White Supremacists," *Washington Post,* December 19, 1998; Thomas Edsall, "GOP Chairman Denounces Racist Group," *Washington Post,* January 20, 1999.
60. Edsall, "Lott Renounces White 'Racialist' Group."
61. Thomas Edsall, "Poor Choice of Words, Lott Says: Senator Apologizes for Recent Remarks About Thurmond," *New York Times,* December 10, 2002.
62. Jackie Koszczuk and Rebecca Carr, "From Ole Miss to Congress: The Lott-Cochran Rivalry," *Congressional Quarterly,* May 25, 1996.
63. Karen Tumulty on *Connie Chung Tonight,* December 13, 2002.
64. Gwen Ifil on *Reliable Sources,* CNN, December 21, 2002.
65. Ibid.
66. Julia Reed, "The Test for Trent," *Newsweek,* January 11, 1999.
67. Trent Lott, *Herding Cats: A Life in Politics,* Regan Books (New York, 2005), Chapter 2.
68. Dan Goodgame and Karen Tumulty, "Tripped Up by History," *Time,* December 16, 2002.
69. Ibid.
70. Ibid.
71. Helen Dewar, "For Lott, Power Rests on Friends More Than Followers," *Washington Post,* December 20, 2002.
72. David Halbfinger and Jeffrey Gentleman, "In Lott's Life, Long Shadows of Segregation," *New York Times,* December 15, 2002; David Halbfinger, "The Constituents," *New York Times,* December 18, 2002.
73. Halbfinger and Gentleman, "In Lott's Life."
74. Reported in Applebome, "Lott's Walk."
75. Halbfinger, "The Constituents."
76. Elizabeth Drew, *Senator,* Simon and Schuster (New York, 1978).
77. Ibid., p. 12.
78. Ibid., pp. 11–12.
79. Ibid., p. 12.
80. Chapters 6 and 7.
81. Ibid., pp. 110–111, 119, 106.
82. Ibid., pp. 105, 127.
83. Ibid.
84. Richard F. Fenno Jr., *Senators on the Campaign Trail: The Politics of Representation,* Oklahoma University Press (Norman, 1996), pp. 123–156. All citations can be found in these pages.
85. Ibid., p. 131.
86. Ibid., p. 132.
87. Drew, *Senator,* p. 111.
88. Fenno, *Senators on the Campaign Trail,* p. 133.
89. Ibid.
90. James Dickenson, "Don't Be Fooled by Charles Grassley's Yokel Image," *Washington Post Weekly Edition,* April 8, 1985.
91. Ibid.

CHAPTER 5

Research: Personal and Professional

A PERSONAL PERSPECTIVE

As a prelude to one person's "What are they like?" explorations, it might be asked of the explorer, "What is he like?" and "What is it like?"—the experience of exploration. If the author is to be the lens through which readers will look at some U.S. politicians, what ought we know about the author—and about life "on the road"? I am often asked questions about my incentives, perspectives, preferences, loyalties, and methods—for the reason, I suspect, that so few political scientists have committed as much time and energy to on-site constituency exploration.

A personal sketch would begin something like this: that before there was political science, there was politics, and before there was politics, there was sports. From early childhood through early college, I participated in unorganized or organized sports. Family celebrations often included trips from our Winchester, Massachusetts, home to Boston Garden for hockey or to Fenway Park for baseball. I courted my wife-to-be in both these hallowed arenas. (Ninety cents apiece for a Sunday doubleheader in Fenway's bleachers.) I played baseball and tennis in college and was the sports editor of a college newspaper. Whether playing or watching or writing, the essential competitiveness of sports—the plotting and the playing, the commitment and the excitement, the winning and the losing, for individuals and for teams alike—captivated me. I was thoroughly predisposed and primed, therefore, when I discovered politics, and all the more so as it became clear that my fellow Bostonians embraced their politics with the same tribal passion as they embraced their sports. Metaphors for one activity served easily as metaphors for the other.

In 1940, an unheralded internationalist businessman, Wendell Willkie, came out of nowhere to become a presidential candidate and won the support of my staunch Republican family. I remember lying in front of the radio keeping score of the state-by-state voting at the Republican National Convention—for six ballots—as the heroic underdog, Willkie, wrested the nomination from the villainous favorite, Robert Taft. Later, in ninth-grade civics class, debating on behalf of Willkie, I overwhelmed—by straight party vote—my pro-Roosevelt opponent. Within weeks, however, I lost my home field advantage, and the agony of defeat swept away the thrill of victory. But I was hooked on politics.

I was not, however, hooked on political science. That came along after a lopsided diet of the physical sciences during officer training in the U.S. Navy revealed a clear preference for the social sciences. My attraction to political science—as having something to do with high-stakes, real-world politics—soon followed. I began to entertain the idea of teaching social studies and coaching athletics in secondary school. When one of my professors suggested that I think seriously about graduate study in political science, I decided to try. I have been teaching political science and writing about politics ever since.

This distinction between political science and politics is not intended to convey a large difference. It calls attention, however, to the sort of political science I practice—heavier on the "political," lighter on the "science." I am an admiring consumer of the mathematical conceptualization and the statistical testing of political relationships that so many of my academic colleagues produce. But my own work leans more heavily than theirs on personal observation. By analogy, I am also an avid consumer of the sports analyses of Alan Barra, in the *Wall Street Journal* and in the online magazine *Salon*. Combining large quantities of data with ingenious statistical measures, Barra's "Mad Max" computer cranks out challenging explanations and comparisons of individual athletes and team performances over time. But another well-known sports analyst, Yogi Berra, describes a perspective closer to my own. "You can observe a lot by watching," he advises.[1] In the informal division of labor among political scientists, I am more Berra than Barra.

At the close of the 2001 baseball season, *New York Times* writer Murray Chass interviewed Lou Piniella, the manager of the record-breaking (116 victories) Seattle Mariners baseball team. Piniella, he writes, "lives with computer print-outs that tell him what each of his hitters has done against every pitcher the Mariners face and what opposing hitters have done against his pitchers." "I don't manage with hunches," the manager told the reporter. "I believe in keeping the percentages in your favor." And Chass continued,

> But if he relies so heavily on data, Piniella was asked, couldn't anybody make out the lineup? "You can get one of the Microsoft guys to come over here and make it out," he said grinning. Then adding, "The manager adds more than just the lineup to the equation, a lot more than just the lineup. I like data. The more data I have, the better I like it. Then you put the human touch into it." What's that, he was asked. "Who knows," he said, grinning even more.[2]

That's where Yogi Berra and I come in.

How, it might be asked, would a political scientist become interested in "the human touch"? My guess is that it's because I had always been especially interested in the activity of high-level politicians—what they do and why they do it. It is a subject political scientists label "elite political activity."

My interest in elite political activity has been a constant since my very first research project—on the president's Cabinet.[3] If presidents and their topmost aides were available to political scientists for observation and conversation, I might never have stopped studying the executive branch. The research question that first sent me to the legislative branch was generated, however, by my work on the Cabinet. It was: why are some cabinet members (and some of their top administrators) more successful in their relations with Congress than others? After looking for answers by reading extensively in congressional hearings, I decided to go to Washington and put my question directly to those members of Congress who controlled executive agency budgets.

That leading question hardly survived my first week of interviews with members of the House Appropriations Committee. I became so intrigued by the complex internal maintenance and decision-making activities of that powerful committee that it became the centerpiece of my research. The original motivating question about executive branch budgetary success patterns got relegated to one book chapter out of ten in a book entitled *The Power of the Purse: Appropriations Politics in Congress*.[4] I spent the following decade studying congressional committees and writing about them in *Congressmen in Committees.*[5] The focus had changed from studying executive elites to studying legislative elites. It has remained there ever since.

The story of my constituency-centered research is very similar. My original goal was to discover and formulate House member constituency perceptions for the purpose of explaining roll call voting patterns inside Congress. Political scientists knew, of course, that votes cast by House members on the chamber floor were strongly influenced by the makeup of their constituencies. And we had plenty of Census Bureau data—and, later, the *Almanac of American Politics*—with which to investigate that connection. It was my hunch, however—growing out of my 1960 experience with my Rochester visitor—that if we could identify and somehow package *member perceptions of their constituencies,* we could factor them into our roll call studies and thus improve our understanding of congressional voting patterns.

Something funny happened, however, on the way to my roll call equations. Real-world experience intruded once again; once again, it changed everything. After I had been traveling at home with a few House members, I became intrigued by all that they were doing in that place, why they were doing it, and with what effect. My scholarly interests were gradually pulled away from House member voting patterns in Washington and toward House member behavior patterns in their home constituencies. The original, motivating research question had led me unexpectedly into a new and more open-ended world of political activity. I did not abandon my basic interest in perceptions, but I began to add substantially to it.

It was the second time that my experience beyond the university, out "in the field," had blown me off course, from my original set of research questions toward a wholly different set. And it was to happen a third time when I switched my attention from the House to the Senate.[6] I'm sure there is nothing novel about a researcher changing focus in the process of doing the research. But the frequency and the magnitude of these shifts in my case seem both extreme and endemic to the kind of research I do.

It is research that requires an openness to a wide range of personal encounters and experiences. You begin with a research question, but you have no strong control over it. And you find yourself in a situation where your research question comes into immediate competition with other possible research questions. You are not tethered to a hardened database, and you're not sure what sorts of data might be available or interesting. You have come to observe one form of political activity, but you observe—and cannot help observing—all kinds of unexpected activity buzzing everywhere around you. When you go out to explore elite political activity, therefore, it is especially easy to be propelled or enticed toward a new course of action. From beginning to end, my research has proceeded more by curiosity than by design.

The constituency world posed a steep learning curve. But there was lots of encouragement, too. The quality and the range of my *conversations* with politicians as traveling companions exceeded anything I had experienced during my one-shot, on-schedule, tightly structured, and well-bounded *interviews* in Washington. Soon I came to realize that among political scientists, a lot less was known about the activities of our elected politicians at home than was known about their activities in Washington. This realization added a sense of adventure to the research. New people and new places provided stimulation, excitement, and a sense of mission. I began to think that my contribution as a political scientist might be to go out into a political world that was not heavily traveled by people in my profession, explore that world, and report back to my colleagues.

The important point is this: that I am a political scientist first and an explorer second. My half-century of research has proceeded, by turns, under the guiding influence of the theoretical umbrellas of my discipline: political pluralism, political sociology, political behavior, and rational choice. Whereas I spend a lot of time close to the real world of politics, many of my colleagues do not. Some deliberately stay as far away as possible. Yet we are all engaged in the same enterprise: to generalize about political phenomena.

My attraction to a world beyond the university sometimes provokes questions. Why, I am asked, would any normal scholar want to leave the comforts of the academic environment—orderly, civilized, and supportive—to endure an unpredictable diet of mundane political activity, amid total strangers in some unfamiliar corner of the land? One answer is that a university is by no means as benign as the comparison implies. Nor is life "out there" in the country necessarily inhospitable. To which it should be added, of course, that all research is something of a gamble. Besides, any personal dislocation, however jarring it might be, is only temporary.

Another answer may be that this reporter is not "a normal scholar." Early in my constituency-level travels, I realized that I suffered from a serious character flaw. I actually *liked* the politicians with whom I traveled—not all equally, perhaps, but all positively. Once outside the academic greenhouse, I turned out to be a "polisymp."

In 1991, I introduced myself to a Texas audience:

I come here as a confirmed politician watcher—and even as something of a politician lover—neither of which places me in the American mainstream. The *New York Post* writer, Pete Hamill, identified the mainstream when he wrote once that "American politicians come and go, but they all get booed at the ballpark." I know he's got it right, because I once sat next to an Iowa senator when he was introduced—and roundly booed—at half-time during a football game. And I read the other day where Governor Lowell Weicker of Connecticut was booed at a Hartford Whalers hockey game. We suffer our politicians at election time; but otherwise our attitude is one of "for God's sake, leave us alone." Well, I happen to be one who can't.[7]

Although I continued and expanded my travels in large part because I continued to learn about politics, it is also a fact that I continued the research because I enjoyed my everyday experiences with politicians much too much to stop. Besides, no one ever told me that doing political science should not be fun.

There is a saying attributed to journalists and editorial cartoonists that "there is only one way to look at a politician—down." A lot of commentary, both written and pictorial, supports that view. Denouncing, demeaning, and mocking our elected politicians is, of course, a national pastime. My view is different. I certainly enjoy the cartoonists' artful thrusts. But, along with those constituents who like their own member of Congress, I came to like those House members and senators I followed and wrote about. When asked to make distinctions among the politicians I have met, I acknowledge only one: "good interviews" and "bad interviews."

My strong sense of indebtedness to them—for letting me come to hang around them and talk with them—explains part of my favorable reaction. But an equal part is the high value I place on what they do. They do democracy's work. At home, I watch them develop, promote, and nourish two-way connections with their constituents. It does not bother me that some like to do this more than others, or that some do it better than others. They all do it. In Washington, where I watch them less, I am willing to give them the benefit of the doubt—that each, by his or her own lights, is trying to do the right thing to make life better for their fellow citizens.

My view is that I do not have to approve of, or agree with, everything each one says or does in order to put a positive value on what each contributes, as a representative and as a legislator, to make our democratic political system work. I hold a personal opinion that a major weakness of our democracy at the congressional level is the woeful lack of electoral competition. But I do not hold the winning individuals responsible for that. I take the politicians with whom I travel as I find them. I choose them for no other reason except to provide diversity. And I depend, of course, on their willingness to have me hang around. When I meet each one for the first time, I always start with a "thanks for letting me come." When I select, I know almost nothing about most of them. My operative premise is that each one has some combination of personal talents, qualities, and experiences that propelled her or him to a very high level of accomplishment, and that each one, therefore, has an interesting story to tell. When Washington people ask me who I'm studying and I mention one, I often get the peremptory judgment: "You don't have much there." I demur, but think to myself, "There's a lot there." My task is twofold: as a reporter to "get the story" and as a political scientist to translate it into the language and the generalizations of political science.

This nonjudgmental stance is made easier, I suspect, by the absence of any strong partisan commitments on my part. The New England Republicanism of my youth—conservative and traditional on matters of business and government, internationalist in foreign affairs, liberal and independent-minded in matters of civil rights and individual conscience—that combination became increasingly hard to recognize in later partisan alignments. As a result, I have never been able to work up or sustain any dominating or enduring partisan preference, enthusiasm, or allegiance. While my long-run research has been propelled by a political scientist's curiosity, my short-run propellant—however flawed—has remained a simple fascination with, and an appreciation for, the people I write about. The politicians I have studied cover the full range of the political spectrum. Not surprisingly, I wanted every one of them to win.

Out in the constituencies, the relationship between researcher and politician is based on an implicit bargain. The politician agrees to let me come and observe and to talk with me about what he or she does; I agree to keep their confidences and to write nothing that would cause them personal or political damage. It is a bargain between two professionals. And that is the context in which the research develops.

When I am at work in their districts, I try to maintain a scholarly distance from them, to stay out of the way, to be nonintrusive and unobtrusive—"up close, but not too personal." Formally, the research method is known as participant observation. More informally, I have labeled my variation as "soaking and poking"—to characterize the improvisational, noncanonical method of gathering and processing the material.[8] The object, of course, is to see the world the way the politicians see it by watching from over their shoulders, listening to them, and talking with them when they are at work in their native habitats.

Out in the constituencies, the task is to observe, ask a little, and listen a lot. I have often claimed that my only special professional talent is a willingness and ability to listen. On the road, my guiding rule of thumb is "when in doubt, be quiet." During a 1994 Kennedy School discussion of journalist-politician relationships, former Louisiana Congressman Buddy Roemer commented, "The greatest reporters of the written word, or the television picture, are those men and women who . . . listen. I don't know if listening is taught at Harvard, but it ought to be."[9] As a one-time student there and as a lifelong listener, I can reply to his question: "No, it wasn't, and yes, it's a good idea." Politicians do know something about politics! Listening to them talk about their subject can be very helpful in the business of discovery.

Given the importance of watching and listening, a "soaking and poking" methodology may seem largely passive. It is not. As political science goes, it is blue-collar, data-grubbing, labor-intensive work. It is time consuming, physically tiring, and psychologically nerve-racking. There is nothing grand, glamorous, or stylish about it. You ride around in a lot of backseats, stand alone at a lot of functions, sit in the back rows of a lot of meeting halls, eat a lot of junk food, and absorb a variety of indignities and a lot of teasing at the expense of your profession. You may find yourself used as a foil or a "prop." If you had ever been touched by a sense of self-importance, this process reminds you to forget about it. You are not central to anything that's going on. The politician is. So, go with the flow, with my doggerel reminder that "If you really let yourself go with the flow, you'll surely write more than anyone wants to know."

The large context in every trip is one of uncertainty. In the beginning, you have to feel your way into a working relationship with a total stranger. A basic decision is whether to wait or to push the conversation, whether and when to watch or to ask a question. It is a decision you face repeatedly in specific situations. The decision may be compounded in the presence of a staffer, a spouse, a friend, a reporter. When in doubt, it is best to wait rather than push. For one thing, it signals your intention to be minimally intrusive. More important, you can learn a lot about what they are like by listening and by observing their interaction with others—by taking in the what, when, how, and how much of their talk and their connections.

At some point in the relationship, a shared experience or emotion will move the connection beyond mere access toward a relationship between two people. The stage of "getting to" a politician will give way to "getting to know" a human being. As I viewed the early days of the relationship, I was being tested to see whether I was a real person and not simply an academic title. And the test involved "doing something" as well as "talking about something." It involved our "getting along" and participating together in addition to any analytical exchange we might have.

Some of the experiences that moved a relationship from access toward friendship were overtly political. Others were not. Shared political activity involved such things as handing out leaflets at plant gates, distributing literature in shops and on windshields, telephone polling, letter addressing, envelope stuffing, parade walking. Among my nonpolitical bonding experiences were changing a tire—once at a rural radio station and once on a mountain road—running out of gas late at night, playing golf, listening to tapes, playing games with the children, staying overnight in the politician's home, and doing anything—eating, riding, sightseeing that involved spending time with a spouse, a relative, or a special friend.

All this had to be tempered by common sense about when to inquire and when to shut up. But it is also important to know that while your task is to observe, in many circumstances you will be forced to talk and forced to decide. On the road, there is no such thing as a one-sided interview. You cannot, no matter how much your protocol requires it, remain "dumb as a post." You will be asked questions; you will be pulled into discussion; you will have to choose whether to do this or that, whether to go to this place or that, with this person or that. You must make choices about talking and choices about doing.

As you learn, you gain an intuition about the nuances of your own relationship and about when and how to ask your questions. In the end, the volume, the subjects, and the pattern of your conversation will be reflective of a personal relationship. And that relationship will, of course, influence your research product.

For the researcher, this type of study obviously requires persistence, adaptability, a high tolerance for ambiguity, a fairly modest ego, and a nonjudgmental, wait-and-see posture toward the people you are with. But the soaking and poking research method also places a burden on *the reader*. There is no shortcut. As I wrote in a preface to an earlier study,

The book will take the reader to the counties, the towns, the homes, the businesses, the churches, the schools, the rallies, the meetings, the restaurants, the coffee shops, the clubs, the organizations, the fields, the streets, and the parks—event by event, handshake by handshake, friend by friend, group by group, visit by visit, question by question, answer by answer, story by story. The research required considerable stamina and patience. Readers will need stamina and patience, too.[10]

On the road, the trick is to remain alert and observant, actively engaged in collecting, organizing, and hypothesizing. The payoff comes in the excitement of exploration, the pleasure of discovery, and a sense of usefulness when "reporting back" to uninitiated students and colleagues.[11]

A PROFESSIONAL PERSPECTIVE

Out in the constituencies, my constant companion is the question: What is there that I'm experiencing that might be of interest and assistance to my fellow political scientists? And how might my observations and conceptualizations contribute to our common enterprise? My inquiries and adventures in the everyday political world have had one ultimate goal: to help other political scientists—who have not "been there and done that" and who probably never will—to think afresh about the large subject of democratic representation. At the end of the day, therefore, the relevance and usefulness of my research will be judged within the community of political scientists.

Between 1970 and 2002, I undertook *five* distinct exploratory adventures, each one consisting of numerous separate expeditions to a great variety of places. All were motivated by an interest in the constituency activities of our national politicians. All were voyages of discovery. And all were concerned ultimately with the subject of representation. Altogether, I soaked and poked in 32 House member districts and in 18 statewide Senate constituencies. I also lived for one year in Washington—watching and talking to ten of the senators there. I want to sketch out each of the five explorations and the ideas that emerged—some cumulative, some not.

For a political scientist whose approach to the study of politics is observational in technique and exploratory in purpose, the narrative, case-study form is especially appealing. It puts the observer front and center in deciding what questions are interesting and allows a richness of detail in presenting explanatory suggestions. Case-study storytelling cannot, however, test and verify a relationship in a language of statistics or probabilities. Nor is it likely to produce propositions that can be easily put in measurable or testable form. That being the case, it is especially incumbent on the storyteller to offer ideas or concepts that might help others think both broadly and carefully about the subject at hand.

As narrator, my obligation is to provide the reader with some organization of ideas that make sense out of my explorations and discoveries. In thinking about how to do that, I have concluded that my contribution has been to offer conceptualizations that would structure observations so as to help others to think about and generalize about the large subject of political representation.

At an abstract level, the five exploratory efforts can be examined in terms of the conceptualizations that grew out of each particular effort and in terms of the ways they were used (or not used) developmentally as my explorations went forward. The explorations produced stories, the stories were told in a conceptual language, and the concepts were embedded in examples. I have come to think of myself as a *conceptual gardener* tending a set of ideas—planting and nourishing, arranging and rearranging, weeding out and adding in. The experimentation and the results to date of this conceptual gardening can be pulled out of five explorations.

I. MAPPING THE HOME TERRITORY: HOUSE MEMBERS 1970–1976

Exploratory details: Eighteen House members, 16 states, 36 trips; anonymity preserved. One study.[12]

Exploratory ideas:

Perceptions: From an electoral point of view, House members perceive four constituencies, nested in a set of concentric circles. The *geographical constituency* is the entire district as legally prescribed, with all individuals and interests therein. The *reelection constituency* consists of those individuals and groups in the district who—the representative believes—have voted for the representative and will, more than likely, continue to do so. The *primary constituency* consists of those individuals and groups who—the representative believes—have provided the strongest support in the past and would stand by the member—with votes, work, and money—in a primary. The *personal constituency* consists of trustworthy friends, family, and advisers in whom the member confides and on whom the member depends for advice and emotional support.

The problem of managing perceptual complexity helps explain why House members feel far more vulnerable electorally and far more uncertain about constituency support than we might expect by examining only their past electoral margins. Caution is advised, therefore, whenever election margins are used to predict a member's legislative behavior.

Activities: House member activities are based on three types of choices they make at home: (a) *allocation,* or How do I divide up my available resources of time, energy, staff, and money? (b) *presentation,* or How do I present myself as a person to my several constituents? and (c) *explanation,* or How do I explain my activities in Washington to my various constituents at home? Presentation of self seems to be the central activity for most individual members, and it is the most discriminating activity for outside observers.

Home styles: The complex patterning of choices and activities produces for each House member a describable "home style." The proximate object of every home style is winning and preserving constituent support. The ultimate object is winning and preserving constituent trust. A variety of home styles exist, and many of them can be arrayed along a spectrum, with a person-to-person emphasis at one end and a policy issue emphasis at the other end.

Constituency careers: House members pursue describable political careers in their home constituencies as well as in Washington. Constituency careers tend to proceed in two stages: expansionist, when members worry about the effectiveness of their home styles in winning constituent support; and then protectionist, as they feel secure in their established home styles. A House member's home style may change over the course of the member's constituency career.

Representation: Heretofore, the empirical study of representation in the United States has been devoted largely to correlating constituency characteristics with roll call votes—especially votes on public policy. That study can be enriched by increased attention to the constituency end of the representative-constituent relationship. As representatives see it, their constituents want much more from them than policy decisions. They want the attention, access, communication, and trust building provided by their House member's allocations, presentations, and explanations at home. The more satisfied a member's constituencies are with his or her home style, the more leeway the representative will have in pursuing policy and career choices inside Congress.

To take individual home styles into account and consider the interaction between the home styles and the Washington behavior of our representatives, the idea of representation should be conceptualized somewhat less in the cross-sectional language of correlation and somewhat more in the across-time language of process.

2. CAMPAIGNING-GOVERNING-CAMPAIGNING: SENATORS, 1978–1986

Exploratory details: Five senators, five states, 21 trips, 59 days, one year in Washington, no anonymity. Five studies.[13]

Exploratory ideas:

Sequence: The six-year term of U.S. senators invites a more textured examination of the home-Washington relationship than was possible in the earlier mapping-the-territory exercise. Given the length of their terms, senatorial activity can usefully be treated in terms of a sequence— as a six-year cycle of *campaigning* to *governing* and back to *campaigning* again. A sequential view also encourages the examination of certain interstitial activities. Three such activities are *interpreting* campaign results as a guide to governing, *adjusting* to the Senate as a legislative institution, and *explaining* governing activity back home as a prelude to campaigning.

Governing: Studies built around the idea of a six-year cycle gave greater prominence to *governing* activity in Washington than did my previous study of House members at home. In addition to 60 days spent in the home states of the five senators, I also spent a year in Washington watching and talking with them about their governing performance. Four of the five studies of individual senators focused heavily on their governing activities. And their titles convey an across-time, sequential perspective: the "making" of Senator Dan Quayle, the "learning" of Senator Arlen Specter, the "emergence" of Senator Pete Domenici, the "failure" of Senator Mark Andrews. [The fifth study, with its focus on (presidential) campaigning, also carried a sequential theme: the "odyssey" of Senator John Glenn.] Whereas the earlier home-centered study had been a counterweight to political scientists' near-exclusive concern for policy, the emphasis on governing in the five later studies restored policy making to prominence.

Careers: Taken together, the macro-level campaigning-governing-campaigning sequence and the micro-level studies of individual senatorial performance gave central importance to the idea of political careers—in the constituency, in the institution, and in both at the same time. (Technically, since I can only claim to have studied a slice of each senator's career, the term should be "career-segments.") What had been a single chapter in the earlier House member study had become a broadly covering concept in each of the five senator studies.

Process: At the end of the *Home Style* study, the idea was advanced that representation could usefully be viewed as a process—one that was rooted in the complexity of a politician's home relationships. No attention was given, however, to how this might be done. In that context, the five senator studies were suggestive, because the campaigning-governing-campaigning sequence *is* process. Thinking about this process makes it easier, in turn, to think about our elected politicians as both representatives and legislators and to be attentive to both parts of their job.

Equally compatible with the sequential idea is an enlarged emphasis on individual careers, at home and in Washington, and their influence on one another. In broadest perspective, therefore, these Senate explorations moved beyond the mapping of activities such as allocation, presentation, and explanation to employ a more longitudinal, more developmental look at our elected politicians.

3. THE POLITICS OF REPRESENTATION: SENATORS, 1978–1992

Exploratory details: Ten senators, ten states, 38 trips, no anonymity. One study.[14]

Exploratory ideas:

Representational processes: Within the broad conceptualization of representation as process, we can consider three individual-level processes:

deciding to become a representative, *campaigning* to win the position as representative, and, having won the position, *maintaining* constituent support. These are the basic, sequential processes that mark the political career of every elected representative.

Campaigns: Election campaigns provide an especially wide and important window through which to view these representational activities. The careers and the campaigns of an elected politician are inseparable, because campaigns launch, extend, and terminate careers. *Campaigns* create, re-create, and test the complete range of a representative's constituency relationships. In my research, representation is conceptualized as a home-centered idea. And campaigning is preeminently a home-centered activity. In this study, the representational activities of senators are studied in the context of their home state election campaigns.

Connections: Campaigning at home is mostly about connecting politicians and constituents, and it is useful to think broadly about representational relationships at home as *connections.* Campaigns connect politicians and citizens, and those connections make possible the accountability of politicians to citizens that our representative government requires. "In short, no campaigns, no connections; no connections, no accountability; no accountability, no representative government."[15]

Negotiation: The many and varied connections sought and made and solidified—while pursuing a career, while campaigning for election, and while building a constituency—are developmental in nature. Each connection can be conceptualized as the provisional result of a cautious, over-time *negotiation* between politician and constituents. The politician wants support and offers responsiveness; constituents want responsiveness and they offer support. Neither can dictate outcomes. Through negotiation, the performance of the politician is gradually, incrementally, and over time brought into some kind of equilibrium with constituency expectations—or it is not.

Only through some such idea as continuous negotiation can we capture the incremental, tentative, changing, uncertain, and essentially experimental nature of the representative-constituency relationship—as I have observed it. Once the representational relationship is recognized as a negotiated relationship, it becomes easier to think of representation as a process. And the representational process can be conceptualized as a continuous negotiation involving the connecting and reconnecting of elected politicians and constituents.

4. REPRESENTATIONAL CHANGE: 1970–1992

Exploratory details: Two U.S. representatives, one congressional district, six trips, no anonymity. One study.[16]

Exploratory ideas:

Representational strategies: A comparative study of the connective activities of individual elected politicians can be based on the interrelationships of three factors: the *personal goals* of the representative, the *constituency context* in which the representative pursues those goals, and the *negotiating sequences* that develop over time between representative and constituents. In combination, the three elements tend to form distinctive patterns of representation, conceptualized and described as *strategies* of representation. Thinking in terms of these three elements—goals, context, and negotiating sequences—facilitates individual-level comparison among and across the full range of elected representatives.

Comparative representational strategies: The quarter-century of extraordinary political-social-economic change in the South provides a golden opportunity for comparative analysis of representational strategies. Personal visits to (essentially) the same Georgia congressional district in the 1970s and again in the 1990s reveal two very different representational strategies: one centered overwhelmingly around personal relationships, the other overwhelmingly centered around policy relationships. Different individual goals and different residential, economic-racial, and partisan contexts contributed to a substantial change from a *person-intensive representational strategy* in the 1970s to a *policy-intensive representational strategy* in the 1990s. This case study of change in the representational strategies of two individuals—from that of a conservative, old-style, rural Southern Democratic House member, to that of a new-style suburban Republican House member—can contribute usefully to our understanding of the historic change from Democratic to Republican political dominance in the late-twentieth-century South.

5. AFRICAN AMERICAN
REPRESENTATION: 1970–2002

Exploratory details: Four House members, three congressional districts, 13 trips, no anonymity. One study.[17]

Exploratory ideas

Experiential learning: The usefulness of the variable in the previous exploration is confirmed in conceptualizing the representational behavior of African American House members. The idea of *experiential learning* (instead of the negotiating sequences of the previous study) appears to improve the paradigm by making it easier to focus on a given representative and to trace his or her path of individual behavior over time.

Group interest and institutional influence: The distinction between person-intensive and policy-intensive representational strategies is strengthened. Two additional sets of personal goals and related strategies are observed and described. One set is dominated by the protection and the assertion of *group interests*, the other dominated by the pursuit of *institutional influence*. The first seems especially relevant for representatives of a minority group seeking political inclusion in the polity. The second seems appealing to any representative. Altogether, their differences in representational behavior are more remarkable than their similarities.

Symbolic and organizational connections: Our working inventory of representational connections between politicians and constituents must be expanded from the personal and policy connections—which dominated in the previous studies—to include *symbolic connections* and *organizational connections*. In thinking about African American representatives (and perhaps those of any other large minority), symbolic connections are crucial to preserving group unity, pride, and strength, while organizational connections are crucial to bargaining for access and power in dealing with white-dominated political organizations.

Context and careers: A quarter-century of slow contextual change from black protest to black politics has brought about a marked change in the prominence, the accomplishments, and the stability of black representation in Congress. For contemporary African American House members, their varied—but solidly established—representational connections at home serve to anchor increasingly successful and important careers inside the nation's most important representative institution.

The research reports that have emerged from these efforts at participant observation are essentially exploratory. The openness to personal experience in shaping questions and the method of participant observation lead to exploratory rather than to verifying work. They lead to formulating hypotheses rather than to testing hypotheses. Research reports from the politicians' world can, at their best, give other political scientists a feel for the real world of politics and a politician's-eye view of the world. And in this process, they may produce conceptualizations that can help others organize their thoughts, discipline their work, and produce, perhaps, new research questions.

Notes

1. "Managers at Ease on Air and in Dugout" from the *New York Times* in *Rochester Democrat and Chronicle,* October 26, 2001.
2. Murray Chass, "Piniella's Numbers Don't Add Up," *New York Times,* October 19, 2001.
3. Richard Fenno, *The President's Cabinet: From Wilson to Eisenhower,* Harvard University Press (Cambridge, 1959). Also, "Now Is the Time for Cabinet Makers," *New York Times Magazine,* November 20, 1960; "The Cabinet Index to the Kennedy Way," *New York Times Magazine,* April 2, 1962.
4. Richard Fenno, *The Power of the Purse: Appropriations Politics in Congress,* Little Brown (Boston, 1966).
5. Richard Fenno, *Congressmen in Committees,* Little Brown (Boston, 1973).
6. Richard Fenno, "Looking for the Senate: Reminiscences and Residuals," in *U.S. Senate Exceptionalism,* Bruce Oppenheimer (ed.), Ohio State University Press (Columbus, 2002).
7. Lecture at Texas Tech University, Lubbock, TX, April 15, 1991.
8. Originally in Richard Fenno, *Home Style, House Members in Their Districts,* Little Brown (Boston, 1978), pp. xiv, 249ff.
9. Buddy Roemer, *The 1994 Theodore H. White Seminar on Press and Politics,* John F. Kennedy School of Government, Harvard University, (Cambridge, 1994), p. 45.
10. Richard Fenno, *Congress at the Grassroots: Representational Change in the South, 1970–1998,* University of North Carolina Press (Chapel Hill, 2000), p. xii.
11. Richard Fenno, *Watching Politicians,* Institute for Governmental Studies (Berkeley, 1990).
12. Fenno, *Home Style.*
13. Richard Fenno, *The Making of A Senator: Dan Quayle* (1988); *The Emergence of a Senate Leader: Pete Domenici and the Reagan Budget* (1991); *Learning to Legislate: The Senate Education of Arlen Specter* (1991); *When Incumbency Fails: The Senate Career of Mark Andrews* (1992); *The Presidential Odyssey of John Glenn* (1990); all by Congressional Quarterly Press, Washington, DC. An appreciative essay on the five studies as a whole is Byron Shafer, "The Senate Quintet," *Journal of Politics,* 56, 1, February 1994.
14. Richard Fenno, *Senators on the Campaign Trail: The Politics of Representation,* Oklahoma University Press (Norman, 1996).
15. Ibid., p. 75.
16. Fenno, *Congress at the Grassroots.*
17. Richard Fenno, *Going Home: Black Representatives and Their Constituents,* University of Chicago Press (Chicago, 2003).

CHAPTER 6

The Salesman and the Old Pro

BOUNDARY CROSSING

Each time I journeyed from classroom to congressional district, I crossed two boundaries—one intellectual, one political. The *intellectual boundary* separated the workaday world of a professor from the workaday world of a politician. It was an imaginary boundary. But it kept me mindful that I had gone from a familiar world to a strange world and that my job there was to do research and report back to my fellow political scientists— most of whom would never go there. The *political boundary* I crossed was tangible and real. In great detail, it marked off the congressional district— the place to which I would travel to conduct my research. My experiences during this boundary crossing—getting acquainted, fleshing out "the bargain," and establishing various personal relationships—were always memorable and sometimes critical.

One midsummer week in the 1970s, I went to two Midwestern states to meet up with two conservative Republican representatives in their home districts. Both districts and both men were totally strange to me. I want to begin my "what are they like?" discussion of House members with them—for several reasons.

First, certain similarities provided a baseline for comparison. Both were in their early fifties, and both were in their second term of service. Each of their districts had one medium-size city or county that dominated the civic, commercial, and cultural life of the district and cast about one-third of its votes. In each case, the dominant county was surrounded by numerous small-town and rural counties. Neither district could be called politically "safe," because both men had come to office by defeating incumbent

Democrats. Both had to work hard to get where they were—and, presumably, to stay there.

In the second place, both men were perfectly ordinary, unaccomplished House rookies, faceless in a chamber long controlled by the Democrats. Neither one produced a headline or a story beyond the district. Because they were of no particular importance in Washington, I could safely focus on their connection patterns at home without having to relate what I was observing to their activity inside the House. Interestingly, neither man ever mentioned the other. If they crossed paths at the Capitol, I never knew about it. And I, of course, did not pursue the matter.

Their lack of notoriety allowed me, thirdly, to write about them anonymously. I could begin, therefore, by demonstrating how much representational activity might be discovered and analyzed without naming names. In later chapters, I will identify the individuals being discussed. But for the first two, I want to proceed without identifying them. In this chapter, readers cannot be guided by any prior knowledge—or any obtainable knowledge—concerning the two individuals involved. The chapter can be read, therefore, as evidence of what can be, or might be, interesting about representational activity, rather than what might have been more interesting about this or that identifiable representative.

I went to their districts to learn about their backgrounds, their perceptions of their job, their districts, and their connections to their constituents. I wanted to learn about their interests, their strengths, their weaknesses, their enjoyments. I wanted to see what they thought about, what they worried about, and what they talked about. I wanted to figure out who they connected with, how, why, how well, and to what effect. I wanted to see how they might connect with me and with my interests, concerns, and puzzles. At the time, I did not think in terms of "authenticity." But this chapter certainly asks the question "what are they like?" Looking back, I was moving in the right direction and going to the right place. I believed that my research would produce a picture that could not be duplicated in, or from, Washington, D.C.

I traveled in both districts during the election seasons of 1972 and 1974. I interviewed each of them once in Washington—but only about representation, *not* about legislation. When I visited their districts, both men were thinking about, and engaged in, an election contest. My report, however, is not about winning and losing—as a visiting Washington reporter's report would have been. I went at campaign time because it provided an excellent context in which to watch them at work—multiple venues, multiple activities. I had no scholarly interest in the election results, and no intention of explaining them.

In the end, the question will be: did I "get it right"? And in truth, I can never be sure. I observed what I was allowed to observe, and I heard what they were willing to say. I went twice to each of their districts. I did eliminate from consideration here any House member with whom I had traveled only once, because I believe that in answering the "what are they like?" question, there is a quantum leap in the value of two trips over one trip. And I do assume that neither person changed much between visits. Would I have learned more or gained greater certainty with three trips—or four—over a longer period of time? I cannot say. For now, my main goal is a modest one: to demonstrate that two district visits are better than no visits at all. And to demonstrate, too, how much of value can be known about "what are they like?" with one comparison and no names.

THE SALESMAN

The representative I met first had not been born in his district. As the son of a Boy Scouts of America executive, he had moved around a lot. He had followed his wife-to-be to her district and secured a job there in the sales department of a major corporation. He had become director of sales training, authored articles on salesmanship, and become a locally recognized management expert. He lived in the central city. I had selected him as "a conservative Midwestern Republican," I had written to him "cold turkey," and he had accepted me sight unseen.

My access experience "at the boundary" proved enormously beneficial. The morning after my arrival, a staffer drove me to campaign headquarters, where I waited for some time for the congressman to arrive. When he did, I was introduced to him, and I waited while he visited with his staff. Then he said, abruptly, "I'm gonna play golf with my son," and he bolted out the door. I had access panic. Whereupon he stuck his head back in the doorway and yelled at me, "Wanna play golf?" I, of course, said "sure"—the first object of my trip being "getting to the politician." His son was waiting in the car outside. We drove to the country club. I left my coat and tie in a locker, rolled up my sleeves, and the three of us played nine holes of golf—a game I had, luckily, tried many years before.

This initial exposure, on the golf course, produced important insights into what he "was like." I knew from his resume that he was a top sales executive for a large corporation. His golfing stories and camaraderie evoked a businessman's connections. Walking along, he joked,

> When I played with _____ of Pepsi Cola, he gave me a dozen Pepsi golf balls, but I noticed he didn't use them himself. He used a Titleist. Then I played with _____ from Alcoa and he gave me some Alcoa golf balls, but he didn't use them himself either . . . no wonder I can't hit the ball as far as they can.

He pointed to a friend playing nearby. "He's general manager of _____ corporation. It must be the best managed corporation in the world because he's out here playing golf every day." And when the man came within shouting distance, the congressman hollered at him, "What are you doing out here? We public employees aren't supposed to work, but you businessmen are." Followed by joking all around.

His willingness to take me along with his son indicated to me that the barriers to access might come down. And they had. The combination of son and golf led him to talk later that day about his three children, their personalities, and their athletic activities. "My wife and I spent half our lives sitting in the bleachers watching one of the children compete in some sport or other." And I noted, "If he said once, he said four times, how many country club swimming records his kids held." His family had remained in the district. "I doubt that I've spent more than ten weekends away from the district in four years," he said. By my own calculations for a single year, he totaled 42 visits and 165 days spent in the district. By any standard, he was remarkably attentive to home.

On my second day, he took me to lunch at his private club, high atop the city's dominant bank building. "Walking from his office to The Club," I wrote in my notes, "he described his every-Friday routine at home. 'I come in (from Washington) Friday morning,' (my wife) meets me at nine and I can be at the office at 9:30. On rainy days, I'll stay in the office till about 11, go over to The Club for lunch and bridge, and come back to the office. On sunny days, I'll stay in the office till 11:59 and then go out to the golf course."

At his club, I experienced more of his golf course camaraderie. "When we first went in, we were seated at a table for two. He said, 'let's go over to the big table where we can shoot the bull,' and we sat down at a big table with eight others. He introduced me: 'He's writing a book about politics and has come to see how we do things here.' Much of the luncheon conversation revolved around golf—money owed, shots made, conversations held . . . and about the congressman's own annual fund-raising golf tournament."

One friend greeted the congressman, "Congratulations for getting on the list of that crazy group that called you names." "There are three of these far-out groups," replied the congressman, "and two of them put me on their 'worst congressman' list. I called the third one and asked them, 'How come you kept me off your list. Didn't you make a mistake?'"

Later, the congressman regaled the group with a long story about a Republican colleague who once knocked Democratic Whip Hale Boggs to the floor with a punch in the men's room during Washington's Gridiron Dinner. "At the climax of the story, the congressman says, 'There's Hale Boggs lying on his back stretched out on the washroom floor waving his arms and calling,' 'Secret Service, Secret Service.' Great hilarity as he reenacts the Washington scene for the boys at The Club." He was, as I would repeatedly confirm, a natural storyteller. It was a salesman's gift.

My notes continued,

> The congressman says to me, "Let's play some bridge." (Once more, luckily, I knew the rudiments of the game.) As we sit down, The Club members gather round to kibitz. My (assigned) bridge partner owns a big farm. The congressman kids him. "The farmers must be in tough shape when they sit around here in the club and play bridge." Another fella says to the congressman, "Better watch it, you'll lose the agriculture vote." A third fella says, "What does he need the agriculture vote for, when he's got the labor vote sewed up." And so on. . . . The wealthy farmer, a real estate developer, the congressman, and I play bridge. The farmer and I win two rubbers, and $19 a piece.

I had no idea we were playing for money. I was nervous the entire game, and, luckily, my partner did all the work. As a follower of politicians, a little lucky experience with golf and cards helped me move beyond access to a helpful human relationship.

More important, from golf and cards I had learned something about the conviviality and the competitiveness of the politician I had just met. About the two venues, I noted, "That is not a bad description of the places I have found him most 'at home,' lunching at The Club, and golfing at the country club." These connections were important clues to the "what is he like?" puzzle. He was a businessman, and he relaxed in the company of businessmen and their social networks.

He was also, I had quickly learned, a very competitive person. In two days' time, we had engaged in two competitions: golf and bridge. And he had talked a lot about a third—swimming. All the while, however, he exhibited the qualities of a trustworthy salesman. He came across as a soft-spoken, straight-shooting, tell-it-like-it-is person. He expressed a particular dislike for "insincerity" and "demagoguery"—by which he meant making promises you can't keep. His "in your face" reaction to the three disapproving rating groups and his delight in describing the knockdown of a Democratic leader, however, hinted at an edgy competitiveness. When I told him I was from Rochester, he told this story: "I once went to Rochester and checked into a hotel with my reservation slip in hand. They said they had no room. I said, 'I have my reservation slip here.' 'We have no room.' 'Then I assume you have covered me at some other hotel.' 'No,' they said. With that I picked up my bag, went over to the corner of the lobby, opened it up next to a couch, hung up my suit coat, and began to undress. I got down to my shorts when they asked me to stop. They found me a room!" His competitiveness, I learned, harbored a taste for confrontation. Put differently, he was not predisposed to compromise.

In his previous salesman-to-sales manager life, the congressman had become a well-established, comfortably settled corporate businessman. He had also become a civic-minded businessman and a civic leader. That is why he had been recruited into politics. Very nearly the first autobiographical comment he made to me was, "I'm not a politician. I came to the job without any experience in politics." His story of how he was recruited into politics is important enough to quote at length.

I was home one day with my two boys, shoveling the driveway so we could shoot baskets, when the phone rang. It was (a former Republican congressman). He said, "What are you doing?" I said, "I'm going to play some basketball." He said, "Can you come down to The Club? There's a group of us here who have something very important to ask you." I said, "If you'll tell me what it is, then I'll come down." He said, "No," that it was very important and secret. . . . I said, "You know I'll do it if you ask me." I always had, whether it was Boy Scouts or Red Cross or United Fund or whatever. My father always told me, "If you have an opportunity to serve, say 'yes' and figure it out later." Well, he said, "If we get a delegation and come out to your house?" I said "no" again, so he finally said, "We want you to run for Congress on the Republican ticket." When I heard that, I said, "Absolutely not, that's the silliest thing I ever heard of," and I hung up. I didn't even think it was important enough to mention it to the family.

I had the normal disdain for politicians and politics that many businessmen have. I was a registered Republican, but I had done nothing whatever politically. I had helped run all the good guy civic functions, but had never turned a finger in politics.

Well, a day or two later, I was sitting in my office and the president of the company came in—something he didn't normally do. He said, "I've been visited by this delegation that thinks you are just the person to run for Congress. If it's your job you're worried about, forget it. You'll always have a job waiting for you. If it's financing you're worried about, forget it and leave it to me. I agree with those men, but I'm not going to tell you what to do." This time I did go back and talk to the family. No way! They didn't want me to have any part of it. So I told my president, the president of the National Bank, and the county chairman—whom I hadn't even heard of and didn't know—and the others. I told them "no."

Then I left to travel in Asia on company business in Australia, Japan, the Philippines, Thailand, Viet Nam, and Hong Kong. . . . I came back just furious about American policy in that area and began criticizing LBJ in talks. Then the same group came back again. They put it to me real hard, that if I felt as strongly as I did, I should run for office or keep my big mouth shut. That put it on the line. I talked to the family again, and they still said "no way." But I thought about it; and three days before the end of the filing period, I went down and signed up. *Absolutely and in every sense of the word, I was drafted into politics.*

When the congressman protested that he was still "not a politician," he meant that he was not a party organization politician. "I'm not going to the national convention. Why, I don't even go to the district political meetings. I'm no politician. I'm probably the most nonpolitical congressman there is. I love the job. I love the casework. But I don't like the cutting and dealing that goes on in politics." He was not personally close to party people, and he openly disparaged the partisan patronage politics that thrived in his rural counties. While he was not active or "at home" in the party, he was heavily dependent on the party. "I'm a 100 percent party man. I work for whomever is in the party leadership. When my county leader is Jones, I work for Jones. When he is beaten by Smith, I work for Smith."

The congressman was a good government, reform-style candidate, who had been the beneficiary of a rising tide of Republicanism in the district's largest county and who had been the choice of the young conservative party activists who had led the resurgence. It helped, too, that he had been elected in a good Republican year nationwide.

When I asked him why he had been picked by others to run, he answered, "I had done a great deal of public speaking in the area, giving management training seminars and speaking in praise of the free enterprise system. They knew I thought as they did philosophically—that we should increase productivity, live within our means, cut down on welfare." His public speaking prowess testified to his communication skills. To which he added, "and they thought I was electable." His philosophical connections to the civic-business community of his district's central city were rock solid. "Financially," he said, "my strong support comes from the Chamber of Commerce, business and professional people."

The congressman had lived in a businessman-civic leader world, one he knew well, and he had been recruited into a partisan-electoral world of which he knew little. He was an organization man without being a political man. But he knew a thing or two about selling and had even written about it, and selling is nothing if not competitive. So he knew about competition, too, and he hated to lose. He had lost his first race for Congress. And when I asked him why he had tried a second time (and won), he said, "Because I hate to get beat. I'm competitive in whatever I do. My whole family is competitive."

For him, campaigning was, quite naturally, selling—selling his product, that is, himself—to voters directly one-on-one and indirectly through larger-scale activities involving assorted other campaigners. Selling himself to constituents meant connecting with them. And he worried a lot about his repertoire of connecting activities, as if connecting, like selling, was his business. And he wanted to get it right.

During my first visit, he worried constantly about the optimal mix of retail selling by one-on-one personal contact, and wholesale selling by vans, caravans, and helicopters. In his city, he walked around amid large crowds at a festival shaking hands, but not as vigorously as I had expected. "I'm shy," he explained, "maybe not shy, but yes, I guess you could say I'm shy. I don't like to go up to someone and stick my hand in his face." "Our two senators go to basketball games, start at the top row,

and work their way around and down shaking hands. I couldn't do that."
(We went to a basketball game together, and he didn't.) He added that if
he wanted "maximum exposure," he would shake hands in front of the
supermarket or at bowling alleys or at festivals. But he acknowledged
that he had yet to do that in his campaign. Later, at a small-town festival
far from home, he said, "the only Republicans who win around here are
the ones who shake every danged hand in every danged county." But,
again, he wasn't doing any. So I asked why. "I should, I should," he said.
"But everyone will know I was here."

As he explained it, any slack would be taken up by wholesale team-
type campaigning, about which he was markedly enthusiastic. "Every
campaign year," he explained, "we have a D-Day. I get in a helicopter
and tour this entire district, setting down in every area, making a short
speech, handing out materials, and taking off. . . . Sometimes we land
right on main street." And later, "Each election we take a caravan of
cars—sometimes with other candidates—and we visit every community
in a county." His youthful campaign staff, he said, liked to drive around
the district—in two vans decked out with plastic GOP elephants on top,
with sound systems singing. He seemed more comfortable with these
wholesale advertising techniques.

Thinking in terms of his background in selling for a large corporation,
he seemed to put more stock in the presentational techniques of his sales
force than he put in a working politician's personal face-to-face contact.
As a "nonpolitician," he seemed to like politics at a distance more than
he liked politics up close—to be more sales manager than salesman. Now
that he was in politics, of course, he had to be both.

During my second visit to the district—with a tougher election
developing—he expressed, again, his preference for large-scale, across-
the-board presentations and connections.

I was talking to (a nearby congressman) the other day, and I told
him I was having a hard campaign. He asked me what I was doing,
and I told him I had these vans with the loudspeaker and the helicopter. He told me that he gets in the car all by himself, and drives
to a little town and goes into the grocery store to talk. He says that
by the time he works his way up to the hardware store, the guys say
to him, "We heard you were in town." He says the small towns
don't like the oompah, the noise. He says that "it's all over town
when he leaves."

Among politicians I knew who represented small-town, rural areas, person-to-person visits were a common practice. But my guy did not do it. His preferred alternative was a campaign by caravan in a rural county. I accompanied him on one of them. My notes:

> Our caravan took us 100 miles or more, through every town in the county. A 27-car caravan can kick up an enormous amount of dust. I chewed it all day. Each candidate had a car. We were about fourth in line, and we played our loud speaker as we went. We drove through some pretty poor rural areas with our music blaring, "Things are gonna be great; things are gonna be grand," i.e., if you just vote GOP. It seemed very incongruous and not terribly sensitive to the problems of the rural poor. But the congressman seems to like it—"Let's give 'em a little music."
>
> We would stop in each little town, overwhelming it with cars and people. Our teenage girls would hop out with their campaign hats on and put leaflets in the doors. I did some "leafletting" too in the larger towns (without a hat!). . . . The congressman would take his recipe books and hunt for hands to shake. In one small town, he went up to a guy and shook his hand. The guy said, "I'm a member of the caravan!" The congressman said, "I can't tell the people in the caravan from the customers." There were far more of the former than the latter.

"The purpose of the campaign," he explained, "is to get hundreds of people involved at the grassroots. A caravan of forty cars in a town of thirty people—that's involvement." His "hoopla" approach to politics reflected a sales manager's preference for mass marketing. But for the salesman himself, it seemed to be a remarkably inefficient use of his time.

He worried about it afterward. "I could have met more voters standing in front of the supermarket for thirty minutes that I did riding all over county all day," he reflected. "Maybe I met only forty voters. But there were fifty good Republicans in the caravan, all of whom will work harder for me because I showed up. There's absolutely no way to judge your effectiveness in this business."

As if to confirm and compound his worries, we had left the caravan early in order to take a helicopter ride to "drop in" on a festival in a distant county—one that was only partly in his district. On the ride back, he lamented,

There's no way that was worth it. I spent two and a half hours and I'll bet I didn't meet more than twelve voters from my district. I had no idea what I was going to do there. I only went because the [party] chairman had been after me for some time and was getting very sensitive about it. . . . Now maybe he'll think I was a nice guy and he'll work harder. . . . [But] I'd have seen a lot more voters if I'd stayed with the caravan and continued on into the county seat.

As he had during my first visit, he talked constantly about the name recognition benefits from one-on-one handshaking. But I did not see him do much of it. Perhaps he had done it in earlier campaigns.

When I was there, however, he had developed a rationale for not doing so by distinguishing between his effort and that of his campaigners. "I'll bet you a million bucks that three good-lookin' kids with their campaign hats on standing in front of the supermarket for one-half hour can do more good than anyone who talks to one person for forty-five minutes. . . . [But] the most productive way for me to spend an hour of my time is to hold a news conference or send a beeper." He elaborated, "When the governor comes to town, he visits each one of the newspapers and each of the TV stations and talks with them personally. I hold a news conference, write up a press release, and send it to those who weren't there. I do in twenty minutes what it takes him a whole day to do. But he believes in the personal touch." More so, apparently, than my traveling companion.

Like a good sales manager, the congressman fretted a lot about productivity and about the trade-offs involved in the use of his time. In an effort to clarify his thinking, I asked him, at the end of my first visit, to rank the 10 or 12 political events—in the order of their "political importance." He gave the top rating to his two-hour walk in a Fourth of July parade—accompanied, I might add, by his blaring sound truck. "Well, folks, we met some voters today. Things went well," he told his staff afterward. And to me he explained, "When you see 10,000 voters, it's got to be important." But, he added, "the most productive event was my news conference that got me coverage on all TV stations and newspapers." As for the rest of the ranking, he didn't seem interested. And he didn't complete the task. Other politicians tackled that prioritizing exercise with care and interest—as a kind of challenge. Not this one. He did not come across, at first blush, as a markedly strategic-minded politician. Technique, yes; strategy, no.

Throughout my second visit, his campaign team was in turmoil, and his campaign was not progressing as he had expected. It produced additional insight into what the salesman-politician was like. He hated inefficiency, and he was very upset. "We have two vans, and all we have done with them so far is to collect $300 worth of parking tickets," he exclaimed. "They've just been sitting in front of the headquarters. . . . So far, the campaign has been going on inside the headquarters. It's about time to take it to the voters."

On the second day, he reported that he had gotten the staff together to straighten things out. "We had a sales meeting this morning. I told the staff the first thing you do is survey the market. We've done that. Then you evaluate your product. We've done that. Then you evaluate the competition. We've done that. Then you plan your advertising and promotion. We've done that. Then you go out and sell your product. That's what we're going to do now. So far, we've all been talking to each other. Now we've got to talk to the voters. We've all got to become salesmen." It was his way.

But his staff's malaise was as much a personnel problem as a sales problem. The staff blamed the campaign director for the organizational disarray, and they wanted him demoted. I had no interest in the particulars. But the relationship of the campaign director to the rest of the staff fascinated me.

I spent my first afternoon at campaign headquarters folding and stuffing invitations to a campaign event. It was the director who met me and talked with me about my schedule and about an upcoming helicopter event in which he hoped to ride along with me. "I love to campaign," he said. I had no contact with the other three or four young campaigners, who sat in an area separated by a counter from the volunteers with whom I worked. Each staff member sat at a desk with a nameplate and campaign title.

The contrast between the disputants captured my interest.

In my view, the director is a big (physically very large) slob—but he was the only one who gave some character to the group. I liked him the best—instinctively. He seemed warm, cranky, impressed with himself, and altogether human. The others were all alike—serious, hardworking, faceless, humorless, cold, and not immediately likable. They are what the congressman likes—neat, clean-cut kids. They look good with campaign hats on. The director would look silly in a hat. But he has zest, and I could imagine him telling a good story. The others could not be storytellers. They do not swear much, they do not reminisce, and I cannot imagine them sitting around like my last campaign group (in Massachusetts), reminiscing and howling with laughter. They seem more mechanical. I could not imagine a volunteer (from the Massachusetts group) with a straw hat on—it's just not conceivable. . . .

Maybe heartland Republicanism is less sophisticated, more concerned with physical appearances, more respectability-oriented, more *conventional* [italics in original]. Here is where the district's social conservatism may come into play. The congressman wants conventional—and conventional-looking—people to give him a conventional image. It is my impression that the campaign director is an individualist and that he irritates the others because he is so unlike them.

The buttoned-up staff seemed to me to reflect the congressman's own concern for the presentational aspects of his work.

My conjectures were reinforced when the director's desire to ride in the helicopter became a burning issue. "I think he wants to ride in the helicopter on D-Day," the congressman told me. "To have him heave his 300-pound body out of the helicopter with one of my campaign hats on, is not the kind of image I want to create. I've had to invent excuses why he can't ride in the helicopter. So I've told him that my daughter is going to do it instead. She's the kind of image I want." The congressman had a sales manager's concern for the packaging and the appearance of his sales force.

His concerns about connecting with his constituents told me little, however, about the constituents with whom he expected to connect. To my standard constituency question, "How would you describe your district?" he answered, "It is a microcosm of the nation. We are a little southern and a little northern. We have agriculture—mostly soybeans and corn. And we have big business. . . . We have a city and we have small towns. We have some of the worst poverty in the country—in X County. And we have some very wealthy sections—though not large. We have wealth in the city and some wealthy small towns. Just about the only thing we don't have is a good-sized ghetto. Otherwise, everything you can have, we have right here." It was, above all, a perception of diversity.

Politically, he described his district as "a marginal district I always win by less than 55 percent. No landslide here." His predecessor, he said, was "a liberal Democrat with a high ADA score." "A person could have the same district I have and hold very different views." Republican Party loyalists—whom he estimated at 22 percent—were not enough. The marginality of the district underscored the importance of the kind of individual he was and the personal connections he had with his constituents. "Issues don't have one danged thing to do about it," he concluded. *"It's an individual franchise you hold, not a political franchise."*

As a political scientist working from his twin emphases—on diversity and on the importance of personal connections—I expected to find a strategy marked by a diversity of connections—different strokes for different folks. All the more so because selling involves a lot of very territorial analysis, and a salesman might be expected to think that way. But that was not the way he talked. He emphasized the whole and not the parts. "I'm probably better known in town than outside," he said, "because of the media. But I'm equally at home in both places. I'll go to the 4-H meeting in the rural part and I'm just as much at home as I am going to the Chamber of Commerce and the Rotary Club. You might think because of my background, that I would be more at home in the Chamber and Rotary, but I don't think I am." "His perception that he's equally at home in diverse contexts squares nicely," I noted, "with his preference for broadside, all-purpose, one-fits-all connections."

To deny differences is, however, to deny politics. And so, when the salesman addressed his district's politics on the road, urban-rural differences *did* appear. For example, he seemed much more in tune with his protective party leader in the city (whom he always praised and never criticized), than he was with his county leaders in the rural areas.

"In A county, the chairman tells me 'we'll collect the money and we'll spend the money.' I never see it." "In B county, the first time I ran, the chairman called and said," "Where's the money? . . . If you don't send me the money, 'I'll stand out in front of the polls and tell people to vote against you.' That year, I lost there by 25,000 votes." "Every time I'd be asked by some group in C county, the chairman would say, 'No, don't come. These people are my opposition.' So I'd say, 'Why don't *you* have an event and invite me to come.' 'No,' he'd say. 'That will only stir things up.' I didn't speak there in four years." "In D county, there are two factions, each of which wants the county chairmanship. That's the whole ball game. So you always have one-half of the county for you, and one-half against you."

During my first visit, as we rode through the countryside, he told a story that suggested (beyond his affinity for storytelling) quite different urban-rural rankings on any "at homeness" scale.

The first time I campaigned in this township, I was scheduled to debate my [incumbent Democratic] opponent. My wife and I and five or six youngsters from the city with their campaign hats and balloons and what not came out in one of our campaign vans going at an exorbitant speed over the narrow country roads, trying to make the 3:30 debate time. When we got there, they had drawn a big flatbed truck with a couple of chairs on it and the crowd was laying all over the truck and sitting all over the ground drinking beer. They'd been there drinking since 10:00 that morning—the Democrats having brought the beer in early. They were all pretty drunk. One fellow had brought a donkey around and had backed him up to my wife and kept poking the donkey to get him to kick her. He'd poke that donkey and then laugh "haw haw," no front teeth. If I'd been able, I'd have seen to it that he had no back teeth either!

When the time came for the debate, my opponent had been "unavoidably detained"—as he always was. I had been challenging him to a debate, chasing him around the district, and using the empty chair to point to and ask why he wasn't here to defend such and such a vote. But the local Democratic leader, a big physical man, got into the chair to take his place and debate me.

The first speaker was the Democratic candidate for sheriff. He got up and started waving his arms, "If I'm elected, you'll have the best danged food in any jail in the country. . . ." Hooray, Hooray! "And I ain't gonna hurt you none." Hooray, Hooray! The crowd cheered and whistled and he sat down. Then I got up, with my glasses on, impeccably dressed and began to discourse on the balance of payments, the international crisis, price-earning ratios, and other great national questions. Silence. Then my "opponent" got up. "I'm full of martinis." Hooray, Hooray! "I don't know what this other fella just said, but he's a dirty rotten liar." Hooray, Hooray! And he sat down.

There were the youngsters from the city, well-scrubbed, clean-necked, and popeyed getting their first taste of rural politics. My wife said she'd never go back to that town again and never has. It was quite an experience.

On the Fourth of July, we joined local party and civic leaders in the executive suite atop the city's largest motel to watch the fireworks. When someone asked if the surrounding areas would have similar events, the congressman joked, "They can sit on their silos and watch ours." It was a city boy's comment, with some of the insensitivity to rural areas that his caravan had shown. Despite his protestations, he seemed to me to be more urban than rural.

Observably, however, he was not equally at home everywhere. During my second visit, I used my "at homeness" scale to puzzle over the strengths of various constituency connections. The notes from my visit to one outlying county revealed different ends of the scale. At a small town country club, "He came in [to the dining room] and started singing with the banjo and piano combo, 'You're A Grand Old Flag' and 'Yankee Doodle Dandy' in a loud voice. When we sat down, it was announced that he was there . . . and all the people eating at the country club clapped and cheered lustily. He stood up and acknowledged the applause from his kind of people—or as he put it when he sat down, 'nice folks.'" His ranking on my "at homeness" scale was high.

Earlier that day, he had presented a flag (flown over the U.S. Capitol) to a local VFW post. "We're in Wallace country," he said as we drove along. "You can tell a Wallacite by his pickup truck, his dog, and his gun. He'll give you his pickup and his dog, but he won't give up his gun." As we entered the VFW parking lot, he spied a row of pickup trucks. "I'd love to get the pickup truck vote," he said, but "that's the kind I never get. The only time I ever get any is with my annual anti-gun control letter. That cuts across the union votes. Most of the people who own pickup trucks are union members—though some are farmers, too." At the VFW presentation, his personal service seemed to be appreciated. But there were no warm embraces, and the presentation was pretty perfunctory. His "at homeness" ranking was low.

His "pickup truck" comment, I wrote, "was one of the most interesting comments of the trip. And what may be as interesting as the comment is how seldom he talks this way. This is the only time I ever heard him mention 'farmers' as a group." He was not at home with political demography. He preferred to think of his connection patterns in across-the-board terms.

Since he did mention his "annual anti-gun control letter" as a strategic success, I asked him about its effect on the campaign. "One of the best things we've done," he repeated, "is the gun control thing. It brought 5,000 letters protesting gun control. I wrote an article in *Gun Week*. We mailed my article to everyone who had written to me." So I asked him about the response. "All the letters I've gotten back have come from outside the district. Not a syllable have I heard from my district." An across-the-board effort, apparently yes; a strategic success, apparently no.

His strong preference for across-the-board connections with his constituents had one major exception—the one he hinted at during our VFW visit—labor unions. "The unions fight me tooth and nail. They send in armies to work against me. . . . Every union hall has a 'Beat the Congressman' sign in it. I'm the prime target of organized labor." He told stories about being "driven off" with a "flying wedge" when he tried to pass out literature at plant gates.

He regaled me with the story of a speech he gave to the machinists union.

I gave a rational, reasonable speech talking about the economy and what I thought should be done. Some of them started shouting, "When [the previous representative] was here, we got this and that." And "How much housing has been built under your administration?" Well, the truth was that no public housing was built while my predecessor was here. . . . But they kept shouting. . . . Then I showed them my literature with the union bug on it, and I picked up a piece of my opponent's literature and showed them that it had no union bug. One fellow rushed up, grabbed the piece of literature from me, and started yelling, "The union bug was here, but the son of a bitch erased it! He erased it!" It was real bad.

But the congressman saw it as a victory. "I've always said that if you can be rational and reasonable, and make your opponent seem belligerent and unreasonable, you will be the gainer." In the telling of it, he seemed to relish labor's hostility and to have been at least as interested in scoring debating points as in winning support.

In my notes, I wrote, "There's a fierce, independent belligerence that comes through that soft demeanor every so often, a hardness under his 'hail fellow well met' appearance." In addition to his Rochester story, there was his story about how he, "the world's greatest expert on how to moderate your opponent's arguments," blew up by telling a profane constituent: "you dumb son-of-a-bitch, if I ever see you, I'll break every bone in your body." There was also his meeting with some anti-war students. "I tried to answer their questions as reasonably and rationally as I could. But I almost took a poke at one guy." He enjoyed telling stories that identified his enemies and highlighted his toughness.

In keeping with his preference for across-the-board connections, he emphasized—and relied heavily on—a one-size-fits-all, *personal* connective link. It was "casework"—helping individual constituents with their government-related "personal problems" like Social Security, and helping the district secure federal money for "projects" like highways and buildings. In his view, casework was a supportive, across-the-board connection—in all parts of, and among all groups in, his heterogeneous constituency. Everyone would be helped. No group would be left out, not even union members. "I get a lot of union member support because of casework," he said. Casework was an across-the-board connection, cut from the same cloth as his wholesale campaign presentations. And he viewed casework as a central, if not pivotal, support-winning activity.

His commentary was studded with comments like "The biggest part of getting reelected is casework." "If you are talking about grassroots support, the most loyal followers are the people for whom we have done casework." Or "I have six years of casework behind me; and I want to run against the toughest opponent they have." He heaped credit for this on his staff—at home and in Washington. "I'm the worst caseworker around." When he came home, however, he made himself available to individuals and civic-minded groups on a strictly "first come, first serve" basis. "I go wherever I'm asked. If someone calls months ahead, I put it on the calendar. I don't do it the way some others do and say, 'I don't schedule that far ahead'—while they wait to see what the biggest invitation will be. I take the one that asks first—big or small." It was another all-purpose approach.

His constant availability seemed to be, for him, a functional equivalent that compensated for any shortage of person-to-person, retail-style campaigning. "My [listed] phone rings constantly when I'm home. And we don't discourage it. . . ." If I retired, "the Republicans wouldn't have a ghost of a chance to win it [this district]. . . . My strength is the result of the casework and all the visits." His reputation in the district, he believed, rested on these constituency-wide activities—connecting him alike with city, small-town, and countryside constituents.

"We took a poll," he said. "And the one thing that came out of it that I was not viewed, in my image, as a hawk or a dove, not conservative or liberal. And this was despite the fact that I supported the [Vietnam] war and that I talk conservatively. The one image they had of me was that I was a hard worker. So I get a broad base of votes. I think I get a lot of votes because of casework."

The poll also told him that "I'm not identified as a person interested in national problems. I'm identified for my interest in local problems." With a slight twist, therefore, his emphasis on "casework" could be expanded to include local "projects"—which were, in fact, the items that dominated his committee work in Washington. His poll reflected his "pork barrel" success. "In our poll, two things stood out. One, he works hard and, two, he works for us. It's the dams, the highways, the buildings, and the casework." "He Gets Things Done" became his campaign slogan. "I've been very successful in getting things for the district and that's what my campaign will be about."

When it came to issues of national policy, the congressman again operated with a set of broad guidelines. His vote pattern in Congress was determined by subject matter. On emotional, social issues such as gun control, abortion, busing, school prayer, and aid to parochial schools, for example, he voted with the dominant view of his constituency (anti, anti, anti, pro, pro), even where his personal preference may have been different. "If you got on the wrong side of those votes, you could be in a lot of trouble here." "People look at one item and drive it to death." "You could be ridden out of my district on a rail of you took the wrong position on those issues." "If I voted no on that, I'd better not come home." While some of these positions might have rested on religious conviction, that consideration never came up in my travels with him. For his list of hot-button issues, he had adopted a clear rule—vote with the most energized single-issue group. "I'm not here to vote on my own convictions," he told me. "I'm here to represent my people."

This "delegate"-style calculus did not, however, apply to economic policy. There, his voting record reflected his business-oriented conservatism and his free enterprise philosophy. And he viewed that, too, as a one-size-fits-all, overarching prescription—equally beneficial for all his constituents. So he voted like the proverbial "trustee." "My district is like Miami Beach," he said. "It's a geriatric district. And I think the senior citizens are a weak spot for us." So I asked him why he did not support legislation to increase Social Security. He answered, "That would be irresponsible. It wouldn't help them. By every principle of economics, it would just fuel the inflation. Every time you put money in people's hands without increasing productivity, you drive prices up." He was strongly opposed to most government regulation—of the energy-producing mining industry and of the workplace (via OSHA) in particular.

For purposes of three types of connections—casework, hot-button issues, and economic and regulatory policy—the salesman adopted an across-the-board perception of his constituents, an across-the-board rationale for his behavior, and an across-the-board performance pattern. By so doing, he finessed issue complexities and strategic variations. He had taken a lot of the politics out of his connections. And as such, he remained, still, more salesman than politician.

The context of my second and last visit presented a unique issue test—one for which the congressman had no guiding category. It was the impeachment of the president. He had chosen a partisan response—total support of the president. Many of his Republican colleagues beat a strategic retreat. That was not his way. He was not afraid of a knock-down, drag-out fight. And he remained steadfast to the bitter end. "I was one of the 20 people who were prepared to defend President Nixon on the House floor. We had a meeting scheduled to divide up the work. Then the president admitted he had obstructed justice. And our leaders said, 'It's all off, we don't have a case.'" The salesman knew he had lost support. He knew he had some trouble at home, but he didn't know how much. And he developed no alternative message. It was a case, I specu-lated, where his competitive and confrontational attitude dominated his actions—at considerable political cost.

The new issue context—first Watergate, then impeachment, and then President Ford's pardon of Nixon—made him nervous. My opponent "is not a better campaigner than any of the others," he said. "It's just that he has these national issues going for him." The salesman had pinned his hopes on his array of all-purpose connections. There was his casework: "Thirty letters a day for eight years has to be helpful. . . ." There was his energy: "If I'm working 80 hours a week, the other fellow ought to be worried." There was his news making: "We are going to turn the cam-paign around 180 degrees. I'm going to hold a news conference every week." There was his attentiveness to home: "My strength is my case-work and all the visits."

His retaliatory reactions were more personal than analytical. Labeling his opponent "a left winger," he asked,

Did you see his literature? That's what I'm up against. My polls show he's making some headway giving me a negative image. He's calling me the tool of the special interests and the tool of the energy barons. It's vicious, gutter politics. Though it's hard on my family, it may hurt him more than it hurts me. I have a reputation as a calm, reasonable person and of service to my constituents. He's just attacking me. He's not dealing with the issues. . . . Did you ever see such dirty politics anywhere else in the country? My instinct is to hit back by being even screamier than he is. But under the constant guidance of my wife and others, I've stayed calm. That's my reputation. He's getting 70 percent of his money from the unions. That's special interest.

It was an exasperated personal outburst, not a competing message or a resourceful strategic response. In truth, he had no plan.

It caused me to think back. Four months earlier, I had talked with the congressman in Washington. He had invited me to sit in on his meeting with his Washington-based campaign consultant. This is how I wrote up that visit.

The impression I had was one of the congressman as a lost little boy, in over his head when he sat listening to and talking to [his consultant]. I almost thought he looked "intimidated" and "frightened" by the big city PR man. He seemed far less confident in this situation than he normally seems to be. Maybe all politicians look scared and non-confident when the professional campaign manager moves in. But this congressman seemed uncomfortable with [his adviser] and almost as if he were waiting for [the adviser] to save him. Maybe he was leading [the adviser] on and keeping his own counsel. . . . But I guess it was the contrast between his normal opinionated, self-assurance that struck me. He may have been in total control of the interaction, but it didn't seem so to me. It was as if the whole thing overwhelmed him.

These earlier notes were a preview of what I was seeing during my October 1974 visit. The congressman had neither the gut instinct nor the talent for strategic maneuver. He was not easily moved away from his all-purpose, across-the-board standardized political activities. The gregarious and competitive salesman had not become a sophisticated politician.

In October, I believed that his across-the-board, undifferentiated perception of the district and his standardized repertoire of political responses had become a handicap. If, indeed, he was faced with a new, wide-reaching, all-consuming issue, he would need to build or reinforce pockets of strength to stop, divert, or contain the new wave. He needed a strategy. But he was bogged down in technique—in the campaign director brouhaha, in the caravan and helicopter inefficiencies. He even seemed unable to rank order the value of his various activities.

His field director told me point blank, "We do not target any group." This common practice was not part of their working vocabulary. Thus, coalition building had been removed from consideration. Reflecting on my visit at the time, I wrote, "I never heard any intelligent talk about strategy or issues or anything from any of the staff—just logistics and organization." And those latter subjects brought mostly dissension and uncertainty.

I rode back to Washington with the congressman. And to the end he remained puzzled about how and where he should spend his time. "Today, there's the opening of a building in _____. My staff thinks I should be there now. All week there's a festival on the city's southside, the biggest event of the year there. You could walk up and down and meet thousands of voters. My staff thinks I should be there. What they don't understand is that I'm better off having my picture taken Tuesday with Henry Kissinger, complaining to him about foreign aid, than to stand at a plant gate." He believed that DC-generated publicity would be most helpful.

Yet he concluded, "How do you know what you should be doing?" It was an unusual question for a politician to ask. But he had spent an inordinate amount of his time worrying about it without any evident forward progress. The congressman had neither the instinct nor the talent for political maneuver. The transformation from salesman to politician had produced a big emphasis on technique and none on strategy. He was long on the "how" of politics, but short on the "when, where and why" of it. And he was right. His way was a nonpolitician's way.

The salesman was defeated for reelection in November. I am not interested in explaining that result, although there are hints in my narrative. It was, perhaps, some consolation to him that his election was not very close and that 1974 was a Democratic landslide year, one that changed the face of the U.S. Congress. The salesman had been swept into office in a good Republican year and swept out of office in a bad Republican year. That is to say, he had never gotten a firm political grip on his self-described "individual franchise."

REPRISE

I did not engage in electoral analysis. But, shortly after the election, I talked with a political reporter from the district's largest newspaper.

He made two observations that resonated with my experience. First, "I don't think his challenger would have won if it had not been for Watergate and if the congressman had not defended Nixon right up to the end. If he had bailed out earlier, he would have won." "Was there strong Republican support for Nixon in the district?" I asked. "Maybe there was in the social circles he traveled in—over at the country club. But the rest of the constituency was more moderate than he was."

Second, the reporter attributed the Democrat's victory to "the most sophisticated campaign this district has ever seen." The opposition, he said, had researched and "targeted" precincts which had previously split their tickets—voting both for the Republican salesman and for statewide Democrats—and plied that group with visits, phone calls, and literature. His explanation interested me in light of the salesman's preference for across-the-board analysis and across-the-board connections. Indeed, as I noted earlier, the congressman had explicitly rejected "targeting" as a strategic option.

As I saw it, the representative thought a lot about the presentational side of politics, but he never learned to think about the strategic side of politics. He remained, to the end, more salesman than politician.

THE OLD PRO

Whatever human relationship you may have achieved with one politician, you begin at ground zero with the next one. Strict comparability is impossible because context and experience cannot be duplicated, much less manipulated. That is the wisdom of my advice to myself: "take what you are given, go where you are driven." Each transition has its own pattern, and each initiates a fresh learning experience. And if truth be told, despite all the uncertainty, it is the learning that is the most fun.

The day after I had left one Midwestern congressman, I found myself in the company of a second one. I had chosen him because of his agricultural constituency, and I had achieved access to him with the help of others. I wrote to a political science friend, who had, in turn, talked with a senior officer of his university on my behalf. That official—also a political scientist—had contacted her friend, the Republican congressman. Her recommendation worked. I met briefly with the congressman in Washington, where we agreed to a summertime visit. "I'll be beatin' the hell out of the district then," he said. Minimal access was assured.

From his biography, I learned that this politician differed in two major respects from his Midwestern colleague. First, he was as deeply embedded in his congressional district as a politician could be. He had been born, raised, educated, and had earned his livelihood as a lawyer in that place. I expected to find, therefore, that his working knowledge of—and his rapport with—the people, the life, and the politics of his district would be more acute than that of the salesman. Second, he was a veteran politician who had been engaged in politics all his adult life. He had already run a close, but unsuccessful, race for public office a few years before.

I expected, in sum, to find greater comfort and more skill in political activity than I had found with his colleague. For the salesman, his recent work experience had been most enlightening; for the new guy, I expected that a lifetime of political experience would hold a key. Two key variables, place and prior job experience, I expected would be critically different.

I caught up with my new guy early one July morning in his district office. I got acclimated by listening while he met with people who had asked to meet with him. (It was a travel-based quirk of fate that I had not actually observed this casework activity with the representative who had placed so much stock in it.) A university professor sought recreation money for an Indian tribe; a filmmaker wanted help in tracking down an old government film on rural America; a group of Jaycees wanted Agriculture Department assistance for a conference boosting the idea of "gasahol"—now ethanol—as a help to corn farmers.

In-between, he filled me in. About his relations with the district's Indian tribe, he said, "We have three Indian tribes in the district. Long before I got to Congress, my wife and I took an active interest in Indian problems. With two of the tribes, I have excellent relationships. . . . We've got a recreation center and housing going up now on the _____ Reservation. The _____ Tribe had a ceremony last year for a boy who was killed in Viet Nam. We both went up, and I danced with them." But with the tribe in question, "I have gone to them on bended knee . . . but we haven't been able to get to first base." He seemed skeptical. About the ethanol conference, he was cautious. "For three years, I was a professional Jaycee. I held every office there is in that organization right up to state chairman. It's one of the greatest organizations there is. But I know from hard experience that sometimes they drop the ball on these ideas." He agreed to help, but he withheld commitment.

At mid-morning, we walked over, with a staff member, to the nearby university to meet with its president for a wide-ranging discussion of higher education legislation, TV education, library financing, performing arts programs, and regional museum development. The president wanted government help on the first four; the congressman wanted help from the president on the fifth. My first observation: "He takes notes on a yellow pad, making sure of names, showing interest, clipping out short questions. Seems very efficient."

Walking back to the office, he spoke as a graduate of the university and of its law school. "I have good rapport with the university. I've gone all out on education legislation. I've been in and out of education for a long time—president of the Alumni Association, president of the PTA." And as a political conservative, he added with evident pleasure, "The student newspaper has endorsed me. I've paid a lot of attention to them, gone over there and met with them and talked with them. It's the personal touch. It will triumph over philosophy every time." His concluding maxim had a more definitive ring than I had heard the week before.

We drove to a luncheon meeting of his campaign finance committee. While he ate and strategized inside, I sat for a couple of hours outside in the parking lot. No offense taken; we were still at arm's length. (And I got no doggie bag.) From there, we traveled to meet with the mayor of "a good-sized (pop. 12,000) city for my district." The mayor was an International Harvester dealer—"a working Democrat, a very popular mayor, and a friendly cuss"—who wanted to help in financing a recreation center and low-cost housing. As we toured the proposed sites, the mayor offered his support in November.

On the way home, a satisfied representative explained: "A congressman has to be a good administrator. He has to follow through—or have a staff that will follow through. You can be sure we'll go back now and shake the trees on those things the mayor talked to us about. He'll get four or five letters from us telling him what we found out. And he'll know that if there is any money anywhere for what he wants, we'll find it." His comments suggested a level of discipline that had been lacking during my visit with his colleague.

"That's what counts with people," he continued. "It's all very nice to go out and visit with them, laugh and shoot the breeze, but if there's no follow through, they'll catch on pretty quick. That was our last governor's problem. He loved people and he'd talk to them all day and all night. But he was all bullshit and didn't accomplish a thing." By contrast, he added that one of his state's U.S. senators "is great on details, but . . . person-to-person, he's not so good. He doesn't look you in the eyeballs when he talks to you and his grip is weak. People have been telling him that for years . . . but he failed the charm school they set up for him." This conversation was my introduction to a pattern that would become very familiar. The congressman watches, measures, and learns from other politicians.

In this learning mode, the congressman critiqued himself as we rode along.

As far as the physical part of the job is concerned, I can keep on going forever. But when it comes to talking to people and getting interested in their problems, I have to work at it. . . . I know the mayors of about 85 percent of the towns in the district. And I'm working hard on the farm implement dealers and car dealers. They are the opinion makers in the small towns—and the grocery store owners, too . . . I'm trying to get to know them so I'll remember their names. I try to associate something with them, some facial characteristic or something, that's how I do it.

He was not, he said, naturally gregarious, but he works at it. And working hard comes naturally to him. The level of personal political detail in our earliest hours together was like nothing I had experienced the week before. He lived in the political world, and he breathed politicized oxygen.

He offered prescriptions for success in reaching groups. "If you can talk to them," he said, "if they identify with you, and if they know you care about their problems, they'll support you and won't care how you vote. . . . Jim Farley [Franklin Roosevelt's campaign manager] always said people vote with their hearts, not their heads. That's true." His earliest travel talk conveyed a strong interest in the craft of politics and a strong sense that he was perpetually enrolled in a continuing education course.

His postuniversity background was about as different from that of the salesman as could be imagined. From the time he became president of his college fraternity and head of the college Republicans, this man had been immersed in party politics: as state chair and national committeeman of the Young Republicans, chair of the State Republican Committee, member of the Republican National Committee, and elected delegate to three national Republican conventions. He was a deep-dyed working Republican politician. And he seemed born to politics.

When I asked him about the possibility of a difficult primary, he said,

I couldn't have a difficult primary. I grew up with the party people [here he listed all the party offices held]. I've been in every home of every person active in the Republican Party in my district. I've stayed in many of their homes overnight. Before we had motels out in the rural areas, it was a tradition that you stayed with the party people overnight. I have an ideal relationship with the party people. Nobody could touch me in a primary. I've been in and out of the party machinery since I was in college. . . . When I was Republican State Chairman, we had an organization that you won't see again. I had a busy law practice, but I spent eight hours a day for the Republican Party.

The week before, I had traveled with a politician who had spent his entire life in business organizations. Now, I was in the company of a politician who had spent his entire life in political organizations. The salesman had been a stranger to political routines; my new acquaintance had been totally immersed in them. As he put it later, "Whenever President Nixon would see me, he would say, 'Here comes *the old pro.*'" The congressman's closest staffer had adopted it. And so did I.

During our conversation on the way to visit the small-town mayor, I quickly confirmed my assumption that his district was overwhelmingly agricultural, and so was the congressman's family background. For him, as for Joe Moakley in South Boston, place was biography. "I was born in the western part of the district on a farm. I hitchhiked over to central city to go to the university." "Two of my brothers still farm." "Agriculture," he said, "is the dominant industry of the district." "Agriculture affects 80 percent of the people in my district. . . . All the businessmen on main street have one eye cocked to the weather and the crops." "People in the city know that their well-being goes up and down with agriculture." And "If there's ever an issue between consumers and farmers, politicians here always go with the farmers just like that (he snapped his fingers) no problem at all. That's not a hard vote." Agriculture dominated the issue politics of the district, imparting overriding policy guidance to this representative—guidance that seemed to have no equivalent in the "microcosmic" district of his Midwestern colleague.

His description of the district began with farming, and he elaborated from that base.

The basic industry is agriculture; but it's a diverse district. . . . It's an independent-minded constituency with strong attachment to the work ethic. A good percentage is composed of people whose families came from Germany, Scandinavia, and Czechoslovakia. I'll bet you they add up to 70 percent. And this goes back to the work ethic. They are hardworking, independent people. They have a strong thought of "keep the government off my back; we'll do all right." That's especially strong in my out-counties. They are very suspicious of big brother government in Washington.

Every drive among the 20-odd counties of his district prompted a running commentary on the fundamentals of farming. "Most of the farms in this area are middle-sized—400 to 500 acres. That used to be large. My Dad had 400 acres and it was the largest farm in the western part of our county. Most of these farmers here aren't rich and they aren't poor. They are making a decent living." Or "The farmers are hardly making it here. The soil isn't so good. It dries out faster and runs right off these hills. You really have to push a tractor up and down these hills." "Corn is still the major crop—some wheat and diversified livestock. . . ." Regarding soybeans, "It's a good crop that's gaining in the area, but it's very hard on the soil." Regarding alfalfa, "It's a rotation crop. It puts nitrogen back into the soil. It's hard to tell from sweet clover." "We aren't going by the big feed lots [for cattle], but we have some smaller ones in this part of the district." "If you are a good farmer, you can make a nice living in this part of the district. One of my brothers is a good farmer. The other one has not been so successful. . . . Agriculture has gotten so competitive that the ones who aren't making it are being weeded out." As a representative from farm country, he operated from a fund of relevant knowledge.

Not surprisingly, he was a member of the House of Representatives' Committee on Agriculture. It had not been his initial assignment, but his first reelection opponent had argued, "He says he's a friend of the farmer. Why isn't he on the Agriculture Committee?" "It was a good issue," said the incumbent. "He didn't get any mileage out of it. . . . But I had heard it; and he was right. . . . It was easy for me and it was good politics." "I may have passed up a chance to go on Ways and Means," he said later. "[But] If I leave Agriculture, I'll leave my people behind. They wouldn't understand that and they would hold it against me. They would say— even though they might vote for me—that I was more interested in the Potomac than I was in their welfare."

The old pro's strategic view of his district was simpler and more sharply delineated than that of my previous House member. As he saw it, the dominant city-county leaned liberal and the "out counties" leaned conservative. Further, the eastern counties—where he was raised and played high school football, and where he is still well known and carries his home county by as much as 92 percent—are the most conservative of all. "I'm very lucky," he said. "I have the best of both worlds. I was born in the east and I practiced law in the west. I'm now stronger than horseradish in the west—and this is an east-west district."

His electoral calculus was clear: that he could not win election without a substantial vote from the liberal-leaning city. The city vote was pivotal. When we first met in Washington, he had said, "I'm more liberal than the average person in my state." It was both asset and liability. His strategic problem was to run as strongly as possible in the city, without losing his "out county" conservative base in the process. "Liberal" and "conservative," city and county, were crucial working descriptions for him, as they had not been for his colleague. For the salesman, the crucial working descriptions had been "political" and "nonpolitical."

Making political calculations I had never heard from the salesman, the old pro discussed his strategic context.

I am lucky because I was born out east and I work in the city. People in both areas identify with me. And I have moderated my record from the last [and losing] Republican. The district is changing—registration figures show it is becoming more Democratic [and] it is becoming more liberal. . . . Some of my old friends, when they spot a vote or two of mine, will say, "What's this?" They are very candid. But the sharp ones will say, "We understand what you have to do. We'd rather have you than any Democrat!" I'm lucky there because these people all identify me from my work in the party. I've been in the vineyards with all of them for 15 years. But they wouldn't go along with some of my [liberal] votes if they didn't identify with me so closely because of my party work.

He relied on his conservative supporters to give him some strategic slack, on personal grounds, when he took actions that resonated favorably in the more liberal city.

If the liberal-leaning city held the key to his electoral success, and if his political skills were organizational in nature, it was only natural that he should devote his maximum effort to *organizing the city* on his own behalf. And that is how he saw it. As important to his success as any of his strategic calculations, then, was his personal effort in organizing the city. In the city-centered county, with its one-third of the district's vote, he described the Republican Party apparatus as "hopeless." "We don't say that out loud. We just smile and organize." He had built his own organization of volunteer workers—200 of them. "They do block work," he said, "covering every block in this city and in the rural part of the county. Other candidates have tried to pirate them away, but we say 'no, we want you to work exclusively for my candidacy. . . . If you don't want to, we'll find someone else.' It takes an awful lot of work to run a campaign." And he praised a reliable money raiser and organizer, "Jack is a doer—not a talker. There aren't too many people like that in politics. There are too many talkers. . . . Our two U.S. senators can't stop talking."

At lunch in his home, he showed me an elaborate organization chart—beginning with his statewide organization and ending with his citywide plan. He was planning a picnic for the 200 workers of his citywide organization. After lunch, as we surveyed the parklike locale of the event, he said, "We've found the picnic to be a very different technique." "'Doer' and 'technique,'" I noted, "are two of his favorite words."

I had left a representative who prided himself on not being a politician and found a representative who prided himself on being a politician. For this second man, politics was not about presentation and hoopla. It was about strategic calculation and concentrated effort.

One day in the congressman's office, I met his most recent Republican predecessor, who told me that his own defeat had been caused by his inability to win the necessary vote in the city. So I asked the old pro what had happened.

He was a political dumbbell. . . . He is a very affable fellow as you saw. He was a good campaigner—a little disorganized, perhaps. If he came up to you on the corner and he liked you, he'd stop and talk to you for a while. That's no way to campaign. Man-to-man he was fine, but you don't have time for that. When I was state chairman, I was at him all the time, "keep movin', keep movin'." And he was very conservative. He was against the Kennedy half-dollar, one of only four [congressmen], and things like that. . . . He carried the Constitution around in his pocket, but he couldn't carry the city!

On my last day, the congressman, his wife, and I rode for three and a half hours to the outer boundaries of the district. Our first scheduled stop was a meatpackers union picnic—a destination I could not have imagined with my previous House member. "I've even had some favorable responses from labor groups," he said. "I go to their meetings and talk with them. Previous Republican congressmen just ignored them, wouldn't establish any dialogue with them. They are Democrats, but they know they can talk with me and that I may be helpful." (Later, he told me that he had worked similarly with the National Farmers Union, the most liberal of his farm organizations.) We arrived at the union picnic too late, however, to do any good. "I knew it was no use after shaking a few hands. They'd had too much beer," he said. "But word will get around and [after several scheduled interviews] I'll be on TV tonight."

In contrast to my previous companion, this man was totally at home in the rural part of his district. During our trip, the sight of farmers driving their tractors in the midsummer heat triggered reminiscences of his boyhood:

> Can you imagine what it must have been like to work as my Dad did with horses in these fields—hot and dusty and having to yell ten hours a day at the horses. My Dad would come in covered with dirt and sweat, and so hoarse he could hardly talk. Then he would do the chores—and up at 5:30 in the morning to begin again. . . . One of our jobs each night was to cut two pieces of cardboard to fit inside Dad's shoes—they were worn through. . . . We used to walk to school barefoot, carrying our shoes. Then when we got to school, we put our shoes on. It was an economy measure.
>
> Once a year we went to the big city. For two weeks before we went, we would talk about the trip and for two weeks afterward. . . . Every weekend, we went to town with a basket of eggs. And we would trade them for next week's groceries. We were really self-sufficient. You got seeds from a neighbor. You grew oats to feed the horses and used the horse manure to fertilize the fields. . . . One year, after we had a tractor, we had to leave it in the barn because we didn't have enough money to buy fuel for it. . . .
>
> My mother was very strong on education. I was the first boy in my whole area to go to college. And I was one of only five or six to go to high school. I hitchhiked to the university with one suit—a secondhand one Mother bought. . . . I was dropped off at the corner

of Maple and 25th Street, and I didn't know which way to walk. I had never been in the town before. So I walked around, found a boarding house, plunked down part of my $60, and started in. . . . I worked three jobs all the time I was in college. . . . Luckily, I was given a wonderful adviser [who] recognized me as a country bumpkin and had a great influence on me.

From these comments, it is not difficult to understand his desire to succeed, his concern for how to do it, and his familiarity with the grinding work it would require.

With respect to his hard work, a chance occurrence in Washington between visits led me to the provisional conclusion that this representative was, indeed, "the hardest working politician I have ever known." One hot summer Sunday noon, I was standing outside the Longworth Office Building, waiting to be picked up by a friend to go to Virginia for dinner. Looking up at the massive five-story building, there was a single open window. Outside, on the street below, a single car was parked. Soon the window was closed. Then a man emerged, got into the car, and drove away. It was the old pro.

When I petitioned for a second visit, he suggested that we meet in Chicago and fly together to the district. I had apparently passed my first test. (Proof came later when, this time, he took me to his campaign strategy meeting!) During our plane ride, he talked more freely than before about his political life—thus demonstrating the critical value of two visits.

I don't know what I'm doing in this business or why I ever got into it. . . . You work so hard to get it and when you get it, you wonder what you did it for. It's like joining a fraternity. I worried about it, but when I got to be president of the house, it didn't matter any more. It's so competitive, and I like that. But you spend so much time and effort—for what? I'll tell you—to get reelected. I'll be more frank with you than I would be with most people. We spend all our time running for reelection. . . . If I could do it over, I'd go to the executive branch. That suits my temperament a lot more. You can get things done. But the legislature? What good is a congressman?

The old pro's interests and his talents, as I saw them, were strongly related to the process of politics, to the organizational how-to-do-it, and only weakly related to the policy why-do-it. He worried and worked for electoral success, and was very good at it. But in a moment of reflection—on the plane—electoral success seemed unfulfilling. In my notes, I wrote, "He doesn't have any policy he wants to get through. He has no specific policy frustrations and he never talks about his inability to get specific things done. He's not policy oriented really. I think he's very reelection-oriented and very political in a technical sense. So he spends his energy on reelection and that frustrates him. But he doesn't try to make policy hay." I suggested to him that his juniority was his problem. But that didn't resonate because, I surmised, he had no strongly held policy goals. Rather than being wrapped up in his own House career, he told me again that he picks out "people to watch" in the House, to see how and why they were successful. He named a few—Pete DuPont, Jack Kemp, John Heinz. And I noted, "It is as if he were still a party official recruiting people to run for office."

He was completely clinical in measuring his political opponents. On my first visit, he expressed respect for his hardworking—"ten hours a day, seven days a week"—Democratic opponent. But he had no respect for that man's political acumen, and he had expressed no fear whatever for his own reelection. Afterward he said, "My God, was he dedicated; but he didn't have any of the right techniques. He worked—a sustained physical effort for seven months—a hell of a campaign. . . . But he was out there trying to convince every voter on every issue, trying to save souls. He'd spend 15 to 20 minutes trying to convert each casual voter. That's not the way to do it. . . . He was duck soup."

On my second visit, I heard a different, but equally professional, evaluation of his current opponent. There was a respect for this Democrat's practical political experience and, with it, some palpable concern. "He has a background in politics and he knows what makes people vote the way they do. He's taken a lot of polls and he uses the information. . . . Any politician would have to worry when someone was spending $120,000 against him—especially if that person knew what he was doing. And now, he's walking the district. He's smart. . . . Our whole strategy is to get our supporters to the polls. He sure will get his out." Issues entered the picture only when he pondered the possibility of a debate—which made him nervous. "I could make a monkey out of him on agricultural issues. But maybe he could study up on others and make me look bad. . . . If he asks, we'll just be busy that day." Verbal combat was not his way.

The congressman's evaluations of his two opponents had almost nothing to do with issues, and everything to do with street-level savvy and organizational proficiency. It was a technician's vocabulary. And it was in sharp contrast to the salesman's personalized, emotional, and nonanalytical assessment of his latest opponent.

During my second visit with the old pro, the issues of Nixon's impeachment and President Ford's pardon of the ex-president were topics of public interest. In sharp contrast to his Republican comrade, this congressman spent his time carefully calculating the effects of his position on his political support. His problem, as always, was to win liberal support without alienating his conservative base.

He had taken no position on impeachment, he said, until the smoking gun. "Either way I voted, I figured I was bound to lose votes about as much one way as the other. We took polls in various parts of the district . . . what surprised us was the 14 percent who would otherwise vote for me and who said they would vote against me if I voted for impeachment—for that reason and no other reason. My hunch is that I would have voted against impeachment."

In his campaign committee meeting, various people reported hearing criticism of that position. His response: "Ask them if they approve overall"—arms sweeping outward and inward—"of the kind of record I have and the kind of job I'm doing—overall, not just individual votes." "After Nixon, admitted he was in on the cover-up, however, I announced I would vote for impeachment." Searching my notes, now, I cannot find any instance where "the old pro" reported taking a resolute, principled stand on any controversial vote.

During our plane ride, he explained his position on *Roe v. Wade*. "I didn't like it. They [the Supreme Court] wrote the law, no doubt about it. So I thought, why not let the states act on it. Maybe it was a political copout. But I'm a strict constructionist and I didn't like the court decision. My wife is all pro-abortion." Reflecting on our plane conversation, I noted, "Most of his positions are politically (i.e., electorally) motivated, I think. He is either the most frank person I'm with or the most overtly political. *I think* [italics in original] the latter—that he is my most perfect weather-vane, wet-finger-in-the-air, ear-to-the-ground politician."

On the ground, the issue of the moment was President Ford's pardon of Richard Nixon. And the representative was trying to figure out how he would react publicly to that event. He started polling the flight attendants on the plane. What did they think of it? And he picked it up with the staffers who met us at the airport, and again at a cocktail party that evening. "I keep taking little polls all the time," he told me. At the party I listened to the following private conversation.

Friend: What do you think about this pardon business?

Congressman: What do you think about it?

Friend: What do you think?

Congressman: Silence.

Friend: I think the same as you do about it. That a lot of shit will fly for a little while and then it will die down.

Congressman: Silence.

As with impeachment, he was hearing criticism of Ford among his hard-core conservatives, and Ford had been one of his House role models. "I watch what Jerry Ford does," he told me two years earlier. "He's a damn good guy, a damn good leader, a damn good congressman, a damn good everything." And he was going to stick by him—if possible. In that context, he said, "District-wide, there isn't anyone whose political judgment I trust. . . . I rely on my own judgment. . . . You learn to listen and then to evaluate and digest what you hear. You have to be especially careful on emotional issues. . . . I must say that what I have heard on the pardon, I don't like. There is more opposition than I thought there would be. When it happened, I thought Ford would get through it all right here. But still we'll have to wait and see on that." "Wait and see" had not been an option in my salesman's strategic vocabulary.

On my last day in the district, the congressman, two aides, and I drove 250 miles (total) to visit seven small communities with a total population of 8,800 people. The adventure took seven and a half hours. "Small town campaigning," he had said earlier, "is hard, hard work. You have to get yourself all psyched up to do it, just like before a big ball game. You have to convince yourself that it's going to be fun. My wife often goes with me, and she goes up one side of the street, while I go up the other side." On this trip, she remained at home. One aide told me that "with her, you get two for the price of one" and "her recipe books are a big hit." When the congressman stopped to talk, he often heard about the recipes and fielded inquiries about the family.

In each town, he would work one side of the street armed with his wife's recipe book, and one aide, distributing matchbooks and palm cards, would work the other. A second aide would visit the grain elevator or newspaper office. I would take campaign cards and put them beneath a car or truck windshield wiper or, if the window was open, on the front seat. I worked both sides, since I did not talk to people. Trying to put a card under a windshield wiper glued to the glass with caked and hardened dust was a reminder of the drought plaguing farm country at the time.

In all but one town, "the street" consisted of three to six stores on both sides: a café or two, a grocery store, a bank, a law office, a filling station, a newspaper office, a farm implement store, a grain elevator, and, perhaps, another farm-related business nearby. "When I campaign out state," he told me, "I stop in every bank, every law office, and every barbershop. And I'd sooner pass up a bank than a barbershop. Do you know how many people a barber talks to in a week? I send all of them a congressional calendar and half of them put it up in their shops." I did not see one this time. But it was a rural rule of thumb that put the nuts and bolts of personal connections front and center in his calculations.

In the one county seat we visited, the congressman made it a point to visit with the newspaper editor and the chairman of the Republican Party. When he completed those two calls, he said, "That was the big one. It's all downhill from here. . . . I guess you can see how important it is—tromping around like this. There's no other way."

It was altogether more personal than the caravans favored by the salesman, and it came from a clearer and steadier perception of representational connections. Not once in our travels did he ever question what he was doing and why. Never did he second-guess himself or worry about a technique or fret that he should have done this or that differently. He knew what to do and how to do it, and he did it. He was an accomplished political man.

On the way home, he dictated a note to everyone he had met, and could name, during his last two days of campaigning—a couple of dozen, I would guess. It was a settled connective technique. He also sent *me* more personal letters than any other politician ever did. It was the personal touch. Never, in my records, did he mention the casework done by his office staff—the people that "the salesman" often credited as so contributory to his political success.

At the end of our trip, I noted: "He's a fairly serious man, but he'll joke a bit about 'beautiful downtown Allen' (pop. 250) or 'I'll sleep better tonight knowing we visited Bloombury (pop. 475) today.' But he does not seem to have a lot of joie de vivre or get a lot of zest out of campaigning." Also, "He never exhibited the storytelling conviviality of my earlier companion. He is every bit as competitive as his colleague. But he is a much steadier—and a less belligerent—competitor."

Reflecting later on where he seemed most "at home" during my visit, I wrote,

> I'm not really sure I've ever seen him unbend. He tends to be a little stiff—or perhaps "studied" is a better word. He certainly loves the university for what it has done for him and means to him. But he certainly didn't lose himself in their football game (which we attended together) and certainly not at the cocktail party afterward. "He was fairly sober, too, in his campaign meeting—even though he knew everyone. . . . He is certainly pleasant—smiles and is quick—but there is nothing that would enable you to say of him: 'here is his emotional base or his (emotional) home.'"

I had occasion to consider my "what is he really like?" question in nonpolitical contexts, too. On the evening of my very first day in the district, for example, my university benefactor had arranged a dinner party at her home with her husband, the congressman, his wife, and two other couples—a group tied together not by politics, but by the friendship of the four women.

Meeting and talking with the congressman's wife on the way to the party reminded me of something I had observed in my previous district, too. "The wives of these guys," I noted, "are quite suspicious of me. The two representatives are so used to talking to other people that they are not suspicious of me. Both wives are very protective. Both of them kept pumping me on why I was there, who else was I with, how I do my research, was I going to write a book, etc."

In both constituencies, I spent time in the company of the wives. I had driven across the district with the wife and daughter of the salesman, to find a place for their daughter to live in her new teaching job. And we had eaten a catfish meal together. But that was it. Now, with "the old pro," I was destined to eat every evening meal—"three nights of good steak"—with the congressman and his wife. She seemed heavily involved in his political life. "Campaigning, that's the real fun," she told me. And she, too, wrote me a nice note afterwards—the only spouse who ever did so.

The first evening's dinner party was friendly and warm with Midwestern hospitality. Conversation focused easily on the city, the university, and the quite varied interests of the individuals. If politics was mentioned, it made no impression on me. Out in the kitchen, however, one of the wives told me that the congressman "had always wanted to be a congressman . . . in

school, you could see his ambition." Then, speaking as an old friend of his
wife, she said, "I hate to see it happen. They've changed. They aren't a family any more. They're an emblem, an image, always wondering 'how am I
doing, how do I look, what are people thinking, why aren't I the center of
conversation.' A hair transplant—now I mean! Who cares?" It was the
evening's only political remark to reach my notes. Though I did not think
about it then, she was evaluating—and bemoaning a loss of—authenticity.

I did, however, take note of the congressman's demeanor in this social
situation, one where the conversation did not naturally flow through him.
"He was strangely quiet at the party. . . . He was not, as I would have
expected, the center of attention. Not at all." And I further reflected, "I
didn't pick up on the transplant. If he had one, it's further evidence—of
which I have a little—of his studied efforts to learn the tricks of the trade."

The next night, one of the original couples invited me to dinner with
the congressman and his wife, plus another friend. And I noted, "Again,
the congressman was quiet." In nonpolitical settings, he was not the convivial, center-stage storyteller that my first House member had been. Neither was he aggressive or cocky—just quiet and self-contained.

On my third night, after the meatpackers' event bust, we had cocktails
with a congressman and his wife from an adjacent state. My congressman did not look forward to this social visit with his slightly senior
colleague—whose wife had been the "big sister" to the congressman's
wife in getting adjusted to Washington. It was another wife-centered
affair. The two men were not particularly friends, the old pro seemed ill
at ease, and the conversation seemed strained.

During a lull in the conversation, my friend asked his colleague, "Dick
was asking me how my voting record compared with yours. How would
you answer that?" They went back and forth on various votes and labels,
with the other congressman more certain and more voluble about his various ratings. Concerning his _CQ_ rankings, the old pro said, "I don't
know. I have them back in the office somewhere. I'll have to look them up
sometime." That these two House members—far from Capitol Hill and
over drinks—should be discussing their vote rankings reflected a distinct
lack of easy fellowship.

In my view, it was the other man who seemed "relaxed and confident"
and "comfortable," whereas my friend "seemed more aggressive, more
edgy, more insecure." And I noted a similar lack of chemistry between the
poetry-writing, Wellesley-educated, "quietly snotty" wife of one politician, and the politically ambitious wife of the other. It was another social,

nonpolitical situation out of his normal orbit in which the old pro seemed ill at ease.

Afterwards, we drove back into the congressman's district for a backyard grilled-steak dinner with his regional campaign director and wife. He was back in his workaday political world, and there was little doubt about his changed comfort level. He complained immediately to his associate that the visit with his House colleague had been "practically a command performance." There is a special place in the old pro's heaven for political operatives who, like himself, do the hard, down-and-dirty, in-the-trenches political labor. And his barbecuing dinner host was one such. "He's a great follow-through person and a good administrator," praised the congressman. "When you ask him to do a thing, it will be done."

Over dinner, the two couples gossiped about politics in that part of the district, gossiped about the Republican congressman we had just visited, and assessed the progress of the old pro's Democratic opponent. "I try to avoid labeling myself conservative or liberal," he offered at one point. Even in this setting, I noted that my companion was "quite subdued at dinner, preferring to listen to the others. He was not a storyteller."

From these several social visits with him, I concluded that this very political representative was, as he had admitted, not naturally gregarious. He had to work at it. He relied on "doing" more than "talking"—on performance more than palaver—in connecting with his constituents.

The old pro was easily reelected in 1974. I did not keep in touch, and I did not see him again. Everything I had learned, however, told me that he would be reelected to the House from that district for as long as he wanted to be. And I was right.

The two conservative Midwestern representatives, whose situation seemed at a distance to be so similar, turned out to be two very different individuals and two very different politicians. One was a civic-minded businessman on loan to politics. He sought political support through salesmanship—especially through personal service to his constituents. In social situations, he was self-confident and gregarious. He seemed insecure and awkward, however, in his adaptations to the environment of, and to the practices of, politics. I could know most of what he was really like, I believe, without knowing much about his constituency. Still, I had to go with him to his political place to find that out.

The lawyerly old pro, on the other hand, was born to politics and to the hard work of politics. He could only be known in the context of his attachments to his rural, agricultural constituency. He thrived on building and exploiting organizational and electoral connections, and he sought political support through his partisan and organizational skills. He tended to be clinical and strategic in his decision making. He was not as outgoing and gregarious as his colleague, but he was more temperate. And he never took his eye off the electoral context.

As for myself, I surely could not have known what these two representatives were "really like" without "going there," learning about their occupations, watching them work, listening to them talk about themselves, and assessing their representational connections in their home districts. Could readers have learned more if my anonymity restriction had been lifted? Perhaps. But readers can judge whether the two stories—the civic-minded salesman and the politically minded old pro—provided convincing evidence that much can be known without naming names. Whatever that overall judgment may be, it can be weighed and revised in the chapters that follow.

CHAPTER 7

Ben Rosenthal 1970–1974: Straightforward Liberal

GETTING STARTED IN QUEENS

As of October 1970, the only New York City I had known was midtown Manhattan—a place of private foundations and welcoming theaters, connected by taxis. Queens was the place where you got in or out of an airport taxi. It was, I quickly learned, a different place with a different pace—faster, louder, and harsher than any in my experience. When I took a taxi to my designated hotel seven minutes from LaGuardia, the cab driver, angered by the short-hop fare, upbraided me in colorful language. And later, at dinner, when the congressman's steak was served too well done, he adopted a similar tone in telling the waiter to take it back and bring him what he had ordered. In this place, people routinely shouted and argued and demanded in dealing with one another. It was not personal. They talked fast and they walked fast. I continually bumped into others on the sidewalk, in elevators, and in revolving doors. For a congenitally subdued and slow-moving upstater, the surface-level strenuousness of Queens had to be an acquired taste.

For a U.S. representative of Queens, however, an acquired taste would not do. My earliest exposure convinced me that *any* representative of Queens would have to have been raised there. Benjamin S. Rosenthal qualified. He was born in Manhattan, moved to Queens when he was four, and was educated in the public schools, at City College, and at Brooklyn Law School. He was totally at home in the hubbub. He was, as he said, "in tune with the district," its rhythms, and its people.

He had this place—his place—well under control. In the car, he issued a barrage of instructions to whomever was driving: "turn here," "watch the car on your left," "stay in the left lane," "slow down, baby, slow down," "don't turn here," "you just missed a parking place," "there was a good spot, you should have taken that spot." To me, he offered a lighter touch: "Did you ever have a ride like that one?" "Are other congressman calm and collected?" "Isn't this just like driving from Rochester to Syracuse?" "If it weren't for the driving, this campaign would be a pretty boring operation." "We'd better go easy on the brochures. We'll need money to pay parking fines." Whimsy was a favorite Rosenthal adaptation mode.

Eating, it turned out, was another. And it gave him—and me—another change of pace. At the end of dinner one evening, he said, "I'm late, but I'll have to have coffee and a cigar. We can't let the campaign interfere with life. Bobby Kennedy would eat a sandwich in the car. But I can't do that. I may have to give up one of tonight's meetings. You eat better on this campaign than any other." Then, "We had a Senate campaign going for about a month. We ate very well, discovered the best restaurant in Buffalo, and ate at Hyde Park. It cost $10,000 and we never got it off the ground." Most days, he punctuated late afternoon campaigning with: "let's go have a malted at 'John's." Once, we ran into writer Jimmy Breslin and went for a beer instead. These pauses invariably led to reflective conversation.

Lucky for me, Ben Rosenthal was an exemplary traveling companion. He tried always to teach and to be faithful to my questions. In those pursuits, he combined openness and intelligence. He was an unpretentious, blunt-spoken, tell-it-like-it-is, what-you-see-is-what-you-get individual. He was issue-driven, but he was not an intellectual. He was at once a passionate reformer and a clinical, cost-benefit pragmatist. He was both analytical and insouciant—sharply critical and engagingly self-deprecating. He was not comfortable as a hand-shaking "meeter and greeter." He described himself as "lazy," he had a short attention span, and he often became impatient. He was, by nature, more a private person than a gregarious one. But he was so earnest and so open that he could never be thought of as aloof or self-centered or "full of himself." Benjamin Rosenthal was a straightforward man.

Lucky for me, too, he took seriously the business of connecting with constituents. He was a good teacher because he was a good learner. "I'm very interested in the subject. I spend a lot of time scrutinizing my operation to make it work better for me. I keep trying to improve. I talk to other people a lot about it." He was markedly self-critical. He talked often with his colleagues about connecting techniques. In the course of my two visits, he mentioned conversations with at least 18 different House Democrats about their retail connection patterns. From baby books, recipe books, telephone messages, newsletters, press releases, to district offices, staff allocations and office equipment, home visits, school appearances, and town meetings, he puzzled out loud over connection activities and patterns. "This is a business," he would say, "and like any business, you have to do time and motion studies. All we have is time and ourselves. So you have to calculate carefully to use your time productively."

He understood that his connection patterns reflected his *choices*. "You have to budget your time and weigh the costs and benefits of everything you do." He took pains to explain his decisions. Often he did this by comparing his choices with those of various New York City colleagues. "He goes to six things every Friday, Saturday, and Sunday, walks in, smiles at everyone, leaves after five minutes. Everyone says, 'Wasn't it nice the Congressman was here.' It's great politics, but it doesn't suit my personality. . . . I want to save myself for meetings, when I can make a speech on an issue." Or "He sits in his New York office every Saturday and sees every constituent who has a problem—sometimes 100 a day. It's good politics, but I could never do that. I couldn't sit still that long." Or "Every Friday night between 5:00 and 7:00, he stands in front of a subway stop handing out literature. . . . I wouldn't make a fool of myself standing in the rain handing out stuff at subways." "X wines and dines every little two-bit group that comes down to Washington from home. He spends all his time with them. He doesn't have anything else to do. But I don't have the patience with these guys—or the time." His conclusion? "Everyone is different. And every operation suits the personality of the congressman." Or "Each of us adjusts to his own metabolism."

He wrestled continuously with these aspects of his constituency connections. And he never subscribed to any magic bullet. As we traveled from event to event, he would counsel, "This event isn't important by itself, but it's all part of a cumulative process, an image-building process. You do a little here and a little there." Indeed, at the end of my visits, he was emphasizing a very different connection pattern than when we first met.

ETHNIC CONNECTIONS

Ben Rosenthal was Jewish. And so were the majority of his constituents. And that was the first requirement that this place imposed upon its representative. *Ethnicity* was a dominant constituency characteristic—which

Rosenthal factored at "55 percent Jewish, 15 percent Irish, 15 percent Italian, and 15 percent mixed." The overwhelming majority of New York City Jews were Democrats, a solid majority were social welfare liberals, and a sizable minority were civil liberties liberals. Ben Rosenthal was all of those. But the rock-bottom condition which the place prescribed for its representative was that he or she be Jewish.

The issues of the day, I would learn, kept him much closer to liberal Jews than to Orthodox Jews. But on matters of their common heritage— particularly their support for victims of Nazi persecution and their support of Israel—he and his Jewish constituent majority were of one mind. "Is there any vote that would kill you?" I asked. "No, I honestly can't think of any. . . . If I voted against arms for Israel, well, that's just inconceivable." And later, "If I voted against aid to Israel, that would be it! If I did something absurd like that, if I voted counter to a massive opinion in my district, I would lose." He sat on the House Committee on Foreign Affairs, where he kept a watchful and influential eye on Middle Eastern affairs. "In terms of Israel, all elements respect me—whether they are Orthodox or the rest of the crowd. They think I've done a good job on my committee." On that subject, he was a textbook representative of a constituency majority.

The first two events of my initial 1972 visit helped establish the prominence of his ethnic ties. He went first to help dedicate an attractive, spacious ("walkway, garden, and fountain") "Home for Displaced Persons," named Kissena #2. It was a private-public development for elderly European Jews, many of them Holocaust survivors. "A self-help, communal spirit shone through everything," I noted, "a strong sense of togetherness." It was an early reminder of the history and the communal compassion that linked this representative to his Jewish constituents.

He did not speak there. The next day, however, he drew a lesson from it. "People will vote for you when you attend openings like the one yesterday. You asked me if one vote could kill me. If you attend all the openings, no vote will matter. I don't want to overstate that, but it's very important. Political scientists miss that." He added, "I didn't want to be an 'openings' kind of congressman, but here I am." Later that day, he replayed his Kissena #2 visit in a talk to members of the heavily Jewish, strongly supportive International Ladies Garment Workers Union. He praised their "moral enthusiasm" and said, "As John and Bobby Kennedy said, 'We can do better.' We have Kissena #2; we should have Kissena #202." Of the ILGWU, he said, "They are strong Democrats. They are 'the people.'"

Our second event on my first day was the installation of officers at the Young Men's and Young Women's Hebrew Association of Greater Flushing, where the congressman was the master of ceremonies and main speaker. The "JY" was a cultural center of the Jewish community in Queens. Rosenthal, I noted, seemed totally "at ease" with a large collection of old friends, former opponents, distinguished judges, and community-minded people. The man who introduced him—an early rival for party endorsement—lauded their guest so lavishly that the audience began urging him to "hurry up!"

Having sipped a little wine, the representative began by saying, "I'm probably the first tipsy installation officer you've ever had." "The 'Y' was the most important influence in my life," he told the group. "It gave me goodness and kindness, and whatever goodness and kindness I have brought to others was instilled in me during my years at the Flushing 'Y.' I belonged from 13 to 19. They were the most important and happiest of my youth. Without my knowing it, they gave me great strength and spirit." At a time of trouble, he recalled, with his just-born child in danger at the hospital, he was drawn to the "Y," and sitting there, viewing the name of its founder, Edward Warburg, on a plaque, "I decided then and there to name our newborn 'Edward' Rosenthal." Whereupon the local Pontiac dealer hollered from the back row, "It's a good thing you didn't name him 'Flushing Y!'" He was clearly among friends.

Afterward, I asked, "What do these people think of you?" "They think I'm a progressive, hardworking, dedicated congressman who brings credit to the community," he said. And he delivered another connection lesson.

> Those people were leadership types. What they want is to be able to have a call on me, to have me present at their functions. And that's far more important than my votes. In a sense, I let myself be used—or my office be used—to give them what they want. It boosts their ego. If you ask me which is most important—my votes or my work in the community—the latter is much, much more important.

When I asked him whether these "leadership types" were also his closest supporters, he gave me some recent history. "They are close supporters," he said,

> but my very closest supporters are the issue-oriented people—the more sophisticated people. These people you saw today are interested in the "Y" more than the issues. That's a fine thing, and people

interested in the community are usually the best people. I'd have to say, too, that my strongest support comes from upper-income people (like these).

But the people in the peace movement are the very strongest. Don't forget, I was one of the first members of Congress to come out against the [Vietnam] war. To the peace people, I'm a semi-hero. We went through hard times together when being against the war wasn't popular, and they worked very hard for me, Women's Strike for Peace. . . . There probably aren't more than 100 of them in all, and they are scattered all over the district. But 100 activists can do a lot. On Moratorium Day, they had 15,000 people marching up Queens Boulevard.

It was the first mention of his leadership in the anti-war movement of the late 1960s. It had brought him district-wide visibility, buttressed his reputation as a fighting liberal, and brought him a devoted following in the constituency.

It was part of a distinctive, issue-centered pattern of behavior—one that would be revealed often during my visits. And revealed, too, in his voting record. In the two congresses while I watched him, Ben Rosenthal had *the most liberal* and *the third most liberal* voting record in the U.S. House of Representatives.[1] He never became a well-known figure in Washington, because he had no skill at self-advertisement in that place. But as a representative, he was best known at home for the liberal policy stands he advocated in Washington.

For him, ethnicity implied policy. When he said, "I'm in tune with the issue-oriented people in the district," he implied that their makeup was largely Jewish and their tune was strongly liberal. In domestic matters, he espoused a large, active, and beneficent role for the federal government. Mostly, he spoke to liberal groups, where his constant theme was that "We are a rich country" and "We can do better." He challenged his constituents never to be satisfied with the federal government's current use of its resources to help needy, problem-plagued urban Americans. "What you and I have to do" was a favorite lead-in line. John and Robert Kennedy were his role models. Richard Nixon and conservative big business were his targets. He was not afraid of new ideas and would test for their merits. He saw himself as an opinion leader, not an organizational leader. He was a needler; he was not a schmoozer.

NEIGHBORHOOD CONNECTIONS

Second to ethnicity, in Ben Rosenthal's perception of his district, was the constellation of its *neighborhoods*—their diversity and their transformations. Queens was not Manhattan. As one denizen put it, "People in Queens, when going to Manhattan, say 'I'm going to New York.'"[2] "This isn't an urban district like some," said Rosenthal. "It's New York City, but it's the outskirts. It's not like downtown Newark. It's the second stage." Or "It's a middle-income, bedroom, New York–oriented district with a large number of subway people." Queens was its own world. And it was a world of neighborhoods.[3] Whether every representative of that district would, out of political necessity, have given the same emphasis to the neighborhoods, I cannot say. It would be hard to avoid it. But that's what Ben Rosenthal saw and what he reacted to, and his neighborhood perspectives tell us something important about what he "was like" as a representative.

During my 1970 visit, we went to places named Flushing, Astoria, Rego Park, Whitestone, Beechhurst, Corona, Bay Terrace, Glendale, Fresh Meadows, and Jackson Heights. Once they had been separate governing entities. Now, all had been incorporated into Queens County. But they retained their identity as "communities"—on maps and in the minds of politicians.[4] Residents who left their "bedroom borough" to work in Manhattan still identified their home places as Forest Hills or Flushing or Corona—not Queens. The congressman viewed the district, too, as a collection of these small communities. Each had its own ethnic mix, its own economic level, its own developmental history, its own housing patterns, its own ideological cast, and its own prospects for stability. Traveling around, the congressman used identifiable neighborhoods as a way of locating himself.

Housing patterns were landmarks. Some places were dominated by private homes; others were marked by high-rise apartment buildings. He had something to say about all of them. Riding along, he would identify (usually unfavorably) both the builders of housing projects and the developers of single-family homes. "Thirty years ago, this neighborhood was developed by X corporation, and a Jew could not buy a house here. My father tried and could not." Or "X built these high rises. He offered $50,000 if anyone would run against me in the primary." When we campaigned outside Lefrak City, people complained of crime inside their buildings. Apartment dwellers, like homeowners, were middle-income people. But personal connections were rare. "They are not joiners," he said. "Not one in 300 is a member of any organization or group. They are unreachable. I send them newsletters." Or "You take Lefrak City (25,000 people packed into high rises)—it's so transient, you don't know who you represent." Or "There are 100,000 people in these buildings here, and I'll get 75 percent of them. They are Democrats moving out from the Bronx and Brooklyn, and they vote the party line."

He saw the district's ethnic and neighborhood patterns as constantly changing, and he saw change as requiring an ability to adapt. It was the intra-urban American story of migration and assimilation, "the melting pot and beyond," the movement of groups across his district, changing the makeup of his constituents in the process. My first trip produced a running commentary on the effects of these constant population waves—moving in, moving on, moving out—and the needs created by efforts to stem or minimize or minister to the constant flux. In a "deteriorating" area, he might say, "This used to be upper upper," or "This used to be middle upper." Every neighborhood was classified by its housing patterns, its relative affluence, and its relative stability.

His own neighborhood was Jackson Heights. When we went there, he commented, "It's still good. Not much change here. In 1925 we moved to Jackson Heights, and I've lived here all my life. I know this district like the back of my hand—everything within 30 blocks of here." Four years later, he described Jackson Heights as "older and more Spanish than before." Elsewhere, it was described as "a two and four family neighborhood of lower middle-income whites and Hispanics."[5] "The great problem," he said, "is whether we can stop areas like this from growing old and deteriorating. I think you can. But it will take massive infusions of federal money." As he saw it, neighborhood change was an inevitable, repetitive, relentless force that all Queens politicians had to contend with and adapt to.

During my first visit, he seemed content with the makeup of his district. He characterized his strongest electoral supporters as "middle upper Jewish." And he touted "middle upper-class" Forest Hills as the heart of the district. "Quite apart from politics," he said, "it gives you a good feeling when you represent homeowners who are stable and not transitional and are concerned about the community." They were his active support base, the people he connected with most easily. "I find," he said, "there is a direct relationship between income and political philosophy—the higher the income, the more liberal the philosophy; the lower the income, the less liberal the philosophy."

When he saw neighborhoods, he saw not only political support patterns. He also saw polarization.

I can win by 500 to 15 in one election district and then, just 20 blocks away, lose in another election district by 500 to 15. We are so polarized in my district. My image is that of a red-hot liberal in Queens, and I'm Jewish. Some parts of my district are totally the opposite of me politically and ethnically. Other congressmen . . . have rolling differences across their districts, a little bit up here and a little bit down there. It's not like the right side of Queens Boulevard and the left side of Queens Boulevard. They are two completely different worlds.

Typical of his "other world" were the communities of Glendale and Ridgewood, heavily supported by Irish and Italian conservatives, which, for the most part, he left alone. "I just don't go there," he said. "There are some groups I'm just not popular with. And I don't try to be. I accept that. It's the way I am. I can't be all things to all people." This comment reflects, again, his penchant for cost-benefit calculation.

One day he decided, on the spur of the moment, to take me to Glendale—pictured on TV as the neighborhood of Archie Bunker. On the way, he had to stop the car (amid some hilarity) to ask a group of students, "Is this Glendale or is it Middle Village? I'm the congressman from Glendale and I'm looking for my district!" Answer: "This is Middle Village." (More hilarity.) When we finally found Glendale, we got out and walked up a busy street. "I've only been here once in my life," he exclaimed. "It looks OK. What's the matter with Glendale? Who said Glendale was different?" Then, "I'll get 30 percent here. I can't see campaigning here. There's nothing I can do. I hope they take these places away from me." A year later, new redistricting legislation did just that. But it gave him two other Catholic, conservative neighborhoods to take their place.

Population flux dictated the redrawing of district boundaries every ten years, and one such change occurred between my two visits. The makeup of his altered district seemed less easily digested by its representative. It was shaped like a lobster with two large claws, and it had less of an identity than his previous one. It was not the worst outcome. "At one time, they had me moved into the Bronx. That would have been horrible. It wouldn't be bad politically, but just psychologically. I don't know the Bronx." As that comment indicates, district change was not a survival problem for him. It was a *connection* problem. "I'll bet there isn't another district as hard to get around in as this one. It's so cut up that I can't deal with any single community as a whole. I'd rather take the political disadvantages of a redistricting if I could deal with whole communities. The way it is now, it's bad for them and it's bad for me. This district is an outrage."

"I don't know whether this area here is in my district or not," he said as we rode along. "It's a nice area, very stable. Let's pull over to the curb and look at the map. It could be, but I'm not sure. That must have been some redistricting when the congressman who represents the district can't tell whether he's in it or not. What a mess!" When we stopped to do some shopping bag campaigning, he pointed out our location on his map. "Redistricting gave us this little bump here. That's crazy. I was the gainer because it's solid middle-class Jewish. But I got it because others didn't want it. . . . I'm the result of everyone else's machinations." "You've got a residual district," I offered. "I've always had a residual district," he replied. He took no part, he added, in the negotiation of his boundaries.

"Until this redistricting, I was a classic representative of the district," he said. "I lost most of Forest Hills—a constituency on the same wave length. And it was replaced by Sunnyside and Woodside, where I'm not on the same wave length." "Forest Hills was the cream of my district— psychologically, sociologically, educationally, politically, any way you want to measure it. They were unhappy to lose me as their congressman as I was unhappy to lose them. I picked up some other areas that were good, but not as good as Forest Hills. And I picked up some incredibly hard areas. . . . They are conservative and Catholic, and there's nothing I can do there . . . except to keep a pretty low profile."

PARTY CONNECTIONS

The ethnic connections and the neighborhood connections of Representative Rosenthal were predicated, of course, on his *partisan* connections. He was, of course, a Democrat. During my time in the district, *any* representative would have had to be a Democrat. It was a third requirement of his constituency.

On the evening of my first day in the district, I was introduced to his party connections when we attended a dinner dance—sponsored by his own Democratic "club."

Every New York assembly district has its own Democratic club, whose members endorse candidates in the Democratic primary—the effective election in Rosenthal's strongly Democratic district. There were ten assembly districts within his congressional district, but he estimated the number of relevant clubs to be twice that number. Club members do the organizational work of the party: securing signatures, manning the polls on election day, distributing literature. Because they make endorsements of candidates, the clubs control the Democratic primary. So attention must be paid.

Some clubs were now in the hands of liberal activists. But others, including the congressman's district club, had remained in the hands of party regulars. When we arrived at the dinner dance, the clubby conviviality which had prevailed at "the Flushing Y" turned palpably cool. To my question beforehand, "Where are we going?" Rosenthal answered, "We're going to a shitty restaurant, to have a shitty meal, and have a shitty time with a shitty club." Over dinner, the wife of the club's leader praised Ben as "intense," "honest," and "a father figure," to whom one could go for help.

"Ethnically," he said, "most members of this Club are with me," he said. "But I supported [Republican] John Lindsay [for Mayor of New York City], and they can't stand that. [For them] party loyalty is everything." He was dutifully massaging them as "the foot soldiers of the party." The extent to which support patterns for the party "ticket"—for mayor and for governor—occupied local political opinion and conversation was a striking characteristic of Queens politics. And the congressman inevitably became embroiled in it.

"Did it live up to advance billing?" he asked after dinner. "I always overreact." "What you saw tonight reflects the state of the Democratic Party. It depresses me so that I want to hide in Washington, tend to my legislative duties, and forget it. It's a political science problem—to know what to do. Sometimes I think I should try to reinvigorate the party—but it would take so much time and effort that I'd have to neglect all my congressional duties. So I do what Jack and Bobby Kennedy did. I leave it alone."

"At the last election," he continued, this particular club had "delayed their endorsements—asking me if I was still a Democrat, because I supported Lindsay. So I went to their meeting and just looked 'em in the eye. They collapsed and endorsed me. They know they can't beat me. . . . I'd say about half the clubs in the district are against me. But they don't want to be against me too strongly, for fear I might go into the primary against them, beat them, and take away their jobs. So self-preservation wins out." And he added, "Even though I have a safe district and never have any trouble in the general election, I always have to keep my eye out for a primary contest. I've only had one, and we beat him eight to one." Both his safety and his vigilance remained common threads throughout my visits.

During my second visit, Rosenthal spent a campaign evening dropping in and out of four Democratic clubs—"a tip of the hat," he called it, to the party faithful. His brief talk called on them to work for "the whole Democratic ticket." Then, "Incidentally, I'm running, too. I hope you'll vote for me. I need the job." ("Big laugh," I noted, "but it wouldn't go over everywhere.")

"This is pro forma campaigning," he explained.

I'm not breaking any new ground. I'm making routine stops and massaging the club members. . . . These people are . . . party automatons. They aren't the thinking man's filter, let's put it that way, not the League of Women Voters. They vote for me because I come and say hello or do them a service or just smile. . . . I show them I'm alive and breathing. Some of these old women have been doing this for 20 years. You don't need them in the general election. But they are the foot soldiers of the organization, circulating the petitions to get you on the ballot.

"What would it take to defeat you?" I asked. "It would take an outstanding, energetic man—a young Jewish lawyer—with $100,000 to run an even heat with me in a primary, and it would take that man, plus $200,000, to beat me. It's important to show strength to keep the young assemblymen and city council members away. If they have the feeling I'm invincible, they won't try. That reputation is intangible. Your vote margin is part of it, but only part of it."

Of his Republican opponent—whose name he could not recall, "they're all the same to me"—he added, "In order to get attention, he would have to attack me; but there's really nothing he could attack me for. If this were a different district, he could call me a radical or he could call me a spender, fiscally irresponsible—the Republican line. But barring some great emotional issue which comes up, there's no way he can attack me or get much attention."

Ben commented that he had no organization. But "I could mobilize 500 people in six days from the Queens community—some inside, some from outside the district. I hate to call on them if they aren't needed. But will they atrophy if you don't use them? I don't know." He understood the power of a "primary constituency." "You can win a primary with 25,000 zealots," he said. "What I'm building up to," he said, "is the thesis that you can't beat an incumbent, barring a catastrophic event."

In career terms, Ben Rosenthal was a product of the Democratic club system. "I got into politics in a prosaic way," he told a reporter. "I joined my local Democratic club in 1949 to help my career as a lawyer. I didn't consider myself anything politically, liberal or conservative in those days."[6] It was the only route for an ambitious young Queens lawyer to make it in politics. When the longtime incumbent congressman resigned midterm to take a judgeship, several prominent officeholders jumped into the special election. So did Rosenthal.

"I tried to get the nomination for kicks," he told the reporter. "I wasn't driven or anything."[7] To me, he said,

> Burt Kohler was president of my club, and he was also the county leader, so he could put the squeeze on some of the other club leaders. I was an unknown. I came from nowhere to get the nomination. It took 13 ballots. . . . I was the lowest on the first ballot. A lot of men stronger than I were candidates. . . . I won because I was the least hated man in the race. The hate of the others for each other cancelled out, and since no one disliked me, I was the winner. Burt Kohler was a gentleman, and he believed the organization should put up good candidates. I was not as provocative a person as I am now, and so I got organization backing.

He was elected to Congress by 264 votes over his Republican opponent. Once in, he was never again seriously threatened.

He always spoke appreciatively of Kohler. "My old district leader— the man through whose beneficence I am here—was an enlightened old-time leader. He had a touch of German socialism in him. For example, his was the first old-time club to solicit blacks for membership. He was a different kind of cat. He said, 'good government is good politics.' And he wanted to produce good candidates."

POLICY CONNECTIONS

It did not take the congressman very long, however, to become "provocative." When he began casting votes in the House, he defined himself, surprisingly, as a very liberal Democrat. Indeed, he soon needed his club's leader to shore up his political support at home. He took a strong pro–civil liberties stand against the congressional investigation of people with unpopular opinions.

> One of the very first votes I cast was against the House Un-American Activities Committee. That was considered heresy. My predecessor had never done it. They even convened a special meeting so that I could explain my vote. Burt Kohler and his support saved me. He took the attitude that if Ben says his vote was right, it must be right. And he had the political wherewithal to make it stick. What really saved me was that Burt himself had been under attack by some group at the time, and I said, "If they can do this to Burt, they can do this to others and we've got to stop it." I even talked to my predecessor about it. He said he wished he had done it—that it was right, but he didn't have the political freedom to do it or the political muscle to survive.

His predecessor had been a faithful, clubhouse-oriented, big-government, big-city Democrat.

Representative Rosenthal's strong defense of civil liberties brought a new orientation to the district. It won him support among groups who had known persecution and/or who worried about the effects of enforced conformity, that is, liberal groups with special strength within the Jewish community. He was charting a new policy course, putting a new stamp on the district, and writing a new personal signature.

In the same vein, he cast another controversial, pro–civil liberties vote against legislation punishing the burning of the American flag. "The flag vote was my toughest vote," he said.

> I got the hell kicked out of me by the American Legion and the Veterans of Foreign Wars. It was a painful vote for me—probably too painful for all the good it did. It was a symbolic vote. There was a law in each of the 50 states against desecrating the flag, so you didn't need it. It was passed in one of those emotional binges, and I didn't want to add to it. But Don Edwards and I practically said afterwards we wouldn't do it again if we could do it over. And if I had a tough district, I probably wouldn't have done it. I'm not captain courageous! John Dow voted against the flag bill, and I think it helped kill him. The difference is that I have 20 points to play with and he was 50-50—he had no points to play with.

Characteristically, he was willing to put his political support to the test—but not recklessly. He stretched the liberal boundaries of his support.

But he did not break them. He often expressed his line-drawing calculation in terms of "points to play with" or having "points to spare" in his election margin. He calculated the degree of leeway available to him, and he used it. Twenty-five years later, when I returned to Queens with his successor, the memories of Rosenthal's HUAC vote and his flag-burning vote remained as prime ideological markers. And they still warmed the hearts of the liberal Democrats I met then.

Superficially, much that I have emphasized about this representative could lead us to expect a Joe Moakley type of representational pattern. The lifelong residency "where he came from," the urban character of the district, the ethnic bonding, the neighborhood-level perspective, the one-party territory—all of them might forecast a dominantly local perspective and a dominantly personal set of connections. To the question "what is Ben Rosenthal really like?" a plausible conjecture might very well be "a lot like Joe Moakley." From a close-up, firsthand look at what Ben Rosenthal "was really like," we can see why, despite their several commonalities, the authentic Ben Rosenthal behaved very differently as a representative than the authentic (as portrayed earlier) Joe Moakley. Ben Rosenthal became best known for the controversial policy positions he took. And they were strongly held. That connection was a large part of "what he was really like." "I never ducked controversy," he said. "I turned controversy into a political plus."

CONSTITUENCY CONNECTIONS

If, as noted earlier, neighborhoods can be described by their housing patterns, it is not surprising that the congressman's most vexing and most publicized connection problems should have centered on perceived threats to established neighborhood housing patterns. And that is what happened—first in "lower middle" Corona, then in "upper middle" Forest Hills. Public housing for needy, low-income citizens was exactly what the congressman's strongly antidiscrimination liberalism prescribed. But as a down-to-earth problem in his constituency, it posed a challenging test.

In Corona, New York City planned to build a new school plus a large adjacent playground—resulting in the condemnation of 69 homes in an established Italian, home-owning neighborhood.[8] Corona citizens erupted in angry protest. "They were hysterical about it [and] used every kind of public pressure there is." They held a candlelight march in front of Mayor John Lindsay's residence. And they held a sizable protest meeting in the neighborhood. As we campaigned up and down Corona's main street, with its small, busy stores and with the subway rattling overhead, Representative Rosenthal was reminded by his constituents that he had not attended their protest meeting. It was a major connection failure, and it triggered a lot of soul searching about the nature of his job and the nature of his constituency connections.

"People are mad at me for two reasons," he explained.

> For one thing, I supported Lindsay [a Republican for mayor], which meant I deserted the Democratic Party and its candidate, Mario Procaccino. They take their party loyalty seriously here—and on top of that, my position was interpreted as anti-Italian. They are mad at me because the 69 homeowners are losing their homes. I worked harder on that than almost anyone, and nearly had a compromise. I could have demagogued those people, but I couldn't bring myself to do it. I should have gone to their meeting and been more visible. These people are mad! They've lost their homes. I don't blame them. But Lindsay got his back up . . . and there was nothing I could do. I wouldn't demagogue. And when [the local assemblyman] got in, I got out. Now I'll just have to suffer. . . . This local thing will cost me 500 to 1000 votes, maybe more. It will cost me more than any vote I could ever cast in Congress.

After the election, he estimated that "the whole thing cost me from 500 to 800 votes."

More interesting to me, however, was the representative's increased interest in the larger representational dilemma. Before the election, he had satisfied himself that "I couldn't have helped them, but I should have been more visible." But when we met afterward, he was worrying the larger question: "How involved should the congressman get in community relations?"

> I'm tending toward the view that whenever anyone is being screwed by the system, the congressman should use the prestige of his office to interpose himself between the people being screwed and the system. Others say that once you get involved in local controversies, you get quagmired in the city councilman role and neglect the congressman role. . . . Of course, I did work privately. I used all my chips to get them to rescind the original order. I know one thing. Private diplomacy is absolutely useless politically. What I think I should have

done . . . was to write a long letter and make it public. But that wouldn't have satisfied the homeowners. Once you're with them, they want you there for every meeting. . . . They want to know, not "where you were last week or last month," but "where were you when we needed you last night." [Their assemblyman-leader] denounced me at one of their meetings. He said, "Where is Rosenthal?" Well, I could tell him that I was back in Washington fighting for aid for Cambodia, working on Vietnam, and the SALT [disarmament] talks. But the little old Italian lady who is being thrown out of the house she built and has lived in, does she give a shit about the SALT talks? These people were being screwed. . . . They knew I was working privately, but the job of the congressman is a political job. You're not just an administrative bureaucrat. Everything you do is political and has political consequences. And I did not do enough.

The details of the Corona case are complex. But in the end, all but 4 of the 69 homes were saved.

No sooner had the housing dispute in Corona been settled than attention turned to a "twin convulsion." The city announced a plan to build a much larger, scatter-site housing project—"three, twenty-four story, low-income, high-rise buildings, housing 842 tenants"—in nearby Forest Hills.[9] The proposal aroused the angry, racially tinted opposition of Forest Hills' upper-middle-class Jewish residents. They flooded Rosenthal's office with 2000 protest letters asking him to do something about it. Even though he no longer represented most of them, he had strong ties. And he became "much more involved," he said, than in the Corona problem. "I was politically, emotionally, psychologically, and spiritually involved." He was a supporter of low-income, scatter-site housing, he said, but not of "warehousing poverty" in "the projects."

This time, he involved himself by opposing the extent of the proposed housing project, and by attacking the "arrogant bureaucracy" of New York City. He advocated a middle ground—cutting the size of the project in half. He praised the people of Forest Hills. "They are willing to pay their dues, more than most people in America. But they aren't willing to pay the dues of the liberals in Manhattan." He blamed Manhattan-oriented Mayor Lindsay for opposing any compromise.

His problem is that he never played stickball in the streets. . . . You can't go to St. Paul's and Yale and live in Georgetown and Gracie Mansion and know anything about the average citizen. Sixty-five to

75 percent of the people in my district will support some low-income housing. They have a conscience, but they have a threshold. Lindsay doesn't understand the people of Queens. He wouldn't have carried Queens without my help. I gave him credibility. And it cost me party support. On every community issue, he was against me: Corona, Forest Hills, and [shutting down] the Flushing airport.

Afterward, the mayor's chief negotiator praised Rosenthal as "the voice of the middle ground."[10] He is "nothing but upright and honest in his work. He's one of the exceptional politicians who have not lost their integrity."[11] Eventually, a project close to the kind the representative had proposed was adopted.

The upshot of the Forest Hills debate, as Rosenthal saw it, was that "both sides want me on the barricades and both extremes are mad at me. I've straddled the issue really—a little this way or a little that way. . . . I support low-income housing, but not that kind of project. I think I've come out all right politically." He was comforted that "The *New York Times* adopted my position." Interestingly, in both Forest Hills and Corona, he had chosen to make his impact by criticizing—and yet negotiating with—the powers that be, the formal citywide decision makers. He had chosen not to get directly involved with the local citizen activists.

But the conflict took a toll. "The strongest opponents have become a political force, and they are talking of running a primary against me." "The Orthodox Jews are on the right side of the ledger. They have become more active against busing, scatter-site housing, and affirmative action problems. I'm not one of their most popular people right now."

People think I'm a pretty decent guy who generally represents their interests. You can find elements who think I'm an SOB. The opposition group is getting larger in numbers. It is not threatening, but it is larger. . . . The Jews are more threatened and have gotten uptight, trying to preserve their last neighborhood. Guys like me who want to keep open conduits to other communities are regarded as only 90 percent loyal, not 100 percent loyal. . . . They regard me as not standing tight enough on the barricades. . . . My 99.9 percent support from the Jewish community has dropped to maybe 80 percent or 75 percent of the Jewish community. Some of them would welcome a viable alternative. It is a very distressing and painful experience for me because I understand exactly how they feel. Forest Hills has crystallized the dilemma.

While he was saddened, he did not feel threatened politically. "I think I'm in good shape," he said.

CAMPAIGN CONTACTS

During both of my visits, I was introduced to urban street campaigning—in heavily trafficked places like shopping clusters and subway stops. He would shake hands while handing out large paper shopping bags to people passing by. The bags carried his name, some his picture. Sometimes he would help people consolidate their bundles into the one bag. And soon the bags could be seen bobbing in all directions as far as the eye could see. At one stop, we handed out 2000 in about 30 minutes. Another day we used 20,000. They were his trademark, and he calculated the benefit to be well worth the cost of supplying them to nonconstituents. "If I were in a really tight race, I think I'd go all the way with shopping bags. They are perfect for a district like this where people walk from their homes to shop. They wouldn't work in Bethesda—everybody has a car. For this district, they are the best thing there is."

They lubricated communication. "Shaking hands this afternoon," he said, "there were three people for whom I had done major favors. Within certain limits, set by efficiency or neglect, the incumbent can stay in office as long as he gives people service." That kind of campaigning, he added, makes him visible to ambitious local politicians, creating the discouraging impression that "I'm all over the place."

By choice and by temperament, he did not relish this kind of nonissue, person-to-person campaigning. In one sense, he was too shy. He couldn't even pretend to be a glad-handing, extroverted campaigner. He was not "smooth." His staff would poke friendly fun at his reluctance to push person-to-person contact. "Look at him, he's standing over there all by himself." "I don't really like it all that much, and I'm glad I don't have to be a congressman in the streets." He would quietly protest. "When my staff wants me to hand out shopping bags on every f—ing street corner in Queens . . . I resist. I have to calculate the benefits of everything I do against the danger to my sanity and my personal lifestyle." But for a couple of weeks every two years, he did it. And the shopping bags provided a facilitating crutch.

My picture of his shopping bags loaded into the car presented a classic juxtaposition to his policy-centered activities in Washington. And I used that contrast to introduce my first book-length study of representation: *Home Style: House Members in Their Districts.*[12]

Along the campaign trail, the congressman's lighter side might emerge—sometimes wistful, sometimes playful—which rounded out his persona. The sight of some kids playing baseball triggered wistfulness. "Bobby Kennedy would stop the car when he was campaigning, jump out, and join kids playing baseball. . . . I used to be on a ball team, too. Only I didn't get to play much." In a similar vein, there was this very unathletic person's attachment to the House gym. "I dreamt last night that I was defeated. . . . And do you know what bothered me the most? The gym! My wife said to me, 'You're a distinguished person. You'll get a job. Don't worry.' I said, 'Yes, I know, but where will I find a gym like that?' I don't know what I'd do without the gym." And later, "The gym is the only place in the House where seniority doesn't count. It's first come, first serve." "The other day, I played paddleball with [Rep. Bert] Podell, and he won 21–20. Did he play hard! Just like a boy from Brooklyn! I don't play that hard. I wish he wouldn't play that hard."

On the playful side, one day he took a bullhorn used for street corner campaigning and walked up the street delivering a series of very loud, piercing squawks. "There's so and so over there, let's give him a shot!" Squawk! And at lunch in the Deli. Squawk! Afterwards, he directed a staffer to drive to us the auto repair shop owned by the local VFW chairman: "He was my strongest opponent on the flag controversy." Once there, he gave the new owner a couple of bullhorn blasts—amid a mixture of staff concern and mirth. Squawk! Squawk! Afterward, he wrote to me—as his accomplice in mischief—"The bullhorn is safe and *sound.*" These moments of "little boy lost" and "little boy misbehaving" kept him down-to-earth amid his serious politicking.

Ben Rosenthal was an effective politician because he could adapt his connection choices to changing constituency circumstances. He was an effective teacher because he could, and he would, explain his adaptations. Years later, I came to think of "experiential learning" as a cornerstone idea.[13] In the 1970s, I had not begun to recognize its importance.

MEDIA CONNECTIONS

When he first got to Congress, Representative Rosenthal had kept his law practice in Queens, and he had kept his family in the district. But as the congressional business year lengthened to "11 months a year," and as family separations lengthened, he adapted by moving his family to Washington. "I was enormously frightened of the political effect of that move. The *New York Times* supported it, however, and took a lot of the heat off. But many people in Queens were upset."

"I can relax and have a more normal family life and tend to legislation in Washington," he reflected in 1970. "But it also removes me from the district. It increases the distance between me and my constituents. I feel all the more strongly that I have to come back and be seen. I come back at least once a week. I'd do more of it, if I had a tight district." And he concluded, "I really don't like it that much, and I'm glad I don't have to be a congressman in the streets."

Throughout the period I traveled with him, he was facing another large adaptation problem: the fading of the Vietnam War issue and the consequent weakening of that strong emotional bond with his strongest supporters. "In the anti-war period, I had a 5000 to a 25,000 floating constituency. I was a hero. That has cooled. They want more but there is no more." "I was way out front on that issue. I organized and I spoke at rallies of 2000 or 3000 people. I had large forums. . . . This year, I decided to forgo large meetings and go back to the neighborhood. . . . I don't see any clearly coalesced large constituency that needed massaging or any large issue I wanted to push." While he puzzled over that replacement problem, he was also absorbing the similar impact of Corona and Forest Hills. "I've changed my thinking about the congressman's involvement in constituency projects," he said. "The public wants us to be involved in their affairs—the problem of alienation, no one cares." And he adapted to the two problems together. "Partly because I think the problem is a legitimate one and partly to make up for the policy change, I've begun to emphasize my interest in constituency projects."

"I am holding town meetings throughout the district," he said in 1974. "They are the most successful things we do. We send out 15,000 invitations. Only 150 come. But the others know I am there. . . . I try to identify each community [so] each meeting has a different flavor." But he held only 13 in 1974. And examining his 1973 appointment schedules, I found only 25 home visits that year, compared to "once a week" in 1970. His district visits had been cut in half.

His major adaptation to change had *not* been to increase his own home visits but to hire two new staff assistants—one full-time and one part-time in the district. Now, during my second visit, he talked a lot about them and what they could do to carry the home load. He called his new group "the best constituency service operation in Queens." He was particularly pleased about the rookie staffer who "goes to every little two-bit community meeting" as an excellent way of cultivating new or undecided groups while presenting a positive face to unfavorable ones. "The staff is so good, it will run without me." And he wanted staff to do all it could. "I may have to get involved in a project, but I can pick and choose."

The improved staff operation also freed him to do what he thought he did best—and what he most wanted to do. "I want to save myself for meetings where I can make a speech on an issue. If there are 20 people meeting in a morning and I have a chance to play tennis, I'll play tennis. . . . But if 400 people ask me to come home—or 150 people—I'll come. I want to engage in substantive public relations, not horseshit public relations."

More even than these adaptations to his Washington-centered life, the change in connections that dominated my 1974 visit was the representative's interest in, knowledge of, and concern for the local media and the work it did to publicize all his activities. In my 1970 visit, he had touched on the media only to make clear his heavy reliance on the validating protection of the *New York Times* editorial page. For example, on his "hard decision" to vote against a crime bill: "Even though I have a sophisticated liberal majority of sorts . . . people are very concerned about law and order. But the *Times* wrote an editorial saying that the 26 who voted against it showed a great deal of courage. I took some comfort in that." So heavily did he weight the *Times'* imprimatur that he went out of his way to explain to me why a vote of his "was not a *Times* vote." He also valued the coverage of the *Long Island Press*. "I have it all to myself," he said. My New York City colleagues "drool when I tell them about the *Press*." He did not, however, test his votes against their editorial page—as he did with the *Times*.

During my initial 1970 visit, the media rated, at most, a dozen lines in my 24 pages of notes. But in 1974, our media-related conversations filled a half-dozen pages. Possibly, the difference was random. But I took it to be reflective of a major adaptation to the loss of his anti-Vietnam issue and to the unlikely prospect that any "constituency project" would, or could, take its place. He had made a self-conscious decision to nurture his publicity-centered connections.

About my second 1974 visit as a whole, I noted:

A thread that runs through the entire trip, and is of special importance to understanding Ben, is his relationship with the press. Half the things he does are measured by their potential for press or TV coverage, especially by the *New York Times,* the *New York Daily News,* the *New York Post,* and the *Long Island Press.* When we first got into the car—Ben, two staffers, and me—one staffer showed him a *Daily News* story with his picture and the other told him, "You've been in the *New York Times* for five days in a row—a new record."[14]

Once in the car, the three of them "talked about press relations, press releases, the cultivation of newspeople, how more press work was now being done in the district, and the need, therefore, for a new office machine to do the job better."

"There was a preoccupation with the papers," I noted. "And I think the papers are a substitute for coming home." From a year's worth of his schedules, I had calculated a drop in home visits from "once a week" in 1970, to a total of 25 trips in 1973. So I asked him point-blank if he had traded home visits for press activity. "Yes, I have willfully and consciously done that," he said.

Some [Democratic] colleagues tell me their papers are Republican, that they can't get their names in the paper, and they have to compensate in other ways. I don't have that trouble. The *Long Island Press,* the *New York Times*—I'm in the paper all the time. . . . I like to do the things that produce news. I like to deal with the issues. My practice does not go against my instincts. It follows my instincts.

And he added, "The press emphasis also suits my personality because I'm lazy."

On the way home that first evening, we stopped off to buy the *Times* and the *News* to see whether they had mentioned his role in overriding a presidential veto that day. They hadn't. "The *Times* didn't play it up, but my colleagues know it was a great victory," he said. The next morning, he asked a staffer to find out whether the *Washington Post* had done so. They hadn't either.

The next day's first event was a hearing on drug abuse and methadone at the federal building. On the way over, he asked me, "Are you going to classify this as congressional performance or as politics? . . . I'd classify it as a waste of time. File it under 'W.'" But when he looked over the audience, he perked up. "The *Times* and the [New York] *Post* are here," he exulted. And afterward, he talked for a while to "The Times" and gave a quick interview to "The Post." He thought it significant that "The *Times* guy sat through the whole thing. . . . If we get a story in the *Times* on the methadone hearing, that will have been the most profitable thing today politically." He got a brief mention in the early *Times* edition, but not in the regular one.

At his second federal building hearing on Social Security, we arrived late, and we met an ABC cameraman who was leaving. "Ben stepped right in and started shaking hands, and his staffer asked the guy if he'd take a picture of Ben. He did and shot quite a bit of footage. They told me he was a friend of theirs." It was the last I heard of it.

That afternoon, there was a discussion of an invitation to visit a high school social studies class. Said Rosenthal, "It is of absolutely no benefit to me in any way, [and my staffer] is not looking out for my interest in pushing me to do it." But to help him make the decision, he searched for a publicity benefit. "Call and see if the [Long Island] *Press* can use the story," he asked. They couldn't.

That same evening, at dinner with two aides, he talked expansively about the media. "I'm a student of the press—of the mechanics of the press. One half of the stories I get happen because we make them happen. If you take a press release to the [House press] gallery after 3:30 in the afternoon, forget it. The *Times* sets up a preliminary front page in the early afternoon and a final page at 5:30; unless the president shoots the president's wife, you can't get a story in after 3:30."

"I'll give you another example. A few days ago, the Walter Cronkite show called and wanted to do an interview on reaction to the president's veto [of a foreign aid bill]. They said they would come [to the office]. I knew if they came out here, the crew might not get back in time to make the program. So I said, 'We'll come right in.' We hopped in the car and went to the studio. At the same time they interviewed us, they interviewed [a colleague] in a downtown restaurant on the same thing. He's more articulate than I. But I told my staff, 'They won't use his interview; they'll use mine!' I knew the technical quality of my interview—the lighting, the sound—would be better than his. They used mine. And I was on the Walter Cronkite show. If I hadn't understood the mechanics of TV newscasting, that would never have happened." He later noted that "There's too much competition among all the New York City congressmen, so we don't do as much with TV or radio as some of them do."

The next day, he sat in his office and talked at length about two *Times* reporters. The details of his analysis were not as interesting as the fact that he did it. "X reports what happens," he said, "very straight and without much color. Y creates news by digging. He thinks of his role as a journalist is to write exposés. Sometimes he doesn't write articles for days . . . you have to play by very special rules when you talk to him. Don't say anything you don't want to see in print. . . . Both X and Y are highly regarded by their superiors, and both are very bright." It was, I noted, "a more sophisticated picture of newsmen than most anyone I've heard." In sum, my 1974 district visit seemed to be "all media, all the time."

His aggressiveness in media relations, I conjectured, was linked to his strong issue orientation, to the heavy competition for publicity among layers of local politicians, his decline in home visits, and his reluctance either to "play the groups" or to handshake his way to "every last vote."

Hand-in-hand with concern for media-oriented connections, I noted a new preoccupation with his personal prominence at public events. He was irate at the seating plan at the Social Security hearing. "Some fool set that meeting up. They put the congressman way down at the end of the table. That pissed me off. I stayed too long—15 minutes, when I should have stayed two." Thinking about an anniversary celebration for its rabbi at "the most important synagogue in my district," he questioned his staff about his prominence there. "Will I be on the receiving line? Am I going to be introduced? Do you suppose they will ask me to say something? How will I meet 800 people—at the cocktail hour? Should we go early?" In matters of scheduling, he was a careful time-and-motion, cost-and-benefit analyst.

Later, during staff discussions, he exclaimed, "Who was that kid who arranged the thing last weekend? I never want to see him again. He said there would be a thousand people there. One hundred showed up and only 20 people spoke English. How come we make such mistakes as that?" Still later: *Rosenthal:* "Why did I ever agree to that Bnai Brith breakfast? It's an insane thing to do." *Staff:* "It's the largest Bnai Brith in New York City. They say 300 people will be there." *Rosenthal:* "I'll tell you how many people will be there—46. I can't believe I ever agreed to do it." *Staff:* "You said 'yes' because you had refused so many other requests from them." *Rosenthal:* "Oh well, I shouldn't have." That same dialogue was replayed the next day, too. In later contexts, I would find such concerns echoed by other House members. But in Rosenthal's context, they seemed to reinforce his increased reliance on publicity-generating connections with his constituents.

THE PRIMACY OF POLICY

During the period I observed him, the Queens representative was defined at home largely by his public policy activities in Washington. For all of his interest in connection techniques at home, they were essentially defensive and protective. Personal service was, for him, essentially a default strategy. In any case, it was left primarily to staff. His positive energies were focused on policy matters and on winning the approval of outside judges—especially the *New York Times*—for his policy choices and for his policy activity. There was his active opposition to the Vietnam War; there was, relatedly, his very liberal voting record.

An unobtrusive indicator of his policy interests and preferences was his frequent mentions in his connection comments of the many House colleagues with whom he compared notes. The sheer number—18—indicated a marked degree of collegial immersion. Most of the 18 also shared his policy views. More pointedly, nine of them were linked with Rosenthal in an informal band of strong anti-war policy liberals, calling themselves "The Group." They met to discuss war-military-peace issues, promote conferences, and publish the results thereof.[15]

A smaller foreign policy issue that energized Rosenthal during this period was one that engaged his small but active Greek constituency. During my first visit, when we walked the streets of Corona and noted the sign over the "Greek-American Democrats" headquarters, he commented, "I have a small but very strong Greek community in Corona. I'm very popular here because I got them all citizenship. It was nothing to do with issues—just naturalization. I don't even talk to them about the issues." When I returned, he had become aggressively involved with their issues. From his foreign policy committee work, he had become active in opposing the harsh military "Junta" when they ruled Greece. He even courted danger by going there to meet with the "underground opposition." Now, he was actively supporting the new civilian government in its bitter disputes with Turkey over the control of Cyprus.

When I arrived, he had recently returned from a trip to Greece, where he had been treated, he said, as "a hero." The new prime minister had told him, "You need no introduction from us." His name had been in the papers, and people had recognized him in restaurants, he said. "All the people I dealt with when I opposed the Junta were now in power. Even the people who had been in prison knew me. It was a very emotional experience." He was on his way, he said, to a dinner for the Greek archbishop—where he would assume "a glory role." "They will stand up and cheer. I'm one of the main speakers and I'll sit on the dais." He had recently succeeded in attaching conditions and strings to all U.S. foreign aid to Turkey—over the opposition of President Gerald Ford. "The *New York Times* did not play it up," he said, "but my colleagues knew it was a great victory." He was in his element: serious issue, tough stand, "great victory."[16]

On the domestic policy side, there was his tenacious leadership in the legislative fight for a national Consumer Protection Agency. I did not focus on that big battle. But I did talk with him a little during a couple of brief Washington visits. His consumer-oriented activity showed me the Washington side of a tough, committed, and relentless policy advocate.

Early in his career, as a member of the Government Operations Committee, his interest in consumer protection attracted the attention of his committee chairman. And he rewarded Rosenthal—despite his low seniority—with the chairmanship of a special ad hoc subcommittee on consumer representation in the federal government. Early on, the congressman forged a working relationship with consumer advocate Ralph Nader. Based on the subcommittee's work, the full committee reported out a Consumer Protection Act in 1970.

His bill was stalled on its way to the House floor, however, by a tie vote in the Rules Committee. A liberal Rules Committee Democrat, vacationing in the Bahamas, refused to fly back to break the tie. It was not clear why.[17] It was very clear, however, that Rosenthal had won the bitter enmity of another Rules Committee member, who could have broken the tie—the very conservative fellow Democrat from "the other Queens," James Delaney.

When we talked in Washington, however, Rosenthal placed the blame elsewhere.

It's taken us years to build the coalition, and this year we finally got everybody in line. I'm afraid it will take us years to bring the coalition back together. The Senate says they won't touch it again until it passes the House. Chet Holifield (a senior Committee Democrat) was the biggest problem we had. He served on two Hoover Commissions, and it was an article of faith with them that independent agencies were bad. We couldn't get it out of subcommittee over his opposition. This year, he folded and agreed to support the bill. As soon as he did, the bill went through subcommittee and full committee. The time was ripe; but who knows about next year.

"It hasn't hurt me at home," he remarked. "I'm the good guy. All my mail—ten letters, I think—tells me that."

The following year, old nemesis Chet Holifield became chairman of the full Government Operations Committee. And he promptly abolished Rosenthal's subcommittee. Why? "For three reasons: he saw me as a potential troublemaker; he had no particular commitment to the issue; it didn't fit with his concept of how he wanted to run the committee."[18] Rosenthal, however, with Nader's backing, reintroduced his bill, whereupon the chairman intervened and directed a "weakened" bill. Rosenthal fought his chairman's version on the House floor; he lost the fight, whereupon he voted against the weakened bill.

After the next election, when Democrats voted to elect all their committee chairmen, Rosenthal escalated his intracommittee conflict by campaigning to deny Holifield his chairmanship. Rosenthal's motion lost decisively, garnering less than a third of the caucus votes. He explained,

> I did it half on the merits and half on emotion. The chairman had screwed me twice and I was mad as hell. I had been wronged. But since the merits were right, I decided to go ahead. I didn't think of the effect it would have on me politically. Outside the House, it has helped me. Inside, I don't know. Around the lunch table, it will hurt some. People will take a few shots at me. . . . But I wanted to put the pressure [on the chairman]. That's the way to put it. I'm going to keep at it inside the committee. . . . The [seniority] system is much more embedded than I thought it was.

For me, the story emphasizes, again, his strong liberal commitments in policy matters—and also, perhaps, his lesser concern for institutional accommodations. In the end, no bill ever passed. No consumer agency was ever created. But Representative Rosenthal received "Consumer of the Year" awards at home. He was a policy hero to his liberal constituency as a consumer protection advocate. Just as he had been a policy hero as an anti-Vietnam protestor.

The authentic Ben Rosenthal was a fighter for his liberal causes, and that was the way he presented himself to his constituents. Consider the relentless, action-oriented presentation of self in his 1974 campaign brochure: "Ben Rosenthal . . . prods, questions, annoys, deflates, doubts, nudges, listens, plots, argues, shoves, performs, worries . . . all for you." Printed nearby were the 100 percent favorable scores given to him by Ralph Nader and by several other liberal public interest groups. "People think," he said,

"I'm a fighting congressman; and that helps." He picked his spots. When he did, his relentless, needling style was honest to his convictions. And his overall performance resonated positively with a constituent majority.

After he lost his final consumer battle, he was forced, by seniority rules, to choose between two subcommittee chairmanships—one with jurisdiction over consumer protection, the other one with jurisdiction over foreign policy toward the Middle East. He chose the latter. And he promptly announced hearings on Soviet Jewry. To the end of my visits, he defined himself to his more supportive constituents by his policy choices. To the others, he did his duty—by maintaining personal service and partisan campaign connections.

TRANSITION

On the last afternoon of my last visit, October 19, 1974, we enjoyed a good-bye malted at "John's." And we chatted broadly about connections and careers. "What worries me," he said,

> is not that I will neglect my district and lose it. That's just not on my schedule. What worries me is that the district will change. How long will that take? I don't know—maybe 10, maybe not for 20 years. Maybe by then I'll be ready to leave, and I should. I hope I'll know when to quit. No one should stay in this job for very long. But the system keeps you in. You lose your law practice and you gain in seniority and you don't want to leave. I'm one of them, I know.

Benjamin Rosenthal succumbed to cancer, at age 60, in January 1983. It was shortly after his constituents had given him an eleventh consecutive election victory.

Twenty-two years later, I returned to Queens to meet and travel with his successor.

Notes

1. Keith Poole and Howard Rosenthal, *Congress: A Political-Economic History of Roll Call Voting*, Oxford University Press (New York, 1997).
2. Jimmy Breslin on Mario Cuomo, *Forest Hills Diary: The Crisis of Low Income Housing*, Random House (New York, 1975), preface, p. v1.
3. A helpful portrait of Queens, with a Rosenthal introduction is: Andrew Hacker, "Does Anybody Really Live in Queens?" *Newsday*, January 9, 1977. It is printed in *Congressional Record*, January 25, 1977, Extension of Remarks, p. E311.

4. See http://www.Queenslibrary.org/gallery/past_exhibits/burgh/map.htm.
5. *Almanac of American Politics,* 1980, p. 590.
6. Jack Newfield, "Courage in Congress: Case of a Quiet Man," *Village Voice,* August 3, 1967.
7. Ibid.
8. Cuomo, *Forest Hills Diary,* pp. 3–23.
9. Ibid., p. 24.
10. Ibid., p. 141.
11. Ibid., p. 106.
12. Richard Fenno, *Home Style,* Little Brown (Boston, 1978), pp. xi–xii.
13. See Chapter 5.
14. According to one compilation, he was mentioned in the *New York Times* 21 times in 1967 and 63 times in 1969. Eileen O. Franch, "Benjamin S. Rosenthal," *Ralph Nader Project,* Grossman (New York, 1972), p. 7.
15. Its members were Abner Mikva (IL), George Brown (CA), Philip Burton (CA), John Conyers (MI), Bob Eckhardt (TX), Don Edwards (CA), Donald Fraser (MN), Robert Kastenmeier (WI), William Ryan (NY), and Rosenthal. Letter from Rep. Mikva staff member Joel Bonder. October 9, 1970.
16. See Andy Logan, "Around City Hall," *New Yorker,* March 27, 1978.
17. Andrea Schoenfield, "Consumer Report," *National Journal,* December 19, 1970, pp. 2771–2779.
18. Franch, "Benjamin S. Rosenthal," p. 12.

CHAPTER 8

Gary Ackerman 1996–1998: Gregarious Local Boy

QUEENS REVISITED: EARLY LEARNING AND EARLY ACCESS

Twenty-two years after I left Ben Rosenthal, I returned to Queens to "soak and poke" with his successor, Representative Gary Ackerman. I went out of curiosity. What, how, and how much, I wondered, might have changed in nearly a quarter of a century? The inevitability of change had, after all, been the one certainty of all my visits in the 1970s. And what, I wondered, was the new guy like—or, really like? Representative Ackerman was then in his seventh term. I knew that in the most recent redistricting, his district—his place—had been radically reconstructed. He had been given large pieces of two new Long Island counties—Nassau and Suffolk—and a much reduced portion of his home base in Queens. His readjustment, I thought, might be a doubly interesting story—about representation in, and representation of, "Queens Plus."

I knew that comparisons would be risky. Between my two sets of observations, I would have spent 20 years learning about a variety of politicians. When I had met Ben Rosenthal, I hardly knew what I wanted to know. And I was six years away from a book. Surely my focus, my ideas, and my interests had changed. The political baseline in America had changed, too. Still, the desire to compare across time was strong. And so, mindful of the need for caution, I decided to go have a look.

> Comparison across time

157

Once again, I encountered the place before I met the person, and the ambiance of Queens, as I had first experienced it in the 1970s, had not changed. In the fall of 1997, I flew in on a Friday morning, checked into the Ramada Inn, and crossed the street to the congressman's district office. My notes record "a cool reception." "The Chief of Staff gave me a desk, but otherwise was totally non-communicative." I started going through the office's file of news clips. "It's a hard talking, busy office," I noted. "Its atmosphere reminded me of Ben Rosenthal's surface brusqueness, hard shell and lack of instant warmth. . . . No one asked me about lunch; no one asked what I was doing." When one staffer "offered me a yellow pad," I noted, "it was a gesture of warmth beyond all measure! [People here] are kind and warm when they get to know you. But they extend themselves to the barest minimum on first acquaintance. It's just New York!" It was a familiar cultural adjustment.

Gary Ackerman's Jewish background and his lifetime residence in Queens were—as with Ben Rosenthal—necessary underpinnings of his authenticity in that place. From reading his news clippings, I soon learned that Ackerman's local sensitivities and local involvements were wider, deeper, and more important to him than those of his predecessor.

Before politics, Gary Ackerman had been thoroughly immersed in local community life. He had been a junior high school social studies teacher in Queens. And soon I would learn that nearly all his staff—at home and in Washington—had been either teachers or principals. Remarkably, there was not a practicing lawyer in either his New York or his Washington office. As a teacher, he had begun a notable crusade to win maternity and childcare leave for fathers. And he had won his case in court. He had then resigned to become the editor and publisher of *The Flushing Tribune,* a community newspaper, which later became *The Queens Tribune.* In that job, he was steeped in community activity. "The philosophy behind 'The Trib' was that neighborhoods count," he said. "A newspaper is a local thing. I told my reporters that all their stories should be about Queens. I used to tell them that if an atom bomb fell on Manhattan, the lead story should be that there was a backup on the Long Island Expressway." Like his predecessor, he thought in terms of neighborhoods. But compared with Ben Rosenthal, Gary Ackerman had been more personally attached to, and affected by, workaday neighborhood life.

Representative Ackerman grew up in public housing, and he melded the sociable side of that place into political activity. "I've always felt I was lucky to have grown up in the projects," he recalled.

I had friends to play with on every floor. My kids never had that. They had a nice house, on a nice street, but not with the numbers of families and friends I had. There were 25 families in our building. My mother was the kind who kept the door open, and, as kids, we congregated in our apartment. We went to school with each other and we stayed in touch with each other, as people moved out of the projects into other parts of Queens. There were 2000 people in these projects. And I had an index card file of 500 of their names when I ran my first race. That's how I started.

It was not surprising that I would find him to be altogether a more gregarious and approachable representative than his predecessor. He did not have to compare matters of technique with his colleagues as Ben Rosenthal did. In connecting with others at home, Gary Ackerman was a natural. *Ackerman's strength, connecting w/ constituents*

His liberalism grew out of his early environment. "I grew up in city housing projects in Flushing. If it wasn't for the social programs helping families that needed a little help, I wouldn't have been able to live in a decent place and get a college education."[1] Politically, he began as a self-starting, independent-minded Democrat. He first ran for city council against the incumbent party regular. And he lost. But the loss proved providential. When the incumbent state senator suddenly decided to retire, Ackerman was geared up to jump into the succession race.[2] He won the primary handily, and he served two terms in the New York State Senate. In that job, he drew notoriety by spending a night, incognito, in a homeless shelter—to publicize the plight of the poor.[3] That early escapade exhibited an outgoing flamboyance that would become familiar—and that was utterly foreign to his predecessor.

Gary Ackerman's political ascent took a radically different path from that of Ben Rosenthal. He was not the candidate from nowhere. And his political path was not smoothed for him by a beneficent party leader— quite the contrary. Ackerman opposed the Queens County leader in two insurgent campaigns—first for the City Council (a defeat) and then for the State Senate (a primary victory). He also worked in "a brutal campaign" to elect a state assemblywoman over the opposition of the county leader. "He sees me as a basic threat to his rule."[4] But Ackerman had also joined with the same leader to help organize the Stevenson Regular Democratic Club—which became, he said, a "hand hold" for his own campaigns.[5] Politically, he was very much self-propelled and very much his own man.

Shortly before incumbent Rosenthal's death, the *New York Daily News* remarked on Ackerman's political prospects.

There may be no vacancies on the immediately foreseeable horizon; but State Senator Gary Ackerman is not one to let one pass if one should occur. . . . His far flung activities for candidates in other parts of Queens in the last (1982) election indicate to politicians that he would be ready and willing to seek and obtain their reciprocal support if a vacancy in a higher office opens up. And, they added, he had already taken a poll.[6]

He was ambitious, he was community-centered, and he had once been a maverick.

When Ben Rosenthal died, State Senator Ackerman was not projected as the front-runner or the heir apparent. Long Island's *Newsday* listed him as one of 13 contenders.[7] The *New York Post* rated the four strongest contenders and did not mention him. The *Daily News* noted that Ackerman "is known to be interested . . . [but] is not known as a loyalist."[8] He was, however, in it from the beginning—even threatening to run as an independent.[9] When his choice declined to run, the Democratic county leader—perhaps fearful of his own position—supported Ackerman. And in a nomination contest with 11 candidates, Gary won the support of 33 out of 36 assembly district leaders.[10] As the official party choice, he was easily elected.[11] On the record, he was a superior strategist and an aggressive campaigner.

 In short, Gary Ackerman had followed a very different career path than his predecessor—more homegrown, more activist, more independent, and more self-propelled. From the news clips, his representational connections seemed to be more idiosyncratic and yet more endemic than those of Ben Rosenthal.

 homegrown, independent, self-propelled

EARLY ACCESS

At the end of my day in his office, the congressman called to tell the staff that he could not get out of Washington. The chief of staff said to me, "Call me in the morning. I'll be at campaign headquarters." My notes described my boundary-crossing access problem. "I don't know *when* to call him," I wrote.

But I'm in my depressing Ramada Inn hotel room; and I decide to call him at 8:45 A.M. I call. "He's not here." "Who is this?" I ask. "Alan Gershuny," the voice says, "Arthur's not here." I recall seeing Alan's name in the news clips. (I tell him who I am.) He says, "I just dropped in to pick up some stuff, and I'm in a hurry." I say, "Is there a chance you can take me with you, wherever you're going? I don't want to spend the rest of the day in this hotel room." He hesitates, then says, "I'm going to Northport for the day. My car's loaded, and I have to be there till late at night." I say, "But I can't stand staying in this hotel room. I don't care when I get back." He says, "Why don't you go to a movie or something, go in to the city." I say, "I came down here to see some politics, and it looks like Gary may not make it." (Pause) He finally says, "Stevie, can we move that stuff in the back and make room for someone?" Then, "Are you ready to go?" "Yes." "OK, be in front of the Ramada in five minutes." I say, "You're a great man." *move pushy here*

The "stuff" that had to be moved to make room for me was a huge pile of shopping bags! (If it's shopping bags, it must be Queens.) Indeed, to that point my experience had been "déjà vu all over again." Queens had not changed. But I had learned in the 1970s that to be heard, you had to speak quicker and louder. And I had succeeded in getting into the flow!

So here I was, headed for an altogether new county—Suffolk. Afterward, I recapitulated,

The luck of the trip was that I happened by sheer *luck* to catch Alan when he was stopping by the office to collect some campaign stuff. Ten minutes later, I'd have been stuck, and Saturday would have been as miserable a day as I've ever had. As it was, we had a great time. As we distributed literature at events in suburban Northport, we became buddies. At one point later, Alan says, "I can't imagine why you didn't want to stay in the Ramada Inn all day!" We did hit it off—several high fives during the day. Every trip has a lucky break in it—and usually a bad break, too. Given that I had a basic bad break—that [Ackerman] never showed up on Friday or Saturday, the lucky break turned disaster into a long-run plus. . . . I got to know the campaign manager . . . in a way that I couldn't have otherwise.

Fenn never actually met Ackerman?

Driving back from Northport, he went out of his way to take me to their two campaign headquarters, where he explained the field operations of his "volunteer intensive" campaign.

"Alan was," I noted, "a very savvy operative in an organizational, streetwise sense" and a self-described "flaming liberal who has calmed down a little." His father and Ackerman's father had been taxi drivers together. With Ackerman, Gershuny had been a founder of their assembly district's Stevenson Regular Democratic Club. When I explained why I was there, Alan responded, "I campaigned for Ben Rosenthal when I was 16 years old. I went to him and asked him one question: 'How do you stand on the House Un-American Activities Committee?' 'I want to abolish it,' he said. 'That's all I wanted to know,' I said. 'I'll work for you.'" Ben Rosenthal's path-breaking stands on civil liberties issues still resonated among like-minded political activists in his territory.

As for Congressman Ackerman's current post-1990 district, Alan told me that only 50 percent of it was in Queens County, with 28 percent in distant Suffolk County and 22 percent in adjacent Nassau County. He explained,

> Our best county in percentage terms is Nassau, then Queens, and then Suffolk. The most interesting is Queens, because the part Gary has now is the most conservative part of Queens. They elect a Republican state senator, a Republican assemblyman, and a Republican city councilman. However, they will always vote for a Jew. Their finger would fall off if they voted for someone other than a Jew. . . . Our benchmark poll showed that 85 percent of the district's Jewish voters are for Gary.

The new district, Alan added, had visibly affected the congressman. "For both philosophical and political reasons, Gary is growing up. Mostly it's for political reasons. The new district has taught him that there are other views. He even voted for the welfare bill. That was a political change. And he got a lot of criticism from his liberal friends." But Alan wanted me to know, "Gary never compromises on the guarantees of the First Amendment."

On the third and final day of my visit, a part-time staffer, Jerry Scharfman, drove me to the airport to pick up Representative Ackerman. He emerged calling out, "Hooray, we're home." And surprisingly, he made a beeline toward me calling out greetings. (His warm welcome was repeated on every subsequent visit.) His staff chief appeared with Ackerman's trademark

same district?
Rosenthal v.
Ackerman

carnation in a vial of water. He pinned it on the congressman. (He gets a fresh one every day.)[12] He had two House colleagues in tow, and we ferried them to their parking lot. As we went, one of them noted Gary's "bubble-ness" and told me how "popular" he was among his House colleagues. As we left the airport, Ackerman called out the window, "We're back!" At first blush, he seemed much more outgoing than his predecessor.

Almost immediately, he started matching wits with Jerry—a law school graduate and a high school Spanish teacher in Great Neck, the wealthiest town in the district—over the unfairness of the property tax as the main source of school funding. Traveling with Ben Rosenthal, I had noted, "He has a fine sense of humor . . . and he delights in being topped by [campaign manager] Mike Goldenthal, who constantly spars verbally with him." Ackerman, too, loved repartee and relished argument. As I listened to him jousting with Jerry, I could imagine I was riding along with Ben and Mike. In my notes, I described my new acquaintance, tentatively, as "jovial, relentless, and bright." Only the first adjective, "jovial," had not applied equally to his predecessor. Ben Rosenthal had a dry, self-deprecating wit; Gary Ackerman had a fun-loving, storyteller's sense of humor.

We soon left Queens and drove into the new, post-1991 part of Acker-man's district. Our destination was the annual parade in suburban Northport, bracketed beforehand by a meeting with a pharmaceutical group and afterward by a Democratic fund-raiser, after which the con-gressman went home for dinner. And I had a pleasant meal with Jerry and a friend of his. As a result of that day, I should add, Jerry Scharfman became my guardian angel during two subsequent visits.

At trip's end, however, future visits seemed very much in doubt. As a commentary on this kind of research, my summary reflections are a reminder of its unpredictabilities. I wrote,

> The trip was a big disappointment. I didn't get the insights I had hoped to get. And since I got to see GA for only one day, I can't tell whether coming back would help any. When we were in the car, he talked with Jerry, who was driving, and I couldn't hear, in the back-seat, what he was saying. After Northport, Jerry had a friend with us, and that relieved Gary from talking with me, since the friend and I were in the backseat. Gary was very tired, and kept saying so from Northport on.
>
> So the afternoon was a bust, pretty much. We never got to talk about Ben or the contours of the district or Gary's career. I told

them I'd be back. They all said fine. But I can't be sure whether it's worth it or not. . . . There was no indication he didn't want me there. He just didn't invite questions. . . . He never asked me what I was doing, so I had no natural way to bring up Ben Rosenthal. He never invited questions. And he kept saying how tired he was.

My instinct is to hold back and not to crowd the people I'm with. That slow, nonintrusive style may have worked against me in this case, first, because I had only one day—and not a lot of that—and second, because I'm in New York City and people here expect you to keep pushing if you want attention.

In retrospect, I was accumulating an indispensable knowledge base.

CONNECTIONS: POLICY ISSUES AND PERSONAL APPEAL

As we left Queens for Suffolk County's Northport, the congressman's travel talk was that of an explorer—which gave me a vicarious sense for the strangeness of his new territory. For starters, we couldn't find the pharmaceutical event. "We came out here before and got lost, and finally found the place by accident," he said. "If we keep this up, we'll find it again by accident." We didn't, and we had to stop and ask directions. As we approached the meeting, he said, "There will be thirty people here, only five will live in my district, and all but three of them will be Republicans. They'll all be against me. But I want to show them I'm not ducking." There was an echo of his predecessor in his assertiveness.

Riding through a farming area, he exclaimed, "This isn't exactly the city. What is a boy from Queens doing out here? Dorothy should be here. It's Kansas!" And when I asked whether it felt "strange" when he first ventured beyond Queens, his answer had more bite. "Strange for me or for them? For them, I was what they had just gotten away from. I was the city chasing them. I was the plague they had escaped from. I was typhoid Mary." Explaining his efforts to adapt, he mused, "I'm getting to be like that Woody Allen movie where he becomes the person he talks with. When he talks to a Chinese man, he begins to look Chinese; when he talks to a Mexican, he starts looking Mexican. That's me." Representative Ackerman's metaphors had an inviting originality.

Nearing our destination, the conversation stirred memories of my earlier visits to Queens. East Northport was at odds with itself over public

Shaws difference in how congress ppl handle tough disputes

housing. A proposal to build 400 units of low-income housing had split this suburban community. And their new congressman had tried—in a move very different from Rosenthal's—to mediate the dispute. The congressman explained,

> For those of us who represent the government, who are on the front line, it is our responsibility to help the people we represent when they have a problem. When they ask for help, what kind of a response is it to say, "It's not a federal problem." They have a right to expect a better answer. . . . It might not have been the politically smart thing to do. Alan didn't want me to do it. He said it would be a big loss politically [1000 votes]. But I feel a responsibility. The community came to me and asked me to bring the two sides together. I did, and we had a blue-ribbon public event, a perfect media event for everyone when we announced an agreement. I stepped aside and let the community leaders—all Republicans—take the credit. And they did. Then a few days later, they backed away. But I'm going to stay with it till we get an agreement.

He continued, "I told them that I had been born and raised in low-income housing projects and now I had a half-million dollar house in one of the pricey districts in the city. So I know which is better. But I had a choice and I believe everyone deserves a choice as to where they will live." I asked him, given that background, whether he would have intervened if the dispute had not involved housing. "No," he said. "If it had been a transportation issue, I would not have been as interested or gotten involved. Housing is an issue I care about deeply. *It is what I am.*"

Ben Rosenthal had never struck as interventionist—or as confident—a stance on public housing as that. He had worried a lot about his involvement. But he had stayed away from front line public meetings, choosing instead to negotiate directly with the city's remote decision makers. Gary Ackerman, given his background, had felt personally involved, and he had plunged in to mediate directly.[13] It was, for him, an authenticating decision.

On the way to the parade, Gary recalled his earliest impression of Northport. "When I first came here, I couldn't even get arrested. It was biblical: 'In the beginning' there was [pause] nothing!" He recalled an early adventure—the annual town parade.

> I went to the place where the elected officials were gathering to march. They said, "You can't walk in the parade. You're not an elected official." I said, "I am a United States Congressman." They

said, "You are not an elected official from this district!" I said, "I will be!" They said, "You can't march in the parade." So I went downtown where all the people had gathered and shook hands for an hour while all the "elected officials" stood around talking to each other waiting for the parade to start!

"And that was exactly what he did this time," I noted. "He shook hands while he had a waiting, captive crowd along the sidewalks. (Moving along in back of him, I picked up the bitterness on both sides of the housing issue.) Then, when the parade and the public officials came down the street, he jumped in and walked the last 100 yards to the reviewing stand." It was not a Ben Rosenthal–style performance. It was distinctively Gary Ackerman.

Watching him work the suburban crowd, he came across, to me, as distinctive and endearing. I wrote,

> In Northport, he stands out—"*because he doesn't look like anyone here*" [underlined in original]. He's about five foot seven, with a big stomach, curly thinning gray hair, loose-fitting (pinstripe) suit (plus carnation), and he waddles instead of walking. He looks very much like a city boy. Northport was all—I mean all—white, with lots of athletic-looking young people. (Alan had called it "an artsy community.") It looks like Gary eats too much and exercises too little. A nice measure of Gary's success at building personal ties in this dominantly Republican town was his relationship with the police chief. "We drove up to him looking for a place to park—all spots having been taken for miles around. He looked in the window at Gary, laughing, 'Who are you? You're a f—ing [Democrat!] I don't let Democrats park here. Fred, show the congressman where to park—over there, right next to the sheriff's car.'"

After the parade, several people thanked him for something he had done. In a recent House vote, for example, he had been "one of 60" voting against legislation banning same-sex marriage. "A man, with his wife, came up to Gary," I noted.

> "I just want to thank you for what you did. I have a daughter who is gay. I have a daughter and three sons. My sons can get married; my daughter can't. We want you to know how much we appreciate your vote." His wife nodded. Gary said something that was sympathetic

"Symbolic" voting

and then, "Let's have a hug on that." And he gave the man a big hug. It seemed warm and genuine. Then he turned to me and said, "I can't tell you how many people have come up to me since that vote and said to me, 'I want to thank you for what you did on that vote!' I know what they mean by 'that vote.'. . . It was a symbolic vote. But there is a community out there that is watching and listening."

That encounter identified a crucial constituency connection that the current representative shared with the previous representative—a liberal outlook and a liberal voting record. From that moment on, I had little doubt that one viscerally strong civil libertarian had been replaced by another. And that the same hard core of "middle-upper" liberal Jewish voters who connected strongly with Ben Rosenthal would connect strongly with Gary Ackerman, too.

At this earliest acquaintance, I understood why, in the news clips, I had found Gary Ackerman so often described as "a colorful character."[14] There was, of course, his omnipresent carnation. And he was often quoted for his suggestion during the House debate on President Clinton's impeachment: "I move that when the House adjourns, we do so adjourn to Salem, a quaint village in the Commonwealth of Massachusetts, whose history beckons us thence." He had garnered notoriety, too, when he sparked his opposition to the anti-flag-burning legislation, brandishing flag-designed articles of clothing—socks, underwear, shirts—on the House floor, while propounding the circumstances under which each might legitimately be worn.[15] He was often chosen to emcee the "roasts" of his colleagues. One of his asides during a party meeting reportedly left his colleagues "clapping, laughing, and stomping their feet."[16] And when he got caught with others in an elevator, "his quips—mostly about food—were awarded with high marks"—from his beleaguered colleagues. He had a ready wit for all occasions.[17]

At the Northport parade, I was introduced to his love affair with food. "All Gary remembered from walking his 100 yards in the parade," I noted, were (in his words) "the tempting, wafting smells as we approached the reviewing stand—first the hamburgs, then the hot dogs!" Several profiles noted his early custom of importing New York delicatessen fare—plus waiters—for his Washington fund-raisers.[18] He joked that "the overriding reason" for choosing to become chairman of the Subcommittee on Asian and Pacific Affairs of the Foreign Affairs Committee was "because I love Asian food."[19] There cannot be many other House members, either, who are looked to for advice on the ethnic restaurants of New York.[20] Or whose gustatory routines are the subject of entire news articles.[21]

Or who would prefer a restaurant as the backdrop for a most influential campaign profile: "Like a master of ceremonies at a Borscht Belt nightclub," it began, "he sails into Ben's Best Deli—a wisecracking character—who oozes New York."[22] In time, sitting beside him, I would sample Jewish deli, Italian, and Indian cuisine. Ben Rosenthal certainly loved to eat, too, but my recollections centered on our late-afternoon malteds at the counter. A final element in Gary's "colorful," "flamboyant" behavior and reputation was his unusual choice of a Washington home—a houseboat on the Potomac River. On its "maiden voyage," the houseboat—christened "Unsinkable"—promptly sank! And he replaced it with "Unsinkable II." When I asked him about it, he said, "Yes, it sank and worse than that, I didn't have any insurance on it. My friends couldn't understand it—a Jew who didn't understand insurance! They were ready to disown me."

For me, however, his houseboat home had a *much larger significance.* It meant that he had chosen *not* to move his family to Washington. It was a career-level decision about place. And it reflected a reversal of Ben Rosenthal's representational priorities—personal and political. It broadcasted Gary Ackerman's intention to stay centered on his home constituency.

CONSTITUENCY CHALLENGES

When I left Queens in 1996, I had become sufficiently intrigued to try a second visit. And I returned for two educational days in the fall of 1997, and again in 1998. Each time, he greeted me in his way—with enthusiasm. I heard much more talk, then, about Ackerman's new "Queens Plus" district, and about primary and general election politics in his reconstructed home place. Neither of these subjects had occupied as much time during my visits in the 1970s. Congressman Rosenthal had been secure in—though congenitally inquisitive about—his political maintenance routines. For Gary Ackerman in the 1990s, local politics was more volatile and more crucial. He had been handed a very unfamiliar and egregiously gerrymandered district, and he had faced tough and strange political challenges in making it his own.

As he explained it, the House incumbents all around him had maneuvered to help themselves, and he got the leftovers. Two Long Island incumbent Democrats "with the help of their friends in the Democratic

State Assembly . . . carved out the Republican areas and left them to be part of the new district." Similarly, two Long Island incumbent Republicans "and their friends in the Republican State Senate carved out Democrats [and] left me with heavily Jewish, heavily Democratic Great Neck." He concluded, "In Suffolk, I was the victim of the machinations of my colleagues, but in Nassau, I was the beneficiary of their machinations. I had no say in the matter. I got the leftover district. . . . It was not to my liking. It was a disaster. I didn't know where it was or anything about it." In Alan Gershuny's opinion, "it was obvious that Gary had been selected for extinction."

Like Ben Rosenthal's, it was a residual district, but it lacked even the small degree of homogeneity that marked Rosenthal's all-Queens district. Ackerman's account (and Gershuny's observation) also suggested that the maverick-minded, two-term state senator may have had comparatively little influence with his fellow legislators in Albany. This fed a further speculation that, in contrast to Rosenthal (e.g., "The Group"), Gary Ackerman's home connections would be stronger—and more prominent in his political world—than his institutional relationships inside Congress.

The new district was, and necessarily so for him, dominantly Jewish— 25 to 35 percent by local calculation. Other than that, he explained, "It makes no sense. I don't know half the time whether I'm in or out of the district. Neither do my constituents. They argue among themselves. 'I'm in Ackerman's district,' 'no you're not,' 'neither of you is.'" He and Jerry were puzzled. "Are we in the district now?" "I think so." "No, I don't think so." "This must be the dividing line. I don't know, but it must be along here somewhere. It's crazy." At one kink in the district, two pieces of it were separated by water. The district boundary "goes under Cold Spring Harbor"—at which point, he would ad lib "burble, burble"—"and it comes back on land somewhere near Laurel Hollow."[23] Even though it was the bane of his existence, he could, and did, treat it with tongue in cheek.

The 1992 redistricting quickly embroiled Representative Ackerman in *three* successive do-or-die political battles, which, taken together, provided as daunting a political test as a politician can face. First, he had to defeat a fellow House Democrat to win the party's endorsement; then, he had to win a Democratic primary election battle against a well-financed attacker; finally, he had to win a congressional election against a strong Republican opponent—and all of this in a district with only a 9 percent population carryover from his previous one. It was a set of challenges the likes of which Ben Rosenthal never faced.

The most talked about, and the most educational, contest during my visits was his 1992 intramural primary contest with his Democratic House colleague, Representative James Scheuer. Ten years earlier, State Senator Ackerman had thought seriously about challenging Representative Scheuer but had backed off. "We were scared into submission by Scheuer's money," recalled an aide, "but never again."[24] In 1992, Scheuer's district, too, had been dismembered, and his only alternative was to run in the new Queens–Long Island district. Because he currently represented much more of its Queens segment than did Ackerman, Scheuer was quickly installed by the media as the favorite.

Ackerman explained,

> The thought was that I would run in a district to the west in Queens and up into Westchester . . . and that Scheuer would run in the new Queens–Long Island district because he already represented 85 percent of the Queens part, and I had only 15 percent of it. Scheuer thought he could scare me out. But what they didn't know was that I had represented a lot of Scheuer's section when I was in the State Senate. Furthermore, I had kept right on doing a lot of constituent work for [those] people. . . . Besides, I knew I could beat Scheuer because he's a different kind of congressman. . . . He didn't relate to people. When we took a poll in the part of the new district he represented . . . more people said Ackerman was their congressman than said Scheuer. . . . When we saw that, we knew we had him. I was well known in the area. I was born and grew up there. My parents were active in the projects. I went to school there. I went to college there. I was a Boy Scout (Eagle Scout) there. I was *the local boy*—not Scheuer. I was the boy who grew up in the projects and went to Congress.[25]

"Scheuer just assumed that [the Queens people] would support him," said Ackerman. "That's the way he was. But he had not represented them well. He was never around. . . . He had no idea that the redistricting had returned me to my home ground. He was completely blindsided."

On Long Island, the Democrats planned to endorse their candidates by party conventions, one each in the Nassau and the Suffolk parts of the district. And there, the Ackerman campaigners simply outhustled Scheuer in the race to line up convention delegates. Indeed, the Scheuer campaign was never much more than a money-based media campaign. That was why he was favored. But Ackerman's ground-level, local-ties campaign was geared to the convention process. "We did it with smoke and mirrors," said Gershuny. "We would nail down one key person in an election district and claim support from the party in that district. Gary made dozens of calls to nail people down." Scheuer took stock before the conventions met, and he backed out of the primary contest. Ackerman became the only incumbent in the primary.

Scheurer's departure left Gary, still, with a Democratic opponent on primary day. His amply financed opponent was the mother of a well-known New York pollster, and she proceeded to dig away at the incumbent's political liabilities—mostly his involvement in the currently raging "House bank scandal." The congressman had 131 overdrafts that had been covered by the House bank—not a large number by comparison with some of his colleagues, but large enough to raise eyebrows at home. They were further raised when a Capitol Hill newspaper reported (without evidence) that Gary had leaked the list of check-bouncing congressmen to the press. "Ackerman used to be popular," wrote *Newsday*. "Not particularly powerful, but at least nobody hated him. . . . [Now it's] Ostracism City."[26] He appeared not to have much media support in reserve. It did not—nor would it ever—matter. He was not a media-centered or a media-dependent congressman.

A primary contest is a rare event for an established member of Congress. The combination of a reshuffled district and the "bank scandal," however, opened the door for an opponent with political connections and money—albeit with no record of public service. I learned about it from the news clips. With a comment that his primary opponent hadn't "a ghost of an idea how Congress works or what she would do there," the *New York Daily News* wrote that "Ackerman is best known for having over 100 checks covered by the ill-fated House bank. But he has been diligent on constituent services and a leader on African famine relief." And they endorsed him.[27] Long Island's *Newsday* wrote, "Ackerman, a tireless campaigner and schmoozer, traveled extensively throughout the district trying to impress voters with his record."[28] The local *Bayside Times Ledger* wrote that although he was "attacked as arrogant and out of touch with voters for his involvement in the bank scandal. . . . Ackerman remained upbeat through the primary and slapped the flesh at bagel stores, train platforms, and coffee klatches."[29] He won with 58 percent of the vote.

The *New York Times* summarized that "The real story was not how Ackerman won, but how his enigmatic [opponent] managed to get as much as forty-two percent of the vote."[30] A local paper agreed that the incumbent "has shown himself to be much weaker than most people had assumed. If [this opponent] can do this well against [him], imagine what a better candidate can do."[31] The *New York Times* echoed that the incumbent had been "weakened by a bruising primary."[32] In November, Long Island's *Newsday* supported the Republican candidate. "On balance," they wrote, "we think his youth and energy offer a better prospect for growth."[33] Similarly, the *New York Times* called the incumbent's record "unremarkable." And they, too, endorsed his Republican opponent. "In a close call," wrote the *Times*, "we endorse [the Republican] for the promise he offers of energetic representation."[34]

Ben Rosenthal, as I knew him, would never have received such a rebuff from the institution (the *Times*) that was his policy polestar and his security blanket. The Manhattan media people seemed not to know Gary Ackerman, and they did not portray him as an influential or effective House member.[35] And he, for his part—aside from his liberal voting record—had chosen to define himself not in Washington but at home. In that place, Queens, he connected in ways that immunized him from lukewarm media judgments.

Ben Rosenthal had a much easier constituency. He never had to navigate anything like "the wacky world of the 5th District where voters from very different communities in Queens, Nassau and Suffolk got to pick one guy to represent them."[36] In completing that electoral task—media or not—Gary Ackerman was remarkably successful. In the general election, he carried the Queens part of the district with 61 percent of the vote and the Nassau part by 59 percent. And he lost the Suffolk part with 38 percent of the vote. When I arrived for my 1997 visit, however, the first words I heard were, "We took Suffolk last time. Can you believe that!" In 1998, he would carry Huntington—and, finally, solidly Republican Smithtown. After 1992, he was pestered by weak opponents—sufficiently sometimes to energize his workers—but he was never seriously challenged.

LIBERALISM PLUS: THE POWER OF PERSONAL CONNECTIONS

When asked to put his arms around the new district, Representative Ackerman described it this way:

It's a conglomeration, an amalgam of communities strung together for contradictory reasons. It's made up of leftovers and remnants, a patchwork quilt. It's a mixture of city and suburbs—50 percent of the population is in the city, in Queens. And 50 percent of the vote is in the suburbs, on Long Island. It has the most liberal Democrats and the most conservative Republicans—but not in a straight line. The most liberal are in the middle; the city is middle-class, working people. Nassau has some very wealthy people—fairly liberal, Jewish. Suffolk has a lot of blue-collar people and some wealthy mixed in along the North Shore. The district is like a man-made lake—artificial.

Sometimes, he would talk about "the three districts I have."
"Is it easy to represent?"

It's a challenge. To one group, the other group might as well have come from outer space. Each one believes that what they believe is all that need be said. So it is hard to synthesize a philosophy. I haven't changed my philosophy. . . . But if it's not a matter of morality or philosophy, if it's not about who I am . . . and I feel that I owe some group consideration on an issue of importance to them . . . I can do that.

As an example of the former, he chose desecration of the flag legislation.

An overwhelming majority of people in my district feel very strongly about the flag issue. They think it's their flag. But it's my flag, too, and I can't vote with them. Where intensity is strong like that, people are most likely to remember and take it out on me. But it's a matter of philosophy. *It's who I am.*

It was not the first or the last time I would hear that policy-based warrant of his authenticity. When I mentioned that Ben Rosenthal had been in a similarly small—and path-breaking—minority in voting against that same legislation, Gary said simply, "*That's why I loved him.*"

To illustrate the positive impact of the new, more Republican district on his thinking and his actions, he chose free trade legislation.

In Queens, there was not any well-honed idea of business concerns and interests. It was just a matter of jobs. There was no long-run view of trade and the future of the economy. I've been forced to grow up. Now that I see both sides of these questions, it makes for tough decisions. . . . I've given a lot of support to the administration on MFN (Most Favored Nation) for China and on GATT (General Agreement on Tariffs and Trade).

An examination of his liberalism rankings on House roll call votes from 1983 to 1998 confirms the "growing up" description. For the period *before the redistricting*, 1983–1990, his vote score marked him as the *forty-fourth* most liberal Democrat. His average vote score *after the redistricting*, 1991–1998, marked him as the *eighty-fourth* most liberal Democrat.[37] He had moderated his policy stance. Still, he ranked easily in the most liberal half of the House Democrats.

When he described what it was like for the Queens Democrat to confront a sea of suburban Republicans on Long Island, he did not emphasize the issue connections that carried so much weight in the city. He emphasized, instead, his personal connections.

My thought processes have changed completely. I used to think of Republicans as people who lived on another planet. It wasn't that I didn't like them. I just had nothing to do with them. As soon as I got redistricted and before I was even sworn in as their congressman, I started going out there to help them recover from hurricane damage. They saw me more in the first couple of months than they had seen a congressman in ten years. I've spent a lot of time getting to know them—proportionately, much more than in the rest of the district. I've gotten to know them, I've worked hard with them, and they have come to appreciate me.

In my 1997 and 1998 visits, I watched him connect with constituents, and I listened to him talk about his connections. I saw a set of connections with groups, and I heard a set of comments about connecting with individuals.

In 1997, we did what Jerry called "the Jewish Circuit" on Long Island, with a talk on the Middle East at a temple in Huntington and ending at the annual Anti-Defamation League banquet in Great Neck. Our four stops in-between were at an outdoor automobile display, a Democratic headquarters opening, a Democratic fund-raiser, and an outdoor antique show. At the temple (about 50 people), he displayed his total familiarity with Middle Eastern politics through his work on the renamed House International Relations Committee.

Afterwards, half the group remained to ask questions and listen to tales about his recent travels to India and Pakistan as well as to Israel. He was widely traveled, and he was widely praised for his efforts to aid suffering and displaced Ethiopian Jews—with food supplies and resettlement planning. He had also been the first American politician to visit the

idea of making a local issue
int'l relations
Liberalism Plus: The Power of Personal Connections   175

premier of North Korea. As we left, he commented, "The Jews are an unusual group. They know so much and they ask so many questions. We've made international relations a local issue," he added, "both for ethnic communities and for the local economy."

From there, we hurriedly toured the Great Neck auto festival. "I'm walking fast by this group," he said. "They are my liberal liberals, the heart of my support. But if I stop, everyone of them will have a question for me." "Great Neck," he said later, "is the most Jewish town in Nassau County. As we say, 'They vote left and live right!'" A few minutes later, Jerry added, "He owns this town." Great Neck was redistricting's richest gift to Representative Ackerman.

Next, we made an "impulse stop" (so named in his schedule) at a large roadside antique show. It gave me a taste of his person-to-person skills as he wandered around, shopped, and schmoozed. I wrote, "He stopped and fingered stuff at every (100 plus) booth, wandered around slowly saying hello or shaking hands when people recognized him or when he felt like it—all very casual. He hit every booth . . . hundreds of people milling around." Later, he said, by way of contrast, "Jim Scheuer would have come to the flea market with a bullhorn and a kid walking up front shouting, 'Come and shake hands with Congressman Scheuer.' Then he would come along . . . looking pretty grand."

"This is the place to campaign," he enthused. "I love garage sales. I buy so much at flea markets and garage sales that I had to have my own garage sale to get rid of the stuff. It's very relaxing and it's a good way to meet people. . . . If I were campaigning hard, we'd have stopped at every garage sale." And then, "That was worth missing our next stop. The thing that amazed me was how many relatives of these people I knew." He was totally involved and at ease. I could not imagine Ben Rosenthal doing, much less enjoying, what I had just seen.

When he talked about connecting with his new Long Island constituents, Ackerman mentioned his group connections. "The Democrats on Long Island were so pleased to have a Democrat in there that they were supportive." And "For the Jewish people on Long Island, I'm the only congressman they ever heard of. We did two rounds of town meetings on Long Island," he added. "We felt we had to because people did not know who I was." In Queens, on the other hand,

I didn't have to have town meetings. *It was my home.* I was always around talking to people. *I was the local guy.* Before I got into politics, I was the editor of the local paper, and I went to all the meetings. People [in Congress] who were not home much felt they had to come back and tell people what they were doing. I didn't.

This pointed comment placed him at the opposite end of the scale from his predecessor—who had moved to Washington and who had, as a result, designated his town meetings "the most important things we've done."

All told, Congressman Ackerman focused more on his new connections with individuals than on his connections with groups. In a manner completely at variance with his predecessor, he emphasized the personal side of politics and talked about his connections that way. Consider his story about the stranger who approached him with the proposition, "If you kiss my wife, I'll contribute $1000 to your campaign." Gary kisses the wife, and the man repeats his promise. Gary forgets all about it. A couple of elections later, he is telephoning from a list of previous financial contributors. A man whose name he does not recognize answers the phone and says, "I already owe you $1000. And I'll bet you don't know why." Says Gary, "As he's talking, I keep racking my brain, 'who is this guy and what is he talking about?' Suddenly it clicked. I said, 'Yes, I do know. I gave your wife a kiss, and you owe me $1000.' He laughed, he gave me $1000, and in the last campaign he raised $17,000 for me. You never know." It was an Ackerman story, not a Rosenthal story.

"How did you colonize Long Island?" I asked. "I went out there a lot and I was me. People would say, 'How come you're here? You were here last week.'" He was a natural storyteller. And he told stories about winning Suffolk County support one-by-one. The covering idea was, as it had been for Rosenthal, that "Politics is a personal service business."

Mass marketing is necessary, but the personal touch is a big plus. A satisfied customer is a lifelong customer. And one that will tell others about it. Even if you don't succeed, people will thank you for trying. Take that guy last night. When I told him I was sorry we couldn't help, he said, "That's OK, you tried."

Both representatives generalized about the importance of personal service, but only Gary Ackerman threw himself into it.

A good part of my Long Island support is personal—even people who disagree with me. One very conservative [Suffolk] town official, who has been a tremendous help to me, disagrees with me on everything. He said to me once, "You fight against me on everything I believe in, but you are the best congressman I ever had." Why? Because I fixed a problem for him—way out in Republican territory—a problem having to do with shorefront erosion and utilities. . . . I walked around in hip boots. And I negotiated for them with Lilco [Long Island Light Co].

"I went out and these people saw me. They told me they had seen me more in two years than they had seen the congressman who lived there."

"Once, when I was out in Huntington, I heard a woman say under her breath, 'We'll see him again in two years.' I made it a point to walk past her on my way out, and I said, 'You'll see me before that.' She had worked for one of my Long Island predecessors, Jerry Ambro, and she was devoted to him. Not long afterward, I saw her at a function. I went over and said, 'It's me again!' By the next election, she was one of the first people at our victory party. She came up to me and said, 'You're the second best congressman in the whole world.' I was pleased. . . . When my mother died recently, she came to pay a shivah call. She said to me, 'You don't remember, but I used to think that you were the second best congressman in the whole world. You aren't. You're the best!' It was so touching, I had tears in my eyes. Jerry Ambro died recently. I went to his funeral. She was there."

The idea I took away from these stories was that he had gone to Long Island facing skepticism and that when individuals got to know him, they became loyal supporters. His one-on-one constituency connections were more "up close and personal" than those of his predecessor.

"When I was given the new district," he said, "I was asked, 'What is your goal now that you have Suffolk?' I said, 'My goal is that when the Suffolk County papers print my name, they will say, 'Gary Ackerman (Democrat, *Huntington*).' And that's what they do now. When people begin to think of you as *the hometown boy*, you've got it made. And when you live 70 miles away, that's the best!" He was reaching for the same reputation among his new voters as the one he had established with the familiar ones.

He had another goal, too—to carry the Suffolk part of his district at election time. Smithtown was its prize Republican town. "A Democratic congressman from Long Island told me that whatever I did, not to bother with Smithtown. 'There is no way they will ever vote for you no matter what you do or say. Don't go out there; it is a total waste of time.' But I said 'I'm not going to concede one bit of the district to anyone. I intend to fight for every inch.'" In 1996, he carried Suffolk County and he got 50 percent of the vote in Smithtown. On Long Island, as in Queens, the persona he wanted—and worked for—was "the local guy," "the hometown boy." It was all about place. And it was an authenticating label.

A 1996 *Newsday* campaign story headlined "Schmoozing the GOP: How Gary Ackerman Learned to Hug Republicans."[38] The simple answer was that it came naturally to him. Before Long Island became part of his district, he had been lumped into "the Long Island delegation" in Congress. And when the Democrats had controlled the House, he had been the acknowledged "head" of that "delegation." "I brought the Republicans in whenever Long Island matters came up. And since they took over, we have continued to work a lot together." One Long Island GOP colleague even called Gary "the glue that holds the [Long Island] delegation together."[39] Those preexisting relationships had already brought him into contact with the leaders of Republican-run Nassau and Suffolk counties, thus lubricating his personal relationships. At election time, their chief executives and supervisors offered praise for his availability, his responsiveness, and his assistance. Indeed, when, in 2002, redistricting took away Suffolk and some of Nassau, the comments of Republican and Conservative leaders emphasized more sorrow than joy.[40] In 2004, when Long Island's *Newsday* rated the performance of the *Long Island* House members, Gary Ackerman was given the *highest* ranking of that group.[41]

THINKING
ABOUT REPRESENTATION

I ended my second visit with a ringside lesson in the study of representation. The subject was trade and an expansion of the president's "fast track" authority on trade matters. The problem was that it might put the recently "grown-up" Representative at odds with his traditional allies in organized labor. My notes were lengthy.

> The meeting with the labor guys was fascinating—so much so I almost missed my plane home! The day before, in the car coming home from ADL event, he was furious with the labor guys. "I am pro-labor. I have 98 percent pro-labor voting record. Now, because I'm undecided on fast track, and I may go to 95 percent, they are roughing me up. They are saying that I want an ambassadorship.

They are threatening to put a picket line around my office. I told them that I've never crossed a picket line in my life, but that if they put one around my office, it will be my first. They are going to push me in the opposite direction if they don't stop these tactics. They're coming in to talk tomorrow."

The next morning, he revisited the balancing problem he faced.

In Queens, there was not any well-honed idea of business concerns and interests. It was just a matter of jobs. There was no long-run view of trade and the future of the economy. I've been forced to grow up. Now that I see both sides of these questions, it makes for tough decisions. I'm grappling with one of them right now—fast track authority for the president. In Queens, the unions are opposed to it. But I have to jump out to Smithtown now, where blue-collar people may be helped by increased trade. I'm leaning in one direction. I've given a lot of support to the administration in foreign affairs—on MFN for China and on GATT. I've accepted a high profile on a lot of long-range issues. But now there are people, you know, who are losing their jobs, real people who have to put bread on the table. You have constituents who need protection. It's hard to know how to equate their jobs with the jobs the business guy is going to create down the road. That is "on the come," and the other is "right now." One is definite; the other is down the road. It's economic triage.

My notes continued,

When they [the union group] came to his office Monday, [there were] five of them led by a NY City Central Labor Council guy [the Boilermakers Union president was the other most vocal one]. I started to leave, and Gary said, "This will be the really interesting one." He told me that he was leaning in their direction. But he battled every argument they gave. I think that verbal battles give him a lot of enjoyment. He loves argument and verbal combat. And he made them shift their ground.

They began with the jobs argument by the Boilermakers guy. "We supported you. Our guys are in such bad shape, we aren't going to be players anymore. We can't put bread on the table." When Gary talked about other jobs being won by expanded trade, they shifted argument to an institutional one. Congress shouldn't abdicate to the president. After Gary had beaten them up on several false starts and arguments, he explained that he had to have good arguments if he was going to support their position. Things lightened up.

But then they got into a wrangle over [Mayor Rudy] Giuliani. Central Labor guy: "Thirty percent of my people will vote for Giuliani. Tell me why? I don't understand it. Pretty soon the labor unions won't be players anymore. There will be a great social upheaval and country will take a right turn . . . ."

The argument seemed to be that Gary had to save the labor movement, save the country, keep the Congress as a viable institution, etc., and the only weapon was to stop fast track, i.e., go slow, to the same end. The labor guys were finding that a reflex, pro-union guy was no longer a sure thing. And that was very upsetting to them.

I had to leave to catch my plane as the labor guy was "betting" Gary that Giuliani would get 30 percent of the black vote, amidst head-shaking, and with Gary challenging the union guys to talk to their membership and educate them. The labor union guys were losing their congressman on one end and their own membership on the other, and the society in general was moving in an unwelcome direction. A real whipsaw situation. And they ended more by pleading than insisting.

On the other hand, Gary is a "middle of the road Democrat now," says Jerry. "He's grown up." That is the same phrase Alan used. And Gary himself had used it, too. The "fast track" decision, giving the president additional leeway on a trade policy, was a test for him and a study in the complexity of representation.

I wrote to myself,

It illustrates a seldom noticed wrinkle. Gary's movement ideologically shows up *in the fact of his indecision* [on trade] and in the fact that the labor guys are after him and are in there arguing with him. In his earlier [ideological] incarnation and [his earlier] district, he would not have thought for ten seconds about how to vote on "fast track." It would have been pure reflex: labor-jobs-Democrats-QED. *The "wrinkle" is that his voting record may not change, and if it doesn't, it will not register the huge change that has taken place in his thinking.* The point is, I guess, that there's a process that goes on prior to vote change that may change the dynamics of representation. And we won't catch it if we only look at roll calls as a measure of ideology. That is: *if Gary listens differently, he's representing differently.* No matter what his roll call vote!

I had witnessed, I thought, encouraging support for my in-depth constituency-centered perspective on the subject of connecting and representing.

On my next visit, I asked him how he had voted on the fast track bill. "I came back to my roots," he said.

I supported labor—the working people. So what did it get me politically—even though that's not why I did it? I got one-half of what I got from them in the last election. I said to them, "I supported you when you told me it was life and death, and you gave me half as much as before." They said, "You're all right. You don't need it." So I lost a lot of business support, and labor did not make up the difference. I hope there are still some businessmen who think I have possibilities.

I did not get to travel with the congressman in his native Queens territory until my final visit in October 1998. But when I did, I recognized much the same Queens that I had experienced with Ben Rosenthal. Again, there was the stressful driving: "turn here," "cross over this curb to get on the highway," "do a U turn," "we've gone too far," "I thought it was a short cut, but it isn't," "go here," "stop here," "take that parking spot," and so forth. Second, there was the familiar running discussion of population and neighborhood change. The ethnic mix had changed in the interim—as a result of the large influx of Asians. There were now 100,000 Chinese in Queens, I was told. "Chinatown is not in San Francisco, it is in Flushing!" From my hotel window in Flushing, I counted 15 storefronts, all Chinese. I was told, "Some of what you see is the very best real estate in Queens."

There were also substantial communities from Korea and India—both large, both growing, both supportive, but neither reliably active. Building on his International Relations Committee membership, Gary had become the cochair of the Indian Caucus of the House of Representatives. My final evening, we had a fund-raising dinner at an Indian restaurant with a religiously oriented Indian group. He was introduced as "truly a great congressman who not only devotes his time to India, but to Indians in

America. He is there for you. He is a man of the people. . . . Hopefully he will make head of Foreign Affairs . . . and next stop secretary of state."[42] Gary made sure that I sat near the group's leader while he told of his worldwide search to locate and save desecrated Jewish graveyards. "Stay close. I want you to hear this." It was the teacher in him. And that relationship extended to his instruction in Indian cuisine as well.

During that final visit, I also observed an enduring difference between the Rosenthal and the Ackerman connecting styles and pleasures. The first day we toured a UPS facility and then campaigned (uneventfully) with shopping bags in the Bayside Senior Center. Our UPS visit provided a chance to see the congressman's mood-setting warmth. In the middle of his informal conversation with a group of managers and employees,

> He turned to a young black woman employee standing nearby listening to his story, and he shook hands with her. She, looking at his carnation, said, "I like that carnation." He said, "I'll send you one." She said, "I'd like 12." Everyone laughs. He says, "I'd hate to be on the other side of the bargaining table from you." Everyone laughs. "What's your name?" Gary asks. She tells him. Whereupon Gary says to (his staff guy nearby), "Call Arthur and tell him to send 12 carnations to Ms.—." Then, to her, "When do you get off work?" Then to his staffer, "Tell Arthur to use the flower shop we use, and tell him to rush them." Amid laughter, she thanks him, he kisses her, and she leaves. Says Gary to the others, "When she gets them, she'll count them, one, two, three. . . . She's management material." More laughter.

I labeled it "the carnation caper." Afterwards, Gary smiled. "That was a fun stop. You've got to make it fun; otherwise, it's boring." Ben Rosenthal would never have performed in such a convivial way—much less labeled it "fun."

"We're running a perfunctory campaign," said Ackerman. "We're doing street fairs and senior centers and shopping bags." We kicked off my last day with an adventure at the "Self Help Benjamin Rosenthal Senior Center" in Flushing. As we began distributing shopping bags, we were ordered to leave—"against regulations," they said. Whereupon Gary got on the phone with the head of the New York City Department of Aging. "I've just been thrown out of a very nice place," he tells her, "*The Benjamin Rosenthal Senior Center* in Flushing. I've been doing this every year for 24 years, and no one has ever thrown me out before. In fact, I've been doing it ever since I broke ground for the building *with Ben Rosenthal!* And I have the hard hat to prove it." She apologized and called the director.

That helped until we got to the Bay Meadows Senior Center, where, again, we were ejected. Outside, another call went out to City Hall. Again, that fixed our problem, where upon we distributed more than 100 shopping bags. I noted, "Gary shoots pool with a group of men who tell him they play 'every day.' Another group serenades him with 'You Are My Sunshine.' Then he leads them in singing, 'For he's a jolly good fellow . . . .' Half the people know him; the rest (I think!) recognize him. And we leave on a bubble of happiness. Says Gary, 'A great stop.'" His easy, enthusiastic outreach effort was very much his own. Ben Rosenthal summoned up a similar enthusiasm when he was talking about helping to make or helping to publicize public policy. More than anything, therefore, it was the shopping bags that reminded me of my 1970s campaign experience in Queens.

REFLECTIONS

Representative Ackerman, of course, knew that I visited, similarly, with Representative Rosenthal. And he knew that I wanted to make comparisons. In this respect, it is noteworthy that he was scrupulous about not influencing my comparisons. He hardly ever mentioned his predecessor. When he went to Congress, he had proposed and passed legislation naming the Flushing Post Office after him—describing Rosenthal as "a man whose wisdom, intelligence and stature towered above the common place."[43] In addition to his civil liberties–related comment, "That is why I loved him," he once said. "I never criticize Ben Rosenthal."

On a single occasion in explaining my research purpose to a staffer, he spoke comparatively.

Different constituencies, different styles, different guys. He was a Washington guy. The heart of my district is still Queens. For Ben, the heart of it was Jackson Heights, where he grew up. [Now] it's Queens several constituent generations later. It's less Jewish and much, much more Asian. But the flavor of the heart is the same. . . . Long Island would have been just as foreign to Ben as it was to me.

Both representatives came from the same place, Queens, and both were embedded in Queens because they were Jewish—by far the largest minority. Given those crucial commonalities of place, they were different individuals working in different times and in different contexts to connect in different ways with their constituents. I went there to observe and learn the constants and the variables, the similarities and the constraints in their representational activities and reflections. And I am arguing that this is the best way to do it.

Representatives Rosenthal and Ackerman were very much alike by virtue of a common ethnicity, a common place, a common base of partisan support, and a common political philosophy. The two men were very different in their personalities, personal relationships, constituency connections, career choices, and workaday priorities.

Ben Rosenthal tended to be reserved, studious, and quietly bemused in his personal relationships. In contrast, Gary Ackerman was by nature outgoing, convivial, and adaptable. He was deeply embedded in the life of his place, his constituency. He savored and sought recognition for his helpful personal relationships, more than for his policy position taking. He wanted to connect—and he did—as "the local guy," "the hometown boy." His constituency connections were altogether closer and more continuous than those of his predecessor.

As Ben Rosenthal had predicted, "his" district did change—more, in 1997, than he could ever have imagined. Gary Ackerman, on the other hand—with his face-to-face talent for extending his constituency connections—made his transition to the reconstituted "Queens plus" constituency much more easily than Rosenthal could have done. Given his talent for extending his media relations and his policy connections, Ben Rosenthal could have moved most easily into another all-Queens district.

For both representatives, I conclude that the question "who is this guy?" or "what is he really like?" can best be understood through the prism of their varied—and varying—constituency connections, which in turn meant "going there" to observe and to listen at close range.

Notes

1. David Armstrong, "Dem Loyalist Ackerman Runs for 8th Term," *Bayside Times Ledger,* October 22, 1998.
2. He acknowledged that "luck" in his Flushing Town Hall installation ceremony speech on December 27, 1978. *Flushing Tribune,* December 28, 1978–January 3, 1979, p. 6.
3. Bernard Rabin and Don Singleton, "State Senator Goes Bumming: Spends Night in Flushing Armory," *New York Daily News,* December 19, 1981.
4. *New York Daily News,* September 27, 1982; William Butler, "Harsh Words over Ft. Totten," *Newsday,* April 8, 1981; John Toscano (no title), *New York Daily News,* December 28, 1981.

5. Gerald McKelvey, "Results of Vote Mixed for Manes," *Newsday*, September 27, 1982; Michael Arena, "Manes and Cuomo After the Election," *Newsday*, November 7, 1982.
6. Bernard Rabin, "With Running Shoes on, Ackerman Looks for Race," *New York Daily News*, January 4, 1983.
7. Michael Arena, "Battle Shapes Up for Rosenthal Seat," *Newsday*, January 9, 1983.
8. Bernard Rabin, "See How They Run for 7th District Seat," *New York Daily News*, January 10, 1983.
9. Bernard Rabin, "Dems Swarming for a Honey of an Open Seat," *New York Daily News*, January 14, 1983.
10. The selection was by weighted vote of each assembly district leader who had 7th District voters in his assembly district. Frank Lynn, "Democrats Pick a State Senator for House Race," *New York Times*.
11. See George Arzt, "Lessons of the Queens Election," *New York Times*, March 4, 1983.
12. The most detailed carnation story is: Jennifer Bradley and Francesca Cantiuglia, "Standing Out in a Sea of Navy," *Roll Call*, September 15, 1997.
13. Vivian Toy, "Soon, Dry Feet for Ackerman," *New York Times*, June 30, 2001.
14. Cathy Delum, "New York Congressman," *New York Times*, May 22, 1994; *Almanac of American Politics 1996*, p. 876.
15. N. Ching-Ching N, "Mum's the Bad Word in East Northport," *Newsday*, March 23, 1997. Elaine Povich, "Serving with A Smile," *Newsday*, October 19, 1998.
16. "Heard Around the House," *Roll Call*, February 2, 2006. When the House closed down because of the post-9/11 anthrax scare, he set up a card table office in the House parking lot and defiantly conducted business. His picture was in the *Times* and in several other newspapers. See *Pittsburgh Post Gazette*, October 25, 2001.
17. Ben Pershing, "House Members Survive Bipartisan Ordeal," *Roll Call*, June 12, 2003.
18. Delum, "New York Congressman."
19. *Almanac*, p. 877.
20. Liza Gutierrez and Sunny Bunch, "Members' Best Bets for the Big Apple," *Roll Call*, August 30, 1994.
21. Albert Eisele, "Young Chow: How the Chinese Influence Congress; Rep. Gary Ackerman Admits Weakness for General Tso's Chicken," *Capitol Hill Publishing*, April 23, 1997.
22. Carol Eisenberg, "5th District Opponents Are Drawn into a Fight," *Newsday*, October 22, 1992.
23. Toy, "Soon, Dry Feet for Ackerman."
24. Arthur Nitzburg, "Rep. James Scheuer Withdraws from Congressional Race," *Bayside Times Ledger*, July 23, 1992.
25. "Collins: Washington Power Co." *Newsday*, May 16, 1993. Another rating of all NewYork House members gave him ratings of "average" for 2002 and "below average" for 2003, www.politicsny.com. February 4, 2002 and March 13, 2003. A third ranking of New York House members ranked him as "average." Enos Throop, "Throop's Scoop: New York Politics in Washington," February 4, 2002.
26. Gail Collins, "Washington Power Co: New York Reps. Some Have It, Some Don't," *Newsday*, May 16, 1993. See also Jack Sirica, "3rd City Rep. Admits Bad Checks," *Newsday*, October 8, 1991.
27. *New York Daily News*, September 13, 1992.
28. Joseph Quinn, "Ackerman Had Struggle," *Newsday,* September 16, 1992.
29. Rupert Lothigan, "Ackerman Wards Off Challenge," *Bayside Times Ledger,* September 10, 1992.
30. Andrew Wolf, "Ackerman Wins Primary," *New York Times,* September 18, 1992.
31. Arthur Nitzburg, "How Badly Has Ackerman Been Hurt?" *Bayside Times Ledger,* September 24, 1992.
32. Stewart Ain, "Ackerman Tries to Parry Newcomer's Challenge," *New York Times,* October 18, 1992.

33. *Newsday*, October 23, 1992. See also Jack Sirica, "A Weekly Report," *Newsday*, June 6, 1989.
34. *New York Times*, October 28, 1992. Later, the *Times* labeled him "a colorful character" and called him "a genial glad-hander." Delum, "New York Congressman."
35. Collins, "Washington Power Co." A rating of all New York House members gave him a rating of "average" and "below average" (2002). While he is not the most effective member of the delegation, he is an effective spokesman for the party's more liberal position on the issues. "Rating the Congressional Delegation" see also www.politicsny.com, February 4, 2002 and March 13, 2003.
36. Joseph Queen, "Candidates Want to Take the 5th," *Newsday*, October 29, 1992.
37. Keith Poole and Howard Rosenthal, *Congress: A Political-Economic History of Roll Call Voting*, Oxford University Press (New York, 1997).
38. Susan Benkelman, "Schmoozing the GOP," *Newsday*, 1996.
39. Ibid.
40. Toy, "Soon, Dry Feet for Ackerman."
41. "Newsday Ranks Queens, Long Island Members," *Roll Call*, June 10, 2004.
42. On Ackerman's importance to U.S. citizens from India, see editorial, "A Friend for All Reasons," *India Today*, June 9, 1997.
43. *New York Daily News*, July 8, 1983.

CHAPTER 9

David McIntosh and Lindsey Graham: Constituency Connections

THE VIEW FROM WASHINGTON

The historic 1994 congressional elections resulted in the first Republican majority in the U.S. House of Representatives in 40 years. The rarity of the event produced an unusual burst of national interest in the 73 GOP newcomers. Who are these people? What are they like? What are they really like?

Washington observers concentrated on the shared characteristics of the newcomers. As a group, they espoused a strong antigovernment, social, and economic conservatism. They shared an allegiance to the reformist "Contract with America," the ten-point policy platform that all but three of them had ceremoniously signed on the Capitol steps. Most of them interpreted their election triumph as a mandate to turn provisions of the contract into legislation. And most of them believed, too, that the new freshmen class had been elected to spearhead that legislative mission.[1]

It was easy to think of them as a collectivity, and that is what Washington analysts did. The Capitol Hill newspaper, *Roll Call*, began its postelection assessment: "If diversity was the buzz word of the last freshmen class . . . uniformity is a characteristic of this one."[2] The *Washington Post* introduced the group with the headline: "A Class of Young Warriors."[3] A GOP strategist immediately predicted that "they're going to be very eager foot soldiers in the [Speaker Newt] Gingrich army."[4] In January, the *New York Times* headlined, "73 Mr. Smiths, of the GOP, Go to Washington."[5] In a

Washington Post article that same month, the author predicted, "In their crusade for a balanced budget . . . the 73 House Republican freshmen of the 104th Congress will not budge."[6] In the next two months, *National Journal* articles about the freshmen class were entitled "The GOP's Young Turks," "The Transformers," and "Force Majeure?"[7] "Outsiders on the Inside" headlined the *Washington Post* in July, "The House and Senate Have Never Seen Anything Like the Freshmen Class of '94."[8]

During their first year, the 73 were bundled together in Washington commentary as "shock troopers," "ideological firebrands," "the firebrand freshmen class," "the 800-pound gorilla of Washington politics," and as "platoons [that] march in lock step with General Gingrich on the vast majority of votes." When their first year ended, *Congressional Quarterly* summed up, "The Class of 1994 . . . has been the driving force in the most remarkable reversal of House priorities in nearly a half-century."[9] Indeed, the Republican class of 1994 was often compared in its potential impact to the 1974 Democratic "Watergate babies" class 20 years earlier. Washington commentary was almost entirely focused on the new members as a group: "What are *they* like?"

As a student of Congress, I also found the "what are they like?" question irresistible. And I, too, wrote a small book about "the class."[10] In writing about it, however, I followed preference and habit by adding an individual-centered "what is he or she like?" question to the Washington-centric "what are they like?" question. And I sought insight into the life and problems of the group by traveling around with two of its members in their home districts.

My choice of traveling companions was not random; it was dictated entirely by circumstance and opportunity. I leveraged my acquaintance with Clemson University political scientist and campaign manager David Woodard to join *Representative Lindsey Graham* in South Carolina, and I leveraged my book about former Senator Dan Quayle to connect with his one-time vice presidential aide *Representative David McIntosh* in Indiana.

The geographical mix—one member from the first-ever Southern majority of House Republicans and the other one from the party's traditional Midwestern heartland—was most welcome. But it is important to emphasize that I did *not* choose them because of this or any other characteristic. I simply took the *only* two that were easily available to me.

Between 1995 and 2002, I made six trips to spend 14 days with Lindsey Graham in northwest South Carolina, and from 1996 to 1998, I made four trips to west-central Indiana to spend 10 days with David McIntosh.[11] These visits gave me a much longer time line than I had available to me in the previous chapters. In turn, the time line provided a focus on their

Washington activity that had not been of particular interest to me in earlier explorations.[12]

When I met up with each representative, I knew only what Washington observers made publicly available. From early Capitol Hill profiles—from *Congressional Quarterly* (*CQ*) and *Roll Call*—I had learned that both men were in their thirties, were law school graduates, and were ideologically conservative. Along with these commonalities, I read that their work experiences had been very different—Graham as a state legislator in South Carolina and McIntosh as an executive branch staffer in Washington. Both the similarities and the differences whetted my appetite for more. So I journeyed to each of their home places, to ask "who is this guy?" And as far as I can ascertain, no Washington journalist ever made either journey—until one went to South Carolina for a day in 2002.

Out in their home territories, I found a pair of ambitious, intelligent, and energetic politicians. Both were electorally secure, and both had pledged to serve no more than 12 years in the House. I found two hard-line policy conservatives who regularly voted the same way on bottom-line roll call votes. At the end of their first term, when the allegiance of individual freshmen to the elements of the party's Contract with America was calculated, McIntosh and Graham had identical 100 percent support scores—a level of ideological loyalty matched by only 26 of the 73 newcomers.

As people and as politicians, however, I found them to be very different. They had come to their conservatism along different paths, with different learning experiences, and had made quite different choices along the way. I discovered different life experiences, different habits of thought, different patterns of action, and different constituency relationships. They had different political strengths and different policy priorities. And they often made very different strategic decisions. Sometimes, they made the same decision for very different reasons. And I developed very different personal relationships with them. In short, my inquiries on the road produced two different answers to my "what is he like?" question. They are answers I could not have found—to questions I might never have asked—in Washington.

THE INTELLECTUAL AS LEADER:
DAVID MCINTOSH, 1995–1996

When I went to Indiana to travel with David McIntosh, I took with me the resumes from *CQ* and *Roll Call*. He was 36 years old, he had graduated from Yale University and from the University of Chicago Law School, he had worked in the White House during the Reagan administration, and he had been chairman of Vice President Dan Quayle's Council on Competitiveness. *Roll Call* noted that he "has the type of high-level Washington experience that most freshmen members yearn for" and that "he has won the respect of the Republican braintrust for championing the ideas of competitiveness." *CQ* emphasized his leadership potential. "Boasting one of the longer resumes of government experience among his freshman colleagues, McIntosh was tapped early on as an up-and-comer. He was one of eight freshmen selected by Speaker Newt Gingrich to be part of the GOP transition team and was later selected by his colleagues as a leadership liaison."[13]

At home in Indiana—13 months into his tenure—he picked up the threads of these promising introductions. Shortly after the election, he said,

> Newt invited seven of us to come back there and sit with party leaders to discuss what to do in the next Congress. . . . It was during that time that the party strategy developed to make the Contract with America the agenda of the House Republicans. At the same time, I decided I wanted to remain active within our class. There were two jobs I thought about: class president, who could call meetings, and class liaison, who could meet every week with the leadership. I decided that the liaison job was the one I wanted. . . . During orientation, I talked to people about the job. I talked about policy and politics. I said that I had the experience on the other side of the government. And I was familiar with a lot of the policies we would be dealing with. On the political side, I said that it was very important for our class to be active and to stick together as a class because we could have unusual influence.

He and a co-liaison were elected. "The freshmen started having regular meetings," he said, "to talk about what we wanted to tell the leadership. The two of us go to leadership meetings every week, and we convey the thinking of the freshmen. . . . And, there is a lot I can do to help them individually."

The Washington profilers were right to emphasize his resume. He came to the House amply certified to think legislatively about matters of public policy, and he came with an ambition for leadership. He came, also, as a product of mentoring and protégé systems. In law school, there had been Professor Antonin Scalia (who, as a Supreme Court justice, swore him in privately before the ceremony in the House) and in Washington, there had been Vice President Dan Quayle.

Prior experience helped him to fit easily into a similar relationship with Newt Gingrich, the man who invited him to join in making the decision to adopt the contract as the party's legislative agenda. Party leaders acknowledged his preparation, they co-opted him, and they treated him as a now and future Republican Party leader. The same protégé-preferment scenario unfolded when McIntosh faced a key institutional decision—the choice of a committee assignment.

I had several choices: Ways and Means, Commerce, or a subcommittee on Government Operations, where I could deal with the same kinds of problems I had dealt with on Vice President Quayle's Competitiveness Council. I decided I could have more influence as chairman of a subcommittee, where you have a staff and can set your own agenda. I typed up a four-page paper describing the reasons why a new (anti-regulation) subcommittee should be created and what it would do. Denny Hastert (Chief Deputy Whip) was very helpful at that point, because he knew his way around. He suggested I stand outside Newt's door. When he came out, I handed him the paper. He looked at it and said OK. I knew that if I chose Government Operations, I would have my subcommittee.

He became the first freshman in memory to become an instant subcommittee chairman. The result was widely reported back home as a warrant of future stardom. As one writer put it, he started his congressional career "in overdrive."[14]

Class leader: My acquaintance with David McIntosh had begun in Washington eight months earlier, when I went there to seal our arrangements. In the Longworth House Office Building, I had met his wife, Ruthie, and the family dog, "Maddy," before walking with him (for ten minutes) to a meeting. "He was strong in emphasizing the special nature of the freshmen class," I noted afterward, "that when he got to Washington, the great revelation was the similarity between his experience and that of the others . . . he clearly sees the class as wanting to accomplish something."

The thematic centerpiece of my first Indiana visit—midway through his first term—was his class leadership activity in the House. The sights and sounds of that visit came mostly from several formal connections—three newspaper editorial boards, two plant tours, a think tank talk, and a town meeting. He was recognized as a leader of the class, and his team-playing persona was central to his presentation of self to his constituents—and in our casual conversation as well. The local newspapers had primed people at home to think of him that way, by describing him as "a player," "a star," "a kid in a candy store," a GOP "poster boy," "the substance guy"—with emphasis on his access to Speaker Gingrich and his inner circle.[15]

At the *Winchester News Gazette*, the editor asked him, "How does the public think the freshmen class is doing?" Answer: "Ruthie and I were in the Marsh Grocery the other night and a couple of people come up and said, 'Hang tough, you're doing a good job.' They want us to work for a balanced budget; but they want us to be honest about it. Go back and tell people what you have done and what you have not done. That's part of the ethic we need in politics; follow through on your promises and develop trust." Instinctively, he was soliciting a collective report card for the 73 newcomers as a group and only, by inference, one for himself.

Similarly, he told the editor of the *Newcastle Citizen News* that the freshmen class had embraced "the ethics of campaigning and governing." "We have rejected," he said, "George Bush's view that you campaigned on one platform and then governed without regard to it. That view bred enormous cynicism; and the new cohort of Republicans is saying 'hold us accountable.'"

Editor: "Was it like you thought it would be?"

Answer: "I was used to turf battles in the executive branch, but I didn't expect it in the House—the committee turf battles."

Editor: "Have the freshmen been able to erode that activity?"

Answer: "Newt and his task forces have picked it up; but the freshmen ethic is that it is wrong. I've picked up the opposite; the freshmen talk to each other across committee lines."

Editor: "Is this a generational thing?"

Answer: "It's partly generational. Linda Smith [a classmate] said to me, 'David, why are you so worried about keeping the freshmen together? Pretty soon we'll be sophomores.' I'll have to figure something out—maybe involve the next class."

This contrast, between his party's freshmen class and its "older generation" of Republicans, had become a staple theme.

In my notes, I summarized, "The media people at home see the freshmen class as a relevant political force [because] David talks about the freshmen class as his reference group, his identification. It's like he's willing to live or die with them. . . . As he put it to me, 'The freshmen class is a real thing.'" Relatedly, his opinion of Speaker Newt Gingrich in early 1996 was benign and favorable. The speaker lunches weekly with the freshmen, he said, telling us, "You have what it takes to help us reduce and reinvent this government. Don't sit in your office and gripe. Tell us how to change things."[16]

David McIntosh's activity as protector, unifier, and shepherd of the freshmen class popped up repeatedly during our three days of conversation. "I have taken my job seriously," he said. On the occasion, for example, when Speaker Gingrich took away a fellow freshman's committee assignment for failure to vote the party line on a key vote, he recalled, "Everyone in the class saw the same threat, and everyone was in agreement that we could not let it go by. Lots of people came up to me said, 'Do you know what happened? What are you going to do about it?'" He went with other freshmen to confront the speaker with the prospect of a freshmen class revolt, and the dispute was resolved. "It was," he told a reporter, "a defining moment for us."[17]

He recalled an instance when one member of the class started recruiting, on his own, a select group of first-termers to form "tiger team" media-watch groups. Some who felt "left out" complained to McIntosh. He intervened quickly to ward off divisiveness by opening up the media-watch group to all interested classmates. When individuals felt pressure to stray from the group, he worked to keep them in the fold. "It's getting to be a problem now for some freshmen to be known as 'freshmen,'" he said. "It hurts Tom Davis to be 'a freshman.' I've talked to him to try to get him to stay with us. The other day, I explained to him about Todd Tiahart from Kansas, who was a nobody when he won—that it's a help to him to be known as a freshman, that it might make the difference for him."

When he talked about his behavior in leadership meetings, McIntosh expressed the same strongly team-centered view of his activity. "You know my style," he told an *Indianapolis Star* reporter. "I don't walk into a room and pound on the table. I just want to be a part of the discussion and see my ideas incorporated into the thinking of the group. I don't have to be the one who walks out of the room and says, 'I led the discussion'— so long as my views are incorporated in the decision." He wanted to be in the room, but he seemed not to crave public credit.

On the road, his pattern of freshmen-centric thought and action, together with a modest expression of self-importance, emerged as a pattern. It underpinned and connected with a broad party-centered attitude toward governing the country. His freshmen-centered perspective was all of a piece with an abstract theory of responsible party government; i.e., that a party makes electoral promises, it delivers on its promises, and it faces the voters on that record. His own enduring campaign slogan was "promises made, promises kept." Notably, it was a team slogan, not a personal one. In this abstract formulation, it was the cohesion of the freshmen class that would provide the partisan muscle necessary to implement partisan policy promises and thereby create a more responsible system of governance. He expressed, and operated with, a strong sense of collective responsibility.

A month after my visit, he was arguing with party leaders that "we want to have a freshman vision for where we're going in the year ahead"[18]—"a second Contract with America or son of the Contract"— that gets back to the core issues that cut across Republican and Democratic lines, a "five or ten item pledge."[19] The idea of a specific contract for which voters can hold you responsible was a trademark formula of the Indiana congressman. For political science believers in "responsible party government," he was a poster-boy dream.

When I returned to the district five months later, he was busy campaigning beneath the banner "Promises Made, Promises Kept." He was still focused on the freshmen class, collecting their poll numbers, and thinking expansively.

> It's important that we keep our presence in the party. Almost all the leaders of the class are going to come back. The idea I've been working on is to transform the class by joining with the sophomore class—because I believe the dividing line was 1992—then bringing in some of the incoming class and form a reform caucus within the Republican party. That group would have a lot of coherence— philosophically as the children of Ronald Reagan with a different view of what we are doing in Congress than the older generation—the view that we are only in Congress for a limited amount of time. . . . [So] we would spend more of our time thinking about philosophy and less time thinking about power of the older generation.

Later, as we watched the first Clinton-Dole presidential debate at home in his upstairs den, his distress over his party's "older generation" candidate was acute. He complained about Bob Dole's inability to "stay on message" and about Dole's "older generation consultants," whose lack of philosophical conviction and whose paramount interest in "who gets what" he held responsible for Dole's inconsistency. It seemed to me that his public policy background had led him to search for a covering political formulation to match his policy conservatism.

To make sense out of his preference for consistency and for success formulas, it will help to rehearse some personal background. David McIntosh's political ambition came very early.[20] But the thread that ties his early and later years together was an intellectual journey that gave his political ambitions a philosophical underpinning.

When writer Nina Easton set out to examine the triumph of Reagan-inspired political conservatism in America, she told her story through the careers of five conservative Republican activists. The one elected politician she chose to profile was David McIntosh. She interviewed widely among his family and lifetime friends. She noted his deep religious faith, and she explored his gradual intellectual conversion to free market conservatism. "He had a mind bent on logic and rational discourse," she wrote; "he liked his arguments orderly."[21] His aunt recalled that "he was the kind of boy who used to sit and read the encyclopedia."[22] All his life, he had thrived on debate—at the kitchen table, in his high school Bible Society, in various ideological and debate organizations in college. Finally, at the University of Chicago Law School, he found "a clean, cool rationalism" to underpin a public political philosophy. And there he organized the conservative "Federalist Society for Law and Public Policy."[23] That organization would become a prominent source of ideas for the conservative movement nationally. Easton's covering term for David McIntosh is simply "wonk." He was an intellectual force before he was a political force.

He embraced a free market, antiregulation, low-tax, limited-government economics and a religious-based social conservatism. But unlike many policy wonks, he had always wanted to be where the action was—in politics. He began his intellectual journey as a liberal Democrat and ended it as a conservative Republican. That journey generated his resume; it fueled and justified his leadership aspirations; it motivated his allegiance to the contract; it identified the partisan, philosophical "team" to which he became attached; it structured the way he thought. He came to the House of Representatives, therefore, with a fully formed and strongly held set of first principles—what he believed, why he believed it—and with ideas about how to turn his ideas into a new body of public policy. He was an intellectual before he was a politician.

"I knew the issues," he explained, "from my work with President Reagan and Vice President Quayle. And the Federalist Society—that was the third part of the triangle. I began with first principles and I worked out the practical policy implications from there." When I noted that the *New York Times* had described him as an "insistent revolutionary,"[24] he demurred. "I know they think of me as one of the strongest supporters of a conservative agenda; but from the beginning, I've been scrupulous about never using the word 'revolution.' I get bothered when [other freshmen] use it. If I had to think of a word to describe myself, the last word I would think of is 'revolutionary.' What I want to do is to return to the government that operated from the time of the founding fathers to the New Deal." Hand-in-hand with these tenaciously held conservative ideas about public policy came his strongly party-centered, team-centered ideas about implementation. And that is the basic way he presented himself to—and connected with—his constituents.

Strictly personal: My initial impressions of my Indiana traveling companion came from a town meeting, one of 13 he had announced for 1996. Two district staffers drove me in a large, brightly lettered "Congressman David McIntosh" mobile office van to pick up David and his wife, Ruthie, at their home—a spacious 1920s wooden house hugging a busy Muncie street. She remembered our initial Washington meeting; he didn't seem to. He said "hello"; I thanked him for "letting me come." We chatted briefly. Riding to the meeting, he talked on the phone with a reporter from the *Indianapolis Star*. Ruthie and I chatted a little. She accompanied us often during my first two visits. She was open, friendly, and knowledgeable. Much to my benefit, she frequently embroidered her husband's careful commentary.

His town meeting presentation to 20 or so constituents focused, lecture-like, with the help of four large charts, on the state of the economy and the benefits of tax cuts. He seemed very knowledgeable. Questions came from political supporters—including one former primary opponent—who spoke favorably about the congressman's support for the recent government shutdown. The meeting had a strong partisan tone. "I'm a Rush Limbaugh fan. He's great." "I'm NRA, let's face it." "Any one of the [Republican] candidates is better than Bill Clinton." *His* summary: "Conservative crowd, good meeting. They were favorable to me, but upset with the Republican Party. 'When are you guys going to get your act together and help us beat Bill Clinton?'" My earliest appraisal: "He was good and informed. He is soft spoken and patient and serious. Not a lot of laughs."

The next day, after watching him with the editorial boards and in business settings, I noted, similarly, that he "never loses his cool or raises his voice. [He] speaks in a very level, even-tempered, almost reassuring tone—nods his head appreciatively when he's listening or making a point."

At the end of my visit, I tried to summarize: "He does not look like a politician or act like a politician. He is not prepossessing. He is neat and ivy-leaguish, and quite self-depreciating. He does not seek the limelight. In the wood-paneled, gracious, old boy network of the Hudson Institute [a think tank where he had once worked], he was at home. As contrasted with the witty, quotable, loosey-goosey attitude of Andy Jacobs [a House Democrat from Indiana who preceded him at the podium], he came across as young, serious, eager to get started, and not good at small talk. He smiles very easily and very quickly, but he doesn't exactly make people laugh. He's quite proper. He *always* speaks of Dan Quayle as *Vice President Quayle* [never 'Dan' or 'Quayle']. Once I heard him say, 'that pissed me off.' He ended his talk with 'God bless you.'. . . The woman who showed me around the Tysons plant said, 'I voted for him. He doesn't talk down to you.' I think that's right. He assumes you have intelligence. And he has a lot. At Brooks Foods, there was his knowledge and inquiries. 'I like to learn how this machine works.' He is generally optimistic—always sees something 'that might help.' He is 'having fun,' he says. He is *not* jaded" (italics in original).

It might be thought that his philosophical certitude expressed itself in personal aggressiveness. It did not. In his personal relationships with others back home, he was soft-spoken, appreciative, and reassuring. He was neither arrogant nor impatient nor full of himself. A reporter who watched him in Washington concluded: "he acted as if he thought" he was a future Speaker of the House.[25] My constituency view, however, was the exact opposite. There wasn't a whiff of hubris in him.

Ruthie told an exemplary story. "On one of our first dates," she said,

David invited me to a banquet of the Federalist Society. I didn't have any idea of what it was. But when I walked in and saw 500 people there, I was very impressed. When I opened up the program, there on the first page was "Founder: David McIntosh." He had started the organization. Typical David, he had never said a word about it to me. He must have been very proud to have watched his organization grow. Others would have made a big thing of that accomplishment. But soft-spoken David McIntosh—he never toots his own horn.

That sounded exactly like the person I had just met.

With me, he was serious, open, upbeat, and helpful, but he was also restrained and impersonal. Before the town meeting, a staffer had said to me, "What David does best is answer questions." That remark proved prescient. Whatever I asked for, I got. Whatever I did not ask for, I did not get. So I needed to push, but in ways that matched his tone. And his tone was accommodating but reserved.

When I returned for my second visit seven months later, he neither recognized me nor knew who I was. My notes: "When David and Ruthie came into the [campaign] office for the first time, he glanced at me and kept going. Ruthie said 'Hi Dick.' Then, when he saw Ruthie and me hugging, he came around and said, 'How are you'—but he could not remember my name. 'How's it going,' I asked. 'Very well, on all levels,' he said and left. It was a little strained for me. I had to tell him that I wanted to travel with him. . . . Later on, he warmed up some as we talked in the car. . . . It was not a great start. The next day, however, was fine and as nice as the last trip."

To the very last, I was known by him, and introduced to others, as "the man who wrote a book about Dan Quayle"—never by name. He never did ask me about the book, and only once, to my recollection, did he solicit my opinion. All the initiatives were mine. Of course, the shortcomings may have been mine, too! He was unfailingly serious and nice. But to the end, I took care to maintain a personal distance that seemed comfortable for him.

Constituency: To find out what any representative is like, I have been arguing, it is necessary to know about his or her constituency and his or her relationship to it. For David McIntosh, it is important to recognize that *he had adopted a philosophy before he had adopted a home constituency.* He was neither born, nor raised, nor educated in the district he came to represent. He moved into the district as an adult with a fully formed, strongly held conservative socioeconomic philosophy, and with equally well-established religious convictions. He brought them *to* the constituency; he did not take them *from* the constituency.

When he moved from Washington to Muncie in 1992, he was a total stranger. "No one knew who we were," he said. He came, however, with political ambitions. "I knew that I wanted to get into politics, and when we got to Muncie I began asking people, 'Why are the Republicans having such difficulty beating [the Democratic incumbent] Phil Sharp?' People would say to me, 'You aren't thinking of running, are you? You don't have a chance.' My friend from the Quayle office, the Republican State Chairman, told me, 'You can't win. But if you want to do it, go ahead and get it out of your system.'"

He and his wife recalled a moment of truth. As the congressman told the story,

One of Sharp's strengths was his moderate voting record. But when Clinton became president, he was pressured to vote with him. He voted for the budget and the tax increase. It was a very unpopular vote. We went to his town meeting two days after that vote and we saw him face an angry crowd. Many of them were union members—his biggest supporters. The union leader spoke and said, "We understand you have to cast tough votes sometimes, and we appreciate all you've done for us." But people yelled, "We do not." The crowd booed and hissed. They would have none of it. When I watched their reaction, I smiled and looked at Ruthie.

Whereupon, Ruthie chimed in, "I saw him smiling and I said to myself, 'Oh, oh, he's running.'" Appropriately, the issue that propelled him into politics—cutting taxes in order to reduce the size of government—would remain his central policy objective throughout his career in Washington.

He decided to run, calling it a "couldn't lose" situation. "The best outcome," he said, "was that we could put it together and do it, and the worst outcome was that I would have gotten around so people would know me for the future." "Win, win," added Ruthie. Fortune intervened. First, 20-year incumbent Phil Sharp decided to retire; then, the front-running Republican challenger botched the filing of her nomination papers. The carpetbagger charge dominated his close (473 votes) primary campaign against a perennial loser who, McIntosh said, "was not in touch with the business community." In the 1994 general election campaign, the district's Republican leanings, in a good Republican year, were sufficient.

The makeup of the McIntosh district is not crucial to an understanding of the kind of representative he became. It is critical, however, to know that his intellectual attachments preceded his constituency attachments and dominated them. "I knew issues, but I did not know how to communicate with people," he said. "Once I started, I found out that I liked people." Compared with most other candidates with whom I have traveled, his sense of constituency seemed more learned than ingrained, more studied than spontaneous. He was *in* the constituency, but he was not *of* the constituency. His travel talk turned more naturally and more fully to the intellectual-political aspects of his work than to the feel, the backgrounds, the sensibilities of the people he represented in the place where they lived. Our travels provoked remarkably little storytelling or reminiscing to connect him to the people or to the place. He was no Joe Moakley.

Questions about his constituency, therefore, were the ones that, above all others, I had to push for to get an answer. Waiting for him to evoke or to capture the complexity of his home context would not work. He was certainly attentive to it—with all the conventional constituency service activities and with the most modern of political techniques. "We took some of Phil Sharp's ideas—the idea of the mobile office van." But the special attractions and attractiveness of the Indiana Third Congressional District and its people were not at the center of his political world. His policies were compatible with district sentiment. But policy came first, independently of district sentiment.

My questioning went like this. And sometimes I asked the same question on more than one occasion.

Question: "What is your district like?" Answer: "It's rural with a large auto parts industry. It's about 50-50 Republican and Democrat—slightly more Republican; but the Democrats are conservative. It's a small-town district. Muncie and Anderson are big small towns. Anderson is becoming more of a bedroom community for Indianapolis."

Question: "Is it an easy district for you to represent?" Answer: "For me, it is. Politically, it is split Republican and Democratic. But the Democrats are socially conservative. The Democrats have a strong base in the unions. But the working class in the district tends to be very church-oriented and religious. It makes it easy to represent them on religious issues." Answer: "I know I'm blessed. I have a district that agrees with my basic philosophy. I don't have to worry about getting out of step. If they do have a problem with something I do, I can explain it to them. Otherwise, they trust me to do the right thing."

Question: "Who are your strongest supporters?" Answer: "The Christian Coalition people, although they are not organized that way here. They are the people who live by faith. Then the NRA—their local director here would walk through fire for us. And then there is the Farm Bureau. They were the first. Those are the three." Answer: "My district is not split. People are socially conservative and fiscally conservative. They are conservative. My base is conservative. Period."

Question: "Is there an environmental movement of any kind in your district?" Answer: "No."

Question: "Is there an organized pro-choice group anywhere in your district?" Answer: "No."

Question: "What are your weak spots?" Answer: "The two main pockets in the district where I'm weak are [the town of Columbus] and Ball State [University]. Columbus is like a little New England town. They are uncomfortable with my social conservatism. . . . As for Ball State, they don't like me. They're just too liberal." Answer: "The only issue on which I'm out of step with the broad constituency view is free trade. Even here, the farmers recognize the need for trade. And so do some small businesses. I don't talk about it a lot."

Question: "What about the carpetbagger issue?" Answer: "I had not lived in the district. But I was raised in Kendallville [Indiana]. And it was just like the district. I knew the carpetbagger issue would come up. I listened to people and their reaction when it came up. It didn't bother them. . . . People could think of Kendallville as part of the district."[26]

For campaign purposes, he had formed his own electoral coalition, beginning with some like-minded young businesspeople and professionals. "The party people are not helpful," said a close adviser, "but you don't want to alienate them. For the most part, they aren't like us. They aren't even the kind of people you like to have in your organization. It's a good feeling when you bring into your organization people who are like you and want to work for you."

Only once did he spontaneously express a feeling of personal attachment. "After the last election, a sense of responsibility came over me," he said. "It's my district now. I became very protective of it. It surprised me because I hadn't thought of it that way during the campaign."

Constituency connections, October 1996: The lessons of my first visit centered around his Washington concerns. The second visit taught me more about his constituency connections. It came during his reelection campaign, and it featured appearances that were more contact and vote-driven than before: two parades, a football game, a chili festival, a Republican rally, and two candidate Q&A meetings, a frosty one with a Ball State gathering and a toasty one with a group of motorcyclists. I also joined the family in church.

Free Methodist Wesleyan Church (Anderson): When David asked, "Would you like to go to church with us tomorrow morning?" I said, "Yes

I would." He said, "We've been invited to go to church in Anderson. It won't be campaigning." In my notes, I wrote:

It *was* campaigning—of the most subtle sort. We got there early. . . . When we walked in, the woman who had invited him came over. She was introduced to me as "the Vice Chair for the Madison County Republican Committee." She told Ruthie how much she liked her TV [campaign] ad. Her husband was introduced [to me] too. Another woman came over to hand out programs. She said, "We've got all our yard signs and we'll be putting them up around the county." The husband and I talked a lot before and after the service—an eighth-grade teacher, very nice, well-informed, community-minded person. Before we went into the main body of the church, the parishioners had to walk near David and Ruthie—and if they wished, they would be introduced to him by the hostess. . . . The minister . . . mentioned David as a guest as soon as he began to speak, and urged everyone to get out and vote, because "it's a privilege."

When services were over, David took a long time getting out of the church, as everyone wanted to meet him. When we left, we stood on the front steps of the church with the hostess and her husband, and they talked politics. She had placed an ad about family values with pictures of the Republican ticket. They talked about plans for a Charlton Heston visit—the tent, the sound system, etc., the need for extra money "to put on a nice event." The husband said, "David, everyone I spoke to this morning said they would be praying for you." David said, "Thank you, that's the most important thing . . . ."

As politics, it was fascinating. These are his people, the core of his political strength. He told me that the woman had never been in politics before.

Abate Motorcycle Club: A meeting, in their clubhouse, with 35 members of a motorcycle club, Abate, was particularly illustrative of his constructive intellectual reach. He shared neither their garb, nor their skin decoration, nor their recreational experience, but he did share, intellectually, their visceral opposition to government regulation. As he answered their questions about personal liberties and government regulation, I sampled the "relentlessly constructive" tenor of his dialogue. "What I've been working on is . . . ." "One way we could deal with that problem is . . . ." "If we could do it this way, I think the situation would not be as hard as it is now . . . ." "I agree with you. What I'd like to see more of is . . . ." "I've been thinking that a better way might be . . . ." Their applause was loud and enthusiastic. He had met them before, and they were libertarian soulmates. On the way out, he smiled and said, uncharacteristically, "Do you think the people at the country club could imagine a meeting like we just had?"

In a concluding note, I reflected again that "the outstanding thing about him is how constructive he is when he talks policy. This was especially noticeable at the Abate meeting. To every complaint or question, his answer would demonstrate that he had thought about some constructive course. . . . He leaves the questioner with an idea about how a problem might be alleviated. There is no promise to solve problems, but only the implied promise to apply his intelligence to a constructive effort. In this way, he is future-oriented, working to make things better. His wonkish quality is constructive."

South Muncie High School Football Game: Saturday night, David and Ruthie shook hands at the gate as people went to a football game, and David was introduced at halftime. It was part of a calculated expansionist strategy in south side Muncie. He had already announced his candidacy there and had attended Catholic Church events there. Ruthie had participated in high school honors programs there. He described the area as "blue collar, working class, a stepchild ignored by the rest of the city." "There's a lot of Middletown left in Muncie," he added.[27] "There's a division between the north side where the affluent businesspeople live and the south side which is working class. . . . We are trying especially hard to expand our support in the working-class areas of Muncie and Anderson" (the two largest cities in the district).

Alexandria and Greenburg Parades: "In the [2-mile] parade, two guys carried a big Congressman David McIntosh banner, and [three staffers] walked behind throwing candy. David and Ruthie ran down the street, shaking hands on either side going onto lawns, porches, store steps, etc., wherever people were. I walked on the sidewalk beside them. They make it look like they like it—and as far as I can tell, they do. No complaints in the car afterward, no cynicism. Pretty open attitude. 'Small-town American parade,' says Ruthie. Says David, 'More and more I meet people at parades' who say, 'I saw you last year at the parade, or I met you some place.'"

"At the Greenburg parade, the entourage was the same except the candy came from a campaign car, and the huge McIntosh dog, 'Maddy,' walked in the parade. I volunteered to put on a McIntosh shirt and march the dog for a while. Once when I got too close to the campaign car, the dog lurched and the car rolled over my toes! No damage, just embarrassment on my part, apologies on the driver's part, and smiles all around. At the afternoon rally, I ran into the driver—and his wife. Driver: 'This is the guy I ran over this morning.' Fenno: 'Didn't hurt a bit.' Wife: 'Who was drunk, Joe, him or you?'"

Anderson: The Hi-Way Restaurant

[After church,] we went to the Hi-Way Restaurant—a classic little dumpy roadhouse. It was packed with a blue-collar crowd—so much so that we had to wait for a table for quite a while. David likes country music, so we spent our time quietly looking over the selections on the jukebox. He knew what was being played. . . . All the people who work there came by and spoke to him at one time or another. Several are collecting his autograph on their placemats. The waitresses came over to get updates, the cook came over, the bus girls did. And then they all gathered for pictures while the 75 or so people there waited for the restaurant to get operative again. I called it "the Hi-Way fan club."

Apparently, they eat there quite often. The workers were all women. And I think since David is a nice-looking, trim person, that the women may cotton to him a little. Ruthie did say at one point, "The women love David." He does not court this, however. He's too serious. For all of his intellectual inclinations, he seemed, in his words, "to like people" when—in cases like this—he touched the everyday lives of his constituents. I could imagine, therefore, that he would win political support on personal as well as philosophical grounds.

Several times in the course of my visit, he emphasized that while he lacked union support, he campaigned at factory gates, where individuals would come up to him and say, "I'm voting for you." His most concerted effort to win union favor, in the face of manufacturing job losses, was his sponsorship of a cooperatively organized and community-supported and well-publicized "job fair" in 1997. It was managed by his district staff and highly praised by all segments of the community. It carried his personal imprimatur, and the effort brought him public credit—warm applause at meetings and favorable editorials. Its success in the job market, however, was unclear.[28]

A comparison: In thinking about representational relationships from the viewpoint of the representative, the politician's perception of the constituency is crucial. It helps to make that point if we ask different people who have represented the same geographical district to describe it for us. In that spirit, I went to former Democratic Representative Philip Sharp[29] to see whether his perceptions of the district and of his constituency relationships might help hone my picture of Representative McIntosh. Before Congress, Sharp had been a political science professor at Ball State University—one of McIntosh's least supportive liberal enclaves. So far as I knew, the two had never met. And the only time David mentioned Sharp was to say that he had borrowed the idea of a mobile office van from him—which, of course, was a technique, not an idea. I talked with Sharp at the Kennedy School of Government in November 1995.

The first characteristics Sharp mentioned were the district's ethnic homogeneity and its religious diversity. "It has very few blacks . . . a few Hispanics . . . no ethnic mix. Ethnicity just doesn't register politically in the district. . . . What there is, is a lot of religious diversity . . . the most stupid mistake any politician could make in this district would be not to take religion seriously. To take it lightly . . . would be the height of stupidity in this district. You might get away with it in some urban districts, but not in this one."

His opening reference to ethnicity touched a subject McIntosh had never mentioned. It was a subject that came naturally to a Democrat. And in Sharp's case, it was meant to indicate that his district was not a typical northern Democratic district and that his constituents, therefore, might not be amenable to some dominant Democratic policy positions. Of special importance in that regard, he suggested, would be policies of special salience to religiously oriented constituents. For Sharp, the religious tone of the district carried strategic warnings and required, therefore, a respectful and cautionary approach. David McIntosh also highlighted the religious character of the constituency. But for him, it identified the hard core of his support and strength. He embraced, activated, and championed the religious groups of the districts. With the two men, very similar perceptions carried very different weights.

Not surprisingly, Sharp gave positive prominence to a different slice of constituents—its industrial workers. "You couldn't be in this district very long," he began, "without noticing the importance of the auto parts industry. It's the most important economic interest in the district—even though fewer people work in the industry than before. . . . One change in the district has been the coming of the Japanese. They have come and opened up a hundred or so small shops making auto parts. . . . They are changing the face of the auto industry here . . . a total change, a revolution in labor-management relations. And it has been all to the good. The Japanese have had a big effect." The district's industrial workers were the core of Sharp's political base. He gave top priority, therefore, to a constituency interest and a connection that McIntosh treated, at best, only in passing—and never as a group.

Phil Sharp's political support problem had been to hold the allegiance he garnered on workingman's issues while not alienating either the business community on economic issues or the conservative religious community on the issues of abortion (about which he held mixed views) and capital punishment, which he opposed.

To elaborate on his connections, Phil Sharp was a vintage "Watergate baby," a surprise Democratic victor in 1974, who had established himself in a traditionally Republican district. He succeeded in doing so, he believed, by fashioning strong and strictly *personal connections* to his constituents.

I always tried to be nonpolitical, to emphasize my small-town background. I did not come on as a politician with loud or strong positions. Wherever I went—in town meetings—I always listened to contending points of view. I always looked for common ground. That's why people liked to come hear me, I think. They knew I might not agree with them, but that I would listen to them and think about what they said. That was my strength in Congress, too. Maybe I was too passive; but I don't think so. I didn't come in and say, "We've got to have a deal now." I let things work themselves out. And [my role in] the '92 Energy Act was a good example of how successful it could be.

In presidential years, his victories were marginal; in off years, his vote was solid.

The district's Republican press, he elaborated, "never campaigned against me—either politically or personally. On the day before election, they would endorse my opponent. But they never came after me on any issue at any time. I attribute that to my dullness. I wanted to stay dull. I didn't want 'thumb up, knock it down.'" (Here, I noted, "he stuck his thumb up and pounded it down"—laughter.) "There's a hard, hard right wing in this district. They never supported me." But "the pragmatic businessmen—country club people—thought of me as 'possible.'. . . I always got some support from business. In the auto industry, I was usually supported by management and labor."

He invoked the idea of authenticity.

> Still, I worried—as politics got more intense—that I didn't have enough of a definition. I wondered whether or not I should not have more bite, more definition, get a little more harsh. But that's not me and I never went through with it. . . . I always knew who I was. [And] I think that is how I survived for so long. I know who I am— or I think I know.

Phil Sharp's enduring political strength, in short, was not ideological, but personal. And it was based, he thought, on personal trust. "It's a conservative district," he said, "in the sense that they are very slow to come to a decision. They want to listen for a while. They are slow to give trust. If you lose their trust, you'll never get it back."

When I traveled with David McIntosh, he was making his way with a different mix of constituency perceptions and connections—more philosophical, more issue-oriented, but less personal, less constituency grounded than his predecessor. And, I judged, with a stronger sense of constituency support as "given" than Sharp had. McIntosh worried less about trust than Sharp. There is, and was, no "one way or best way" to think about, or cultivate Indiana's Fourth District. Each representative saw it and did it "his" way. From all I could tell, however, only the type of Democratic tide that had once swept Phil Sharp "in" would ever sweep David McIntosh "out." And *my* subject would remain the distinctive "McIntosh way."

Washington judgments: Back in Washington, Congressman David McIntosh had concentrated on two initiatives in his first term. As subcommittee chairman, he shepherded legislation that would put a temporary freeze on all new federal regulations on business—"to get the government off our backs." It grew directly out of his work on Vice President Quayle's Competitive Council. He pushed his bill through the House, but it was killed in the Senate.[30] He worked with a colleague as cosponsor of the Istook-McIntosh bill, which was designed to limit the ability of nonprofit groups that received federal money from lobbying Congress. It was aimed at liberal public advocacy groups. Supporters described it as stopping "welfare for lobbyists"; opponents called it an effort to "defund the left." It, too, passed the House as a "rider" on a spending bill, but it, too, was dropped in negotiations with the less conservative Senate.

Citing these two legislative efforts at year's end, he was given a full-page, "Worth Watching" profile in *Congressional Quarterly*. McIntosh's "steely resolve to dismantle the federal regulatory structure," it said, "had made him a powerful and controversial figure in his first year on the job."[31] He was clearly a politician on the upswing.

At the close of the 104th Congress, when Washington observers evaluated its performance, McIntosh was given high marks for his early impact and for his future promise. *Roll Call* rated him as one of three "freshmen who've already been pegged with bright futures."[32] At least two journalist-observers said that if the freshman class were to vote for the member most likely to become speaker of the House, David McIntosh would win."[33] He was one of three first-termers whose names were presented by their classmates to Bob Dole for his consideration as vice presidential running mate.[34] After his 1996 reelection, he was one of two House members (the other was a nonfreshman) described by conservative intellectual David Brooks as an "emerging leader" of the party's conservatives.[35]

At home, in October, I heard Indiana's highly respected veteran Senator Dick Lugar introduce David at a large "farm fest" Republican rally as "a leader of the Republican revolution, a leader of the freshman class and a leader of the whole Republican group in Congress." It was hyperbole. Like the kudos from Washington, however, it reflected an unusual degree of respect, accomplishment, and promise.

THE LOCAL BOY AS PLAYER: LINDSEY GRAHAM, 1995–1996

Lindsey Graham's introductory *Roll Call* and *Congressional Quarterly* profiles revealed that he was 39 years old, a graduate of the University of South Carolina and of its law school; that he had seen military service as an Air Force prosecutor abroad; and that he had been elected to one term in the South Carolina House of Representatives. *Roll Call* described him as "soft spoken and self deprecatory," quoting him as saying, "I still hang out with the same crowd I grew up with and I enjoy being with people that I don't have to worry about what they think or what I say."[36] CQ began: "The first Republican to represent this district since 1877, Graham campaigned on a call for congressional reform and arrived in Washington still looking for ways to shake up the system. While the GOP was organizing as the majority party after the election, Graham suggested adopting term limits for the Speaker."[37]

In South Carolina in April 1995, Graham picked up where these early profiles had left me. Soon after we met, he mentioned his first splash.

I was the person who suggested term limits for the Speaker. We were sitting in the conference voting on term limits for committee chairmen and I said to the guy next to me, "Why shouldn't the speaker's terms be limited too?" He said he agreed with me, that I should speak up, but he didn't want to. People were thinking that it was intellectually inconsistent to give the speaker an unlimited term, but no one wanted to say it out loud. The next day, at a Heritage Foundation seminar, I mentioned it to several people. All of them agreed with me, but no one wanted to speak up. A reporter heard me talking and came up to me and said, "Are you in favor of term limits for the Speaker?" I said that I wasn't pushing it, but that "yes," I did believe that if we were intellectually consistent, the speaker's term should be limited, too. The next day my comment appeared in *Roll Call*. And the next day, Newt announced that he was in favor of term limits for the speaker—eight years, like the President. He got out ahead of the train; I'll give him credit for that. He never spoke to me about it and to this day, we have not had one word about it. It's a good example of the difference between Newt's view of Congress and mine. He has a vision that looks outward, but he doesn't look inside the institution.

Later that day, shopping in Kmart for a new TV, he turned to whimsy. "I like TV; Newt likes books; that's the difference between Newt and me." From our earliest acquaintance, Graham came across as a feisty and independent spirit, sending off signals very different from those of his sober, freshmen class–oriented colleague.

Graham's activity within the freshmen class furthered that impression. "I took the lead," he said,

in trying to get the freshmen and the sophomores to join us in voting for the Democrats' retroactive term limits amendment. I gave a speech to the freshmen class saying that we should call their bluff and vote for their bill—that if we lost, we would have exposed their hypocrisy and that if we won, we would have a term limits law on the books. Newt Gingrich popped into our meeting right after that and said what a bad idea it was. I got 34 freshmen to go with me— almost half of the class. That's pretty good. I said if you're for term limits, you ought to be for all term limits.

Then, echoing a McIntosh distinction, he concluded, "The old guys didn't like making it retroactive. It proved to me the old guys were not really in favor of term limits—and Newt wasn't either." It was an old versus new thing. He enthused often about term limits as "the most important idea of the contract." In contrast to McIntosh, his early enthusiasms centered more on the reform of governmental processes than on specific policies.[38]

On opening day, he was one of a handful of newcomers to venture a one-minute floor statement, saying, "If you want to out-reform me, I challenge you to do so."[39] "I felt the pressure to get off to a good start," he explained. "I went almost immediately from raising my hand to take the oath of office, to a major fight over the three-fifths provision for raising taxes—in the balanced budget amendment.[40] I campaigned on it; I believed in it. I got really upset when the leadership dropped it." "Newt gave in to pressure," he explained. "He wanted to get a bill. I didn't care. I wanted to force people to stand up and be counted. That's why I went into politics. That's what makes me different from Newt." From his first day in the House, Lindsey Graham wanted to be a "player."

He was plunging in and drawing lines of division as he charted his course. He could not be understood, as the Washington press would have it, as a Gingrich "robot" or "foot soldier." He had openly challenged the party leadership and split the freshmen class—a far more individualistic and far less team-oriented pattern of thought and action than that of his Indiana colleague. And he had entered into a vastly different relationship with Speaker Gingrich. David McIntosh's first decision was to join the leadership. Lindsey Graham's first decision was to challenge the leadership. They were not clones.

Predictably, Graham received none of the early preferment accorded his colleague. "Did you get the committee you wanted?" I asked him. "No," he said, "I wanted Commerce because of my interest in the Savannah River [nuclear power] Project. It didn't work out. I got Science, which has some oversight. And Economic and Education Opportunities has worked out well for me. . . . The way Newt runs the House, committees don't mean as much as they once did. It's government by task force." So I asked, "Are you on any of the task forces?" "No. I may be put on Air Power [task force]. I think Newt likes me. But I have been something of an unruly child." Whereupon he reeled off four amendment votes in which he had already opposed the party leadership.

No one could be found touting Lindsey Graham as a future "player" inside the House. *Roll Call*'s early "report card" on the freshmen, which described McIntosh as "a conservative policy wonk . . . favored by the GOP leadership," said of Graham only that "he has gained a reputation as something of a freshman class comic."[41] In a companion scouting report on the "GOP's Next Generation of Leaders," *Roll Call* listed 13 freshmen. McIntosh was a top-three choice. Graham was not mentioned.[42]

The self-styled "unruly child" and "rowdy child" had never been anyone's protégé. He had not come to the job with an outstanding resume or influential references. His name never appears in Nina Easton's study of influential conservatives. He was not the product of any distinguishing intellectual movement. He had no visible mentor. He had no history as a team player within any political organization. In the South Carolina legislature, he had described his behavior as "rambunctious." Lindsey Graham had never been an "insider" of any kind. He had always been very much on his own—and very much his own man. When I met him, he was at the *beginning* of an uncertain political career, in sharp contrast to David McIntosh, whose career seemed to be *continuing* on a predictable upward trajectory.

Strictly personal: Throughout my first home visit, Graham greeted everyone he met: "Hey, I'm Lindsey Graham. I'm your new congressman." He could hardly contain his enthusiasm. "I have the overpowering desire to go into every home in the district to thank people for their support, and ask them if I can do anything to help them." He seemed happy, even eager, to talk with me about himself and his experiences. The very first sentences of my notes read: "He was the most talkative congressman I have ever met. He seemed eager to please and anxious to know how I felt about everything." It was as if recalling his experiences and his reactions would help him make sense out of who he was, what he was doing, and why he was doing it—both in Congress and at home. He had gone into politics to make a contribution, he had started from scratch, he had been making it up as he went along, and it seemed natural to rehearse his experience with the "book writer" from out of town.[43] His exuberance contrasted markedly with the reserve of his colleague. Our relationship involved more give-and-take than the one with McIntosh. One was as inquisitive as the other was self-contained. Because I came to Graham under the auspices of the political scientist who had managed his election campaign, he may have credited me with having useful political knowledge. Try as I might to remain quiet and observe, he often pumped me for my reactions. Whereas McIntosh would leave me to go elsewhere to meet with his political advisers, Graham often arranged lunch or dinner so I could meet *with* his political advisers. He told the local newspaper about my presence; thus generating a headline in the *Greenville News,* "Political Scientist Studying Graham."[44]

He was personally solicitous in numerous ways: sometimes sending staff to meet my plane, calling to make sure I got in safely, or picking me up in the morning to start the day together. When we toured MCI, the posters welcoming "Congressman Lindsey Graham" also welcomed "Author, Dr. Richard Fenno." He invariably greeted me with, "Hey Doc, have I been busy since you were here. I've got a lot to tell you." I did not have to push. He never stopped quizzing me. It was some comfort that our relationship never evolved to include the correct pronunciation of my name (I was always "Dr. Feeno"). Still, I had to work extra hard to keep an arm's-length distance and a scholarly perspective. And I was not always successful.

After three months on the job, Graham knew that he liked it. His reform enthusiasms were bringing favorable reaction back home.[45] "If you have the slightest interest in politics," he told a reporter from the *Anderson Mail,* "if you ever wanted to be involved and see the fruits of your labor, the experience would make you happy. In a sea of clams, I am the happiest clam." But he hardly ever "clammed up"!

My earliest and strongest impressions centered on Lindsey Graham's attraction to political combat. The impression became even stronger when contrasted to McIntosh's concern for team unity. In Graham's case, some-thing instinctive and ingrained—a moth-to-the-flame syndrome—seemed to be at work. When a reporter asked him, "What were you like growing up?" he answered, "If I thought you wanted me to go left, I'd go right; if I thought you wanted me to go right, I'd go left. I loved getting arguments started. I would argue with a sign post." "I loved law school," he said later. "I loved debating the professors. I was doing what I had always done. I had been a lawyer since sixth grade and didn't know it."

"People admire a fighter," he said, "and they don't mind it when I'm feisty because they know it isn't personal." "I've always been a fighter. I'm a short guy. People like it when a little guy gets in and fights for his position. Besides, I like a good fight. When I see an argument starting, I want to run over and get in on it. After all, you've got to have a little fun. Politics let you inject these quirks of personality into the process." I took it as more than a quirk—as a preference and a pattern. A year later, when some colleagues asked him to run for class president, he declined. "Who wants to be class president? You just call meetings. I want to be out front when there's an issue—partly because of the issue, but partly, too [smile], because I'm attracted to a fight." As much as David McIntosh seemed born to theorize, Lindsey Graham seemed born to do battle.[46]

Graham certainly acknowledged the reality of the freshmen class. "We have the same agenda. You could take my campaign literature and put an overlay on it for anyone in the class. There is a lot of camaraderie and spirit." Like McIntosh, he divided Republicans into new and old generation—and was highly critical of the latter. But he tended to focus on ways he was different from other "new guys." "I'm more traditional than most of my class. I served in the legislature. Half of them, 40 percent, never held elective office. . . . I served one term in the state legislature, but I'm not a sophisticated politician." "I'm more practical . . . [and] not as ideological as most of them. I'm a swing person, because I get along with all groups in the class." When I asked why his colleagues wanted him to run for class office, he answered, "Because politics is a personal business, and they like me." He articulated no team concept. And he did not think of himself as a member of any "team."

In making room for the personal side of politics, he also allowed himself room to maneuver—while maintaining a strong conservative posture. He was a strong conservative, and he favored very conservative social policies—but not for doctrinal reasons. Unlike McIntosh, he was not constrained by party status or by conservatism as ideology. You could sense this difference in his (unsolicited) 1996 reviews of his colleague: "He's a very intense person, very ideological. He believes strongly in what he believes. He's a good guy. He's very smart. . . . He has a bright future in the House. I have no interest in moving up in the House." To Graham, election meant access to a playing field where "the fun thing is to affect public policy." Thus positioned, he could—and he would—thrive on legislative combat, legislative maneuver, and political risk taking in general. He could, in a word, become a player.

It will be helpful in understanding Lindsey Graham's affinity for combat and risk taking if we rehearse some of his personal background. As much as David McIntosh's view of politics tended to be intellectual and formulaic, Lindsey Graham's view of politics tended to be experiential and personal. As much as one leaned toward a macro-view of politics, the other leaned toward a micro-view. For McIntosh, his prepolitical intellectual journey proved particularly helpful in explaining his outlook and behavior. With Graham, it is his unfolding success story that is most helpful. At first encounter, McIntosh presented a more finished picture of himself as a politician, and Graham came across as very much a political work-in-progress.

"I'm what America is all about," he said when we met. "Neither my father nor my mother graduated from high school. I'm the first person in my family on either side to go to college. I think that's why I'm so much in awe of the job I have. You think about these things, but you never think it will happen to you. Then one day you wake up and it did." Driving past Anderson College, he said that he was going to be their commencement speaker. "Can you imagine my giving a commencement speech? Nobody ever cared what I said. Now they want to hear my message. The transition from Lindsey Graham to Congressman Lindsey Graham makes all the difference." "I take myself a little more seriously now than I used to. The role of congressman has had that effect. I'm still Lindsey, and I hope I will grow into the role." "He may be a little surprised at where he is," I noted. I would never have made that comment about David McIntosh.

Unlike David McIntosh, whose mother was a local judge, Lindsey Graham came from a working-class family environment. His family ran a bar and restaurant (some called it "a beer joint")—catering to the textile mill workers of his hometown of Central. Most of them were white, and many of them lived next door in a company-owned development, Central Mills Village, where "the houses, substandard and segregated . . . in rings around the mill, rented for four dollars a month." "My parents worked 18 hours a day," he said. "We lived in one room in the back of the restaurant—the Sanitary Restaurant. We sold food and beer. . . . I stocked shelves and waited tables. . . . I can remember the shift changes at 3 o'clock when mill workers would come in all covered with lint and cotton, some with fingers missing. . . . We were a close family. It was a successful small business, and they made a pretty good living."

By the time he was 22, both parents were dead, and their medical bills had eaten up their savings. An aunt took Lindsey and his younger sister to live with her. Lindsey became the legal guardian for his sister and helped put her through college. And he spent his entire military service "paying on my parents' horrendous medical bills."

"I was in the bottom half of my class in high school," he recalled, "involved in sports and having a ton of fun." Yet high school "shaped my life," he said, "because I was around people who expected to go to college. Your friends mold you. They changed my outlook. I have always been my best critic. [So] I pushed myself. I was very self-motivated." When he could not get into law school on his first try, he took a summer school course, passed, and was admitted. He summed up, "I had a supportive family and great friends, and they brought out the best in me. I've exceeded many expectations, including my own. . . . I have a good mind. I'm not the most talented person in the room, but I try hard. You don't have to be the most talented to succeed, but you do have to want it the most." "I think his constant questioning of me is not because he's suspicious," I noted, "but because he wants to learn . . . there is a strong self-improvement strain in Lindsey." Nothing had ever been handed to him. He came to the House as a battler, because he had been a battler all his life.

And a bit of a gambler, too. Why, I asked him, did someone raised as a Democrat become a Republican? "I placed my bets," he answered.

I had never been to a Republican meeting of any kind. I had always been conservative, I wanted to go into politics, and I asked myself what I would feel comfortable doing and where was the country going in the future. I looked at it like a business. It was a gamble. It would be hard to win as a Republican, but if I did, I would be in the best possible shape for the future. It didn't take a rocket scientist to see what direction the country was moving in. It was a risk, but not a huge risk since the Republican Party was the party of the future. Any young person who wants to go into politics in the South today will be a Republican.

The philosophically minded David McIntosh became a Republican by intellectual conversion. Lindsey Graham became a Republican by personal calculation.

The participation-minded Graham's good fortune was Democratic incumbent Butler Derrick's decision to retire. "I had already announced a run for the State Senate," said Graham.

> [But] when Derrick announced, it took me 48 hours to decide to run, instead, for his seat. My friends all told me not to run. "You haven't had enough experience," they told me, "wait, run for the State Senate and move up later." Two state senators with 10 or 12 years of experience had already been thinking of running (for Congress). . . . It's hard when your supporters tell you that it is not the right time. . . . I believe there is no right time. They had the old, farm-team theory. That theory is gone. I saw it as my opportunity, that it would not come around again, that this was Lindsey Graham's time, and I went for it.

In the manner (but not the context) of a storied local politician, "he seen his opportunities and he took 'em."[47]

For Graham, "local" is the right word. He is, in every sense—and unlike David McIntosh—the child of his constituency. For him, *place* is, indeed, key to biography and to politics. In recounting his electoral success, he emphasized the importance of his local connections. The feature event of his first congressional race was a rally in his hometown. "We had the biggest rally ever seen in the district—500 people," he said. "And getting people to come to that rally was my campaign." The rally organizer, who had known him since boyhood, recalled its local impact.

> In high school, there was not the slightest indication of what was to come. He was just one of the boys. No one thought he would go anywhere special. When I tried to get people to come to the rally and I said, "Lindsey's running for Congress," the reaction was, "Oh, isn't that cute." Everyone was surprised, and no one took it seriously. Then he got up, and they saw all that intelligence. People were amazed. The reaction was: "Lindsey Graham? Where in the world did *that* come from?"

It was not the last time the question would be asked.

When he explained his 52 percent congressional primary victory, he again emphasized his personal connections. "The person who has a base, wins the primary. My home county gave me a 6000-vote margin (80 percent) in the primary because they knew me. A lot of it was word of mouth. People who knew me called their relatives in other parts of the district. It was personal. In the general [election], I carried every precinct in my home county. I do best where people know me, where I grew up. My family left me a good name. They were well thought of."

His core support in the general election was broader, but still dominantly personal. "We blanketed the district with volunteers." "I carried every precinct in my home county." "My base is the people I've met . . . family and friends in the business community, working families, conservative groups, the NRA. It all goes back to the personal thing." As much as a member of Congress can be, Lindsey Graham was the local boy who made good.

He liked to picture himself as "just Lindsey." He told a local reporter, "The only way I know is to be nice to everybody and not over promise—just be Lindsey. . . . Being nice, approachable, and honest is a good way to be anything—friend, spouse, parent, or congressman. . . . If you act that way outside politics, you can bring it into politics. The people I hang around with, go to dinner with, are the people I'm like." This newspaper interview was headlined in the two major local papers: "I'm Still Lindsey" and "Graham Still Sees Himself as Hometown Guy."[48] They were vastly different from the early hometown headlines touting the power and promise of David McIntosh. When we shook hands at the end of my first visit, he said, "I've just been Lindsey."

In sharp contrast to David McIntosh, Graham's early travel talk centered on his idea that politics is personal and that representation, therefore, centers on personal connections at home. "To me, the best part of the job by far is what you can do to help people. And when you help them, they will be with you for life." Or "What I like best about the job is getting out in the community and meeting with people. I think I have a talent for letting people know I care, that I've thought about what I say, that I'm sincere and honest. It gives you a good feeling when you meet people, talk to them and feel a part of the community." During our MCI visit, a young woman questioned him about Medicare. "My numbers meant nothing to her," he said afterward. "What she wants to know is whether I'm the kind of person who will hurt her grandmother. For people in the South, politics is personal. If they like you, and they think you are trying hard, they will vote for you."

He seemed to enjoy—as well as value—his connections with the people of the district. After two plant tours: "This is what I like most about the job—seeing the people of the district at work, learning about how they make their living. Everything we do, in education, in the work place, is to get people into the economy. I like to watch that, and I like to go to festivals to meet the people of the district that way." To a small dinner group of businessmen, "My job is to represent the values of the people of my district—nothing more, nothing less. I think I do that well. I was born and brought up here. I've lived my entire life here and I think I know how people feel and what they want. If I'm wrong, they can fire me."

"There's a split," he said later,

> that's always there among politicians—between those who want to find out where the public is so they can go there and those who want to move the public from where they are to where they ought to be. If you take ten politicians, seven of them will lack the self-confidence or the aggressiveness to move the public. They will give the public what they want and do it responsibly. The other three will try to move the public. Newt is one of those three. Some of those three will grab you by the neck and pull you along. Some others are people that the public will listen to and say to themselves, "I like that guy. I think he's right and I trust him." You can't get away from it. Politics is a people business.

Clearly, he put himself in the last category.

"It is important to Lindsey that people like him," I noted. "And, feisty and stubborn and determined as he is, there is that desire to be liked . . . and to be *trusted* [italics in original]. He speaks of trust a lot. He uses it repeatedly in talking about Medicare." "After the senior citizens have heard me explain what the situation is and what we tried to do to save it, they trust me." In talking to one group about Medicare, he relied heavily on his personal background. "First person in my family to go to college, father worked in cotton mills, mother and father ran a small business, parents dependent on Social Security and Medicare. I know where you're at. My life has been as close to yours as is possible for people in my generation. I am not you, but I know what the system has done to you."

As kickoff speaker at an urban development conference in Anderson, the district's largest city, the new congressman told his unfamiliar, skeptical, and racially mixed (50-50) audience that, "The Community Development Block Grant to me is the way to go." And to buttress his credibility, he made a personal connection, saying,

We'll do things differently; that doesn't mean we don't care. I can assure you that I care. I'm the first person in my family to go to college. Neither of my parents graduated high school. I was born and raised in Central, South Carolina. I'm not a country club Republican. My mom and dad died when I was 22 years old and I had a 12-year-old sister. She went to college on a Pell Grant. It helped me to help her. . . . That's what it takes to get by sometimes—all the help. I just wanted the government to help me when I needed them . . . and they were there. But the system we have now spends too much money, too inefficiently.

He often invoked his life story as a warrant of his connectedness and his trustworthiness—something David McIntosh did not do.

Lindsey Graham was more emotionally embedded in his constituency and more a product of his constituency than David McIntosh ever was. Graham's constituency immersion produced a torrent of commentary during our travels—in the sharpest possible contrast to my experience in Indiana. As naturally as his colleague discoursed on the mission of the freshmen class in Washington, Graham spoke about the makeup of his constituency. I did not have to pry that perspective out of him. He had lived it, and it was in his bones. It was all about place. And in sharp contrast to his Indiana colleague, he loved talking about it.

"It's not a typical Republican district income level. It's a typical Southern conservative district." "It's rural; it has a low average income, and pockets of prosperity; energy issues are very important; and basic employment is in manufacturing; environmental issues are important because there's so much water. It's hard to describe the district. It's very diverse. God, country, and guns, I guess. But you can't represent the district well without understanding the SRS [Savannah River Site] and nuclear energy generally." Or "It's not like a compact suburban district. . . . At the southern end of the district is one of the most advanced nuclear power facilities in the world. At the northern end is one of the most sophisticated water treatment plants in the country. In between, it's 160 miles of pickup trucks and guns." During his campaign, Lindsey had described Anderson County (his largest) as "the most God-fearing, gun-toting, in-your-face county in the state." "We worried about the local reaction," said a staffer. "But they said, 'Yeah, that's us all right!'"

In that vein, his travel talk produced memorable snapshots. "A good friend of mine wants me to keep the ban on assault weapons. There's no way I can help him on that. This is a gun district. Everyone in the district has a gun. Even children have guns—to make it a fair fight." On Sunday blue laws, "I'm with the Baptists. Whatever the Baptists want, I want. There are more Baptists in this district than any other group." "If I had my choice of one person to come into this district to campaign for me, it would be [legendary auto racer] Richard Petty. Isn't democracy great." Eight years later, political pundits began talking about "NASCAR Dads" as election targets.[49] Graham had them in his sights from the beginning.

On my first day with him, we drove past a huge flea market, and it moved him to elaborate on the politics of his district. "That's a big event every Wednesday. . . . It's a great place to shop and a great place to campaign. They are good people, many of them work in the mills. They may make nine dollars an hour. Nine dollars an hour is a good wage in this district. You wouldn't think that kind of a district would set up very well for a Republican. It's probably a good thing that I'm the kind of Republican I am—a personable one. I'm not a country club Republican. Many of those folks at the market have the same core beliefs as the Republicans, but there is a social barrier that keeps them from being Republicans. I can break down that barrier. And when you do, the dam will break. Democratic support will just collapse in no time. That's what happened in Anderson County where I won by 65 percent."

The exemplary story of his election campaign went like this. "I spoke to the Rotary Club one day at noon and I couldn't get any response— couldn't get a laugh, nothing. In the afternoon I went to a mill. The manager took me to meet the workers out back. One guy says, 'What party are you?' I said, 'Republican.' The guy broke into a big smile and said, 'No more Democrats, no more damn Democrats.' The others—all poor, white mill workers—started slapping me on the back. That's when I knew we were going to win."

His electoral accomplishment was to forge a coalition between well-to-do and working-class white voters. In a district with a bloody history of management-worker conflict in its textile industry,[50] his electoral coalition reflected large changes. Driving along, he pointed out residential manifestations. "Over there is the new housing development I was telling you about. Those people are moving in from out of town and they all vote Republican. But these [older, smaller] modest homes you see right along here and the trailers—these people are also voting Republican now. And that's the big change. They don't like what they see going on in society and in the government. The income levels between these groups are different, but the values are the same." "They share the same values—getting the government out of my life. If you're business, it's economic. If you're social, you are against homosexual rights and abortion. They are the congressman's values, too."

In social matters such as abortion, gun control, sexual preference, and treatment of the flag, McIntosh and Graham were equally strong conservatives. For McIntosh, this social conservatism seemed grounded in personal philosophy and religious beliefs. Graham's social conservatism, on the other hand, seemed derived from the white, middle-, and working-class constituency he had described when he discovered racial segregation and homosexual rights. On matters of social policy, he looked to prevailing community values, opinions, and standards for guidance. Place was crucial in large part because that is where his social conservatism came from.

Speaking of his family's restaurant, he said, "It was a bar where blacks came in, bought beer, and took it out with them. I used to think, 'Why is it that way?' We knew it shouldn't have been that way. . . . Later on, everyone could come in and sit. . . . It's hard to determine good and bad sometimes. My parents accepted the situation. But they were not evil people. It wasn't right and it wasn't fair, but it didn't seem like evil when you lived it every day." Whatever constituent views on these matters might be, he absorbed them, and he reflected them. In my notes, I wrote, "I was struck when he handled the race question . . . by how inarticulate he seemed and how unsettled and unformed his formulations seemed to be."

Only twice during my days with him did he mention black voters. Driving through a black neighborhood during my first visit, he said, "I went into that store there once during the campaign. Some Republicans say there's no use campaigning among blacks. I disagree. I talked in some black churches. And I'm going to try to get some middle-class blacks involved. In the past, I have gotten 15 to 20 percent of the black vote, which is just as much as Strom Thurmond gets. The way politics is moving now, it's going to be the white party against the black party. And that's bad." I noted, "He's riding the main tide and isn't about to put that in jeopardy."

On the road two years later, he commented, "I do better with blacks than most Southern Republicans because I have the kind of district where you can make a lot of friends through personal contacts. I go to black churches. And when I talk about reforming the welfare system, I get Amens as loud as anywhere else. The average support is about 10 percent for most Southerners. I get 15 percent. That's pretty good. We're becoming a black party and a white party in the South and that's bad." Nothing had changed in the two years between touches. He did give two articulate, "tough love" speeches—one each year—to the racially mixed urban development group in Anderson. But neither one triggered a discussion of race relations afterward. He was content to go with his constituency flow.

In matters of sexual preference, too, he reflected prevailing constituency views. But on this question, he had taken a lead. His one state legislative success was his bill to bar homosexuals from serving in the South Carolina National Guard.

He explained to a local reporter, "In the military, you need cohesion; and a display of the homosexual lifestyle in the barracks would lower morale. When Bill Clinton tried to introduce that lifestyle into the military and legitimize it, it bothered people. And I was doing my job representing my people. In my part of the country, people don't knock your door down to see what you're doing. But they do feel uncomfortable when you push it on them. . . . I spoke out on it and my bill passed 90-20. I pat myself on the back. I had the guts to go out and say what other people wanted to say, but didn't. President Clinton felt it was something he had to do. I did what I had to do. I responded to what Bill Clinton did." In social policy matters, he was easy with accepting constituency standards and not about to support or entertain any personal or maverick points of view. As he put it to one group, "I want my voting to be like y'all."

For political purposes, Graham was content to encapsulate his social conservatism in his anti-Clinton rhetoric. "By far, the biggest factor in my [first] election was Bill Clinton," he said. "People here were against almost everything he did. My opponent tried to run away from Clinton, but he couldn't. When I first heard about 'The Contract,' I was reluctant. I was not real enthusiastic. I was happy running against Bill Clinton." "You could shoot Bill Clinton out of a cannon and he could spread $100 bills all over South Carolina and he'd never carry the state." At the end of his first term, he claimed proudly: "My constituents know I'm not Clinton."

With respect to his social conservatism, however, he never once mentioned the Christian Coalition. Because David McIntosh had given topmost rank to his Christian Coalition–type supporters, I asked Graham about that. And his answer pointed up his more personal, less philosophical connections. "I agree with them on a lot of things. And I listen to them. But I am not one of them," he said. "And I do not need their support. They did not support me in the primary. I beat them. I'm not a 'Coalition' candidate." To which his campaign manager added, "After they lost [the primary], their leader came over to us and started to tell us what they wanted Lindsey to support. I told him not to bother talking to Lindsey, that Lindsey knows what he thinks about all those matters. 'You should go home and decide whether you want to support him or not.'" It was a vastly more tentative relationship than that which McIntosh had with the same group of people. And it allowed Graham maneuvering room as a freewheeling, unencumbered player inside the House.

The greatest source of constituency worry for Graham was the federally operated Savannah River Site (SRS) nuclear facility, which was in the process of being downsized (from 25,000 to 16,000 employees). To my very first "how's it going" question when we met, he exclaimed, "First 100 days and 2,400 people laid off by the biggest single employer in my district. It's a monumental job." "It's an easy district to represent," he said later, "except for the Savannah River Site. I've worried myself sick trying to reconcile its problems with the kind of [antigovernment] congressman I want to be. How many other congressmen have been faced with the loss of 9,000 jobs? I've tried to tell them the truth—that the site has an important and honored role to play in our nation's security, but that 25,000 employees is not viable. I told them that 15,000 to 16,000 is more like it." "Here I am, a congressman from a rural district spending 60 percent of my time thinking about nuclear energy, tritium production and the reprocessing of nuclear waste." "I spend 50 percent of my [committee] time on Savannah River. I go wherever the subject leads me." His conservatism carried him toward smaller government; but SRS pulled in a different direction.

Politically, SRS meant the town and the county of Aiken, as distinctive a place as the facility itself. He campaigned one afternoon in and out of the stores in Aiken on a broad street with a grassy median. And he drove me around the town, "a lovely Southern town, big trees, big homes." "The people in this part of the district are very different from the rest," he said. "The average yearly salary in the district is $13,000. At Savannah River, it's about $40,000. They are better educated and have higher paying jobs. Sixty percent of them were not born in South Carolina. The good news is that they vote Republican. Which is a good thing since they make up 25 percent of the voting population." David McIntosh had no such conflicted configurations. For him, one overarching conservative philosophy seemed to fit all.

Aside from the constituency's dominant conservatism on social issues, therefore, Graham did enjoy considerable maneuvering room in promoting his district's interests. Speaking of the district's economy, he elaborated: "The district is rural to live in, but the economy is not rural. The economy is 'the country.' Textile mills are closing, and Michelin, BMW, and Fuji are coming in." "I'm going to Japan to visit Fuji next year. My rule is: 'you bring one billion dollars into my district, I go to your country.'" "This is an exciting district—some businesses leaving, more businesses coming in. It's a business-friendly district, a quality-of-life district, where money goes a lot further than elsewhere. My job is to get the district ready for the future. That's why I'm so interested in infrastructure." "Some people say a congressman should stay out of local politics. I think that's wrong. If you can help to get people together on a problem and get things moving, you should. Otherwise, nothing may get done."

His victory and his constituency, he believed, had given him the freedom to run reform missions in Washington. "We didn't win the election," he began, "they lost it [because] people got fed up with Bill Clinton–type politics as demonstrated by the northeastern Democrats. A new type of representation has become popular. I am against this, I am for this. . . . I established a new standard of politics for this district. That makes it possible for me to pass along something different to the next generation of politicians. I feel a lot of pressure to do that . . . ." "I believe that showing a hard edge on political reform is good politics, that it is just as popular as the old formula." Working off his strong constituency base, Graham would, indeed, run numerous political reform missions—campaign finance reform, for example—in the House.[51]

At home, Graham leveraged his pioneer's prominence to grow his party in the district, by encouraging Republicans to run and by persuading Democrats to switch. Early on, it was a frequent topic of his travel talk.

> For two full days after the [1994] election, I was on the phone persuading Democratic officeholders to change to Republican. Of the six state representatives from Anderson County, all but one were Democrats in 1994. Two became Republicans, three retired, and in 1996 all six will be Republicans—I spent a lot of time with the state senator from Anderson telling him now is the time to do it. Two years from now will be too late. He switched. . . . (So did the senator from Oconee County.) The sheriff of Pickens County became a Republican. (As did the sheriffs of Oconee and Anderson.) It's amazing; and it's not going back to what it was.

"I'm trying to create a farm system among Republicans. I watch every legislative race and every county council race to see who is coming along, and I try to energize people everywhere I go. I want that to be my legacy, a strong Republican party." "I try to talk to as many groups as I can, groups that Republicans don't normally talk to. I want to enlarge the party."

His long-run musings were not just about the party. They were also about himself. Unlike his Indiana colleague, Graham mused openly about his career during my earliest visits. "I'm not sure what will happen to me. I know that eventually you get co-opted by any institution you belong to." "I don't care whether or not I become a committee chairman." "I have no interest in moving up in the House." "This is such a hard job that I imagine people will want to change after 12 years. But that is such a long way off and how do I know. Right now, I'm trying to be a politician and get reelected. I don't have time to think ahead . . . with term limits I think what we'll see is politicians moving from job to job."

"I don't think you'll find many people going back where they were. I'm 39, and that's about the average of my class. After 12 years, we'll still be in the prime of life. What will we do? Won't we have been away too long to pick up where we left off? Will we go into lobbying or some private interest group? That's not much to look forward to." "I tell people that if I want to stay in politics, I'll run for the Senate or come back home and run for county council."

> I'm creating a farm team of my own in the district. If I ever want to run for another office, I will have a team in place. . . . I was down in Columbia [the state capital] yesterday, talking to some of my buddies, keeping up old ties. You have to do that if you are going to run statewide. You need an organization in place. . . . I think eight years in Congress might be about right. . . . In 1998, the governor's two terms will be up. If I wanted to go that route . . . and I'm thinking of it—I'd have to have an organization in place.

If ever there were other opportunities, he would most likely continue to "see 'em and take 'em." In the meantime, he was primed to remain a player inside the House of Representatives.

Postscript: Representative Graham's predecessor, Butler Derrick, was (like Representative McIntosh's predecessor) a 1974 "Watergate baby" who retired voluntarily after 20 years. To help sharpen my picture of Graham, I went to talk with Derrick in October 1996 in his law office at the Washington, D.C., firm of Williams, Jensen.

His theme was change—district-level and region-level. "I took a district that was overwhelmingly Democratic," he joked, "and through 20 years of hard work, turned it into a district that is overwhelmingly Republican."[52] But his explanation began with a broader perception.

For a long time, the district had been becoming more Republican. And the catalyst was race. For years and years and years, the Democratic Party was the party of the white man and the Republican Party was the party of the black man. Now, that has been reversed. It's a subtle thing. But the Republican Party has become the party of the white man. It is now not socially respectable for a young person rising up the corporate ladder to be a Democrat. You aren't accepted at the country club if you are a Democrat.

If a career-oriented young lawyer were to ask him about joining a party, said Derrick, "I'd advise him to become a Republican." It was the same dynamic that Lindsey Graham recognized and on which he had bet his political career.

Derrick's focus on race as a change catalyst and as a change indicator highlighted—and confirmed—for me, the notable absence of serious race-centered conversation and meaningful black citizen connections during my early visits with Graham. It confirmed my conclusion that he had decided to go with the constituency flow on all such social issues—and to be content with whatever black support came his way. For the time being, at least, civil rights attitudes and issues would get incorporated, unsaid, within his strongly held, strongly voiced, all-purpose anti-Clintonism. My conversation with Derrick helped explain why I, a stranger, heard so little race-centered talk during my visits. "Thirty years ago," he said, "you would have had no trouble picking it up. But it has become 'not respectable' to make racially tinged commentary. So anti–civil rights talk has gone underground."

Butler Derrick's congressional career shed light, too, on the importance of Graham's tight constituency connections. Derrick had chosen to become a major player within the House Democratic Party, as a top lieutenant to the leadership. Indeed, both he and Phil Sharp had worked closely with Speaker Tip O'Neill.[53] "I had advanced higher in the party leadership than any South Carolinian since 1857," said Derrick. He had, he said, "one of the two most progressive voting records of any of the Southerners"—voting in support of civil rights and gun control legislation. He traveled in Democratic

Party establishment circles. Indeed, I had met him in 1980 when he had come with House Speaker Tom Foley to a three-nation conference on democratic legislatures in Selsden Park, England.[54]

His choice of a Washington career became increasingly incompatible with his conservative, Republican-trending district. "If I had wanted to, I could have stayed in Congress forever," he said. "If you come up here [to Washington] and don't get too involved and go back home a lot and damn the government, you can get reelected forever. I could have been the Strom Thurmond of the House. But that doesn't fit with my values and I had no interest in doing it that way. I love our government." Derrick's rewarding Washington connections collided increasingly with his less pleasurable connecting activities at home.

"I was the first congressman in my district," he recalled, "to hold public meetings—one a year in every county and sometimes more in large counties." But time eroded these connections. "Toward the end," he said, "I got into trouble with my district by voting for gun control. Every time I would hold a meeting, there would be ten of these guys up front and all I would hear was 'guns.' I got tired of that."

On the occasion of Lindsey Graham's first town meeting, the local paper editorialized, "Butler Derrick often met hostile audiences . . . [but] Mr. Graham's was a veritable love feast . . .."[55] Derrick had surrendered his constituency to a local boy, with fresh constituency ties at home—ties that buttressed his career. It was Graham's strong personal connections with his constituents that freed him to become a player in Washington. And he seemed most unlikely to become a party establishment player or to lose touch with his constituents.

Notes

1. I did not inquire into the early lives of the two men, but I learned about a common experience that may be worth noting. Both men lost parents when they were young, and both accepted responsibility, early in life, for their siblings. David McIntosh's father died when he was five. "Now I have to be the man of the family," he declared. And he helped his mother raise three siblings. Lindsey Graham lost both parents when he was in college. He took his younger sister to live with him in their aunt's home, became her guardian, and helped put her through college. Because representation is in essence a relationship of responsibility—politician to constituent—I have wondered whether people who assume responsibility for others early in life might bring some extra maturity and judgment to their constituency responsibility in their later political life. But I have nothing to add. On McIntosh, see Nina Easton, *Gang of Five*, Simon and Schuster (New York, 2000), Chapter 2.

2. "Introducing the Class of 1994," *Roll Call*, November 14, 1994.

3. Kevin Merida and Kenneth Cooper, "A Class of Young Warriors," *Washington Post Weekly,* December 19–25, 1994.
4. Bob Hohler, "Most in GOP's New House Army Likely to March with Gingrich," *Boston Globe,* November 21, 1994.
5. Robin Toner, "73 Mr. Smiths, of the GOP, Go to Washington," *New York Times,* January 8, 1995.
6. Guy Gugliotta, "They Flat Do Not Care," *Washington Post Weekly,* January 1–7, 1995.
7. Paul Taylor and Helen Dewar, "Outsiders on the Inside," *Washington Post Weekly,* July 17–23, 1995.
8. Graeme Browning, "The GOP's Young Turks," *National Journal,* February 25, 1995; Richard E. Cohen, "The Transformers," *National Journal,* March 4, 1995; Jeff Shear, "Force Majeure?" *National Journal,* March 11, 1995; Karen Hosler, "Humbled Freshmen Regroup," *Baltimore Sun,* January 26, 1996.
9. Juliana Gruenwald, "GOP Freshmen Are Determined to Defy One-Term Tradition," *Congressional Quarterly,* October 28, 1995. Also, Jerry Gray, "Grading GOP Freshmen in House," *New York Times,* April 11, 1995; Rhodes Cook, "Republican Freshmen Voting Support for Party Agenda," *Congressional Quarterly,* October 28, 1995; David Rogers, "In Budget Impasse, Gingrich's Control of GOP Rank and File Is Never Clear," *Wall Street Journal,* November 16, 1995.
10. Richard Fenno, *Learning to Govern: An Institutional Analysis,* Brookings Institution (Washington, DC, 1996).
11. My trips to South Carolina were April 1995, April and October 1996, December 1997, February 1999, and April 2002. My trips to Indiana were February and October 1996 and August and October 1998.
12. See Chapter 6.
13. *Congressional Quarterly,* "David McIntosh," January 7, 1995, p. 61.
14. George Stuteville, "With a Speech to Pre-Assess, McIntosh Puts It in Overdrive," *Indianapolis Star,* January 24, 1995.
15. George Stuteville, "David McIntosh Has Already Become a Player in GOP House," *Indianapolis Star,* December 11, 1994; Brian Fransisco, "David's the Substance Guy: McIntosh Attracting National Attention," *Muncie Star,* January 2, 1995; Charles Wilson, "Why Is David McIntosh Smiling," *Rushville Republican,* December 30, 1994; Ken Goze, "Mr. McIntosh Goes to Washington," *The Republic* (Columbus), December 21, 1994.
16. David Broder, "At 6 Months, House GOP Juggernaut Still Cohesive," *Washington Post Weekly,* July 17, 1995.
17. Jeffrey Goldberg, "Adventures of a Republican Revolutionary," *New York Times Magazine,* November 3, 1996, pp. 48–49; Lloyd Grove, "Hard Boiled Eggs, No Waffles, No Pork; Upstart Freshmen Hash Out Their Agenda over Breakfast," *Washington Post,* September 27, 1995; Jackie Koszczuk, "Freshmen: New, Powerful Voice," *CQ,* October 28, 1995.
18. Mary Jacoby, "House GOP Freshmen 'Taking Control' with New Task Forces to Shape Agenda," *Roll Call,* March 18, 1996.
19. NPR, *Morning Edition,* April 3, 1996; Jake Thompson, "Republicans Call to Dole," *Kansas City Star,* May 1, 1996.
20. Nina J. Easton, *Gang of Five,* p. 60.
21. Ibid., p. 51.
22. *Almanac of American Politics* (1995), p. 959.
23. Ibid., p. 65.
24. Michael Wines, "Fervor of Freshmen Wanes as Reelection Time Nears," *New York Times,* March 24, 1996.

25. Linda Killian, *The Freshmen: What Happened to the Republican Revolution?* Westview Press (Boulder, CO, 1998), p. 16.
26. Judging from Nina Easton's description of Kendallville, he was probably right. Easton, *Gang of Five*, pp. 58–59.
27. Sociologists Robert Lynd and Helen Lynd wrote a famous book in the 1930s about Muncie, its small town life and civic boosterism, entitled *Middletown U.S.A.*
28. "Jobs," *Muncie Star Press,* July 5, 1998; Brian Fransisco, "Thousands Expected to Attend Job Fair," *Muncie Star Press,* July 9, 1998; Brian Bransisco, "Employers, Job Prospects a Varied Lot," *Muncie Star Press,* July 10, 1998. McIntosh press release in *Rushville Republican,* July 8, 1998.
29. Interview with Philip Sharp, November 28, 1995, Cambridge, MA.
30. Cindy Skrzycki, "A Gentle House Freshman Presses for Not-So-Gentle Change," *Washington Post,* January 20, 1995; Tom Kenworthy, "House Passes Temporary Freeze on Regulations," *Washington Post,* February 25, 1995.
31. Alan Greenblatt, "Worth Watching," *Congressional Quarterly,* October 28, 1995.
32. Timothy Burger, "Preparing (Early) for Post-Newt Era; Who Will Be House GOP's Next Generation of Leaders?" *Roll Call,* September 11, 1995.
33. Killian, *The Freshmen,* p. 16; Wines, "Fervor of Freshmen," p. 47.
34. George Stuteville, "McIntosh on Some Veep Lists," *Indianapolis Star,* April 3, 1996.
35. David Brooks, "Winners and Weepers," *Washington Post Weekly,* November 18–24, 1996.
36. *Roll Call,* November 11, 1994.
37. *Congressional Quarterly,* "Lindsey Graham," January 7, 1995, p. 93.
38. *Congressional Record,* March 28, 1995, p. H3858.
39. Speech: "A Historic Night with Votes on Term Limits," *Congressional Record,* March 29, 1995, p. H3971; Killian, *The Freshmen Class,* p. 48.
40. Alissa Rubin, "Super Majority Requirement for Tax Increase Criticized," *Congressional Quarterly,* April 13, 1996; Killian, *The Freshmen,* p. 28ff.; Jerry Gray, "For GOP Freshmen in the House, Political Reality Arrives All Too Quickly," *New York Times,* January 28, 1996.
41. "The Freshmen, Report Card on the Revolution," *Roll Call,* September 11, 1995.
42. Burger, "Preparing (Early) for Post-Newt Era."
43. On his cell phone, in the car, he would mention me and ask, "How do you spell your last name? Oh, we'll just call him Dick." Or "We'll just call him 'the book writer.'"
44. Michael Dumiak, "Political Scientist Studying Graham," *Greenville News,* April 16, 1995.
45. Lisa Buie, "I'm Still Lindsey," *Anderson Independence-Mail,* June 25, 1995; AP, "Graham Still Sees Self as Hometown Guy," *Index Journal* (Greenwood), July 20, 1995.
46. See also (and later) Charles Pope, "Graham Was Born To Do Battle," *The State,* July 25, 1997.
47. William Riordan, *Plunkitt of Tammary Hall,* E. P. Dutton (New York, 1963), p. 3.
48. Buie, "I'm Still Lindsey"; AP, "Graham Still Sees Self." For early portraits, see also Lauren Markoe, "Senate Race Provides Challenge That Graham Relishes," *The State,* October 2, 2002; Brian Hicks, "Graham Discounts a Guaranteed Victory," *Portland Courier,* October 20, 2002.
49. Liz Clarke, "Fast-Track Politicking: Candidates Gear Their Messages to NASCAR Dads," *Washington Post Weekly,* August 11–17, 2003.
50. A vivid picture of this conflict, in his district's town of Honea Path, is in Peter Applebome, *Dixie Rising: How the South Is Shaping American Values, Politics and Culture,* Random House (New York, 1996), Chapter 7.

51. An early notice is Michael Dumiak, "Rep. Graham Joins Finance Reform Battle," *Greenville News,* November 7, 1995.
52. Interview at office of Williams and Jenson, 1155 21st Street, N.W., Suite 300, Washington, DC, October 10, 1996.
53. See, for example, Richard E. Cohen, "Tip O'Neill—He Gets By with a Little Help from His Friends," *National Journal,* September 2, 1978.
54. See conference report, Norman Ornstein (ed.), *The Role of Legislature in Western Democracies,* American Enterprise, Institute for Public Policy Research (Washington, DC, 1981).
55. Editorial, "The New Congressman," *Anderson Independent,* February 8, 1995.

CHAPTER 10

Washington: The Leader
and the Player

INTRODUCTION

mod cqos

In the years from 1995 to 1999, the House Republicans faced two serious crises. The *first* was their unsuccessful attempt, in 1995 and 1996, to pass the balanced-budget item of their contract. That crisis was punctuated by a 21-day partial shutdown of the federal government. It featured their sharp conflict with President Bill Clinton and their eventual acquiescence in a major compromise defeat. The *second* crisis, partly related to the first one, was the growing intraparty dissatisfaction in 1997 and 1998 with the performance of Speaker Newt Gingrich. It boiled over in an attempt to overthrow him.

Happily, for my purposes, Representatives McIntosh and Graham were active during the two party crises, and both men received more than their share of Washington media attention. Frequently, they appeared together on talk shows or were quoted in the same newspaper article. As Washington saw them, they were peas in a pod—a pod of conservative ideologues and party activists.

In 1995, they were among the 26 out of 73 newcomers with 100 percent support scores in voting for the Contract with America.[1] In 1997, *CQ* lumped them together with only six others as noteworthy first-term "revolutionaries"—for "insisting on unalloyed conservative principles and pushing their party to take a hard line—even if that means political defeat."[2] Again, in 1998, when *CQ* profiled a variety of inside institutional behavior patterns, Graham and McIntosh were listed among six House members as "possibilities" for recognition as "Staunch Defenders of Conservative Faith."[3] Conventional roll call analysis placed both representatives solidly in the most conservative half of their party—with McIntosh consistently ranked more conservative than Graham.[4]

Along with these large similarities, however, there were large differences. These differences, in turn, were rooted in personal and constituency factors that were especially visible at home. Moreover, the content, the changes, and the core of each member's thoughts and behavior patterns could best be observed and comprehended through a *sequence* of home visits. In short, to know them in Washington was to emphasize their commonalities, but to know them at home was to emphasize their differences.

FIRST CRISIS: THE GOVERNMENT SHUTDOWN

When the freshmen class held its first press conference on the budget standoff, class leader David McIntosh spoke for his team. "The Republican freshmen in the House will not back down," he said. "We will handle him [the president] and we will send him a firm message . . . and we will keep sending him a balanced budget until he finally signs on." When a reporter inquired, "Are you saying there's no room for negotiations?" McIntosh replied, "Yeah, that's what we're saying."[5] Then, when an early, temporary agreement broke down, he accused the president of breaking a "sacred agreement," a "solid contract."[6] "We realize that President Clinton can't be trusted . . . and we are going to take this back to the American people."[7]

During the protracted shutdown that followed, McIntosh often carried the freshmen message on Washington talk shows. A *Crossfire* host, for example, described him as "sort of a radical out-front guy of the freshmen class keeping the government closed." To which he replied, "We're not going to move forward until the President puts a serious proposal on the table."[8] His class leadership role, as expected, kept him and his "no surrender" posture in the limelight.

For Lindsey Graham, Washington's preoccupation with the budget deadlock became an opportunity to emerge from the obscurity of the faceless freshmen class. His policy position was identical to that of McIntosh. But "I" was more prominent than "we." By year's end, he was beginning to sense the possibilities for influence. "One thing I've learned is you can be a player up here without a whole lot of time on station if you really get into the ballgame."[9] In the budget fight, he spoke only for himself, not on behalf of the freshmen class. He emphasized a personal obligation rather than the abstract notion of a "solid contract" or a "sacred agreement." And more than McIntosh, he emphasized his constituency context.

"Let me just say this as respectfully as I can," he said of the president's position.

> One of the things that we need to understand is that there's an obligation to keep your word that should be just as genuine up here as it is at home. I've only been here a year. I practiced law. I didn't win all my cases, but other lawyers and judges could expect Lindsey Graham to keep his word. . . . We need to make our commitments mean something in Washington just like they mean in South Carolina.[10]

"I'm tired of negotiating against myself," he said. "I'm new to politics, but I'm not new to life."[11]

Early in his tenure, his choice of words had attracted attention when he had said of his speaker term limits proposal. "I trust Newt Gingrich to lead us to the promised land," he said, "but the good Lord never let Moses go. We'll do to him what the good Lord did to Moses."[12] The Washington media favor combatants who have a mind of their own and who can display it in other than boilerplate language. Lindsey Graham was coming into focus as one of them. Twice during the budget fight, the *News Hour with Jim Lehrer* chose him to debate head-to-head with experienced Democratic senators.[13] My two traveling companions were becoming Washington sounding boards—one because of his position, the other because of his presentation.

After 21 days, with public opinion tilting toward the president, Speaker Gingrich negotiated a settlement that would reopen the government. But it did not produce the balanced budget the party had demanded. The roll call vote to agree to the less-than-optimal settlement was a defining decision for the party, and it called for a defining vote by each freshman. David McIntosh (with 61 classmates) voted "*yes.*" Lindsey Graham (with 10 classmates) voted "*no.*"

While the policy positions of the two representatives could hardly have been more similar, their votes could hardly have been more different. And when a final agreement on the terms of the budget was reached in April, McIntosh again voted "yes," and Graham, with nine other freshmen, again voted "no."[14] I went looking for explanations at home as well as in Washington.

David McIntosh and the shutdown: On one level, David McIntosh's vote with the overwhelming majority of his party to reopen the government is easy to explain. He was a team player. That was his precongressional behavior pattern, and it was reinforced by his position as leader of his "freshmen class team" and as a member of the party "leadership team." He voted, not a bit surprisingly, with the overwhelming majority of his party.[15]

When we traveled together back home, however, he did not let it go at that. He thought about it, reflected on it, worried about it. Because I touched base with him over time, I could watch the process of reconsideration, as he peeled back layers of reaction and reflection. Maybe all the layers had been there from the beginning. I doubt it. But even if they had been, neither I nor anyone else could have absorbed them all at once, and the tracing certainly could not have been accomplished in Washington. A sequential rendering may help, therefore, to underscore the contribution to be made by observation and conversation up close, over time, and in the constituency.

February 1996: When I joined David McIntosh in Muncie, my first question had been—as always—"How's it going?" And his answer had set a tone for that initial visit. "I was at the grocery store yesterday and people came up and said, 'Hang in there, keep it up.'" With summertime's budget defeat in mind, I asked, "Is sentiment different from August?" "There was a lot of optimism in August," he said. "We had passed the contract and we were working on the balanced budget. Now you hear some pessimism. We lost the balanced budget. Shutting down the government didn't work. But I'd say there's still an undercurrent [of optimism]."

His vote to reopen the government had been a no-brainer. He had, after all, voted with his party. No one was criticizing him for it. People at home were telling him to "hang in there." And he spent much of his time there touting the freshmen class and its mission: "promises made, promises kept." Still, the shutdown strategy had failed, and the outcome of the vote had taught him some lessons. "We overstated what the freshmen could do, with the Senate able to disagree with our ideas and with the president able to knock them down."

At the same time, however, he believed that he knew a lot more about presidential power than some of his colleagues in the leadership. "I said several times," he told a reporter,

> that we should think of Clinton's budget position as the start of his reelection campaign, and that we should deal with it appropriately. The senior guys would say, "we hear you," but they didn't take it seriously. They probably thought that here was some freshman who hasn't had any experience. [But] I had served in the Executive Branch and I know how they see things.

So, while his vote was no problem, his inability to influence his party's leaders during budget negotiations was personally discomforting.

With respect to his party leader, McIntosh was ambivalent. In private, he wondered about Newt Gingrich's negotiating judgments. "Sitting outside the room, it was clear to me what Clinton was doing. . . . [But] Newt lost track of the insight that Bill Clinton was a political animal and would veto our budget. I remember saying, 'Why was anyone surprised that he vetoed the bill?' I had the advantage of having seen it from the Executive Branch." As Newt had not.

Among his constituents, however, McIntosh was protective of the speaker, expressing praise and admiration. "Listen to one of his speeches," he told an editor.

> He's much more thoughtful than people think. He's also thoughtful about running the Congress. I wanted us to keep super majorities on all the committees. But he said, "No, we may pass something in committee, but it won't pass in the House." He was right. He listens to the freshmen. He knows that will help him run the body. He really does use his listen, learn, help, lead management philosophy.

He told a reporter, "He's the only man with the tactical skill and energy to lead us."[16]

In sum, McIntosh had expressed mixed feelings about the causes and effects of the shutdown. But he expressed no second thoughts on his team-centered vote, and he had no public second thoughts about his leader.

October 1996: Six months later, on the reelection campaign trail, I asked, "What was your biggest disappointment during the 104th Congress?" He quickly chose the budget showdown. And his observations were more nuanced than before.

> I remember how disappointed I was when Newt came to the [party] conference with the series of articles on the budget fight from the *Washington Post*[17] and suggested that we read it because it was the best story of what happened. What the article showed was that Newt wanted to engage Clinton three weeks before he should have. Clinton had convinced him that there would be a deal—that he [Clinton] had to have a fight, and that if the Republicans shut the government down, he [Clinton] would then cave in on the balanced budget.
>
> I remember being worried in August when Alice Rivlin sent me a memo saying in essence, "If you are going to shut the government down, you had better be ready to tell us what programs you want to sacrifice and which ones you want to save." That told me they meant serious business. So, I suggested to the leadership that we should be ready with our priorities in case they put that question to us. They said that wasn't necessary, that if the government were shut down, it wouldn't be for long.
>
> I've wondered a lot since then whether I shouldn't have been more forceful. As liaison to the leadership, I felt I had two roles. One was to act as a conduit from the ideas of the freshmen to the leadership, and the other was to bring my own experience in the Executive Branch into the leadership. It was a disaster. Worst of all, it left us without a plan for the summer. And more than most, I think, I could see it coming.

And he said flatly, "When we lost the balanced budget, the momentum of 1994 came to an end."

These reflections were similar to his earlier ones. But they were more detailed, more personal, and more regretful. They contained the suggestion that he should become less immersed in the freshmen class and more attentive to a wider sphere of influence. His retrospective on the shutdown had led him to think "outside" the freshmen class "box."

Despite his "disappointment," he continued to judge his party leader sympathetically on the historical-institutional level. "He's a historian. He has the greatest respect for the institutions of our government, a tremendous respect for the presidency. When he was with the president, he sometimes forgot what his party was willing to do philosophically. Some politicians are more interested in power than philosophy. It's a balance between the two." He would use this intellectual distinction to render a harsher, more permanent judgment during my next visit.

August 1998: Nearly two years later, at the time of my third visit, it might be thought that the 1995 budget battle had finally been put to rest. It hadn't. "It's receding," said McIntosh, "but it's still there." Indeed it was. And he was still reformulating his postmortems. His strategic thinking had changed from confrontation to incrementalism. "The biggest lesson overall is that you don't challenge the president with one big all-in-one legislative package." And on another level, he added, "You don't outrun your mandate."

His thoughts on the party leader had also changed:

At the time we passed our first budget, I had begun to have reservations about our leadership. But I was put under a great deal of pressure to go along. And I did so at that point, maybe because I did feel as though I was a part of the leadership. But that feeling began to change. And the turning point came when Newt told us all to read an article in the *Washington Post* about the government shutdown. What the article said was that Newt was saying one thing to us in the leadership and in the conference and then saying something different when he was with the president. That's when I began to distrust his leadership.

Neither "pressure to go along," nor "reservations," nor "distrust" of the leader had appeared in his earlier reflections.

The congressman's final 1998 portrait of Newt Gingrich illustrates the broad-gauged, intellectually disciplined way he approaches politics.

I have a theory that all politicians fall along a spectrum. At one end are those most interested in philosophy and at the other end are those most interested in politics. We are all arranged along the spectrum, and there is a little of both in all of us. The philosophical types need power to implement their ideas, and the power types need ideas to guide them. Newt, it seemed to me, had gone from one extreme to the other—from a man of ideas to a man concerned with power. I had been attracted to him in the beginning because of the forcefulness of his ideas—but I began to see him as a person increasingly concerned with power. I don't want to put a value judgment on the two types of politicians. But I think of myself as a philosopher. And I hope I am guided by a philosophy. Other people who were disappointed by the leadership saw what I saw. They saw what was happening. But they didn't have a theory about it as I did.

Few politicians construct their arguments this broadly. His construction tells us a lot about what David McIntosh is like. So, too, I believe does his sequence of reflections over time. They were a theorizer's reflections. They provided some intellectual underpinning for the acceptance of political conflict. And, unlike Graham, they reflected a greater appetite for political agreement than for political skirmishing.

Lindsey Graham and the shutdown: On the defining vote to reopen the federal government, Lindsey Graham was unmoved by team loyalties. His vote against reopening the government was a matter of principle. He voted his oft-stated position—that the purpose of a legislative vote was less to produce an outcome than to take sides, define differences "to stay on message and define who is for you and who is against you."[18] His assessment of Speaker Gingrich was less sympathetic, less institutional, less philosophical—and altogether less nuanced—than McIntosh's. Gingrich was his foil in highlighting his own preferences. "Newt compromised. He wanted a bill. I wanted people to stand up and be counted." Unlike McIntosh, Graham had no conflicting ties to the speaker, he owed him nothing, and he did not depend on the speaker to advance his ambitions. From day one, he had been "an unruly child," and one generally suspicious of the speaker. And he did not flinch from combat.

In defending his defining budget vote, Graham invoked his attachments to his constituents, rather than to any Washington-centered team or strategy. "There comes a time when you have to pick your district over the party."[19] "I know that Lindsey is doing what the people of the Third District want me to do."[20] "Shutting down the government is not a problem in this district. My constituents are all in favor of it."[21] "Newt is not popular in my district. He's too partisan. 'I'm right, you're wrong.' He's a polarizing force. He just has a hard time connecting with people."[22] As he, Graham, surely did not. His constituency-centered defense of his position and his disregard for the speaker were widely at variance from those of his Indiana colleague.

April and October 1996: During my first district visit, Graham never mentioned the balanced budget fight. But in two subsequent visits to South Carolina, he was anxious to rehearse these events, reactions, and outcomes. He went into detail about his own role.

> Our poll numbers were dropping, but I believed they had slipped as far as they were going to go. I was one of the fiery ones saying "no,

no, no, don't give in." The president had agreed that we would each put a balanced budget on the table. We produced ours. He did not. The issue was keeping his word.

Bob Dole put a continuing resolution through the Senate that provided for opening the government. . . . When that resolution came to our conference, I was madder than I've ever been in politics. I asked Newt, "Did you know Dole was going to do this?" He said he did, and I asked, "Why didn't you tell us?" He was proposing that we compromise by sending people back to work, even though there was no appropriation to pay them. I got up and said, "How am I going to explain this to the *Greenville News* when they go to the Forest Service and ask them what they are doing and are told, 'We are doing nothing.' 'Why?' 'No money.' How am I going to explain to the working people of my district that we are sending people back to work without paying them?" Newt listened, and he came up with a compromise plan.

Later, he explained,

I was excited about the opportunity we had, and I wanted to get everything at once. . . . Looking back, I think it was a mistake. We didn't need to get it all in one Congress—not even the balanced budget. The worst thing was that we didn't have an exit strategy. We knew how to get started, but not when to stop. . . . The president . . . had a budget all the time, but they held it back so long as our [poll] numbers were dropping and we were getting the blame. He played us like a fiddle.

"I guess," he told *USA Today*, "I underestimated the power of the President to keep the [budget issue] moving around."[23] From the budget fight, both McIntosh and Graham learned something very important about legislating—that it is an incremental, not an all-or-nothing, process.

The large strategic proposition—that in political decision making you should factor in some notion of what other players might do—was prominent in Graham's postmortems. He saw what David McIntosh saw, but he focused on the terms of engagement. "We had all been saying to ourselves, 'This is so neat, everything is going to work out for us' that we forgot to worry about what other people might be thinking or what other people might do."

On my next visit, he greeted me with, "Here's a question for you. What happened in 1994? Did we win or did they lose? It's very important that we decide which it was . . . so we can decide what to do." And he picked it up again when I returned.

When the Republicans held their very first conference after the election, there was a question I was dying to ask. And I've been kicking myself in the butt ever since for not asking it. Did we win or did they lose [the 1994 election]. . . ? If you think we won, give me five things you think we should do. If you think they lost, give me five things we should do. You can't figure out where you want to go until you take an inventory of what got you there. The other question I wanted to ask but didn't was, "if you were in their place, what would you do?" We acted like we thought we won. And we never asked ourselves what the Democrats would do.

In the same vein, he recalled his earlier confrontation with the speaker. "When I stood up in conference and opposed his idea of putting people back to work without any money, he listened. . . . When I asked that question, I think he saw me for the first time as a guy who thinks. . . . Since then, I've been sort of the designated Freshman . . . who tries to picture what the other person is thinking." Out of hard experience, he seemed to be developing and articulating a strategic sense he had lacked in the blush of victory in 1994.

SECOND CRISIS: THE COUP

In the long view, Speaker Newt Gingrich never recovered from the budget shutdown debacle. It sowed doubts about his leadership among hard-line party conservatives. Two months after the budget vote, Lindsey Graham and 10 others took the unusual step of voting against the party leadership on a routine motion to take up legislation that funded House committees. "Subcommittees had been turning back money," Graham recalled. "And the leadership wanted an increase. It was outrageous. So we held it up. It was the first shot in the war."[24] The group of 11 included nine freshmen, four of whom (including Graham) had dissented on the defining government shutdown vote. Once again, he was on the cutting edge of opposition to the leadership.

Speaker Gingrich "hauled the eleven into a closed door meeting of the GOP caucus and demanded that they explain themselves."[25] When he moved to discipline them (by canceling his fund-raising visits to their districts), Graham called him "incredibly petty." "When I need to go on a different route, I'll go a different route, and I won't be intimidated."[26] In his role as protector of his classmates, David McIntosh—who had voted the party position—agreed, calling it "an outrageous step," and admonished the speaker "to stop the cry baby attitude with people who don't agree with you."[27] It was the team player's first public criticism of the party leader.

In the ensuing weeks, the words "rebels" and "rebellion" became commonplace in media headlines. And Graham's picture and commentary became increasingly prominent on Capitol Hill.[28] The Capitol Hill newspaper, *Roll Call*, described Graham as "the spokesman for the rebellious group of eleven who broke with leadership" on the procedural vote.[29] And the *Washington Post* later described the "gang of eleven" rebels as "the hard core of the (eventual) dump Gingrich movement."[30] David McIntosh was not among them.

Several weeks later, the GOP leadership suffered a decisive defeat— using a strategy identical to that in the budget shutdown fiasco. They challenged the president on a flood disaster spending bill, provoked a veto battle, and ended up in wholesale surrender. "The President spent days beating us up," complained McIntosh, "and we were nowhere to be seen."[31] Other June headlines finished the story: "Strange Partisan Tactics for Flood Relief Bill Could Be GOP *Disaster*," "Clinton Signs 'Clean' Disaster Aid After *Flailing* GOP Yields to Veto," "GOP Support for Gingrich Shows Signs of *Fraying*"[32] (italics added).

In July, the Capitol Hill media reported that an enlarged dissident group of "15 or 20" members was holding meetings—mostly in Graham's office. "Graham," wrote *Roll Call*, "emerged as the leader. He organized meetings, rallied members and coordinated the rebels' strategy. . . . [He became] lead spokesman for the dissidents to the press and to the leadership."[33] His reputation as "ringleader" was ratified at home by the district's top columnist, to whom Graham commented, "I'd hire [Gingrich] to express ideas and a vision to where you want to go. I wouldn't hire Newt to negotiate a deal for me."[34]

Occasionally, the rebel group included an increasingly alarmed David McIntosh, whose role oscillated between that of a class leader and that of a dissident. Though he termed leadership action on the flood disaster bill "a terrible performance" of "bad strategy and bad leadership" and a "cave to the President," McIntosh counseled caution.[35] So, too, did Graham. For a time, "cooler heads prevailed after Reps. David McIntosh and Lindsey Graham implored members to focus less on Gingrich and more on changing the leadership structure."[36] "At that point in time," Graham explained later, "it was wait and see . . . [that] if things didn't get better, we may have to do something about the Speaker. We were very serious and we talked about serious things. But at that point, we had no plan to do anything."[37]

Everything changed, however, when some top House leaders came to meet with the group and expressed interest. Plotting against the Speaker became serious, and scenarios were discussed. In the end, they did nothing. But thousands of words were written about "the abortive coup"—who, what, when, why, and with what consequences.[38] In retrospect, it put Newt Gingrich on a slippery slope. And it had effects on the behavior and the careers of my two companions.

Lindsey Graham and the coup

April and October 1996: I followed up my initial 1995 visit to South Carolina with two visits in 1996. During those visits, Lindsey Graham began to talk a little bit about his influence inside the party. One thing was clear: He wanted some. And he savored the amount he already had. "For me personally, the greatest impact has come from banding together with like-minded freshmen who were not afraid to say 'no' when necessary. From working inside the conference, I learned that 15 votes meant influence. And I learned it through the school of hard knocks. . . . I'm amazed at how much influence one freshman can have in the Congress."

He focused his complaints and his energies on the party conference. "The leadership [is] putting oil on every squeaky wheel trying to get unanimity," he complained.

I want to make people in my conference take hard votes on tough issues. . . . I'm tired of changing our whole program because 25 or 30 moderates object to it. My attitude is . . . if they can do it, so can we. We can get 15 or 20 conservatives to hold out. Let's have a vote. If we lose, we lose. With a margin of only 15 Republicans in the House, 25 or 30 votes gives you a lot of bargaining power. And with the organization we freshmen have, someone like me can actually get 25 votes. That's influence.

Halfway through the following year came "the abortive coup," and with it an enlarged base of influence for Graham—not in numbers, but in recognition.

"The most dramatic moments of the failed coup occurred in Rep. Graham's office," wrote the *Wall Street Journal*.[39] His appearance in the media as "ringleader" of and "spokesman" for "the cabal" gave him a short but notable burst of publicity. For a few days, the national media fed on the party's intrigue and turmoil, and their fascination boosted Graham's name recognition. Afterward, when one of the party leaders tried to publicly absolve himself of any participation, Graham had to be physically restrained from grabbing the microphone to issue a rebuttal.[40] It was definitely not a McIntosh-style move.

"Were you here last time before or after the coup?" he asked me in October. "I've got to get you all the articles. I've been having a lot of fun." For any blow-by-blow account, the articles would have to suffice. But his attitude toward Gingrich—always suspicious—had hardened. "I told people I was making the test of Gingrich's leadership the management of the tax cut. Could he manage a one and a half percent cut. He couldn't! He agreed to give the tax cut to people who didn't even pay taxes. Every time he came out of the White House, he came out with more spending than he went in with. . . . Gingrich has got to go. Our leadership is all over the place, and we are rudderless."

He told a before-the-coup story. "I said to him, 'Newt, you're trying to build a spaceship, but there's a train coming.' I thought this was pretty funny. Don't you think that was pretty funny? Newt didn't crack a smile. That's when I knew he had to go. We would never have won a majority without Newt. He was the only person for that job. But he could not lead us in the House. He couldn't see the train coming."

On the last evening of my October visit, I had dinner with the congressman and a longtime adviser—in his hometown of Central. As we walked to the restaurant, he pointed out the nearby structure that had once housed the family business, and the next-door restaurant, now Villa Luigi, that had once been his home. As we entered the restaurant, he pointed out what used to be his bedroom. And we ate dinner in what had been his parents' bedroom! From a pleasant evening, I recalled only two comments. From the long-term adviser: "It has been wonderful watching an average kid blossom into such a good congressman." From the congressman: "Newt Gingrich is not a nice person." Why? "He lies to you."

When the dust from "the coup" had settled, the *Wall Street Journal* singled out Graham as one of the five "key players" in the "House Soap Opera." He was described as "a leader of the coup attempt"—the only freshman to be so recognized. And he was given the label "Provocateur."[41] In *Congressional Quarterly*'s year-end selection of "Twelve Key Players Who Made a Difference: Key Players of 1997," Graham was, again, the only freshman selected. His picture was set atop a column-length citation "for his leadership of a group that did *not* bring down Speaker Gingrich, but did have a profound effect on GOP House leadership."[42] And, they might have added, on Lindsey Graham's visibility in Washington.

December 1997: At year's end, I returned to South Carolina to ask, "How's it going?" "We did 15 town meetings last month," he reported. "In Clemson we had 200 people, but most meetings were about 30 people. I said the same thing to all of them: cut the size of government."

I had read that his performance during the time of the coup had resonated favorably back home. In the DC press, a top South Carolina party leader had described him as "approaching sainthood in Aiken County." And the leader had characterized Third District opinion as, "Thank God for Lindsey Graham . . . the only one with the gumption to stand up and say what everyone else is saying."[43] When I arrived, his pollster reported that Graham's approval record was "in the high 60s." And they bantered about it. Graham: "I told people that Newt Gingrich was less popular than I was—*before* you took your poll." Pollster: "Then I took the poll and you were right."

At a breakfast meeting of four local chambers of commerce, he was introduced as "the man who took Newt Gingrich to the mat for going back on his principles." He spoke about taxes, budgets, and entitlements. Afterward, the president of the group said to me, "We think of Lindsey as a young statesman. He's not up there trying to make a name for himself or make a career out of politics." And the master of ceremonies said, "We're proud of Lindsey and what he's trying to do." "It was a good turnout—50 percent better than normal," said another. "People like to listen to Lindsey." He was hometown's David against Washington's Goliath.

Besides the chamber talk, my district itinerary centered around three small-town Christmas parades. They are a tradition in the district. There were 48 parades that year; he received 30 invitations and he accepted 20; his staff fretted about the other 10. "I love parades, but a little less so this year." And hopping out of the car to join one, he explained, "I've got to go right over and talk to the people running the parade. They are the people who run everything in town." My next glimpse came when he rode by in an open parade car, waving and calling out "$500 tax cut."

In private, his themes were a continuation of familiar ones. "The only thing that's fun is to be a player in the arena—if you like policy." "We are not going to let anyone not talk about policy. People like me will not let them. . . . My rule is: make sure the debate continues." "It's frustrating but it's also fun; I'm having fun because I'm making a difference." "As you know, I'm not climbing the ladder in the House. If I am, I'm doing it the wrong way!" "I'm speaking out about Social Security, and about entitlements. They are the biggest problems." In Washington, he helped write some education legislation in committee. And "I spend 50 percent of my time on Savannah River—and I go wherever that problem takes me."

He talked a lot about constituency relations and the glue of trust between himself and his constituents.

> Accountability is more important than ever. When you are bringing about major changes, to carry them out you need people's trust. And that means you've got to go see them. You don't have to choose between being articulate and having a sound message. You have to convince people that you have their interests at heart. That takes all the skills now. It means a solid understanding of entitlements and the ability to communicate to the average citizen. You have to sell yourself to people while you have their attention, so that they will trust you.

And

> It doesn't bother me one bit to argue with Newt. And I think people should know it. I could come back and BS people. But I won't, and people know I'm right. Sometimes people will say to me, "You can't do everything by yourself." It's as if they want to protect me—to keep me from doing something that may be too risky or dangerous. You know what I'm saying? When they say that, it makes me want to do *even more*! A lot of people don't like to argue. But I'm the guy they sent up there to argue for them.

David McIntosh and the coup: David McIntosh, like his classmate, became identified with the abortive coup. Graham was a charter member of the originating Gang of Eleven. McIntosh joined the conversations later. And he became a voice of caution. For McIntosh, his philosophy of responsible party government—"the team," "promises made, promises kept"—was, as always, his bottom line. The Republicans had been elected, he believed, because of a set of distinctive, principled, policy positions, and it was their obligation, in Congress, to carry out those policies. The corollary was that they should sharpen their differences with the other party. While he might, as a last resort, give in to some sort of compromise, he would argue against it and oppose every move away from his party's electoral promises. He would, on principle, be the last person to give in. The greater the differentiation from the Democrats, the better. In practice, his formula earned him press descriptions as "ideological fire breather" and "enfant terrible."[44]

In 1997, while calling Gingrich "a brilliant leader," he nonetheless was complaining publicly that "there's a real sense of malaise" and that "we need to get moving back on the agenda that we talked to the voters about in the last two elections."[45] He was complaining, too, about the leadership's "decision to not engage the President on any fundamental issues."[46] His talk, however, was bolder than his action.

When he joined the dissidents, he proposed warning the speaker. "I urged my colleagues," he told an interviewer, "not to take this to a vote, but to go to the Speaker and tell him we have some real problems and say, 'If we have another 18 months . . . of drifting, no agenda, breaking promises to voters, they're going to throw us out. Something has to change. . . .'"[47] Apparently, he had some effect. He described the outcome. "We came together yesterday and agreed we were going to develop a complete agenda, fighting for the tax cut, and the Speaker apologized and said he had made mistakes."[48] But he had put his leader on probation. "If the Speaker does cave on tax cuts, he should leave."[49]

The collapse of the attempted coup did not mute his philosophical misgivings. "Our whole leadership team in the last six months was acting in a way that was giving up the Contract with America and our conservative principles."[50] "We don't have an agenda of our own. We've agreed to let Clinton lead and we'll react; and that led to our coalition falling apart."[51] The party's job in Congress is to "send out a message that the bulk of the Republicans still believe in those conservative principles . . . [and are] willing to fight for those principles."[52]

Describing his cautious contribution to the coup effort, he added, "I'm still very much involved in the leadership group as a representative of my class."[53] While he clung, in a formal sense, to that relationship, it was in the process of changing.

August 1998: It was not until a year after the failed coup that I had a chance to pick up the threads with the congressman. On the road in 1998, he talked about a gradual change in his relationship with the speaker. At the time of the coup, he said, that change was already in the air.

> After the 1996 election, Newt told Sue Myrick and me that he wanted us to stay in the leadership . . . and we agreed to stay. But I had begun to feel a great burden in trying to speak or think in terms of the freshmen class. And I did not want to continue in that role. So I suggested to the leadership two or three projects that I might undertake to help. And they knocked all of them down. One was a proposal that we have a study of regulations of all sorts, so as to coordinate our efforts. I think Newt was afraid of the chairmen on that. I had suggested ways he could harness my energies, and he rejected them. . . .

And he revealed a related feature of his earlier association with the speaker.

> I don't tell people I'm a lawyer because in my experience, it does more harm than good. It makes people suspicious. But recently, in a meeting with Newt, I made a legal analysis. And he said to me, "I didn't know you were a lawyer. That explains it." He never knew anything about my background, or about the Federalist Society. I guess he never thought it worth his while.

Apparently, David's rather cool, formulaic way of approaching political decision making had yielded him an equally cool formulaic relationship with his leader.

In late 1997, however, his relationship with the speaker underwent a permanent and radical change. "Some of the people in CATS [Conservative Action Team] wanted me to become the leader of the group. Which I did. . . . It was a surprise. I was going along, minding my own business, when some members came to me to discuss the leadership of the group. So I gave them some names. I should have seen it coming, but I didn't."

CATS was a loosely organized group of the most conservative House Republicans who met periodically to discuss policy and influence, with the intent of becoming players in legislative and intraparty decision making. When he took it over, the membership was near 70. His first action was to "slim down" membership to 30 to 35 hardcore, confrontational, right-wing conservatives.[54] As its leader, McIntosh became a dominant spokesman for enacting conservative principles—especially tax cuts. While he remained as a class liaison, that role had been eclipsed by his new one. He was no longer simply a class leader. He was a conservative, intellectual leader. And he was a factional leader. As such, he was given front-page picture-and-profile treatment in *Barron's*.[55] The team player had found a new team.

"It was a great relief," he said as we rode through Indiana, "to be able to be just what I wanted to be—a conservative, an active conservative, pushing the agenda I believed in." And he elaborated,

> It has given me a different standing with Newt. Until now, he has thought of me as a kid who was useful to have around to keep the freshmen happy. Now, he knows he has to listen to me, because I can back up what I say. But I don't think he will ever trust me again the way he did. He will know that on substantive matters, when I say I'll back him, I will. When we disagree, I will be aggressive in pursuing my view.

He added, "The question I get at home is, 'What do you stand for?' Now I can tell them what I stand for." David McIntosh was finally among philosophical soulmates. He was free at last.

He was free to speak truth to power. And he spoke with the assurance of solid constituency support. "Standing up for what you believe in can be perceived as being extreme here" (in Washington) and "seen as a virtue outside of Washington."[56] And when he spoke, Washington listened. During the tax and budget battles of 1998, when reporters wanted to know what "the conservatives" or "the confrontational conservatives" or "the House hardliners" were thinking or were going to do, they frequently went to McIntosh. When, for example, liberal columnist E. J. Dionne wanted to portray doctrinal conservatism, McIntosh was a favorite source.[57] He was like the canary in the coal mine, warning his party's leaders whenever he whiffed any abandonment of conservative doctrine.

In 1998, CATS had not waited on the party leadership, but had proposed an agenda of its own—"ensure a balanced budget," "enact tax relief," "champion family values."[58] "We are not waiting for the leadership to come up with initiatives and then react." Early on, McIntosh expressed wary optimism that "party leaders would listen to them and accommodate them."[59] But he made it clear that the leadership was on trial.

At one point, he was harshly critical of "the incredible shrinking Republican budget leadership, without the will or the heart to fight for what is right."[60] At another point, he held a press conference to "attack his own party's leadership" for settling for compromise.[61] Always, he fretted about the party's lack of definition. In May, "all of us went home and heard from the voters that there was no difference between Democrats and Republicans. We told Newt he had to do something about this."[62] He even suggested shutting down the government, if necessary, to make their point. "I think we win this time around."[63]

When the Republicans lost House seats in 1998, he explained, "The message was not that we were 'too extreme,' it was that we failed to be faithful to our core principles."[64] A month later, however, he was emphasizing both the party "team" and the need for accommodation with "the other side of the aisle."[65] At which point, McIntosh's own problems had become a part of a larger and more serious Republican Party problem—a problem widely and variously described as "a frustrated GOP," as an "identity crisis," as "GOP vs. GOP," as "moderates vs. conservatives," as "pragmatists vs. ideologues," or as "a permanent insurrection."[66] He was not one of his party's deal makers. He was a divisive activist in an increasingly divided party.

TWO CRISES, TWO AUTHENTICITIES

The two crises—budget and coup—left an indelible mark on the House Republicans, and on Lindsey Graham and David McIntosh. Their similarities were obvious. Both men came across as ambitious, energetic, intelligent, and competitive. Both were electorally secure at home and recognizably active players in Washington. Both were strong policy conservatives who had caught a national conservative wave. Neither man came across as arrogant or "in it for himself."

In the Washington press, their performance commonalities seemed enduring. In January 1998, the two men were pictured together, along with six freshmen colleagues among "a dozen [who] stick closest to the revolutionary flame, insisting on unalloyed conservative principles and pushing their party to take a hard line even if that means political defeat."[67] In

March, Capitol Hill's *Roll Call* coupled them as "leadership critics like Reps. Lindsey Graham and David McIntosh."[68] A *New York Times* March analysis coupled McIntosh's criticism of his party's "incredible shrinking leadership" with Graham's complaint that "a basketball team that tries not to lose, invariably loses."[69]

In July of 1998, *Roll Call*'s feature article on the "anniversary of the coup" carried only two pictures, one of McIntosh and one of Graham. Both were quoted at some length—Graham as "a founding member of the original 11 GOP rebels, and the person who eventually emerged as the de facto leader of last year's aborted coup"[70] and McIntosh as "a quiet but active member of the gang that eventually huddled last year."[71] For the purpose of Washington's reporters, it seemed almost natural to lump them together. Such differences as might have existed went unnoticed and/or unreported.

After the 1998 election in which the Republicans retained control of the House, Newt Gingrich resigned from the speakership. On the following Sunday morning, my two companions were placed side by side for the last time. Representatives Graham and McIntosh appeared on *Meet the Press*—along with fellow House members Jennifer Dunn and Steve Largent. Their presence was a Washington indicator of the prominence the two men had achieved in four years' time. But with their common target gone, two quite different authenticity profiles were put on public display.[72] Now, their differences were given more play than before.

To Tim Russert's first question, "Who do you support for [the next] speaker?" they had different answers. McIntosh supported Representative Christopher Cox; Graham supported Representative Bob Livingston. McIntosh argued for Cox on conservative, programmatic grounds that "He'll do a good job of very calmly, very carefully and thoughtfully getting the job done to get us back focusing on tax cuts and shrinking the government." McIntosh had previously criticized Livingston, as an "old style pork caucus kind of guy, who would lead us back to the minority . . . [as a person] who had demonstrated an appalling lack of judgment . . . and recklessness." He knew Cox as a responsible fellow member of the leadership team. Livingston was not.

Graham (who was participating via a remote connection) answered the question discursively. "Well, I want to say first, this is brought to you by the students at Buena Vista University in Storm Lake, Iowa. This has been a fun morning. I'm out here trying to pheasant hunt." Then, he said, "The dam is leaking for the Republican party," and he identified the government shutdown as the beginning of the trouble. "We need to get a leadership team that understands we've got to produce . . . HMO reform, [stop] the federalization of your school system . . . save Social Security . . . and produce a new tax code." It was a very different agenda from the one set by his colleague.

Finally, Graham got to Russert's question. "I said I would support Bob Livingston [for speaker] early on when he threw his hat in the ring. . . . Bob Livingston is telling me I was 'full of it' a couple of times and nobody else has done that. I admire and respect that . . . you can put me down as keeping my word to Bob Livingston." Again, he emphasized personal relationships.

When McIntosh spoke next, he conceded that his vote to end the shutdown had been a mistake. "I didn't vote the way he [Graham] did; in retrospect, I wish I had." Then he took up their differences. "If we fight on the issues the President has laid out there—health care, education—and ignore our agenda of tax cuts, shrinking the size of government . . . we'll fall into the same trap we did last time when the President set the agenda." Next he sought to "make up" with Graham, saying, "[We] differ about who should be Speaker, but I admire him because he's keeping his word [to] Bob Livingston," an act that, he said, exemplified "moral values."

But Graham stuck with his expansionist themes. "I want to let it be clear that one Republican believes HMO reform is a Republican issue . . . [and that] education is a Republican issue. . . . If we don't produce for people the things that affect their lives, like their health care and the education of their children, they're going to throw us out, and they should." Graham was not a member of CATS. Its ideological underpinnings would have been too confining for him.

The contrast between the maverick adventurism Graham brought to his connections and the catechismal care McIntosh brought to his connections was striking. A stylistic difference was reflected, too, in the amount of time consumed by each participant during the *Meet the Press* interview. A line count gave Largent 38 lines of "talk," McIntosh 44 lines, Dunn 71 lines, and Graham 114 lines. I was not surprised.

The contrast between the principle-centered reasoning of one representative and the person-centered instincts of the other—here in the choice of a new leader—was familiar to me. So, too, was the difference between the tightly bundled free market issues central to one representative and the one-at-a-time constituency-generated issues central to the other. Their responses to Russert suggested that they were trending ever more in different directions. The cerebral, team-centered McIntosh—the intellectual—seemed to be holding fast to the like-minded, safe harbor conservatism of CATS. The more provisional, less predictable Graham—the player—seemed to be reaching experientially toward a broader playing field.[73] Relatedly, perhaps, one man had grown in public prominence with each crisis, while the other had remained pretty much in place.

These comparative perspectives had not come from any Washington reports on their activity. In all the reading I did on the budget and the coup, I never came across any conscious effort to make distinctions between the two freshmen representatives. If anything, Washington press accounts tended to lump them together. I learned about their very different patterns of preference, interest, and habit by watching them and talking with them, over time, in their home constituencies. And I believe that way—at a distance from Washington—is the only way it could have been done.

Notes

1. Jonathan Salant, "Republicans May Be Squeezed in Defending the Contract," *Congressional Quarterly,* February 24, 1996.
2. Carroll Doherty and Jeffrey Katz, "The Class of '94," *Congressional Quarterly,* January 24, 1998.
3. "CQ Fifty," *Congressional Quarterly,* October 30, 1999, p. 63.
4. Poole, Rosenthal scores placed McIntosh at 17th, 18th, and 37th most conservative House member for the 104th, 105th, and 106th Congresses, with Graham ranked at 80th, 83rd, and 76th most conservative member during the same period. See Keith Poole and Howard Rosenthal, *Congress: A Political-Economic History of Roll Call Voting,* Oxford University Press (New York, 1997).
5. CNN, "Text of House Republican Freshmen News Conference," November 17, 1995.
6. Linda Killian, *The Freshmen Class,* Westview (Boulder, CO, 1997), p. 226.
7. Transcript, *Crossfire,* January 4, 1996, p. 3.
8. Ibid., pp. 7–8. See also Transcript, *Both Sides with Jesse Jackson,"* January 7, 1996.
9. Steve Piacente, "Failure of Term Limits in '95 Linked to Career Politicians," *Charleston Post and Courier,* December 31, 1995.
10. Transcript, *The News Hour with Jim Lehrer,* January 3, 1996, p. 6.
11. Transcript, *The News Hour with Jim Lehrer,* December 18, 1995.
12. *Investor's Business Daily,* December 14, 1995. Another rendering was captured in *Congressional Quarterly,* January 7, 1995, p. 93.
13. See notes 8 and 9 in this chapter.
14. Steve Piacente, "Sanford, Graham Reject Spending Bill, *Charleston Post and Courier* April 26, 1996.
15. Killian says that "McIntosh was informed that if he didn't vote with Gingrich, he would have to resign from his position as freshman delegate to the leadership." See Killian, *The Freshmen,* p. 256. McIntosh denied it.
16. Tony Snow, "Republicans Have Strayed from the Tenets of Their Revolution," *Idaho Statesman,* May 3, 1996.

17. Michael Weisskopf and David Maraniss, "Behind the Stage: Common Problems," *Washington Post Weekly,* February 5–11, 1996. See also Elizabeth Drew, "Can This Leadership Be Saved?" *Washington Post Weekly,* April 15–21, 1996.

18. Michael Shanahan and Miles Benson, "Moderates Can't Stand Heat, Leave Kitchen," *Cleveland Plain Dealer,* December 14, 1995.

19. Steve Piacente, "Gingrich Snub Riles Freshmen," *Charleston Post and Courier,* January 12, 1996.

20. PBS, *The Newshour,* December 18, 1995.

21. Steve Piacente, *Charleston Post and Courier,* January 29, 1996.

22. Piacente, "Gingrich Snub."

23. Jessica Lee, "New Course for GOP Freshmen," *USA Today,* January 30, 1996.

24. Steve Piacente, "Palmetto GOPer's Irk Newt," *Charleston Post and Courier,* March 27, 1997. See also Guy Gugliotta, "Rebels with a Cause," *Washington Post Weekly,* April 13, 1998; Jennifer Bradley, "Panel Funding Waits 'Til May After Rare Defeat on Rules," *Roll Call,* March 24, 1997.

25. Jackie Koszczuk, "Gingrich's Friends Turn to Foes as Frustration Builds," *Congressional Quarterly,* March 22, 1997.

26. Piacente, "Gingrich Snub."

27. Killian, *The Freshmen,* p. 257.

28. Jennifer Bradley, "GOP Rebel Says Leadership Rebuff Was Coordinated," *Roll Call,* March 27, 1997; Jennifer Bradley, "To Placate Rebels, Gingrich Supports House Fund Freeze," *Roll Call,* May 1, 1997; Jennifer Bradley, Juliet Eilpern, and Jim VandeHei, "Several Rebels Urge Ouster of the Speaker," *Roll Call,* June 19, 1997.

29. Jennifer Bradley and Jim VandeHei, "Disaster Bill Disaster Engulfs House GOP," *Roll Call,* June 16, 1997.

30. Ceci Connolly, David Broder, and Dan Balz, "A GOP House Divided," *Washington Post Weekly,* August 4, 1997.

31. Jim VandeHei, "What They've Got There Is a Failure to Communicate," *Roll Call,* June 16, 1997.

32. Stuart Rothenberg, "Strange Partisan Tactics for Flood Relief Bill Could Be GOP Disaster," *Roll Call,* June 12, 1997; Andrew Taylor, "Clinton Signs 'Clean' Disaster Aid After Flailing GOP Yields to Veto," *Congressional Quarterly,* June 14, 1997; Chris Black, "GOP Support for Gingrich Shows Signs of Fraying," *Boston Globe,* June 18, 1997.

33. Jim VandeHei, "Inside the Republican Caucus," *Roll Call,* September 15, 1997.

34. Dan Hoover, "House Freshmen Regret Budget Dealing," *Greenville News,* February 4, 1996.

35. Interview: "McIntosh Walks Through His Role in the Coup Attempt Against Gingrich," *Howey Political Report* (Indianapolis), July 30, 1997.

36. Bradley, Eilpern, and VandeHei, "Several Rebels Urge Ouster."

37. *Roll Call* circa July 20, 1997.

38. Jackie Koszczuk, "Coup Throws GOP Off Legislative Track," *Congressional Quarterly,* July 19, 1997; "McIntosh Walks Through His Role"; "Jackie Koszczuk "Party Stalwarts Will Determine Gingrich's Long-Term Survival," *Congressional Quarterly,* July 26, 1997; Juliet Eilpern and Jim VandeHei, "House GOP Forgives Its Leaders," *Roll Call,* July 24, 1997.

39. Greg Hill, "Feud with Gingrich Leaves Paxon Bloody but Unbowed," *Wall Street Journal,* November 7, 1997.

40. Jim VandeHei, "Gingrich May Ask Ouster of Leaders," *Roll Call,* July 21, 1997; David Espo, "House Leaders Alleged Effort to Dump Gingrich May Cause Backlash," AP, July 17, 1997.

41. Gregg Hill and David Rogers, "Beleaguered Gingrich Faces Test over Budget Talks," *Wall Street Journal,* July 22, 1997.

42. "Twelve Who Made a Difference: Key Players of 1997, *Congressional Quarterly,* December 6, 1997.

43. Rachel VanDongen, "Coup Bolster Rebels at Home, but May Threaten GOP Hold on House," *Roll Call,* July 24, 1997. See also Editorial, *Greenville News,* July 23, 1997.

44. Janet Hook, "GOP Class of '94 Clamoring for Confrontation," *Los Angeles Times,* September 15, 1997; Morton Kondracke, "Dear Newt: Don't Quit. Pay Your Debt. And Fight," *Roll Call,* April 7, 1997.

45. Jim Abrams, "Republican Critics Say It's Time for Gingrich to Show Leadership," AP, April 7, 1997.

46. Ron Brownstein, "GOP Congressional Leaders Wrestle with Rebels Spoiling for a Fight," *Los Angeles Times,* July 28, 1997.

47. "McIntosh Walks Through His Role," *Howey Political Report.*

48. Ibid.

49. Associated Press Report, July 23, 1997.

50. Ibid.

51. E. J. Dionne, "The Republicans' Fine Mess," *Washington Post Weekly,* August 4, 1997.

52. Hook, "GOP Class of '94 Clamoring."

53. *Howey Political Report.*

54. "Morning Business," *Roll Call,* February 5, 1998; *Howey Political Report,* March 5, 1998, p. 6.

55. Jim McTague, "Dogged CATS," *Barron's,* August 10, 1998.

56. Michael Weisskopf, "Not a Newtoid Says It All," *Washington Post Weekly,* July 6, 1996.

57. E. J. Dionne Jr., "The GOP vs. the GOP," *Washington Post Weekly,* May 18, 1998; E. J. Dionne Jr., "After Impeachment: What We Need Is Real Partisanship," *Washington Post Weekly,* February 22, 1999; E. J. Dionne, "The Republican's Fine Mess," *Washington Post Weekly,* August 4, 1997.

58. David McIntosh, "CATS in Congress," *Washington Times,* March 13, 1998. E. J. Dionne Jr.

59. Jim VandeHei, "McIntosh New Leader of House Rebels," *Roll Call,* February 12, 1998; Jim VandeHei and Francesca Contiguglia, "A Year Later, Rebels Work Is Not Done," *Roll Call,* July 13, 1998.

60. Rick Yencer, "McIntosh Criticizes GOP Leadership for 'Anemic' Tax Cuts," *Muncie Star Press,* March 5, 1998.

61. Ethan Wallison and Jim VandeHei, "GOP Members Ask: Where's the Message," *Roll Call,* October 19, 1998.

62. Jim VandeHei, "GOP Leaders Rev Up for Campaign," *Roll Call,* May 4, 1998.

63. Ethan Wallison and John Breshnehan, "Conservatives: GOP Can Win Shutdown Fight," *Roll Call,* August 10, 1998.

64. Dan Balz, "Don't Expect Peace in the Party," *Washington Post Weekly,* November 16, 1998.

65. Guy Gugliotta and Eric Pianin, "If You Can't Beat 'Em, Join 'Em," *Washington Post Weekly,* March 8, 1999; Dana Milbank, "Whatever Happened to the Class of 1994?" *New York Times Magazine,* January 17, 1999.

66. David Hosansky, "Clinton's Biggest Prize Was a Frustrated GOP," *Congressional Quarterly,* January 9, 1999; Richard Berke, "An Identity Crisis in U.S.," *New York Times,* January 31, 1999; E. J. Dionne, "The GOP vs. the GOP," *Washington Post Weekly,* May 18, 1998; Andrew Taylor, "GOP Leaders Less Than Eager for Fiscal Face-Off with Clinton," *Congressional Quarterly,* September 12, 1998; David Grann, "The Permanent Insurrection," *New Republic,* November 30, 1998.

67. Special Report, *Congressional Quarterly,* January 24, 1998, p. 157.
68. Jim VandeHei, "Paxon Gone, GOP Rebels Fret over Gingrich Budget Plans," *Roll Call,* March 5, 1998.
69. Alison Mitchell, "House GOP Content to Make Ripples," *New York Times,* March 9, 1998.
70. Jim VandeHei and Francesca Contiguglia, "A Year Later, Rebels' Work Isn't Done," *Roll Call,* July 13, 1998.
71. Ibid.
72. Transcript, *Meet the Press,* November 8, 1998.
73. For Graham's elaboration of his leadership choice, see *News Hour with Jim Lehrer,* PBS, November 9, 1998. His maverick views on health care and tort reform can be found in Rachel VanDongen, "HMO's Take Center Stage," *Roll Call,* June 15, 1998; and Caroll Doherty, "Lots of Inertia, Little Lawmaking as Election '98 Approaches," *Congressional Quarterly,* July 18, 1998.

CHAPTER 11

Constituency Views
and Washington Views

David McIntosh and Lindsey Graham were among the very first of their 1994 colleagues to develop a noteworthy presence inside the House. As children of the contemporary term limits movement, however, both men had promised to serve no more than six terms (12 years) in that body. So, both of them faced the question: what to do next? Ambition is the engine that drives individuals into the House of Representatives, motivates their careers inside the House, and sometimes propels them toward political careers beyond the House. Both representatives decided to seek office beyond the House. After three terms, David McIntosh challenged the Democratic incumbent governor of Indiana. Two years later, Lindsey Graham reached for the vacant South Carolina seat in the U.S. Senate. McIntosh lost; Graham won.

DAVID McINTOSH: AMBITION

In August and in October of 1998, I returned to Indiana to look in on David McIntosh's third and last campaign for the House.[1] In the two years since my previous visit, there had been continuity and change. On the one hand, he had continued to gain unusually favorable recognition in Washington—and by reflection, at home—for his brainy conservatism and his steadfastness on policy. He had achieved unquestionable electoral security. On the other hand, he found it increasingly difficult to relate to his more temporizing, give-and-take, deal-making colleagues—even the speaker himself. And the indeterminacy of system-wide, party-wide, and institution-wide decision-making processes seemed frustrating.

He had assuaged these disappointments by taking on the leadership of CATS, a like-minded group of unalloyed and aggressive conservative policy wonks. With CATS, he had found satisfaction. But he had become a spokesman for an increasingly smaller and less consequential team of out-lying conservative dissidents. These continued limitations on his influence, I believe, gradually sapped his enthusiasm for legislative life in the House. The team player's team had shrunk, and its prospects for success seemed diminished. By the end of his second term, he had begun to think about a move—to House leadership or to the Senate or to the governorship. The idea was not, of course, to abandon his strongly held conservative values or his derived policy positions, but to implement them more effectively from a different office.

David McIntosh's reputation as a policy conservative remained his core connective strength at home. In August, he was introduced at a fund-raiser as "a man with a reputation as a strong conservative" and at a noontime Rotary Club luncheon as "a conservative voice." When asked afterward by a reporter, "David, what should the Republican strategy be for the fall election?" his answer was familiar. "Aggressively lay out a vision of where we want to take the country—a tax cut, regulatory reform, strengthening our values in our schools and in our communities, be strong in standing up for our values and in implementing our values." On the regulatory side, he had found a recent application in the Kyoto Treaty on global warming—which he vehemently opposed. On the social values side, he confronted a recent application in President Bill Clinton's alleged improprieties, which he treated with quiet circumspection.

The day I arrived in the district was the day of the president's prime-time television defense of his public and his private behavior. And what the congressman called "the presidential stuff" was in the air. At a friendly country club fund-raiser, McIntosh expressed himself in moral and legal generalities. "I know it's not politically correct to say this, but its wrong to commit adultery and cheat on your wife." "If he tells the truth and asks forgiveness, as Christians we should forgive him." "It is also important that the rule of law be upheld."

The next day at the Muncie Rotary Club, in the Q&A period after his broadside attack on the Kyoto Treaty, the "presidential stuff" came up.

And the representative finessed the "what did you think?" question by turning it back to his audience, "What did *you* think?" "When I get back to Washington," he told them, "people will ask me what the people back home were saying." So he asked for a show of hands from the hundred or so guests. "How many think it's a private affair?" Zero. "How many think there should be a different standard for the president?" Zero. "Well then, let me ask you this. How many think the president should be impeached?" My quick count was about 25 "yes" votes. The congressman said nothing.

Later, in the car, he estimated that "a quarter to a third" were "yes" votes. "I was really surprised," he said. "I thought more people would say it was a private matter. At the country club last night, several people came up and said they thought it was a private matter. There may have been social pressure [at Rotary]." On his car phone, he reported, "I was at Rotary today and I think sentiment is changing. The president did not answer their questions."

"How do you think I did at Rotary?" he asked afterward. "I thought you navigated it well," I said. And I seized the opportunity to ask, "Was that group representative of the district?"

It was mostly Republican with some Democrats. Most of the opinion leaders in town were present. I'd expect most support for impeachment elsewhere. Muncie would be a little less harsh than some places. Except for Columbus, whose self-image is that they are part of the establishment. Muncie is not establishment, but they tend a little bit that way. If I went to Russellville [a small rural county seat], I know they'd say "string him up.". . . We'll see what the Muncie paper picks up.

It was a familiar calibration of his representational strength: Columbus on his skeptical left, the rural areas on his supportive right, and the conservative-leaning city in the middle. In the spread of district opinion, Muncie seemed to be his reliable connective compass. Impeachment never became a central concern of his. He voted, predictably, in favor of it. But he remained out of the spotlight.

My October visit consisted of a daylong drive across the state. His Indiana PAC had raised $374,000, and he was delivering campaign checks to local candidates.[2] His travel talk had familiar themes. "Our freshman class," he asserted, "has a special responsibility to do what we said we would do and complete the Contract with America." In South Bend, he drew a local candidate aside and advised him, "My philosophy is that you campaign by telling people what you will do, and if you win, you do it.

That gives you a philosophy to guide you. Some politicians get buffeted and blown by the political winds. If you have a basic philosophy, that won't happen to you."

Within those established boundaries, however, were a set of new reflections about his past legislative activity and his future office ambitions. Most striking, because it was not prompted by me, is the frequency with which the word *learning* appears in my notes.[3] There are job-related lessons. "I didn't know how to conduct an oversight hearing. I *learned* how to conduct an investigation." "I *learned* to have a review, every six months, of my priorities." "I had to *learn* (that when a staffer) whose work I have not followed in detail got into trouble, to create a stink and back him up." "I've had to *learn* as I go along. My whole career had been as a staff person who had to know everything. I had to give up that idea first in my personal office, then with other members, too."

There were also broader political lessons. "I *learned* about the powerful combination of [policy] subcommittee and the Appropriations Committee." "I've *learned* that political capital increases when you use it. If you don't use it, you lose it." "I could see that it was not helpful [in a disagreement] for us to bash the [local] mayor, so I stopped. I called him and said, 'Let's move on and work together.' I *learned* a lot from that." "I like to *learn* new campaign techniques. On absentee ballots, let's take some ideas from California and bring them to Indiana." And finally, "I had to *learn* to be friendly with the opposition [Democrats]. Later on, you may need them."

There were new ruminations about Speaker Gingrich and intraparty relationships. Here, I believe, his new job as leader of an ideological faction, CATS, had forced him to come to grips with intraparty factional relationships—to recognize them and to cope with them.

> Newt began to play one group in the party against the others. He would tell conservatives that the moderates will block this, and he would tell the moderates that the social conservatives must have that. He would fabricate demands. We need joint projects with the moderate group so that we can *learn* to trust one another and be willing to compare notes with one another. We need to improve our *learning* curve. Playing one faction against the other cost us a lot of proactive energy with our agenda.

He seemed to be gathering up his lessons before plunging forward. Calling the party "multi-multifaceted," he commented that, "The way the party leaders keep us together is by finding common ground . . .

they have to ask each group for their priorities, how that fits into the party agenda, and what is unacceptable." There was, in all this, a new appreciation of the intraparty accommodation problem. When push came to shove for McIntosh, however, "accommodation" was strictly a second thought. "On issues involving abortion, like parental consent, we would tell the moderates, 'you can be against it, but we are the party and we are going to do it. On this issue you will have to be dissidents.'" Relatedly, he told a story: "I had a very interesting conversation with Nancy Johnson [a moderate]. She said to me, 'There is not one evangelical church in my district. Every time I associate with you, they think I'm not one of them.' That was a good conversation for me." He had learned something. So what was his reaction? "I guess our allies will have to evangelize in districts that are not accepting." Ideas like reaching out and bargaining to a compromise had become part of his working vocabulary. But putting them into practice remained a daunting enterprise for him.

At the end of the trip, I puzzled over his broadened outlook and its new complexities in his thinking. "He always talks compromise," I noted, "but when it comes to cases, he takes the hard line." His policy views fit closely with like-minded colleagues and fit easily with his culturally conservative district majority. What he learned about political compromise and bargaining, I concluded, came more gradually and more tentatively.

His emphasis on political learning came during my third visit—much later than the same emphasis had come to his South Carolina colleague. Lindsey Graham had been talking about political learning from day one, and he had been a political risk taker from day one. I could only speculate that perhaps my Indiana companion was pulling together lessons that might be of help to him in his adventures beyond the House.

Between my 1996 and my 1998 visits, he had begun to entertain a new set of ambitions. When a U.S. Senate seat had opened up in Indiana for 2000, there had been Capitol Hill speculation about a possible McIntosh candidacy. When queried about that possibility, he had said, "You never say never."[4] And in a February 1998 *Roll Call* interview about his new role in CATS, he had denied having leadership aspirations in the House. Being in the leadership, he noted, is "much less valuable than it used to be." He had, however, offered an alternative. "Where I see myself is taking a shot" at the governor's race in 2004.[5] The week before I arrived, a leading statewide political writer highlighted his presence at a regular Republican Party meeting at the State Capitol in Indianapolis: "What was new was that McIntosh was there. So, what was a federal officer doing there? He's running for Governor."[6]

When I arrived, his campaign director asked, "Do you know what David is doing this time? It's called the Indiana Family and Freedom PAC and [a former campaign manager] runs it. David is all over the state fund-raising to help other candidates, especially in the six state races in our district." Another top campaign aide chipped in, "David is dividing his time—one-third to Washington business, one-third to state business, one-third to campaign business." And he added that when scheduling conflicts arose, primacy was always given to fund-raising activity. It all sounded very much like groundwork for a statewide campaign.

His PAC director filled me in. "We thought long and hard about running for the Senate [in 2002], and we spent several weeks talking to people. David decided not to do it. A lot of people came up to us, however, and told us there was a void in the party . . . so we decided to organize a statewide PAC to raise funds solely to support candidates. As a result of our campaign audits, we have talked to 15 or 16 campaigns. We will play very heavily in six or seven races and less in three or four." Home state comments about his appeal as a candidate highlighted his fund-raising prowess.[7]

Our travel talk began with his party leadership prospects in the House. "Some have suggested that I try. If we decide to make a career in Indiana, I would not run for a leadership position. After the election we will make a decision about whether or not to concentrate on Indiana."

"I will have a strategy question in the fall," he said. "My question is: Now, after four years working hard to be a successful member of Congress, what should be my plan for the next step—Indiana or House leadership?" He was assuming that there would be a "next step." And he named "my planning circle"—the seven people with whom he would consult in making his decision: "Ruthie [his wife], she's first," plus two from his Washington office, two from his district, a political consultant, and a statewide party leader.

Obviously, he was thinking statewide. He talked a lot about the disunity of Indiana's Republicans in the state legislature. And he traced his efforts to unite them around a platform of property tax cuts and education reforms. So I asked him whether a campaign for governor would be same as a campaign for Congress. "I've thought a lot about that," he said. "In six [congressional] districts, it will be very much the same, a lot of grassroots activity. In the other districts, it will be mostly media. The last Republican candidate made a mistake. He tried to do it all with media." Our October drop-in drive from Muncie to South Bend had been a thread in the statewide web he was weaving in preparation for a gubernatorial race. I concluded, "He's thinking more already about the governorship than about the Congress."

He was easily reelected in 1998 with 61 percent of the votes. Immediately, the Indianapolis press focused on his "many . . . long-term options."[8] They reported that he had quickly tested the waters for a challenge to Speaker Gingrich. "Being cautious about his ambitions is not a McIntosh trait," wrote *Indianapolis Star* reporters.[9] They quoted him: "Now I have to say I think it would be more interesting to come back to the state"—the idea being that he could have more success and a bigger impact implementing his ideas in "the smaller state arena."[10]

In February, he said that "the desire [to run] is in my heart. In my mind, I've got to make sure this is the right time to do it."[11] In May, he told *Roll Call,* "It's more of a green light." "Essentially," he said, "I became interested in state issues. Indiana has been falling behind in the last ten years on a lot of national measures."[12] In July, he formally announced that he would run for the governorship against the one-term incumbent, Democrat Frank O'Bannon.[13]

His platform was consistent with his free market economic philosophy. "I look for market-based approach on regulation and let decisions be made lower in government rather than higher. A lot of these reforms are reforms for a governor." And he emphasized lower property taxes and educational reforms. "I relish the opportunity to show that some of these ideas are very practical and can be done."[14]

When I left David McIntosh in the fall of 1998, I was quite certain that he would run for governor in 2000. I had to make a decision about following him in that quest. There were two deterrents. First, he was leaving Washington and immersing himself in a new political arena, and I would have to learn state politics. Second, my visits had convinced me that I had learned all I could about what he "was really like."

I wrote,

> After the warmth of the [Gary] Ackerman campaign, the essential coolness of the McIntosh campaign is striking. It is professional, very much so. David answers questions—politely and carefully—with just the slightest hint that he may be telling you something very special, but the steam never comes out of his ears as it often does with Gary.

He cannot seem to remember my name, so when he has to introduce me, I introduce myself. Gary walks into headquarters and toward me. "Hello, Dick" and says how glad he is I've come. David says, "Hello, how are you," and I thank him for letting me come. Each time I come here, I get the feeling I'm starting all over. He tells people, "He wrote the book about Dan Quayle," as that's still what he knows most about me. . . . This may be the way he is with everyone. He is very nice . . . but no belly laughs, no heartiness, no letting his hair down. He thinks a lot about politics, but he doesn't seem to have a love of politics. . . . He has juices, but they are invisible.

On the positive side, he is self-effacing, not pushy, loud, or arrogant. He is not a credit claimer. He is very reserved. He is very ambitious, but his ambition does not stick out all over him.

I was not being smug or self-satisfied about what I had learned. It was simply a cost-benefit problem. The odds of my learning more about "what he is like" seemed very long. He would, I believed, always remain at the same personal distance—accommodating yet aloof. No matter what new experiences and new relationships he might be involved in, I had come to the end of my exploration.

In May 2000, Representative McIntosh swept the Indiana Republican gubernatorial primary with 72 percent of the vote. In the general election, early polls found him far behind the incumbent governor, and he never came close.[15] In November, he was defeated—52 percent to 47 percent.[16] Private citizen David McIntosh joined a large Washington law firm.[17]

His statewide political ambition, however, did not die. In 2003, with the incumbent now term-limited, McIntosh launched his second campaign for governor of Indiana.

This time, President George W. Bush announced his preference for his own former budget director, Mitch Daniels—another aspiring and accomplished Indiana politician. The president's choice was understandable. He saw Daniels as a loyal member of the Bush team and a person of broad experience. His decision was preemptive. Once he had spoken, McIntosh withdrew. "The team is coming together," he said. "I am a team player. I have always been a team player. And I am going to be a part of that team." I thought to myself, "That comment is authentic David McIntosh." His team-playing preferences had been an early, crucial, and durable building block as I worked to figure out what he "is really like." His team-playing orientation had surely helped to underpin his political success in the House. Yet here he was using that very strength to cushion his second straight political rejection—first by Indiana's voters and now by the president. I knew nothing about these two decisions. But the familiar ring of his withdrawal statement led me to wonder whether my adventures with him might shed light on them.

My speculation began with my other defining answer to the "what is he really like?" question—his disciplined intelligence. These two authenticating characteristics—team player and policy intellectual—had combined to give him definition as a politician. They combined to underpin his support at home and to fuel his rise to prominence inside Congress. They enabled him to become a high-definition team player in the Republican ranks—freshman class, liaison to the leadership, subcommittee chairman, and prominent media source. They were the central answers to my "who is this guy?" inquiry.

I speculated that his ambition, plus his team-playing and intellectual strengths, had led him, step-by-step, to the leadership of CATS. It was a position for which David McIntosh—as I knew him—was ideally suited. It was a group within which he was comfortable and to which he was devoted. But it was a group that provided no help in furthering his expanding ambitions. It was too small numerically and too narrow philosophically to serve as a springboard to weightier and broader ambitions. To the degree that he had defined himself as a leader of CATS, he had maneuvered himself into a political cul-de-sac. Had he been a more flamboyant, outgoing, experimental person, perhaps he could have moved beyond his CATS persona. As I saw it, he had won extraordinary respect. But I had never sensed extraordinary devotion. I ended with two speculations. I had discovered the authentic David McIntosh. In so doing, I had also discovered the impediments to his constituency-based, representational ambitions.

LINDSEY GRAHAM AND THE WASHINGTON MEDIA

Between the time I left Lindsey Graham in late 1997 and the time I returned to South Carolina in early 1999, his political career had been radically transformed. And I had a sweeping sequence of events and decisions to absorb: his appointment to the House Judiciary Committee, his participation in the impeachment of the president, his prominence in the national media, his adventure in presidential politics, and the start of his campaign for the U.S. Senate. I had secondhand knowledge of these changes, and I took special notice of the treatment given to him by the Washington media. I could not, however, grasp the impact of events on him until I talked and watched on the ground in South Carolina.

When he first saw me there, he called out, "Hey Doc, how are you doing? We'll have a lot of time to talk. What has happened to me is unbelievable." And when we did sit down later, his first exclamation was: "These have been the wildest four months of my life. Everything in my life has changed."

With respect to the Judiciary Committee, he explained: "Any lawyer would want to get on that committee. There were two vacancies. I talked to [Committee Chairman] Henry Hyde. He wanted me. [Jim] Rogan and I were his two picks." With his request still hanging, Speaker Gingrich happened to visit Clemson University, and Graham seized the moment.[18] David Woodard, his friend and pollster, recalled, "The two men had not spoken to one another since the coup. Gingrich came in one door, Graham came in the other door. They went into a private room. And when they came out, Lindsey was on the Judiciary Committee. Everyone has been dying to know what went on in that room."

Graham recalled, "I took him [Gingrich] around and introduced him to people, and he asked me to take it." But a top Graham staffer added, "I heard Lindsey lobbying the Speaker. He lobbied hard for it." "I learned," said Graham, "that others had already spoken on my behalf. . . . Impeachment was in the air. We were preparing ourselves for that eventuality, and Newt wanted people with prosecutorial experience. No one imagined it would go all the way." His continuing ambition, his timely lobbying, and his instinct for the main chance had positioned him to participate in a history-making, career-shaping activity.

Impeachment: I cannot trace Lindsey Graham's participation in, or his effect on, the impeachment of President Bill Clinton. Nor can I parse his many public—and private—commentaries. One thing, however, is clear. As a politician who was "born to fight," he thrived in the thick of the impeachment conflict. In the middle of it, he told a reporter that "he had begun to like Congress when he realized it was a street fight."[19] He was Br'er Rabbit in the briar patch.

On the Judiciary Committee, known to be one of the most partisan of all House committees, Graham may have been the least partisan of the Republican majority. Early on, he was part of a small bipartisan "Breakfast

Group" working to find procedures to minimize partisanship.[20] He was widely described as "a model of restraint," "more tempered," "a man who has calmed down and softened his hard-edged rhetoric," and as "the conservative firebrand . . . with a penchant for moderation on the impeachment issue."[21] In the beginning, he actively explored the idea of a censure resolution, and he was described as "struggling with his stance on the impeachment matter."[22] Later, he was the only Republican committee member to "give the President the benefit of the doubt" and vote against one article of impeachment on the final House vote.[23]

"I was," he said, "more moderate than the others. Which is why Henry [Hyde] used me on TV. I did two for everyone else's one. He liked the way I answered the media's questions." But the media liked him, too, because, as a trial lawyer, he could help them untangle legal niceties.[24] His positioning helped to turn him into one of the—if not "the"—most visible and most quoted members of the committee. National visibility translated into increased constituency visibility.[25] And constituency visibility translated into strengthened constituency support.

His description of his behavior emphasized: "All the models I worked from during impeachment go back to my trial experience." He talked at length about his most important case as a military lawyer when he defended a soldier against a drug charge by demonstrating faulty procedures in the lab tests, after which he succeeded in shutting down the offending Army laboratory. "I committed to a worthy cause and got people to help. I thought 'I can change anything.' People trusted me and came forward. I had taken on 'city hall.' Now, I was up against another big institution and a popular president. Here again, we were the underdog." And he went about it in the same careful way.

"As a trial lawyer I'm not as likely [as some other members] to get wrapped up emotionally in a case," he emphasized. "Politicians pursue causes . . . [and] 80 percent of the guys in our [House Republican] conference just wanted to 'get him out of there.' As a trial lawyer you have to fall back—and advance—strategically." Near the end, he even told CNN, "I like those White House counselors. When this is over, we'll go out and have a coke—not a beer—a coke together."[26] It was very much a trial lawyer's comment.

Graham's strategy was to pursue a bipartisan censure resolution and, when that failed, to push hard for impeachment. In his words, "The best thing to do was to find bipartisan ground, and let the president meet us halfway. We could have met our legislative responsibilities with a resolution of censure. . . . I could have voted for censure if the president had reconciled himself with the law." "I worked hard to find a bipartisan way out—one best for the party and the country. But once censure failed and bipartisanship broke down, I shifted gears and went all out—'balls to the wall'—in the other direction. I'm a prosecutor and a prosecutor fights as hard as he can to convict." "To that point, I had been the most balanced. But I knew my role had to change if we were to succeed—that I would have to get much tougher."

His attack began with his question: "Was it Peyton Place or Watergate?—Was it about sex or abuse of power?" He called it an abuse of power. "I was involved in painting broad themes," he said. "Starr had the facts, but he had no broad theme. Lying and covering up is not a broad theme. The broad theme was abuse of power—the humiliation of women, starting with Paula Jones. What Nixon did to the political system, Clinton did to the legal system. That's why I asked: Is it Watergate or Peyton Place? When you use your office to intimidate women and ruin their lives, that's not about sex. It's not Peyton Place. That's Watergate. It was always Watergate. . . . My goal was to define what he did as Watergate."

Washington media story I: Graham's bipartisanship, his strategic outlook, and his thematic approach—when combined with his constituency-honed presentational skills—captured Washington media attention. In the summer of 1999, Graham led all House members in the number of appearances on Sunday news shows.[27] As one of the 13 House prosecutors at the president's impeachment trial in the Senate, Graham's presentations commanded the most attention. For example, when the Judiciary Committee voted four articles of impeachment and Graham cast the one dissenting vote, a *New York Times* reporter wrote that he "has stood apart from the rest with his vivid, concise remarks, the kind that made sense to his grandmother over the kitchen table, not just to a roomful of lawyers. He likes to speak right off the cuff without the full text notes that most members would never dare to ditch." And she noted his comment to the president's lawyer, "I can only believe your defense if I check my common sense at the door and I forget the way the world really works."[28]

Calling him "the maverick," the *New York Times* wrote, "folksy, confessional and shrewd," Mr. Graham's address to the House "as a child of the south" stood out among the more technical presentations of the other twelve Republicans."[29] And they editorialized: "Representative Lindsey Graham put the prosecution argument in its most forceful and emotional terms."[30] Graham's plea to "cleanse this office" commanded the lead paragraph in the *Washington Post*—and in many other papers nationwide.[31] CNN commentator Wolf Blitzer singled out Graham: "I was struck during listening to the 13 House prosecutors [that] one of the most effective parts was when Lindsey Graham, in a soft-spoken sort of folksy way, said, 'We begged you, Mr. President, don't lie to the grand jury.'"[32] His appearance on *Face the Nation* the next day drew widespread attention.

At the close of the presentation by the House "managers," the *New York Times* summed up their report by quoting Graham's opinion: "It's never been hard to find out whether Bill Clinton committed perjury or whether he obstructed justice. That ain't a hard one for me. But when you take the good of the nation, the up side and the down side, reasonable people can disagree on what we should do." "That concession," concluded R. W. Apple, "was the most dramatic moment of the . . . last day of questioning."[33]

The *Washington Post* gave what they called Graham's "outstretched hand" even greater prominence. Taking note of Graham's friendly, boyish persona, David von Drehl wrote,

> Graham has been the Hamlet of this impeachment, wrestling his way toward certainty in a series of long, compelling soliloquies. His framing of the dilemma. . . . "Is this Watergate or Peyton Place," has been as close as anyone has come in this drama to "To be, or not to be?" Like Hamlet, Graham has registered as a very human figure in a tragedy full of schemers, blowhards, stalking horses and madness. Like Hamlet, his on-the-one-hand, on-the-other-hand speeches may grow exasperating. And like Hamlet, he is the character who keeps surprising. . . . Impeachment, however, has elevated him from the pack of House Republicans. The camera loves him and that love is requited. He makes jokes, tells stories, says "ain't." "Baptists love repentance," Graham declared. . . . "I'm a Baptist. In my church everybody gets saved about every other week . . . ." Will he be remembered as a man of principle who tried to respect his opponents? A civil voice in the middle of a knife fight? Or will he find himself unemployed in a couple of years, like so many others who got famous by opposing this President?[34]

It was a long-term question. But the short-term answer was favorable. In the near term, there were positive reactions beyond the state. When the trial ended with the president's acquittal and Washington pundits handed out their inevitable performance ratings, Lindsey Graham was near the top of the class. From Robert Novak: "The political buzz in Washington now, as you know, is that Lindsey Graham turned from an absolutely unknown back bencher to a prominent person and became a Senate candidate," and he called Graham "the best new face of 1998."[35] Albert Hunt named "the folksy but intellectually gifted Rep. Graham" as "one of the three House managers who came out of this mess as a larger figure with a promising future."[36] Fred Barnes declared that "Lindsey Graham is a star [and] I predict he will be the one" to succeed Senator Strom Thurmond."[37] Mort Kondracke pictured Graham and called him one of three "winners" among House managers. "[He] is a winner for doggedly pursuing Clinton's 'stalker strategy' against Lewinsky."[38] These were, of course, Washington judgments about Washington behavior. When Graham said to me, "I went from the back of the pack to the front of the pack during impeachment," he, too, was talking about Washington.

Outsiders who watched and judged him were impressed with his presentation and style. Indeed, "folksy" and "down home" soon became his name and address! Media critic Andrew Ferguson wrote in *TV Guide*: "Graham's talk was casual, rambling and sprinkled with references [like] . . . 'my father and mother owned a restaurant—a beer joint.' Well, terrific, but what does that have to do with impeachment?" "The question turned out to be irrelevant. The next day, pundits and even some Republicans decreed that Graham's presentation was by far the most effective—perfectly pitched to the TV age."[39] Graham's presentational style, he wrote, was like that of the president himself. Clinton, too, he wrote, "shows the TV audience he can mingle with them, and draws anecdotes from his own history."[40]

In a similar vein, a *Newsday* critic wrote, "Graham has a Clintonesque ability to talk in a folksy manner that connects with people. Of all the House managers, he appears to be the least dogmatic, the most genuinely torn by the pain this impeachment is causing the country."[41] Presentational style, they were saying, leads to favorable substantive judgments. And the combination—carrying, as it did, the sense of a nourishing constituency—was an underpinning of authenticity.

Had these various commentators been interested in Graham's representational relationships at home, they would have tied his presentational style directly to his constituency support. But that was not their interest. Moreover, the few media people who did make a connection between his style and his constituency tended to express disdain for his constituents. If you were on trial, suggested one, and "your jury was a panel of back-woods, vacant-eyed moonshiners and good old boys . . . you might want to [hire] the drawling Lindsey Graham."[42] And another wrote, "Does anyone seriously believe that Lindsey Graham is going to voluntarily give up his television network limousines and go back to hosting town hall meetings in Chickenbone, S.C.?"[43] These were the familiar Podunk putdowns of a Washington-centric world.

Back home in South Carolina: In South Carolina, where judgments mattered most, the reviews put a "rising star" emphasis on what had transpired. The state's largest paper, *The State,* editorialized: "Rep. Lindsey Graham did the state proud. . . . Using common sense, personal touches and plain talk, Mr. Graham framed [his argument] in ways senators—and average citizens—could relate to . . . even White House lawyers conceded that Mr. Graham, a maverick who doesn't always side with fellow Republicans, was particularly effective."[44] Next door, the *Augusta Chronicle* editorialized, "A Star Is Born."[45]

South Carolina's reporters headlined his future career prospects: "Lindsey Graham in Position for Standout Political Future" *(Charleston Post and Courier),* "Graham Rising on SC's Radar," and "The Case Is Over for SC's Graham, but His New Found Fame Continues" *(The State).*[46] "Trial Boosted Graham to All-Time High," wrote his neighboring *Greenville News.* And its columnist, Dan Hoover, opined, "Seneca's Graham is riding a wave of popularity and attention that could put him beyond meaningful challenge."[47] The headline in the district's own *Anderson Independent* read, "Small Town Legislator an Overnight Sensation."[48] South Carolina political scientists, too, weighed in with positive judgments. "I can't think of many other people . . . who have done as well," said Jim Guth. And John Cavanaugh agreed, "Lindsey came across as the most rational and reasonable Republican."[49]

The State's Michelle Davis concluded with circumspection. "The case catapulted Graham into the national limelight, making his face and his South Carolina accent well known across the country. But depending on whom you ask, Graham either did South Carolina proud with his homespun, down-to-earth speeches, or he was a small-time politician who let all the big time attention go to his head."[50] It was David VonDrehle's question. And only time would tell.

Two weeks after President Clinton's acquittal in the senate, I went to South Carolina. I accompanied Graham to two town meetings in

Greenwood and in Laurens, two counties that had supported him at modest levels. I can best convey my impressions and their unusual impact on me by printing my lengthy notes.

About the Greenwood and Laurens town meetings, it's hard to describe them. I had *never* [italics in original] seen anything like it in all my years of traveling. There were 325 people at Greenwood (275 in chairs—not one empty one) and another 50 standing or sitting on tables around the room. It reminded me of a gymnasium at [high school] graduation time. When he walked in the back door, they got up and started clapping, which they did as he walked down the aisle and got up on the stage. Then they kept clapping. It was a two-minute standing ovation, hard clapping for the most part, warm, appreciative, a salute, a thank you—all of that. He called it a "welcome home." But it was a phenomenon—in a country of presumed cynics, skeptics, anti-politics people. Here, on a week night, not in his home town, on a raw evening, this huge crowd had come out to see him, hear him, thank him for something he had done as a politician.

It was a working people, small business crowd, more than any elite kind of crowd—lots of couples, very few if any suit-and-tie people. Elderly to middle age with a sprinkling of young people (in each meeting, at least one teenager asked a question). When we drove up, there were hundreds, a sea of cars in front of the building and all around it. LG was stunned. "I can't believe it." (To the crowd, he said, "This is unbelievable! I thought they were giving away a truck or something.")

I've seen major political rallies with that many people, but never a town meeting or any other kind of meeting like it. And no political rally could have the emotional wallop that this one did. It wasn't about politics. It wasn't about promises. It was about someone who had stood up for something—something these people wanted very much to have said on their behalf—however "popular" it might have been. In a sense, too, they were thanking a loser. He had lost! So it wasn't a victory celebration. It was as if they had discovered a champion. And in their midst—"one of them"—they never knew they had. In a time of apathy, here was emotional commitment. It was an American Legion Hall, and when we came in the door, a friend said to Lindsey, "There's a lot of emotion in there." There were lots of good policy questions of the normal town meeting sort, but the ambience was very different.

On the way to the Laurens meeting, I asked LG to guess the attendance there. He guessed 75 people. There were 150! They were packed into a much smaller room in a county library and some had to listen in the hall. Again, a standing, hand-clapping welcome that continued for a bit while he just acknowledged it with thanks. Again, he talked for a while about the trial and then about Social Security, Medicare, and taxes. Then he opened up for questions.

Until I heard LG speak on these two occasions, it hadn't seemed to me that he was senatorial material. Now I think differently. He is smart enough, sufficiently policy oriented and policy knowledgeable to hold his own with anyone. He is certainly articulate, good humored. He has a strong, consistent, thoughtful, anti-government, free enterprise theme that carries philosophical punch. You would always pretty much know what he thought. He's energetic, telegenic, down home. He remains upbeat in the sense that "there's hope" and in the sense that he wants to work things out. "I'm going to get together with Pat Moynihan when I get back to see if we can work out a Social Security package." And "I'm going to see if I can't sit down with Barney Frank and see if we can come up with a bipartisan solution to the independent counsel problem."

He has the conservative base with him, and he has a religious grounding, but he does not parade religion as the basis for what he says. He keeps religion as underpinning, but does not push it as David McIntosh does. . . . That will give him broader appeal. Anyway, I now believe he has the stuff to be a U.S. Senator. He's certainly got guts, too. All the rest remains to be seen.

Town meetings, of course, are all about connections. Reflecting afterwards on the two town meetings, Graham talked a lot about his constituency connections and constituent trust.

They see that I'm consistent in what I say at home and in Congress. People saw a side of me during impeachment—a tough prosecutor with serious views—that was not unknown to them when they sent me to Washington. They know me as aggressive [and] engaging, that I tell jokes and talk plain, and they get reinforcement when they see those positive traits during impeachment. They have pride that I'm not just "one of 435," that I'm carrying the ball in a major event. They know I'm credible and they trust me. I told them I was going to vote against Article Two [of the impeachment charges] and

I did. ["Did you get pressure on that vote?"] You wouldn't believe the pressure I got.

"My politics is defined by what I do in Washington, and the trust I have is defined by what I do at home," he explained. "My activity in Washington is dominant because of the media. What I do there gets home in twenty minutes. . . . But home is still the under-footing, the floor. When I talk about 'my district' in Washington, I'm not talking about 'some people.' I'm talking about people I was talking to at home the day before." "People think of me as the hometown boy. I'm just Lindsey. I've been adopted in all ten counties. I've grown into being their hometown boy." The week before I arrived, he had told a Washington reporter, "I'm getting hammered up here; but let me tell you something, they think I'm a hero back home."[51] There was no other conclusion. Lindsey Graham remained more solidly embedded than ever in a supportive constituency.

Washington media story II: Four days before I arrived, *New York Times* political reporter Katharine Seelye went to Graham's district to cover his town meeting in Anderson. Both her curiosity and her visit were admirable and unusual, and they provided added testimony to Graham's newfound visibility. She saw the same activity I saw. But her take on the activity was so different from my own that it exemplifies, once again, the gulf between a constituency-oriented view and a Washington-oriented view of our House members.[52]

Seelye begins her account with a Washington-generated question: "Didn't Lindsey Graham see the memo?" The "memo" was the plan of Washington Republicans "to shuck the scandal and delve into the real issues that affect real people." And she found that "the folksy southerner is not inclined to do that just yet." Washington's Republican Party orthodoxy, she writes, "holds that no good can come of reliving impeachment wars."

She had come, therefore, posing a question formulated in Washington, to which she gets a South Carolina answer. Her question has no relation to what is going on here. Graham tells her that he wants "to tell them what I did and why" during impeachment. He is, quite simply, doing his job. She calls it a "kind of victory lap for the hometown boy, even though Republicans lost the case and the Senate acquitted Mr. Clinton." But the win-lose outcome of the Washington saga had no relevance for what she was observing. Representation is not a win-lose legislative idea.

She observes further that "an overflow audience cheered and yelled and gave him a standing ovation." Then she remarks that his rhetoric was designed "to prompt the collective memory of his audience." If she realized how rare that kind of audience reaction was, she would have put a different interpretation on what she was seeing, and she would know that this audience surely needed no prompting. They knew what they came for. As Graham put it, "they came to say thanks." When Graham says, "My God, I can't believe this," she treats it as nothing extraordinary. Yet his staff assistant puts the normal town meeting number at 20 to 30 and guessed there had been "over 200 at Anderson [the meeting she saw]—filling the hall and stretched way down the hall to the back of the building."

The *Times* reporter described Lindsey's presentational skills in familiar language. But she did so by invoking standards established in Washington, not in Anderson. The town meeting, she wrote, "was a chance to demonstrate a down-home folksiness that stood in sharp contrast to the dour scowls and legal mumbo jumbo of many of his fellow managers. He became an instant hit on the all-Monica-all-the-time cable channels." She sees Lindsey as Washington sees Lindsey, she contrasts him with other Washington players, and she judges him by Washington standards.

She has no interest in how the people of the district see—or judge—their representative, except that she deems it worth reporting a Graham supporter's platitude, "it was entirely appropriate that Mr. Graham devote so much time to impeachment." As if it were a serious question. This same woman also opines, "He's got a bright future." And the article ends, for balance, with some less sanguine local observations.

In sum, a fine Washington reporter has come to report on a representational activity without any interest in representational relationships or connective questions. She has, to her credit, come to the district to observe. But she has come with Washington glasses and a Washington perspective. The connections between politician and constituency—and the town meeting as an essential medium—are of no interest to her. To belabor my theme: A Washington mind-set and a constituency mind-set are very different. Not better or worse, just different. One is no easy substitute for the other.

The next day, Washington public affairs analyst Jeff Greenfield brings his Washington mind-set to a constituency setting–by catching Lindsey Graham live during his constituency visit to the small town of Walhalla.[53] Again, the fact of a Washington journalist's interest is a tribute to Graham's raised profile. But again, the journalist has no interest in the phenomenon of representation.

Greenfield certainly recognizes the constituency context as he connects with Graham. "People talk all the time of going beyond the beltway," he begins. So "We'll try Walhalla, South Carolina, a town in the western part of the state, population about 4,000." "Glad to be here in Walhalla," says Graham. "I have a hunch that's right," parries Greenfield. "You've been out talking to some of your constituents earlier this evening. And I assume they're as anxious to talk about the future as we are and as you are. What, specifically, are they telling you about how politics is to be conducted in the future or where they want Congress to go?"

It is, as with Seelye, a question from Washington about legislative activity in Washington. As with Seelye, it draws a South Carolina answer about a representational activity in South Carolina. "Well," says the representative, "the first reaction was [that] about 700 people stood and clapped for about 20 minutes. So it was a very good welcome home for me and I'll remember it for the rest of my life. I told them why I voted the way I did. They wanted to talk about the case. . . . Then we got into where we're going to go as a nation. We talked about Social Security, surpluses, control over some of your money, health care, taxes. But we still, at the end of the evening, came back to this case. And I think [for] people in my district, the take home message is . . . ." Greenfield: "Well, congressman, I'm sure you were delighted to find that the people you talked to were pleased with the job you did. Our challenge tonight is to try to look beyond that case. . . . In your own sense, do you look forward to a political atmosphere when you go back to Washington, assuming you look forward to going back to Washington and leaving Walhalla . . . ?"

There is, in this interview, a tone—or an overtone—of impatience with the local story and a taste of "Washington patronizes Podunk." Washington is, or is declared to be, finished with impeachment. And the implication is that representatives who are touching base with, talking with, reporting to, and connecting with—and thereby closing the impeachment loop with—their constituents are not vitally engaged in the nation's business. The tone is "get over it," or forget representational activity and get back to your real job.

For the studio analyst in Washington who imagines the home scene, as for the Washington reporter who visits the home scene, lifeline representational activity at home is not intrinsically interesting and not much appreciated.

The Senate and John McCain: During my February 1999 visit, when Graham was not in town meetings, he was fulfilling some postimpeachment prophecies by firing the opening gun in a race for the U.S. Senate.

On my second day, he gathered 35 to 40 people in the Clemson Holiday Inn—charter members of his newly formed, fund-raising *Capitol Club*—to tell them "for the first time right now," that he was going to run for the U.S. Senate in 2002. "I wanted you to be the first to know because you are the people who have been with me from the start."

"I'm not making any public announcement until after the next congressional election," he told them at lunch,

> but the Senate is my goal. I want it and I'm in it to win. Once I decided to run for Congress, I never looked back. I've made my decision now and there's no looking back. I don't care who else runs, I'm running. And from now on, I'm thinking primary politics— not general election politics—that would be foolish. Anyone who runs in the Senate primary is going to have to run over me. Right now, I enjoy a lot of popularity. I know it won't last long. And I want to capitalize on this opportunity to start building on that popularity.

"These were my friends who were with us from the first campaign," he explained afterward. "I feel especially close to them and they do to me. I didn't want them to hear about it until they heard it from me." It was, a friend said, "the worst kept secret in South Carolina."

I caught a glimpse of Graham's characteristic determination when he discussed his most likely primary opponent.

> If he runs, I'll beat him. If he knows he can't scare me out—and he can't—he won't want to run in a tough primary. He knows I'll be there. I'll never look back. He knows it will be a hard, hard fight. . . . He would go after me for being too far to the right. But that would be risky because with the party's base, I'm solid. And I have strength beyond the base, too, because people know I have worked for bipartisan solutions in Congress. I don't think he wants it unless it is handed to him.

And on a more positive note, he said, "My strategy is the 'heir apparent' strategy. I want to get known as the heir apparent to Strom Thurmond.

That's a strategy that will hold right up until election day." It was altogether a familiar risk-taking stance.[54]

At dinner the night I arrived, my friend—and his friend—Dave Woodard had summed up the Graham's postimpeachment status—national and state.

He's the golden boy of South Carolina politics right now. The national papers call me a lot. The national media love him and he gets standing ovations here. . . . The media likes him so much because he's not typical. He came out of nowhere. He's not glamorous. He's not the most polished. He's not the smartest. But he's smart. And he has the best political instincts.

Graham's instinctive move toward the Judiciary Committee, he said, was only the most recent example.

Shortly before I left the state, Graham hinted at yet another instinctive decision—one that might divert his attention from the Senate, and even threaten his popularity. A Republican presidential nomination campaign was on the horizon. And expressing his distaste for "anointing anyone," he said, "I like [U.S. Senator] John McCain. I may end up supporting him. He's independent. If I disagree with him, I can tell him so, and we can go right on to other things. I know he may have some problems. But they don't bother me." He was invoking the same straight-talk standard in assessing personal relationships that he had used in explaining his support for Bob Livingston as Speaker of the House.

In addition, though he did not mention it then, he had a strong process reformer's affinity with McCain's signature issue of campaign finance reform.[55] From Graham's earliest public appearances in 1995—and against the majority of his party in the House—he had pushed for campaign finance reform. And he would continue to do so until its passage in 2001.

When Senator McCain, citing Graham's "feisty, free spirit," came calling a short time later, the congressman signed on.[56] He embraced McCain as "a fighter's fighter."[57] He praised the senator for his "guts" and for his "willingness to take on the status quo."[58] And for his authenticity, "People trust him. They think he's sincere. They believe he is the real thing."[59] "I broke out of the role of being just an impeachment guy," he said. It was, potentially, a career-shaping decision. Predictably—and perhaps crucially—McCain's presidential primary contest with Texas Governor George W. Bush would come to South Carolina. And when McCain did triumph in the New Hampshire primary, South Carolina loomed pivotal in national politics.

By November 1999, Lindsey Graham was being identified in the national news as the "risk taking" cochairman of McCain's South Carolina campaign.[60] Soon he became his candidate's "most visible"[61] local surrogate in what was said to be the most bitter and most bruising intraparty contest of the 2000 presidential nominating season. Graham was even called "strategist" and "leader" of the campaign there.

He was, once again, omnipresent on the news, talk, and call-in shows. "I was being interviewed," he said later, "by the newspapers and TV two or three times a day, every day for two weeks—*Hardball,* CNN, the networks." Calling him "the star" among McCain supporters, a *New York Times* reporter wrote: "Ever since the senator swept into the state with his populist assaults on special interests, Lindsey Graham has been at his side like a younger brother, working his heart out day and night. . . . [He] never fails to rev up the crowds with his down-home flights of rhetoric designed to harness home-state pride and stoke anti-establishment fever."[62]

In the end, the South Carolina primary dealt candidate McCain a defeat from which he never recovered. And it created problems for the aspiring U.S. Senate nominee who had been his champion.

Campaigning for the Senate: Two years later, in April 2002, I visited South Carolina for the fifth and last time. There I found Lindsey Graham running at full throttle for the U.S. Senate—and talking at full throttle, too. Just before I arrived, the filing period for the Senate primary had closed. And he was, against all odds, running *unopposed!* He was pumped up with wonderment and energy.

> I'm a lucky guy. I cannot believe how lucky I am. Of course, I was not lucky earlier in my life—losing my parents. But right now, I am. If I had been at any other place at any other time, I would not be in the circumstances I am in right now. So much in life is timing. . . . All the right windows have opened up for me—the Republican take over in 1994, the Contract with America, the first chance to elect a Republican congressman for this district in a hundred years, the trouble with Newt, impeachment, the South Carolina primary and John McCain, Strom Thurmond's retirement, the first open Senate seat in 50 years. . . . And I am in the right place at the right time to take advantage of it.

And do you know what was the most important window of all? Impeachment. The recognition I got from impeachment put me where I am today. In our [recent] poll, my name recognition is 74 percent statewide. . . . If I live to be 100 years, there will never be any opportunity or any moment like that.

If timing governed opportunity, he realized, it also opened up risk. "The timing has been absolutely flawless for me," he told a reporter. "But every time the spotlight shines, that could be two steps backward, not one step forward."[63]

After impeachment—and as a result of it—the opening "window" had been the presidential candidacy of John McCain. His support of McCain was another risky choice, and it, too, put him in the spotlight—taking his chances.

He rehearsed that choice as it intertwined with his Senate campaign. "When I saw you," he recalled,

I had begun to think seriously about McCain. I came out in support of him a month after my Capitol Club meeting. I didn't agree with him on a lot of things, but I thought the party needed to go in a different direction and he would represent a new direction. . . . He's a great guy. He came courting, I liked him, and I signed on. On March 9th at the Silver Elephants dinner, he was my guest. If you think the town meeting receptions you saw were something unique, I got ten times that from the party base—three standing ovations at the Silver Elephants dinner.

He continued,

So there I was, getting all the rave reviews you could ask for, planning to run for the Senate and starting to create the best machine I can, and I have decided to help McCain! My problem was: How much will that decision screw up my chances for the Senate? At first, it was not a big problem. But pretty soon, I really got into it. I'm a competitive person. So, during the presidential primary, everything about the Senate took a back seat to presidential politics.

He added,

Then my candidate lost badly, decisively. That was a low point for me—a bummer. It created a problem for my aspirations. Some of the attacks on me had gotten out of hand. It was gut-check time. It was a dilemma. But I decided that I was going to keep helping John, that I was not going to bail out. So I went to Michigan. John can be difficult, but I liked him a lot and I still do.

Then he gave a quick analysis.

In setting a new direction, he [McCain] totally alienated the party's base. He had a very conservative voting record, but the way he said it left "the base" behind. He spent too much time with the media. They told him he could repeat New Hampshire in South Carolina. But it was the independents that gave him victory in New Hampshire, and there were no independents to give it to him here. . . . We won Michigan, but with independents and Democrats. After the South Carolina primary, I knew it was all over.

Graham's support of McCain carried peril for what he had earlier described to his Capitol Club friends as the "primary election strategy" of his Senate race. "The last thing I wanted, the thing I feared most," he recalled, "was a [Senate] primary—because it would have opened up the old wounds from the presidential primary. The Bush-McCain fight in South Carolina was the most brutal, the nastiest, the dirtiest, the most divisive political fight anyone could imagine. It was war. Friendships were destroyed; grudges were opened up. And a [Senate] primary would have been a repeat of that war."

So, how had he avoided a Senate primary election? By being the first to jump into the race and by conducting what he called "my primary" to "clear the field" of all possible rivals. He turned his connection skills to a monopolistic plan. "It took me all of 30 seconds to decide that the situation was made for me and that I was in the Senate race to stay. A lot of people are afraid to pull the trigger. And now, all the others have been frozen. . . . As soon as I decided to run, my goal was to *clear the field*. Whenever anyone's name would pop us as a possible opponent, I moved to knock it down."

"When the attorney general indicated his intent," he explained, "I went and got the support of the three state senators from his home area . . . when the lieutenant governor put out his feeler, he found out I had already hired his political consultant. When another congressman was all revved up and ready to hold a press conference announcing that a former governor was going to endorse him, he learned that the governor was already supporting me." "There were six possible opponents. And you can see most of them now," he said, "crowded into the race for governor!" He had cleared the field in spectacular fashion.

But the "bitterness" from his McCain apostasy remained. So, he worked to repair his Republican Party ties. Armed with early February poll results that gave him 74 percent name recognition and a 45-11 percent "favorability" rating, he worked the party establishment.

> I went to the man who had been chairman of the Bush campaign and asked him to be the statewide chairman of my senate campaign. He agreed. . . . I knew that the members of the party's finance committee were cold to me because of McCain. So I went around the state, meeting personally with each member of the committee and asked each one, individually, for his or her support. Many of them were not crazy about it, but they read my poll numbers and they agreed to help me. Ever since, they have worked for me on the money side. The financial director of the state committee agreed to be the financial chairman of my Senate campaign. All that work discouraged prospective opponents.

"My primary campaign," he concluded, "was all about endorsements and money to drive out the opposition. For months, I bopped back and forth from endorsements to money to endorsements to money . . . [and when] nobody else filed, my worst worry was over."

With his nomination secure, he moved to mend fences with the national party. "Do you know what helped me the most with the party people? That when McCain and I lost, I did not pick up my ball and go away." To the contrary, he explained,

> When John withdrew, it opened up a new opportunity for me to get engaged on behalf of Bush against Gore. I was well known by the national media, and it was easy for me to get on TV to challenge Gore—who was trying to win over McCain supporters. Very slowly, I got [the McCain supporters] thinking positively again. . . . Then, because of the "squirrelly" nature of the election, I had another opportunity to help the party. I got involved in the Florida recount and again, I was on TV all the time. The Bush people saw that I could help. So the presidential campaign gave me a chance to prove I was a value-added product.

Shortly before my own arrival, President Bush had come to South Carolina to help Graham raise money. "We talked [about the primary] analytically, like two lawyers talking after a case," said Graham. "He told me not to worry about it, that he knew I had helped in his election. I told him he was doing a great job and I was honored to serve with him and to help him. He agreed the primary was tough, but he wanted to talk about the general election which, he said, was a lot tougher." Graham concluded, "His visit was a home run. We raised over a million dollars." At Graham's speech to an outdoorsmen's club that evening, his only applause lines were his mentions of Bush. "It's that way everywhere when you mention Bush," he said, adding, "I've got to put more of him in my speeches."

As Graham saw it, the election was his to lose. "South Carolina is a Republican state, and a Republican should win—if the Republicans turn out. The Republican governor lost last time because he was complacent and didn't get around to talk to people. He took them for granted, and he paid for it. People like to be asked." Not a problem for him. His weakness, he said, was geographical—in the unfamiliar coastal region farthest from his district.

> The election will be won on the coast—from Myrtle Beach to Charleston. Clinton carried the coast, and the Republican governor lost his election on the coast. They are more liberal, more upscale, and more environmentally conscious than the rest of the state. . . . My plan is to get a place on the coast, live there for two weeks and do retail politics—meeting as many people as I can—just like I was running for the state legislature. My whole Senate race will be like running for Congress all over again.

On the Carolina coast, he was sure that his support for John McCain would be a plus. "John is out there now pushing big issues . . . winning some big victories. . . . He's coming down here for four days. He's going to help me up and down the coast where they love him." He reflected, again, on his support for McCain. "I took a big risk. I got lucky. And my association with him is going to help me in this election." Time spent sharing that "spotlight," he hoped, would produce "one step forward."

Meanwhile, he was enjoying himself campaigning. We spent most of one morning walking up and down in a sea of several thousand people at an outdoor festival. "There is nothing more exciting than beginning a campaign," he enthused. "If you don't get excited, you're in the wrong business. Walking around as we're doing this afternoon, looking people in the eye, and getting a response—that's exciting. It's like a salesman making a sale, securing a customer. My Dad had that attitude in his store. When people opened the door and the bell went off and someone came in, he always put on a smile and greeted a customer. . . . Walking around today is getting your foot in the door; a vote for you is closing the deal." At day's end, he characterized his morning stroll as "foot in the door" and his evening talk to the outdoorsmen as "closing the sale." Of the latter group, he said, "I enjoyed meeting them on their own terms . . . and they will vote." "Today was a testing-the-water day," he said later. "It was the first time I have gone to a mass outdoor event outside my district. I wanted to see what, if any, recognition there was. I concluded that we need to raise our ID [identification]. I made some good contacts. The guy from the real estate PAC was worth the whole visit. But there was not much recognition . . . so we are going to have to spend $250,000 on a media buy."

"You can be good at campaigning," he said, "and not be good at governing. But if you aren't good at campaigning, you can't be good at governing. You won't know what your people are thinking, and they won't trust you. Trust is the name of the game." When I asked him to "define" trust, he worked at it. "It's the feeling your constituents have that when the crunch comes, this person will put my interest ahead of his. It's the feeling on the part of the constituent that 'I know he will do the right thing.' It's the feeling 'I know that the method of decision he uses will be fair and not just for himself.'" As a first-cut, working definition, I thought, that was about as good as it gets.

My visit took us across the state, from "upstate" Anderson to "low country" Charleston and to Columbia in "the midlands." It was a visit with long rides and leisurely meals. It was, I wrote, "short on events, but long on talk. It is still true, only more so, that Lindsey wants to . . . ask me questions as much as I want to ask him questions. A little bizarre. But [unlike McIntosh] he doesn't leave much dead air. If I don't have a question for him, he always has one for me . . . what I had been doing, thinking or traveling with, etc." "He asked me questions about the Senate, whom did I like best, what different kinds of senators there were, and grilled me on individual senators. . . . He grills me on people all the time, but never shows an interest in my books or what's in them."

It helps, I believe, to explain Graham's relentless curiosity to note that, among the politicians I have known, he is surely among the most self-reliant. He keeps his own counsel. He relies on no McIntosh-style "planning council" to help him with political-career decisions. He trusts less than a handful of old friends. He is a risk taker who adds instinct to calculation.

I once talked with a person who had worked for him in Washington. When I described Graham as "a one-man band," the staffer agreed vigorously. "The congressman's chief of staff," he said, "once told me, 'Only twice since I've been with him has he asked me for advice—on impeachment and on McCain—and twice he did the opposite of what I advised him to do.'" His usable information comes from personal experience and personal contact. And he is a shrewd and practiced judge of other people.

He is not a reader. We never talked books or articles. But he exploits every opportunity to push and probe and learn whatever he can from whomever he thinks might provide usable perspective or knowledge. Every so often, that person happened to be me. His drive for self-improvement that had been so prominent in my first visit seemed alive and well during my last one. And I, of course, was the real beneficiary.

In quiet moments during that last visit, he looked ahead. A couple of times I caught him saying, "When I get to the Senate . . . ." "The Senate," he generalized, "is made for a renaissance-type person like me. In the Senate, I can be whatever I want to be. And I can have a much wider influence than I could in the House. The media presence means that you can 'hit higher than your weight' early. I could become known as a valued ally or as a worthy opponent. But if I wanted to be more than that, I might act differently. When I get there, I will have to choose."

My trip ended with the two of us in the Columbia airport waiting for different US Air flights. We bought soft-serve ice cream cones and talked. His last comment, as scribbled in my notebook, was this: "My goal is not to be in Congress. I like being a congressman, but I don't get my kicks out of being a congressman or being called 'Congressman.' Some people do. I don't. I'm in Congress to move the ball, to bring about change. And I'll have a better chance to move the ball in the Senate than I will ever have in the House. It's that simple. *And if I go to the Senate, I'm going to have a blast.*" I was certain he would.

I have not seen or talked with him since. In November 2002, he was elected to the U.S. Senate with 54.4 percent of the votes. He carried the seven coastal ("low country") swing counties with 56 percent.[64]

Postscript: During my final South Carolina trip with Lindsey Graham, I crossed paths with journalist Joe Klein. He had come to watch and talk with the two Senate candidates and, I assumed, to write something about the race. Lindsey identified him for me, and, as bystanders, we chatted aimlessly a couple of times. I did not ask him what he was writing about or where it might be published. He did not ask me who I was or why I was accompanying the congressman. "I think he'll be good to me," Graham said afterward. "But it won't make any difference one way or another at home." It didn't. But it did influence the thinking of the outside world about the race. Unexpectedly, too, it produced support for my arguments about the importance of authenticity and the relevance of constituency-based research.

I was a fan of Joe Klein. He was the author of *Primary Colors*, in which he offered the idea of authenticity as the crucial characteristic of his book's embattled and successful politician.[65] With that in mind, I figured that he had come to South Carolina to ask of each candidate: "Who is this guy?" "What is he really like?" I resonated favorably to his effort on two counts. First, he was, again, asking the authenticity question. And second, he had chosen the constituency as the place to find answers. He was doing what I had been advocating. And I was anxious to read his perceptions and his appraisal of Lindsey Graham.

Five weeks later, Klein's lengthy report was published in the *New Yorker*.[66] He had, indeed, been looking for an authentic individual. And he had found one. But it was not Lindsey Graham. It was his Democratic opponent, Alex Sanders. It is Sanders who gets the full-blown "what is he really like?" treatment. And Graham is a stick figure in the background. I had not gotten what I had hoped for, but I had gotten something better—an article that confirmed my emphasis on place and on connections in that place.

The author, it turned out, had traveled around with Sanders off and on for two months—flying with him, driving with him, eating with him, meeting members of his family, talking with him, and listening to him. Most of all, listening to him. Klein saw Sanders as a special kind of candidate—a yarn-spinning throwback to a time when connections were slower, more down-to-earth, and folksy. "Every word he utters is carefully unpacked, inspected, reassembled and inflected, usually in the service of drollery." Being with Sanders, Klein quotes a friend, "is like hanging out with Mark Twain." His talk conveys who he is. He connects with people through his talk. Sanders's varied experience gave him lots to talk about—his adventures as a carnival performer, lawyer, schoolteacher, state legislator, judge, college president. The article's subhead asks, "Can a cracker-barrel fabulist capture South Carolina's Senate seat?"

Klein records his long, leisurely talks with Sanders on many different subjects. But Klein's talks with Graham—the ones I witnessed—took place during lulls at public gatherings. From what I could detect, they were boilerplate exchanges. In Klein's article, Graham is not portrayed as doing anything or talking to anyone. Sanders gets ten times as much print space as Graham. And Klein writes about Graham primarily to state his issue positions as they contrast with those of Sanders.

On the electoral side, Klein concludes carefully but hopefully. "Lindsey Graham's positions certainly seem a more comfortable fit with the majority of South Carolinians; but the campaign may turn on who has the size and the presence to replace Strom Thurmond in the Senate. . . . Sanders has the advantage of seeming more mature, substantial and, well, unusual than Graham." Klein offers more hope to Sanders's supporters by quoting the upbeat judgments of veteran South Carolina political analyst and reporter Lee Bandy. He tells Klein that Sanders is "doing surprisingly well," that he is "doing better—in terms of fund-raising and word of mouth—than he was expected to do," and that "the race may turn out to be a dead heat."[67]

Washington's reaction to Klein's article was fascinating. Political Washington believed it, and the pundits came to rely heavily on it. They did so, I believe, because it came directly, firsthand, from the constituency battleground. The report had credibility, not simply because Joe Klein wrote it but because he wrote it from his immersion *in the constituency*. No stay-at-home journalist could have produced as authentic a picture. The moral: There is, in Washington, a market for constituency-produced answers to "what are they like?" questions.

So taken was political Washington, in fact, that one week after its appearance, *Roll Call* columnist Stuart Rothenberg felt obliged to comment on "the rampant romanticism that has run amok" because of Klein's article. "Democratic party strategists have crowed about Sanders' personality and resume," he wrote. "Political analyst Joe Klein has written engagingly about his sense of humor, storytelling ability and unfettered naturalness. And CNN's website has characterized his race . . . as if it were close to a toss up." Rothenberg advised, "It's time to turn the volume down a wee bit. Klein's piece about Sanders is entertaining, but that's primarily because of Klein's writing ability . . . rather than the candidate's electoral prospects."[68]

Nonetheless, the Washington political community remained captivated by Joe Klein's constituency perspective. Calling Sanders an "engaging candidate," the *Cook Report* in August said that "Joe Klein wrote a profile . . . that captures [Sanders] perfectly; he is smart, witty and a wonderful storyteller."[69] *Congressional Quarterly*'s analysis of the race also follows the Klein portrait. Sanders is described as "folksy, storytelling . . . a people's politician [who] makes a connection with almost everyone he meets . . . who has a down home manner."[70] Lindsey Graham, by contrast, rates *not* a single adjective in either of these reports. Indeed, adjectives that Graham had once earned and owned—"folksy," "personable," "down to earth"—during impeachment, had now been lifted from him and, thanks to Joe Klein, bestowed on Alex Sanders.[71]

Again, following Klein, *Congressional Quarterly*'s final election report relied on local analyst Lee Bandy for sustenance. "This election day," Bandy tells them, "is about style and personality. . . . And if people vote style and personality, that would work to Sanders' advantage."[72] Capitol Hill's *Roll Call* eventually rated the race as "surprisingly competitive" and "a takeover possibility" for the Democrats.[73] The *Wall Street Journal* concluded that the race "could well surprise."[74] The Joe Klein–centered story remained alive and well—in Washington.

Political handicapper Rothenberg stayed focused on the Graham-Sanders race. When it was over—affected as he had been by Klein's article—he indicated his surprise at the outcome. He did so by giving Lindsey Graham's winning campaign "top honors" as "the best campaign for 2002." Sanders, he wrote, "was older, had a more interesting personal story to tell and looked more like a senator from South Carolina than Graham." By comparison, "Graham didn't seem to have the gravitas or the maturity. . . ." But, said Rothenberg, Graham "turned out to be a tenacious campaigner and aggressive debater, and really never allowed Sanders to get any traction in the race."[75]

It was a remarkable comment. Anyone who knew anything at all about Graham's constituency relationships and campaign performance would have known all this from the outset. Lindsey Graham had always been a smart, strongly connected campaigner—as his preparations for the Senate campaign clearly demonstrated to anyone who watched. But of course the Washington-centered punditry had only Klein to go by.

A month later, campaign-watcher Rothenberg returned a third time to the Graham-Sanders race to admit openly that he had, like others, been overly influenced by Klein's portrayal of the combatants. In a column entitled "Not So Great Eight: The Most Over-Hyped Candidates of 2002," he ranked Alex Sanders in second place. "The likeable Sanders . . . simply didn't deserve all the hype he received. A folksy storyteller . . . Sanders' early fund-raising and his quirky appeal raised Democratic expectations far too high. Sometimes national magazines are the worst place to look for any evaluation of candidates."[76] A Washington-centered punditry could hardly be faulted for giving too much credence to a journalistic rarity—a constituency-based, authenticity-seeking report.

Had Joe Klein gone to South Carolina with any intention of observing and evaluating Lindsey Graham's representational strength in connecting with constituents, Rothenberg and his colleagues would have been better served. Had Klein allowed Graham's strengths to become part of his campaign story, pundit predictions would have been very different, and the campaign outcome would not have been noteworthy.

In the manner of his *Primary Colors,* journalist Klein had gone looking for authenticity. He had found it in Alex Sanders, and he had endowed Sanders's quest with political significance. It had none. Lindsey Graham was the significant political story. He was the authentic *political* figure. He had exhibited strong and durable constituency connections. He was a proven political fighter, learner, risk taker, and decision maker. Alex Sanders was an interesting individual. But Lindsey Graham was the politically relevant story. It is a big help when journalists go to the constituency; it would be an even bigger help when they go there to research the most important story.

The Joe Klein story validated, for me, both the importance of authenticity as a question and the relevance of the constituency as a place to go looking for the answer. At the same time, the eagerness of the Washington press to embrace Klein's story nurtured my belief that much room remains for constituency-based research on our Washington politicians.

Notes

1. August 17 and 18 and October 29, 1998.
2. Susan Glasser and Juliet Eilperin, "Don't Ask—They Don't Have To Tell," *Washington Post Weekly,* May 24, 1999.
3. Chapter 6 discusses the importance of learning as an idea in the study of the representational connections of elected politicians. For a McIntosh case study, see Alan Freedman, "GOP's Anti-Regulation Drive Takes Path of Least Resistance," *CQ Weekly,* September 5, 1998.
4. Jim VandeHei, "McIntosh Keeps Wary Eye on House GOP Leaders," *Roll Call Monthly,* March 1998.
5. Jim VandeHei, "McIntosh Now Leader of House GOP Rebels," *Roll Call,* February 12, 1998.

6. Mary Beth Schneider, "Parties Polish Election Routines," *Indianapolis Star,* July 9, 1998.
7. Jim McKinney, "Stakes for McIntosh Bigger in Senate," *Shelbyville News,* February 7, 1997.
8. Mary Beth Schneider and George Stuteville, "McIntosh's Long Term Options Are Many," *Indianapolis Star,* November 15, 1998.
9. Ibid.
10. Ibid.
11. Mary Beth Schneider, "Gubernatorial Landscape Grows Denser for GOP," *Indianapolis Star,* February 25, 1999.
12. Rachel VanDongen, "McIntosh Leaning Toward Go Bid," *Roll Call,* May 17, 1999.
13. Rachel VanDongen, "Heading Home," *Roll Call,* July 8, 1999.
14. David Shribman, "Indiana Republican Tackles a Tough Nut," *Boston Globe,* October 10, 2000.
15. Stuart Rothenberg, "A Maverick in D.C., McIntosh Is Proving a Hard Sell in Indiana," *Roll Call,* September 14, 2000.
16. AP Newswires, "Campaign Memo Says Blunders Cost McIntosh Public's Trust, Election," June 11, 2001.
17. Ibid.
18. Daniel Hoover and James Hammond, "Gingrich: Be Cautious in Judging Clinton," *Greenville News,* January 23, 1998.
19. Evan Thomas, "Why Clinton Won," *Newsweek,* February 22, 1999.
20. Juliet Elperin and Dan Morgan, "Can't We All Just Sit Down and Talk?" *Washington Post Weekly,* October 19, 1998; Dan Carney, "GOP's Next Task: Managing the Impeachment Juggernaut," *CQ,* October 10, 1998; Joe Conason, "Riders on the Storm," *Boston Magazine,* February 1999; James Jefferson, "Congressmen: Some on Judiciary Committee Eyed Impeachment Altlernatives," AP Newswires, June 15, 2001.
21. Dan Carey and Andrew Taylor, "105th's Final Vote May Be Against Impeachment," *CQ,* November 21, 1998; Carroll Doherty, "Braced for Impeachment Inquiry, Democrats Still Lobby for a Deal," *CQ,* September 26, 1998; David Rogers and Jeffrey Taylor, "Judiciary Panel Moves Toward Approving Impeachment Inquiry," *Wall Street Journal,* October 6, 1998; "Investigating the President," *Roll Call,* September 14, 1998; Lizette Alvarez, "Graham Votes Yes, No on Articles of Impeachment," *New York Times,* December 12, 1998.
22. Amy Keller and Jim VandeHei, "GOP Impeachment Goes On," *Roll Call,* November 23, 1998; Ed Sealaver, "Graham Says He Could Accept Censure of Clinton," *Anderson Independent Mail,* December 29, 1998. See also NBC *Meet the Press,* September 20, 1998; NBC *Today Show,* September 22, 1998; NBC *Meet the Press,* November 29, 1998; ABC *News Sunday,* November 22, 1998.
23. *Fox News Sunday,* December 13, 1998. All of Graham's six official public statements during the impeachment proceedings can be found on www.house.gov/graham.
24. For example, on the matter of calling witnesses before the Senate, see *Fox News Sunday,* January 10, 1999, where he appeared along with four U.S. senators.
25. For example, John Monk, "Graham Not Checking His Common Sense at House Door," *The State,* December 11, 1998; Chris Collins, "Congressman Is Media Darling for Clinton Comments," *Greenville News,* October 12, 1998; Chris Collins, "To Graham, Hearing Is Exciting Time," *Greenville News,* December 11, 1998.
26. CNN, January 26, 1999.
27. See "Face Time," *Roll Call,* June 10, 1999; July 8, 1999; and August 22, 1999. See also the "mentions" compilation in Chris Collins "Graham Suddenly Enveloped in Fame," *Greenville News,* February 14, 1999.
28. Alvarez, "Graham Votes Yes, No."

29. Frank Bruni, "The President's Trial: The Maverick," *New York Times*, January 17, 1999.
30. Editorial, "Judgment Day," *New York Times*, January 24, 1999.
31. Ruth Marcus, "Respect Election Results or 'Cleanse the Office,'" *Washington Post*, January 17, 1999. See also Lynn Swett, "GOP: 'Cleanse This Office,'" *Chicago Sun Times*, January 17, 1999. Sun National Staff, "Senate Told to 'Cleanse' White House," *Baltimore Sun*, January 17, 1999. Excerpts are in the January 17, 1999, *Times* and *Post*."
32. *CNN Late Edition*, January 17, 1999.
33. R. W. Apple Jr., "The President's Trial: Reasonable People Can Differ on Penalty, A Prosecutor Says," *New York Times*, January 24, 1999.
34. David VonDrehle, "A Manager Makes Room for Doubts," *Washington Post*, January 24, 1999.
35. *Evans, Novak, Hunt, and Shields*, "Rep. Graham Discusses the Acquittal of President Clinton," February 13, 1999; and *The Capitol Gang*, December 26, 1998.
36. Albert Hunt, "Losers and Winners," *Wall Street Journal*, February 11, 1999.
37. Fred Barnes, "The Beltway Boys,"Fox News, February 7, 1999.
38. Morton Kondracke, "Clinton Scandal Has Few Winners, Multiple Losers," *Roll Call*, February 15, 1999.
39. Andrew Ferguson, "Today Everyone is Phil Donahue," *TV Guide*, January 30, 1999.
40. Ibid.
41. James Klurfeld, "Who Wins, Who Loses in the Impeachment Case," *Newsday*, February 4, 1999.
42. Robert Reno, "Reno on Sunday," *Newsday*, February 14, 1999.
43. Frank Rich, "From Here to Eternity," *New York Times*, February 3, 1999.
44. Editorial, *The State*, January 19, 1999.
45. "A Star Is Born," *Augusta Chronicle*, February 16, 1999.
46. "Lindsey Graham in Position for Standout Political Future," *Charleston Post and Courier*, January 31, 1999; Michelle Davis, "Graham Rising on SC's Radar," *The State*, February 14, 1999; Michelle Davis, "The Case Is Over for SC's Graham, but His New Found Fame Continues," *The State*, January 24, 1999.
47. Dan Hoover, "Trial Boosted Graham to All-Time High," *Greenville News*, February 21, 1999. See also Dan Hoover, "Politics See No SC Voter Effect, but Graham's Star Rising," *Greenville News*, February 13, 1999.
48. Ed Sealaver, "Small Town Legislator an Overnight Sensation," *Anderson Independent Mail*, February 17, 1999. And his hometown paper editorialized "Small Towns Like Seneca Have Voice on National Scene," *Seneca Journal Tribune*, January 27, 1999.
49. Jeff Wilkinson, "Some SC Voters Have Graham Fever, but Others Not Impressed," *The State*, February 14, 1999.
50. Davis, "The Case Is Over."
51. Howard Fineman, "Beyond Monica's Story," *Newsweek*, February 15, 1999.
52. Katharine Seelye, "An Impeachment Sequel Stars Lindsey Graham," *New York Times*, February 17, 1999. All subsequent quotations come from this article.
53. CNN Transcript, "A Conversation with America: We the People," February 16, 1999.
54. His stance was later reported more extensively in John Mercurio, "South Carolina Republicans Looking at Post-Strom Senate," *Roll Call*, November 18, 1999.
55. See Heather Higgins (moderator), *Progress Report With Newt Gingrich*, October 31, 1995.
56. Mark Lacey, "Forever Linked to Clinton, Ferociously Loyal to McCain," *New York Times*, February 7, 2000.
57. Peter Savodnik, "McCain: Principle or Ambition?," *American Enterprise*, April 2000.
58. Jim VandeHei and Amy Keller, "Bush Gets Six More Endorsements from GOP Members," *Roll Call*, February 2000; Bobbie Batista, *CNN Talk Back Live*, February 2, 2000.
59. *CNBC Hardball with Chris Matthews*, February 3, 2000.

60. "Team McCain: Risk Takers," *Newsweek,* November 15, 1999.
61. David Rogers, "McCain Invokes Spirit of Reagan As GOP Rebel," *Wall Street Journal,* January 14, 2000.
62. Allison Mitchell, "The 2000 Campaign: The Supporter." *New York Times,* February 14, 2000.
63. Bruce Smith, "Lawmaker Running for the Senate Always Seems in Right Place at Right Time," *AP News Wires,* September 2001.
64. The counties were Beaufort, Berkely, Charleston, Colleta, Dorchester, Hampton, and Jasper.
65. Anonymous (Joe Klein), *Primary Colors,* Random House (New York, 1996), see p. 366.
66. Joe Klein, "After Strom: Can a Cracker Barrel Fabulist Capture South Carolina's Senate Seat?" *New Yorker,* May 13, 2002. All Klein quotes are from this article.
67. In March, around the time Klein was beginning his travels, Bandy had been talking up the Sanders's candidacy. So much so that *National Journal's Hotline* had used Bandy's reporting to speak of Sanders as having "generated excitement" and "sparked a buzz across S.C." One wonders whether Bandy's reporting was what piqued Klein's interest in the first place. See *National Journal, The Hotline,* Senate Report, South Carolina, March 25, 2002.
68. Stuart Rothenberg, "A Dose of Reality About South Carolina's Senate Contest," *Roll Call,* May 20, 2002.
69. National Journal Group, *The Cook Report Analysis,* August 7, 2002.
70. Mary Clare Jalonick, "Battling to a Drawl in South Carolina," *Congressional Quarterly,* October 10, 2002.
71. Ibid. See also David Shribman, "South Carolina Democrats Are Fighting the Tide," *Yahoo News,* October 30, 2002.
72. Jalonick, "Battling To A Drawl."
73. Chris Collizza, "Democrats Put Money on SC Senate Race," *Roll Call,* September 30, 2002; *Election Preview 2002,* "Can Sanders Keep Up with Graham in SC Race," October 7, 2002.
74. Jackie Calmes, "Black Vote in Democrats' Mantra in Dixie," *Wall Street Journal,* October 31, 2002.
75. Stuart Rothenberg, "Stu Makes His Picks: The Best Campaigns of Election 2002," *Roll Call,* November 18, 2002.
76. Stuart Rothenberg, "Not-So-Great-Eight: The Most Over-Hyped Candidates of 2002," *Roll Call,* December 16, 2002.

CHAPTER 12

Conclusion

What are they really like—our national politicians? It's a large question, and it drives a very large body of political science inquiry. Most of that inquiry focuses on the activity of our U.S. representatives and senators in the place where our national politics is played and our national decisions are made. That place is Washington, D.C.—in particular, Capitol Hill. We spend a lot of time studying our politicians' behavior in that place. And we have produced careful, complex, and useful answers to our questions.

There is, however, a different place in which our national politicians also play politics, make decisions, and shape outcomes. That other place is the constituency from which each individual is elected and to which each one returns for ultimate political judgment. It is a place less traveled to, and it deserves more attention than it gets. Or so I have argued. If, that is, we want to answer the question, "Our politicians—what are they really like?"

If we do pay more attention to a politician's activity in a home constituency, we will be pulled away from the organizing subject of legislation and toward the organizing subject of representation. Having first asked, "What are they really like?" our follow-up question will be: "How do they connect with their constituents?" Which takes us—or should take us—to the kind of empirical description that comes from going there, spending time watching politicians connect with citizens, and talking with them about it. A focus on legislation is not an entitlement to discourse on representation.

At several points, I have compared Washington-driven analysis to constituency-driven analysis. They are different. In a politician's home territory, goals are set, exchanges take place, and observations are expressed that simply do not occur in Washington. Journalists and others who take the view that there is nothing to be learned "out there" should be asked to assume some burden of proof in making that case. Especially so if they have not, themselves, ventured "out there" with the political figures they are discussing, and even more so when they begin, as some do, by describing our politicians in Washington as fundamentally inauthentic—as "chameleons" who alter their skins, as politicians who shuffle their "fake personas" and manipulate their "images" and their "reputations." It is a risky proposition for political scientists to farm out the discovery of constituency-based, representational variations to the ministrations and the intuitions of stay-at-home reporters in Washington, D.C.

In view of my many years of research inside a few constituencies, the temptation to add some autobiographical sections was impossible to resist. My early explorations, reflections, and tracings were used here and there to help set up the more recent ones. Three sets of pairwise comparisons illustrate, elaborate, and play out the ideas in the early chapters. To the extent that these cases demonstrate the relevance and the usefulness of detailed, in-the-constituency research, my hope is that others—with a keener eye to generalization—might think it worthwhile to continue.

The first comparison contains an anonymous discussion of two Midwestern Republicans. They were equally new to Congress and equally unaccomplished there. One was a civic-minded businessman, a transplant, and a self-proclaimed nonpolitician in a very mixed constituency. He was a sales manager, and he was naturally sociable. His other connective strengths were his policy-based business connections; his civic-minded, service-oriented presentation of self; and his natural competitiveness.

He was an amateur recruited into politics. He was not, by instinct or by preference, a strategic thinker or a coalition builder. He seemed to think that if he tended the civic duty side of his constituency connections carefully, election day would take care of itself. When faced with a tough reelection, however, he relied on his hard-nosed instincts, unleavened by any strategic flexibilities. Before he could settle on any recognizable authenticating patterns, he was defeated.

The second representative was a lawyer and a lifelong politician, with deep roots in a dominantly agricultural district. He took to politics early. His connective strength was derived from his farm-boy work ethic, his local sensitivities, and his organizational abilities. By the time we met, he could claim a long string of political involvements. In contrast to his nonpolitician colleague, he was not an ideologue. He was a pragmatic deal maker. As a working politician, he presented himself to others as knowledgeable, seasoned, and dependable. He was not, however, policy-oriented or notably decisive on nonagricultural policy matters. His work-horse energy, his organizational mastery, and his leadership results seemed to have underwritten a durable authenticity in his home place.

In contrast to my two contemporaneous travels with the politicians of Chapter 6, 22 years elapsed between my travels in Chapters 7 and 8, the second pair of representatives. Here, my purpose was to capture a representational succession from Benjamin Rosenthal to Gary Ackerman in the *same* New York City constituency. While the district boundaries were altered, the political heart of both their districts was the Borough of Queens, and the authenticity of the two Queens residents was solidly grounded in that one place. The salient characteristics of Queens were its large Jewish population, its urban culture, and its Democratic politics. Because of the district's continuing ethnic, urban, and partisan base, the two men also shared an authenticating policy liberalism.

Representative Ben Rosenthal was a local pathbreaker. He established his authenticity as a liberal when he attacked the House Un-American Activities Committee and became an active protector of civil liberties. His strong liberal stance drew marquee notice because he had not had to campaign on any policy issues in winning his clubhouse-brokered nomination. He burnished his liberal reputation by fighting high-profile battles—against the Vietnam War and, later, in favor of consumer protection. He balanced his policy aggressiveness with a dry wit and an appealingly modest, self-deprecating view of himself. He did not, however, display or tend any notably strong personal involvements with his constituents. Nor, indeed, was he attached to the abstract idea of a home place. He was one of the first New York City representatives to move his family to Washington. To compensate for a deficit in personal attentiveness, he directed much of his energy and that of his staff to increasing his local media coverage. The combination produced a 20-year career without challenge.

Gary Ackerman continued the strong policy liberalism to which a majority of his Jewish, Democratic constituents had become accustomed. Unlike his predecessor, he had to fight to get the job. Unlike his predecessor, too, he achieved a distinctive personal authenticity through his sustained community involvements, the cultivation of his personal connections, and his skillful maneuvering in local politics. Faced with extinction, he fought for his seat by out-organizing a fellow representative in a ground-level, intraparty showdown. And he successfully parlayed his personal service and networking skills into connections with his new and unfamiliar Long Island Republican constituencies. He was not widely known for his liberal policy battles, nor by his publicity obsessions. Unlike his predecessor, however, Representative Ackerman touched his constituents with compassion, exuberance, and warmth. Along with his policy liberalism, those personal qualities underwrote an authenticity that has already sustained a career longer than that of his predecessor.

The three-chapter, two-person comparison of Republicans David McIntosh and Lindsey Graham is the most ambitious part of the book. For that reason, it is the best test of the basic question: Do personal visits to home constituencies give observers an improved chance to understand what our congressional representatives are really like? The McIntosh-Graham comparison provides us with the longest time line (1995–2002), with the greatest number of constituency visits (ten), and with the most opportunities for connecting home activity and Washington activity. It also gives us a longer look at Washington journalists in action. I did not go to Washington to talk with them there. But because the two men received more than their share of journalistic interest, I could follow a fair bit of their Washington activity in the newspapers. Washington journalists often treated the two men as peas in a pod. They were not.

David McIntosh's authenticity at home rested on his certified intellectual conservatism, his prior executive branch experience in Washington, his quiet confidence, and his attention to public policy. It did not depend on place. He was a fully formed newcomer to his district, and though he seemed quite comfortable there, he did not give off any strong sense of connectedness to his constituency as a distinctive place or as a special repository of judgment. His serious cultural and economic conservatism and his constructive decency served him well there.

His previous career gave him a head start in Washington, and he became a leader in that place. He was very team-oriented. He was not a freelancer. He was "mentioned" often by Washington journalists, and he frequently topped their insider lists of young conservative politicians "worth watching." As time went on, his fluctuating relationships with party leaders and with various Republican "teams" became a trace element of his career and a consistent thread of our Indiana conversations.

Lindsey Graham was as outgoing and inquisitive as his colleague was reserved and circumspect. The two men were equally ambitious, and they usually voted together. Whereas his colleague was intellectually grounded and programmatic, Graham was down-to-earth and pragmatic. He was not attracted to any overarching, full-blown philosophy. In matters of policy, he was a constructive counterpuncher. He did not think in terms of any team, and he thrived on legislative and political combat.

Graham's authenticity was grounded in his strong sense of a home place. He was totally a child of his economically energetic, white, working-class, Republicanizing, up-country constituency. He drew direct support from and nurtured its social and economic conservatism. And he talked a lot about shared values and constituent trust, as his colleague did not. Gradually, Graham's feisty, down-home, independent-sounding presentations of self carried him into David McIntosh's league—in attracting a greater than average amount of journalistic coverage. Eventually, Graham attracted a few journalists to his constituency, as McIntosh did not. Graham's encounters with them helped me to think about Washington journalism and constituency politics.

Congressional Travels has detailed one person's encounter with a few of our national politicians. It is autobiographical in outline and constituency-centered in focus. Its large subject is representation. Its researchable subject is the connection patterns between representatives and constituents. The connections can be studied in the place where they occur and where they make a difference. That place is the constituency. And yet, among the public places where the actions of our elected politicians can be observed, their individual constituencies are the most neglected. Relative to Washington, D.C., that is, they are neglected by political scientists and journalists alike. Going to that place is crucial because context—and perception of context—is crucial. Where perception matters and authenticity is the question, an *Almanac of American Politics* on a desk in Washington will not suffice.

There are some obvious reasons for benign neglect—little interest, competing interests, few incentives, few resources, no models. Against these negatives, the suggestion offered here is one important idea or ingredient that might be examined to best advantage in the constituency. The idea is authenticity. The authenticity question "what are they really like?" is a connections question. It is a contextual question. It can be answered best, or at least advantageously, by observing and talking with politicians when they are at home actually connecting with an array of constituents. Seeing, hearing, questioning, and reflecting in the constituency makes a difference. Although my summaries may look as if they can easily be obtained from Washington, my argument is that they cannot be.

For any political scientist or journalist interested in the subject of representation—or in the smaller question of authenticity or simply in finding out what goes on between an elected representative and the people he or she represents—there is something to be learned by taking these questions to the main place where representational connections occur. If "what are they really like?" is a good question, then "go visit a constituency" is a good answer.

Index